Empires of Print

At the turn of the twentieth century, the publishing industries in Britain and the United States underwent dramatic expansions and reorganization that brought about an increased traffic in books and periodicals around the world. Focusing on adventure fiction published from 1899 to 1919, Patrick Scott Belk looks at authors such as Joseph Conrad, H.G. Wells, Conan Doyle, and John Buchan to explore how writers of popular fiction engaged with foreign markets and readers through periodical publishing. Belk argues that popular fiction, particularly the adventure genre, developed in ways that directly correlate with authors' experiences, and shows that popular genres of the late nineteenth and early twentieth centuries emerged as one way of marketing their literary works to expanding audiences of readers world-wide. Despite an over-determined print space altered by the rise of new kinds of consumers and transformations of accepted habits of reading, publishing, and writing, these changes in British and American publishing at the turn of the twentieth century inspired an exciting new period of literary invention and experimentation in the adventure genre, and the greater part of that invention and experimentation was happening in the magazines.

Patrick Scott Belk is Assistant Professor of English in the Multimedia and Digital Culture program at the University of Pittsburgh, Johnstown, USA, principal investigator for The Pulp Magazines Project, and webmaster for the Joseph Conrad Society UK.

Empires of Print
Adventure Fiction in the Magazines, 1899–1919

Patrick Scott Belk

Routledge
Taylor & Francis Group

LONDON AND NEW YORK

First published 2017 by Routledge

2 Park Square, Milton Park, Abingdon, Oxfordshire OX14 4RN
52 Vanderbilt Avenue, New York, NY 10017

Routledge is an imprint of the Taylor & Francis Group, an informa business

First issued in paperback 2019

British Library Cataloguing in Publication Data
A catalogue record for this book is available from the British Library

Library of Congress Cataloging in Publication Data
Names: Belk, Patrick Scott author.
Title: Empires of Print: adventure fiction in the magazines, 1899–1919 /
by Patrick Scott Belk.
Description: New York: Routledge, 2017. | Includes bibliographical
references and index.
Identifiers: LCCN 2016050703| ISBN 9781472441140 (alk. paper) |
ISBN 9781315565767 (ebk)
Subjects: LCSH: Serialized fiction—United States—History and
criticism. | Serialized fiction—Great Britain—History and criticism. |
American fiction—20th century—History and criticism. | English
fiction—20th century—History and criticism. | Publishers and publishing—
United States—History—20th century. | Books and reading—United
States—History—20th century. | Publishers and publishing—Great
Britain—History—20th century. | Books and reading—Great Britain—
History—20th century.
Classification: LCC PS374.S446 B45 2017 | DDC 823/.087090912–dc23
LC record available at https://lccn.loc.gov/2016050703

ISBN: 978-1-4724-4114-0 (hbk)
ISBN: 978-0-367-88029-3 (pbk)

Typeset in Sabon
by Florence Production Ltd, Stoodleigh, Devon, UK

To Joe Kestner, for your passion, limitless spirit of adventure, and unwavering mentorship over the years, I warmly dedicate this first monograph.

Contents

Figures and Tables

Figures

Tables

Acknowledgments

This monograph is based on my Ph.D. dissertation, completed in 2012 at The University of Tulsa under the guidance of Sean Latham, Joseph Kestner, and Robert Jackson. I want to thank them for their combined advice and support, which helped me turn a jumbled mass of ideas into a proper scholarly argument. Their tough criticism and uncompromising standards made me a better writer, even when I did not want to become one, and I hope to repay them by being the kind of teacher, mentor, and colleague they taught me to be.

Chapters of this book would never have seen the light of day without Kate Macdonald, who continues to inspire me with her tenacity and imagination; Mike Ashley, David Finkelstein, and Stephen Donovan, who answered an interminable barrage of questions; and especially David Earle, who taught me to read magazines. To Patrick Brantlinger for early advice on the proposal, coffee, and conversation, thank you. Hugh Epstein, J.H. Stape, and Allan Simmons, onwards and upwards.

Research for this book was made possible through the generous assistance of librarians at research institutions around the world, including Richard Walker and Christine Holmes (British Library); Anne Mouron (Bodleian Library, Oxford); David McClay (National Library, Scotland); Tal Nadan (Berg Collection, New York City); Adrienne Sharpe (Beinecke Library, Yale); Nicole Dittrich (Special Collections Research Center, Syracuse); Rosemary Cullen (John Hay Library, Brown); Linda Dobb and Richard Apple (CSU-East Bay); Helen Beardsley (Stirling University Library, Scotland); Elizabeth Fields (Cushing Memorial Library, Texas A & M); David Frasier (Lilly Library, Indiana); Matt Turi (Wilson Library, UNC-Chapel Hill); Heather Home (Queen's University Library, Kingston, Ontario); and Maria McWilliams (Coates Library, Trinity).

Parts of Chapter 5, "Deciphered Codes: John Buchan in *All-Story Weekly* (1915) and *The Popular Magazine* (1919)," have appeared previously in a revised form as "John Buchan and the American Pulp Magazines," in *John Buchan and the Idea of Modernity*, edited by Kate Macdonald and Nathan Wadell (Pickering & Chatto, May 2013).

To Shirley Edrich at I.D. Edrich Books, London, and John Gunnison at Adventure House, Silver Spring, Maryland, thank you for all the magazines.

Abbreviations

ARL	All Red Line
ASM	*All-Story Magazine*
BJP	*British Journal of Photography*
BOP	*Boy's Own Paper*
CBS	Columbia Broadcasting System
CF	Conrad First
CL	*Collected Letters*
EPU	Empire Press Union
ER	*English Review*
FNP	First National Pictures
HAL	Hamburg-American Line
ICA	International Copyright Act
ICS	International Correspondence Schools
ILN	*Illustrated London News*
KFS	King Features Syndicate
MJP	Modernist Journals Project
NBA	Net Book Agreement
NR	*New Review*
NSW	New South Wales
NYT	*New York Times*
OSC	Oceanic Steamship Company
PM	*Popular Magazine*
PMP	Pulp Magazines Project
PO	Post Office
RDF	Resource Description Framework
RED	Reading Experience Database
RM	Royal Mail
S&S	Street & Smith Corporation
SQM	Standard Quality Monthly
UFS	United Feature Syndicate

Introduction

Print in Transition: Magazines, Adventure, and Threats of New Media, 1880–1920

From 1880 to 1914, the publishing industries in Great Britain and the United States underwent dramatic expansions and reorganization. By 1900, the annual production of new books in Britain had climbed to nearly 6,000, up from just 370 titles a century before;[1] by 1914, this figure had doubled.[2] In the field of periodical production, the total number of annually published titles, not including newspapers, more than tripled, from 3,200 to more than 10,000 by the start of the First World War[3] (see Appendix A). In roughly the same period, the number of Post Office Directory listings for professional literary agencies in London rose from just 2 or 3 in the early 1880s to more than 30 by 1913,[4] a tenfold increase reflecting the industry's growing demand for skilled managers to facilitate and direct the increasingly international flow of a rapidly expanding volume of printed material. Alongside newspaper syndicates and authors' societies, literary agents helped navigate the complexities of an increasingly fragmented print culture field, which, by 1925, could include 26 different rights to a single work.[5]

These seismic shifts in literary production at the turn of the twentieth century had far-reaching effects beyond the British and American publishing industries and transatlantic print cultures of the period. Anxieties of "overproduction and Darwinian competition among novels, journals, and newspapers"[6] in late-Victorian Britain, for example, were paralleled in Australia in the mid-1920s, when a "significant presence of English and American magazines" on Australian bookstalls "was seen as a threat to local industry" and the "national character of an emerging culture."[7] The collapse of the three-decker novel in 1894 may have signaled Mudie's recognition that this new era in global trafficking of affordable reading matter had arrived. In 1899, the UK's Net Book Agreement (NBA) attempted to rein in some forms of supply more efficient than others,[8] but the industry-wide measure—which was regarded by *The Times*'s general manager, C.F. Moberly Bell, as "simple extortion"—would do little to check the early twentieth century's "unfettered free trade in books," and especially that "great mass of popular literature," that is, fiction.[9] Book and periodical production rates climbed, prices fell, publishers diversified, and technological capacities expanded. In 1901, G.M. Trevelyan warned that a "white peril" would inundate British and American cities beneath a sea of "[j]ournals, magazines, and the continued spawn of bad novels."[10] Trevelyan's image of these drowned urban centers had its counterpoint in the tentacle-like extension of the modern trade, transportation, and distribution networks that helped channel this alarming accumulation of print culture materials ever farther afield.

By 1900, most leading publishers in London, New York, and Edinburgh had established some form of printing, binding, distribution, or sales operations overseas. In many cases, these highly organized networks of export agents, news dealers, post office (PO) masters, and subscription managers extended as far away as Johannesburg, Melbourne, Calcutta, and San Francisco. They orchestrated multiple-market media campaigns; helped synchronize complex overseas legal and contract negotiations; and together they created the phenomenon of the modern best-seller.[11] Of course, the competition between publishers for shared global media markets could be fierce, but, despite rivalries at this level of commercial production, reading communities in Australia, India, England, and South Africa developed common literary vernaculars with their counterparts living many thousands of miles away, in New Zealand, Barbados, Hong Kong, and across the

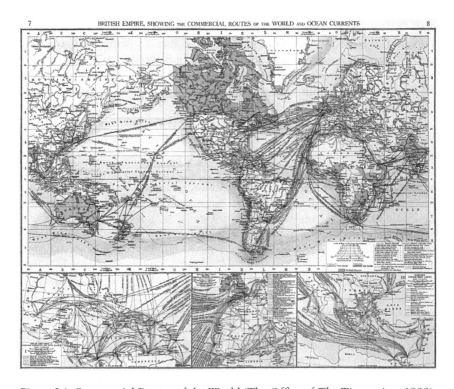

Figure I.1 Commercial Routes of the World (The Office of *The Times*, circa 1900).

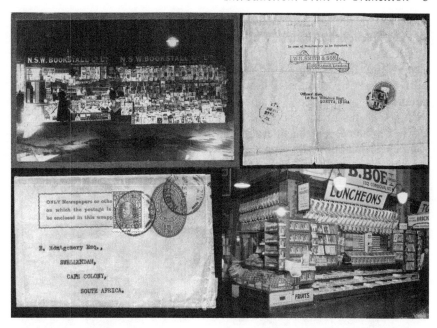

Figure I.2 (Clockwise, from Top Left) N.S.W. Bookstall Co. Ltd. (Sydney, 1920);
W.H. Smith & Son 4d Magazine Wrapper (1901); and Newsstand and
Luncheon Counter (Vancouver, 1924); New Zealand ½d Newspaper
Wrapper (1909).

American Midwest. At a time when the emergent technologies of film
and radio were still in their infancy, long before television or the Internet
were even on the horizon, both old-established[12] firms such as William
Blackwood & Sons (UK) and new, large-scale commercial publishers of the
1890s such as the Frank A. Munsey Company (US) were already exploring
and shaping the early contours of globalization. Their pioneering efforts
brought textbooks, magazines, and paperback reprints shipped and bound
for timely delivery to overseas markets, which were sold to "an increasingly
imperial, global audience for novels and other [. . .] books produced by
British [and American] publishers."[13]

Today's megalithic, multinational media entertainment corporations are
a far cry from the operations of Blackwood and Munsey at the turn of the
twentieth century, but the difference is one of degree, rather than kind.
Although most readers today would not readily associate celebrity authors
such as H. Rider Haggard, H.G. Wells, or Conan Doyle with sweeping
technological changes in global modernity and large-scale revolutions in early
twentieth-century print culture, it was best-selling professional writers like
them—along with their agents, editors, and commercial publishers—who
rode the wave of sea-changes taking place in modern book and periodical

publishing. And they continued to dominate global print media markets well into the twentieth century. With the trend toward revisionist histories of Anglo-American modernism of the past two decades offering valuable new insights into modernism's complex engagements with new media, celebrity culture, and the commercial marketplace,[14] it is important to keep in mind that few authors of the period ever approached a level comparable with Haggard's literary success, Wells's intellectual and cultural clout, or Doyle's influence on the international press—and certainly not with their commercial viability (see Appendix B).

From their publishers' central offices in London, Edinburgh, and New York, authors of popular literary fiction sold commercially, and their

Figure I.3 Six Covers: *Munsey's Magazine* (June 1906); *The All-Story* (October 1912); *The Popular Magazine* (February 1905); *Pearson's* (April 1897); *The Royal Magazine* (December 1898); and *The Strand Magazine* (April 1912).

works were marketed aggressively on the global scale. By 1900, this business involved several new, discrete British, American, colonial, and continental territorial markets.[15] Across an increasingly diversified range of major new media markets, such as film and reprint publishing, they were courted by American magazine editors such as Charles Agnew Maclean (*The Popular Magazine*; Street & Smith [S&S] Corporation) and Robert H. "Bob" Davis (*Munsey's Magazine, The All-Story*; The Frank Munsey Co.); and championed by British editors Percy Everett (*Pearson's Magazine, The Royal Magazine*; Pearson Ltd.) and H. Greenhough Smith (*The Strand Magazine*; George Newnes Ltd.). These were four of the most influential editors and most widely read fiction magazines in Great Britain and the United States during the first decades of the twentieth century.[16]

Literary agencies, particularly A.P. Watt & Son (1883–1924); newspaper syndicates, such as W.F. Tillotsons, S.S. McClure, King Features Syndicate, and United Feature Syndicate; the Society of Authors (UK) and Authors' League of America facilitated further the widespread dissemination of their stories, often reaching hundreds of thousands of readers of romance, westerns, mysteries, and adventure fiction around the world.

Many of the most profitable literary properties of the day have long been forgotten. Few readers now, besides a handful of scholars, recognize the names Charles Garvice, Marie Corelli, or Hall Caine.[17] Others have demonstrated a remarkable degree of cultural endurance, however, and, as much as they were shaped by the late-Victorian era, continue to help shape the course of the twentieth century's new media and electronic cultures. Their direct influence can be seen, for example, in a cross-section of Hollywood films (*Sherlock Holmes*,[18] *John Carter, King Kong*, and *Conan the Barbarian*), radio programs of the 1930s ('Flash Gordon' and CBS's 'Detective Story Hour'), today's comic books (*The League of Extraordinary Gentlemen*), TV shows ('The Lone Ranger'), and video games (from Atari's *Pitfall!* to Xbox's *Call of Cthulhu*). Blockbuster films of today demonstrate the longevity of literary forms popularized by them in newspapers and magazines over a century ago, and tomorrow's sequels will attempt to recapture these same magic formulas yet again. Iconic Hollywood "tomb raiders" such as Indiana Jones, Lara Croft, and Rick O'Connell are all drawn straight out of American pulp magazines and Saturday matinee serials of the 1930s,[19] which borrowed extensively from literary traditions handed down through Haggard, Doyle, R.L. Stevenson, C.J. Cutcliffe Hyne, and H. de Vere Stacpoole.[20] Some of the first silent film adaptations of *King Solomon's Mines* (1918),[21] *Dr. Jekyll and Mr. Hyde* (1920),[22] *The Blue Lagoon* (1923), and *The Lost World* (1925) were also the major critical and commercial blockbusters of their day. Adaptations in film, radio, and subsequent new media of the twentieth century "gave a new lease of life"[23] to the works of these popular authors, and, as Nicholas Daly points out, classic novels such as *Treasure Island, King Solomon's Mines, She*, and *Dracula* have not been out of print since.[24]

This study shows that a cross-fertilization of adventure fiction, periodical publishing, and the "new mass entertainment culture" was already at work in the late-Victorian popular "revival of romance" itself.[25] The emergent forms deployed in romance and adventure fiction at the turn of the twentieth century, moreover, developed in direct response to the practice of serialization in the popular and well-established magazines of the day. Exploring the high-stakes professional field of publishing, marketing, and circulating works of popular fiction in the early twentieth century, *Empires of Print: Adventure Fiction in the Magazines, 1899–1919* shows how popular authors not only competed commercially in an expanding global market, but also actively and successfully participated in key developments transforming print and periodical publishing. It demonstrates how massive readerships around the world shared reliable access to contemporary popular fiction through key periodical forms, and argues that the emergence of distinctive tropes and character types in popular fiction at the turn of the twentieth century is inseparable from authors' negotiations of these global markets. Focusing on adventure fiction in the magazines, it suggests further that authors' complex engagements with the foreign markets through periodical publication inspired them to create and develop new modern subjectivities, successfully adapting conventions of nineteenth-century adventure fiction in order to navigate modernity's new media landscapes and changing cartographies and engage its new technologies.

Popular adventure fiction emerges from this account of modern periodical publishing as something more complicated and more sophisticated than just "light holiday literature."[26] I argue instead that popular fiction from the turn of the twentieth century—with the emphasis on *adventure* fiction, in particular—must be viewed critically through the lens of the modern media landscape. It developed in ways directly correlative to authors' experiences in the periodical publishing market, and its proliferating subgenres emerged as one way of marketing their works in this over-determined print space, altered by the rise of new kinds of consumers and transformations of accepted habits of reading, publishing, and writing.[27]

In the process, this study also examines the production and circulation of the magazines that first carried these popular new forms of adventure fiction and modern best-sellers to nearly every known corner of the world. It illuminates an alternate history and reading of imperial romance at the turn of the twentieth century, relocating this enormously popular genre within the expanding volumes of print and visual material of the period. It shows how the themes and emergent forms deployed by romance and adventure writers developed in direct response to serialization in old-established magazines such as *Blackwood's*, rough-paper pulps such as *The All-Story*, and illustrated general-interest monthlies such as *The Strand*. Asserting that large-scale expansions of the global trade in literary publishing dramatically altered the conceptual horizons of modern adventure fiction in magazines, I ask how writers Joseph Conrad, Wells, Doyle, and John Buchan responded to this crisis, and I discover that it was often through new and emerging literary genres that extended the limits and enlarged the contours of modern adventure fiction's imaginary domains.

The book is divided into five chapters, each focusing on a different set of adventure texts, and arranged chronologically in order of the texts' first serializations. Chapter 1, "Empires of Print: An Imperial History of Late Nineteenth-Century Periodical Expansion," gives a brief historical overview of the expansion of overseas markets and publishers' attempts to supply those markets from 1880 to 1914. This chapter surveys some of the periodical forms in which readers may have encountered adventure fiction during the nineteenth century. It also argues that a close, symbiotic relationship existed between magazines and adventure fiction, and that this relationship would play a critical role in the literary debates between Romance and Realism at the turn of the century. As new and emerging markets were developed worldwide, publishers such as Macmillan, Bell, and Blackwood & Sons established networks of distribution to supply these markets with up-to-date shipments of print and periodical reading material. The globalization of literary culture had not yet been fully realized, but, as this chapter shows, by the late nineteenth century, the tastes and reading habits of British and American readers were dependent on, and in some cases dictated by,

Figure I.4 Edgar Rice Burroughs, "Tarzan of the Apes," Unidentified American Newspaper (circa 1912).

the preferences and buying habits of foreign, international, and colonial readers living in large, increasingly more lucrative markets overseas.[28] This chapter's expanded portrait of modern periodical print culture acknowledges the horizontal and global production of magazines in the early twentieth century, and subsequent chapters examine key texts by individual authors more closely, situating them against this wider material background.

Chapter 2, "Imperial Technologies: Adventure and the Threat of New Media in Conrad's *Lord Jim* (1899)," examines the original periodical context of Conrad's *Lord Jim*, first published as a protracted serialization in *Blackwood's Edinburgh Magazine* from October 1899 to November 1900. This chapter argues that *Lord Jim* anticipates the threatened displacement of an older, heroic, and mythic literary tradition by the spread of worldwide information networks that, in 1902, had fully encircled the Earth's surface with crisscrossing lines of telegraph cables.[29] This erasure is registered on the four interrelated subgenres of late nineteenth-century adventure fiction featured in the novel: imperial romance, exotic love story, pirate tale, and the lost world romance. *Lord Jim* acknowledges the widespread cultural currency of a robust and multifaceted literary tradition. It draws on conventions of adventure literature derived from sea stories, travel books, confessional diaries, captivity narratives, and discovery journals of the past two centuries, while it interrogates this tradition's contingency and diminishing possibilities in an increasingly integrated, more mobile world. This position poses complications for an author of sea stories and adventures whose career depended on expanding new markets for periodical publication, but it also marks the creative tension between *Lord Jim*'s Patusan section and the material context of its serialization in a magazine such as *Blackwood's*, which not only "took [Conrad's] name wherever the English language is read,"[30] but also aimed to develop new, larger, and ever-growing markets of those readers worldwide. Finally, with this chapter I show how reading *Lord Jim* in its original periodical context adds an important dimension to the novel's notoriously complex composition history, and I argue that *Blackwood's* own transitional identity at the turn of the twentieth century offers a cogent explanation for the novel's "structural rift,"[31] or what the author called its "plague spot . . . [the] division of the book into two parts."[32]

Chapter 3 then considers the uneven, shifting development of adventure fiction during the first two decades of the twentieth century. In "Transatlantic Crossings: The Technological Scene of H.G. Wells's *Tono-Bungay* (1909)," I begin by reassessing H.G. Wells's comic portrayal of Conradian adventure fiction in Part Three of *Tono-Bungay*, "How I Stole the Heaps of Quap from Mordet Island." Several scholars have already shown how Wells's unflattering caricature of the "Roumanian [*sic*] captain" suggests an attitude of contempt toward Conrad, his style, and subject matter. In command of the doomed sailing vessel, the *Maud Mary*, the captain "had learnt the sea in the Roumanian navy, and English out of a book."[33] Andrew

Glazzard labels the episode "an extended piece of Conradese" and concludes that, "recollections of Conrad in *Experiment in Autobiography* (1934) confirm *Tono-Bungay*'s captain was based on [him]."[34] According to Wells's narrator, George Ponderevo, he was "an exceptionally inefficient captain"; was "perpetually imagining danger"; and, in the end, he must be "bought off."[35] I note, however, that there were two distinctly different "first" appearances of Wells's novel, through its simultaneous transatlantic serialization in both Ford Maddox Hueffer's *The English Review* (UK) and S&S Corporation's *The Popular Magazine* (US); any reading of the novel's material history, print culture, or first periodical contexts should therefore take into account this expanded field of modern literary production.

Finally, I argue that this critique of the Conradian adventure story should be read alongside contemporary advertisements for around-the-world holiday cruise ships, express tour packages, resort hotels, and deluxe travel accommodations. Wells's dark, comical dramatizations of familiar colonialist themes—violence, escape, and surveillance in the jungle—are here more likely regarded as an attempt at relocating Conrad's romantic posturing within the shifting signs and representations of foreign and faraway places found in the posters, travel brochures, and popular illustrated magazines of the period.

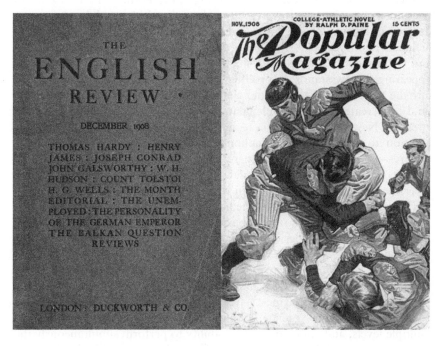

Figure I.5 Two Covers: *The English Review* (December 1908) and *The Popular Magazine* (November 1908).

My fourth chapter, "Spectacular Texts: Conan Doyle's Essays on Photography and *The Lost World* (1912)," foregrounds relationships that existed commercially and professionally between print and competing forms of popular media in the early twentieth century. It examines Doyle's expert command of modern publicity, his fascination with spirit photography, and his knowledge of innovative photographic techniques. It shows how Doyle mobilized international celebrity, the American press, film, and trick photography in order to cast doubt on scientific materialism, and argues that new media technologies could also help reinstate a diminishing body of evidence for geographical frontiers separating civilization from the unknown. It examines the first periodical publication of Doyle's *The Lost World*, which was serialized in *The Strand Magazine* from April to November 1912, and argues that Doyle appropriates photography and its representation in the popular illustrated magazine as a seemingly objective form of proof and documentary evidence. In doing so, Doyle postulates new imaginary avenues for escape and transgression in the modern world. Modernity is not a threat, but an opportunity to reveal hidden avenues and to unlock other worlds. This chapter emphasizes that paper, printing, publishing, and authorship did not exist in a vacuum, but that print and new media were complementary forms of a "new mass entertainment culture."[36] Books, magazines, and newspapers gave cinema and radio some of their earliest plots, stories, and iconography. From 1911 to 1938, 60 consumer magazines and nearly 90 trade and in-house publications were devoted to cinema, movie stars, and movie production.[37] Some early titles included *Photoplay* (1911), *Picture Play* (1915), and *Screen Play* (1925), and "[t]hroughout the twenties, thirties and forties, new titles were forever appearing on newsstands . . . proliferation of movie magazines . . . continued into the 1940s."[38] Magazines and cinema shared "similar subject matter . . . [and this created their] complementary effect, rather than a displacement effect."[39] New electronic media technologies such as cinema and radio—in addition to the airplanes, telephones, tanks, spiritualism, and celebrity culture—were just some of the many variations and multiplying indices of modern life, offering volumes of new books, magazines, and newspapers a diversified range of new subjects in which to specialize.

The convergence of modern media, where every story gets told across multiple platforms, is also the subject of the fifth and final chapter of this book, "Deciphered Codes: John Buchan in *All-Story Weekly* (1915) and *The Popular Magazine* (1919)." This chapter examines Buchan's wartime spy novels, *The Thirty-Nine Steps* (1915) and *Mr. Standfast* (1919), in the transatlantic context of their first North American serializations in the popular pulp-paper magazines.[40] It shows how Buchan's own professional command of literary agency, publishing, and authorship operated on multiple levels, and contends that his ability to perform simultaneously the roles of agent, publisher, and author effectively informs his development of a new kind of modern hero. Buchan's protagonist—the South African expatriate turned decorated soldier, Richard Hannay—emerges from these rough-paper pages of American pulp magazines as an expert navigator of modern media environments and manager of texts and information. As an amateur agent, he successfully adapts conventions of late nineteenth-century adventure literature, in order to engage with and navigate modernity's threatening new landscapes and emergent new technologies. This new kind of modern adventure hero traverses geographies composed of paper and wields weapons of printer's ink and pen. This chapter concludes my study by demonstrating how Buchan—one of many best-selling adventure novelists of the early twentieth century—engaged Conrad's literary concerns regarding the threat of new media directly and successfully. The spy hero engages, and, by doing so, exerts power and mastery over, these dark, new forces. Drawing connections between the business of transatlantic periodical publishing in the First World War and Buchan's development of the spy hero as expert reader of new media and cultural codes, this chapter suggests that Buchan's own successful career as a literary publisher, which involved his real-life expert navigation of the competitive transatlantic markets for popular fiction, illustrates the highly sophisticated literary and cultural contexts out of which Hannay—one of modern spy fiction's early[41] new forms of adventurer—first emerged.

These five chapters demonstrate the complex range and versatility of adventure fiction in the first two decades of the twentieth century. This dynamic mobility of the form allowed writers to harness and manipulate traditional formulas, narrative structures, and expectations of the genre in modern, sophisticated, and often unforeseen ways. Adapting the conventions of a nineteenth-century tradition handed down from Sir Walter Scott, James Fenimore Cooper, Captain Frederick Marryat, Alexandre Dumas, and R.M. Ballantyne,[42] modern adventure's engagement with the "systematic reduction of the Empire to grids and projections"[43] called for invention and variety. Insisting on the importance of the novels' first serializations in magazines, *Empires of Print* finally suggests that, within the much wider range of genres and print media forms taking part in the phenomenal expansion of early twentieth-century periodical publishing, an urgent and profoundly generative tension developed between modern adventure fiction and the context of its material distribution and circulation in popular magazines, throughout the empire and around the world. Expansions in the British and American publishing industries at the turn of the twentieth century inspired an exciting new period of literary invention and experimentation in this genre, and the greater part of that invention and experimentation was happening in the magazines.

Notes

1   James G. Hepburn. *The Author's Empty Purse and the Rise of the Literary Agent*. London and New York: Oxford University Press, 1968, pp. 15–16.

2   According to *The American Library Annual* for 1915, the total number of books published in Britain in 1914 was 11,537, down from 12,379 in 1913. "International Statistics of Book and Periodical Production, Great Britain, Book Production," *The American Library Annual 1914–1915*, New York: R.R. Bowker, 1915, pp. 267–69.

3   Figures compiled from *N.W. Ayer & Son's American Newspaper Annual and Directory*, Philadelphia, PA: N.W. Ayer, 1880–1915; Frank Luther Mott's *A History of American Magazines, 1885–1905*, Boston, MA: Harvard University Press, 1957; *Mitchell's Newspaper Press Directory*, London: Mitchell, 1880–1915; and *May's British and Irish Press Guide*, London: F.L. May, 1880–1915. See also Hepburn; Philip J. Waller, *Writers, Readers, and Reputations: Literary Life in Britain, 1870–1918*, New York and Oxford, UK: Oxford University Press, 2006; and Mary Ann Gillies, *The Professional Literary Agent in Britain, 1880–1920*, Toronto: University of Toronto Press, 2007.

4   According to Hepburn, "From 1874 to 1894 the Directory listed a total of nineteen agents in London. In all these years no more than six agents were listed at one time, and as late as 1891 only two appeared. Except for three men, none of them survived more than four years; and one of these three, Henry Stevens of Vermont, never seems to have been a literary agent in the conventional sense of the word. The other two were A.M. Burghes and A.P. Watt, who are the first nameable agents known to be true agents" (49). See Hepburn, pp. 45–66.

5   These included first and second serial, book, reprint, syndication, translation, dramatic, cinematic, radio, and gramophone rights, which were frequently negotiated for British, American, colonial, and continental markets simultaneously. See David Finkelstein, "The Globalization of the Book 1880–1970," *A Companion to the History of the Book*, Simon Eliot and Jonathan Rose, Eds., London: John Wiley, 2011, p. 336.

6   Patrick Brantlinger, *The Reading Lesson: The Threat of Mass Literacy in Nineteenth-Century British Fiction*, Bloomington and Indianapolis, IN: Indiana University Press, 1998, p. 185.

7   Roger Osborne, "A National Interest in an International Market: The Circulation of Magazines in Australia during the 1920s," *History Australia* Vol. 5, No. 3 (2008), pp. 75.1–75.16.

8   Ostensibly designed by Frederick Macmillan to combat the "evils of underselling," the UK's Net Book Agreement (1899) formalized an industry-wide publishers' ban on any bookseller, agent, or retailer in the UK who offered the publishers' fixed-price books to the public at discounted prices. For more on the NBA, see Waller, pp. 36–42.

9   Letter (1907) published in *The Times*, quoted in Philip J. Waller, p. 39; Waller, fn., p. 37; Frederick Macmillan, *The Net Book Agreement 1899 and the Book War 1906–1908*, Glasgow: Robert MacLehose, 1924, pp. 17–18, quoted in Waller, p. 36.

10   G.M. Trevelyan, "The White Peril," *Nineteenth Century* 50 (December 1901), pp. 1049–50.

11   See Lynda J. King, *Best-Sellers by Design*, Detroit, MI: Wayne State University Press, 1988, pp. 74–76.

12   The term "old-established" was in commonly use in the magazines and trade journals at the turn of the century. It is used less often today, but here it refers to publishers such as Macmillan & Co., William Blackwood & Son, Sampson & Low, Kegan Paul, Wiley & Putnam, Richard Bentley & Son, Longman, John Murray, Methuen, and George Bell. The term was also often applied to the periodicals published by, or associated with, such houses. In an 1882 article,

Herbert Thurston thus describes the characteristics of "an old-established periodical": "The independence which can afford to disregard the general rush and scramble is now-a-days a mark of distinction. It is unmistakeable evidence of a sure circulation, and it probably implies also . . . a more than usual care in revising proofs and a wish to include as many recent changes as possible. . . . [It] is a highly respectable institution, and . . . deserves to be valued accordingly," Herbert Thurston, "An Old-Established Periodical," *The Month* Vol. XXV, No. 212 (February, 1882), p. 153.

13   See Brantlinger, p. 186.

14   For some examples of the New Modernist studies, see Mark Morrison, *The Public Face of Modernism*, Madison, WI: University Press Wisconsin, 2001; Patrick Collier, *Modernism on Fleet Street*, Farnham, UK: Ashgate, 2006; David M. Earle, *Re-Covering Modernism*, Farnham, UK: Ashgate, 2009; Robert Scholes and Clifford Wulfman, *Modernism in the Magazines*, New Haven, CT: Yale University Press, 2011; Carey Mickalites, *Modernism and Market Fantasy*, London: Palgrave Macmillan, 2012; and Alissa Karl, *Modernism and the Marketplace*, London: Routledge, 2013.

15   For more about the influence of territorial markets, and global marketing, on the culture of publishing and literary authorship at the turn of the century, see George Parker, "Distributors, Agents, and Publishers: Creating a Separate Market for Books in Canada 1900–1920: Part I," *Papers of the Bibliographical Society of Canada* Vol. 43, No. 2 (2005), pp. 7–65, and Eli MacLaren, " 'Against All Invasion': The Archival Story of Kipling, Copyright, and the Macmillan Expansion into Canada, 1900–1920," *Journal of Canadian Studies* 40.2 (2006), pp. 139–62. For a nineteenth-century French perspective, see Christine Haynes, *Lost Illusions: The Politics of Publishing in Nineteenth-Century France*, Cambridge, MA: Harvard University Press, 2010, especially Chapter 6: "The Divorce Between State and Market," pp. 187–231.

16   In the pages of their publishers' flagship titles, Charles Agnew Maclean, Robert H. Davis, Percy Everett, and H. Greenhough Smith launched Ayesha, Tarzan, an "Invasion of the Earth," and Professor Challenger, respectively, onto the world. *The All-Story* and *The Strand Magazine* also nurtured the writing careers of Edgar Rice Burroughs (from 1911) and Conan Doyle (from 1891). Sherlock Holmes had first appeared in "A Study in Scarlet," which was published in Ward, Lock, & Co.'s *Beeton's Christmas Annual* (December 1887).

17   By 1914, Charles Garvice had published more than 150 novels, which had sold more than seven million copies worldwide. According to Arnold Bennett, he was "the most successful novelist in England." Marie Corelli's novels sold more copies than those of Doyle, H.G. Wells, and Rudyard Kipling combined, although critics derided her work as "the favourite of the common multitude." Hall Caine's *The Christian* (1897) became the first novel in Britain to sell more than a million copies.

18   According to Alan Barnes, Holmes has appeared on screen more times than any other fictional character. See Barnes's *Sherlock Holmes on Screen: The Complete Film and TV History*, Chicago, IL: Reynolds & Hearn, 2009.

19   There were dozens of single-character hero pulps from the 1930s: *The Shadow* (1931–49), *Doc Savage* (1933–49), *Phantom Detective* (1933–53), *The Spider* (1933–43), *G-8 and His Battle Aces* (1933–44), *Operator #5* (1934–39), *Secret Agent X* (1934–39), and *The Avenger* (1939–42). From 1936–45, a golden age of film serials featured the adventures of Flash Gordon (Universal, 1936), Dick Tracy (Republic, 1937), Zorro (Republic, 1937), the Lone Ranger (Republic, 1938), Captain Marvel (Republic, 1941), Spy Smasher (Republic, 1942), and Smilin' Jack Martin (Universal, 1943). They included jungle and "lost world"

adventurers, such as Bruce Gordon (Super Serial, 1935), Clyde Beatty (Republic, 1936), Jungle Jim (Universal, 1937), Frank Buck (Columbia, 1937), Terry Lee (Columbia, 1940), Nyoka the Jungle Girl (Republic, 1941), The Phantom (Columbia, 1943), and Congo Bill (Columbia, 1948).

20   In Chapter 5, "Deciphered Codes: John Buchan in *All-Story Weekly* (1915) and *The Popular Magazine* (1919)," I bring attention to the fact that these and many other British popular-fiction writers published widely in pulp magazines as well. Edgar Wallace, Talbot Mundy, Baroness Orczy, E. Phillips Oppenheim, William Le Queux, and Rafael Sabatini were featured often, in fact, and Kipling, Anthony Hope, G.K. Chesterton, A.E.W. Mason, Max Pemberton, Ethel M. Dell, and Sax Rohmer all, at one point or another, were published in the pulps.

21   Nicholas Daly writes: "By 1916, the English film maker, H.L. Lucoque, had bought the seven-year film-rights to six of Haggard's novels, including *King Solomon's Mines*, *She* and *Allan Quatermain*, and Haggard received some £9000 in royalties from 1915 to 1916." For more on the interrelationship between early silent cinema and popular romance and adventure novels, see Daly, *Modernism, Romance and the Fin de Siècle: Popular Fiction and British Culture, 1880–1914*, Cambridge, UK: Cambridge University Press, 1999, pp. 151–58.

22   *Dr. Jekyll and Mr. Hyde*, dir. John S. Robertson, perfs. John Barrymore and Charles Lane, Famous Players-Lasky Corp., April 1920, 80 min. Several other film adaptations of R.L. Stevenson's 1886 novel were produced earlier in the century, however, including the earliest known version, released March 7, 1908, from Selig Polyscope Company.

23   Daly, p. 151.

24   Ibid. As Daly asserts, moreover, "It is difficult to discuss the longevity of the romance without mentioning the role played by [film]. . . . The film industry seems almost from its inception to have been a bulwark of imperial culture. . . . Indeed . . . the appearance of both film and romance as components of a new mass entertainment culture is far from a coincidence . . . the imaginary pleasures that film offers follow directly from those developed by Haggard, Stevenson, and [Bram] Stoker," p. 155.

25   For more about the 1880s' and 1890s' "revival of romance," see R.L. Stevenson, "A Gossip on Romance," *Longman's Magazine* 1 (February 1882), pp. 69–79; Rider Haggard, "About Fiction," *Contemporary Review* Vol. 51, No. 302 (February 1887), pp. 172–80; Conan Doyle, "Mr Stevenson's Methods in Fiction," *The National Review* 14 (1890), pp. 646–57; and, for a contemporary perspective, John McClure, *Late Imperial Romance*, London and New York: Verso, 1994.

26   Joseph Conrad, *Lord Jim* (1900), Thomas C. Moser, Ed., Second Norton Critical Edition, New York & London: W.W. Norton, 2006, p. 8.

27   See Kate Macdonald and Nathan Waddell, "Introduction" to *John Buchan and the Idea of Modernity*, London: Pickering & Chatto, 2013, p. 14.

28   See Priya Joshi, *In Another Country: Colonialism, Culture, and the English Novel in India*, New York: Columbia University Press, 2002; and her essay "Trading Places: The Novel, the Colonial Library, and India," in *Print Areas: Book History in India*, Abhijit Gupta and Swapan Chakravorty, Eds., Delhi: Permanent Black, 2004, pp. 17–64.

29   In 1901, the British cable ship *Colonia* set out from Bamfield, British Columbia, to lay 4,000 kilometers of cable to Fanning Island (1,600 kilometers south of Hawaii). The trans-Pacific telegraph line between Bamfield and Fanning Island was finished October 31, 1902. The next day, the first telegraph messages to

circle the globe were relayed along this line, known as the All Red Cable Route. See Daniel R. Headrick, *The Tentacles of Progress: Technology Transfer in the Age of Imperialism, 1850–1940*, Oxford, UK: Oxford University Press, 1988, pp. 104–10.

30 Conrad, Letter to J.B. Pinker (February 1908), *The Collected Letters of Joseph Conrad, Volume 4: 1908–1911*, Eds. Frederick R. Karl and Laurence Davies, Cambridge, UK: Cambridge University Press, 1990, p. 49.

31 Daphna Erdinast-Vulcan, "The Failure of Myth: *Lord Jim*," *Lord Jim* (1900), Joseph Conrad, Thomas Moser, Ed., Second Norton Critical Edition, New York and London: W.W. Norton, 1996, p. 493.

32 Conrad, Letter to Edward Garnett (November 12, 1900), *The Collected Letters of Joseph Conrad, Volume 2: 1898–1902*, Eds. Frederick R. Karl and Laurence Davies, Cambridge, UK: Cambridge University Press, 1986, p. 302.

33 Wells, "Chapter IX: How I Stole the Heaps of Quap from Mordet Island," *Tono-Bungay*, Part 3, *The Popular Magazine*, Vol. XII, No. 2, (December 1908), pp. 130, 134. The full installment runs from pp. 125–39.

34 Andrew Glazzard, "Book Review of Linda Dryden's *Joseph Conrad and H.G. Wells: The Fin-de-Siècle Literary Scene* (Palgrave Macmillan, 2015)", *The Conradian: The Journal of the Joseph Conrad Society* (UK), 41.1 (2016), on the Society's website, at www.josephconradsociety.org/reviews.htm (last accessed May 5, 2016).

35 Wells, "Chapter IX: How I Stole the Heaps of Quap from Mordet Island," pp. 130, 134.

36 Daly, p. 155.

37 S. Lomazow, *American Periodicals: A Collector's Manual and Reference Guide*. West Orange, NJ: Horowitz, 1996.

38 Theodore Peterson, *Magazines in the Twentieth Century*. Urbana, IL: Univ. of Illinois Press, 1956, pp. 281–82.

39 P. Lazarsfeld, and R. Wyant, "Magazines in 90 Cities: Who Reads What?" *Public Opinion Quarterly* (October 1837), pp. 29–41.

40 See also The Pulp Magazines Project, "an open-access archive and digital research initiative for the study and preservation of one of the twentieth century's most influential print culture forms," at www.pulpmags.org/ (last accessed October 22, 2016).

41 Examples also include Carruthers (Erskine Childers, *The Riddle of the Sands*, London: Smith, Elder, 1903), and, as for the "most famous," that would likely be James Bond (Ian Fleming, *Casino Royale*, London: Cape, 1953).

42 Sir Walter Scott (1771–1832), James Fenimore Cooper (1789–1851), Captain Frederick Marryat (1792–1848), Alexandre Dumas (1802–70), and R.M. Ballantyne (1825–94). Of these five authors, no doubt Scott, Cooper, and Dumas represent the nineteenth century's undisputed triumvirate of romance and adventure writing.

43 James Morris, *Pax Britannica*, New York: Harcourt, 1980, p. 60.

1 Empires of Print

An Imperial History of Late Nineteenth-Century Periodical Expansion

The rapid expansion of the British and American periodical press during the last three decades of the nineteenth century was, as many critics have noted, not unprecedented. Simon Eliot records the "almost relentless" increase in both new titles and circulations "from 1800 to the mid-1850s" in Britain. It was followed by a period of relative "quiescence" in the 1860s, which was "similar to the one visible in book production figures for the same decade."[1] Eliot cites at least 1,564 new periodical titles established in England and Wales during the 1850s (a 51 percent increase over the 1840s), and he notes that these figures do not include the "vast quantities of unstamped weekly papers," which "probably accounted for a significant proportion of total newspaper and magazine production."[2] From 1800, the periodical industry had grown intermittently, but at an accelerated pace, in London, Manchester, Liverpool, New York, Chicago, and Edinburgh. It experienced two major "surges in production" in the UK, which were roughly between 1830–55 and 1875–1903.[3] In the US, a similar "dynamic of development" occurred, although, as David Reed argues, it was "late but explosive," and the process "happened earlier in Britain than in America."[4] According to Reed:

> [T]he dynamic of development within both Britain and the United States proved remarkably consistent whether judged from the point of view of an industrialist, an advertising executive or a magazine publisher. The energies of urbanization were released in the first part of the nineteenth century in Britain and towards its end in America. The rise of the popular magazine was a part of this process in each country.[5]

The nineteenth-century periodical industry developed in tandem with the increasing centrality of the industrialized, metropolitan cities as major hubs of culture, information, and political power. It also radiated outwards, alongside "the evolution of the railway system (1830s on)" in the UK,[6] and again, "in the 1870s, when ... railway managements [in the US] were able to organize efficient long-distance services ... [which] also meant regular and faster postal and small package services, important for both business communication and the distribution of magazines."[7] Eliot reminds us that:

the history of text involves the history of its dissemination and . . . as part of the context, we need to know what was happening to the distribution of printed matter in the nineteenth century. This deserves and needs a large-scale study in its own right.[8]

Part I of this chapter focuses on that critical "part of the context . . . what was happening to the distribution of printed matter" during the period Eliot terms the "second phase" of British book and periodical expansion in the nineteenth century (1875–1903). In the process, I explore the under-documented global expansion of colonial and foreign markets for British periodicals, and British publishers' attempts to supply those markets, from roughly 1880 to 1914. In Part II of this chapter, I survey some of the many periodicals and periodical forms in which readers first encountered adventure fiction during the nineteenth century, and argue that a close, symbiotic relationship developed between these periodical forms and the evolving genre of late-Victorian adventure fiction. Within the phenomenal expansion of British and American publishing at the turn of the twentieth century, this chapter identifies an important link between adventure fiction, its serialization in magazines, and concerns about the globalization of literary markets that was exploited by authors Joseph Conrad, H.G. Wells, Conan Doyle, and John Buchan. This chapter's macroscopic, historical overview then serves to contextualize the following four chapters of this study, which examine key texts by these individual authors more closely, while situating them against this wider material and economic background. I argue that important serializations of their works across a variety of magazines evince a particularly urgent, profoundly generative tension between the texts of modern adventure fiction and the global and material context of their periodical publication, distribution, and circulation throughout the Empire and around the world.[9]

Part I: "The History of Text Involves the History of its Dissemination"

The revolution in distribution and transportation that began in Great Britain in the 1830s culminated in the creation of a national network within 20 years. The completion of the main inter-urban railway system in the 1850s gave publishers rapid and reliable access to nearly all of Britain's local markets. Improvements in the Royal Mail services in 1830–53 were made possible by the greater speed and reliability of these railways,[10] and, without this combination of speed, reliability, frequency, and affordability, the "first phase" of British periodical expansion during the nineteenth century (1830–55) could scarcely have materialized. The late nineteenth century's unprecedented global diffusion of trade, technology, and commerce abetted further extensions of print culture networks around the world. This "second phase" of British periodical expansion in the nineteenth century

(1875–1903) was, in many ways, an accelerated version of previous "surges in production" that occurred in 1830–55. The access to new markets was again made possible by revolutions in distribution and transportation, but this time the markets were far larger, owing to international and imperial processes of the nineteenth century (see Appendix C).

Thousands of miles separated Wellington or Victoria[11] from industrialized metropolitan centers in nineteenth-century Britain, but the increasing range, reliability, and speed of shipping, travel, the electric telegraph, and Imperial Penny Post allowed a degree of physical and imagined immediacy with the cultural comforts of home unavailable to previous generations of emigrants. Janet C. Myers coined the term "portable domesticity" to describe the significant role played by English books and printed text in British emigrants' establishing of domestic lives in Australia.[12] Citing estimates to suggest that, "between 1821 and 1915, 10 million emigrants left Great Britain for non-European destinations," Myers argues that, "the imperial project depended not only upon territorial expansion . . . but also on various kinds of texts and writing" transported by the British mail steamers and transformed by colonial readers into mobile forms of cultural capital.[13] Bill Bell notes that emigrant-oriented journals[14] relentlessly praised books and periodicals as "a continued flow of valuable and correct information," and argues that, "the thousands of books, tracts, letters and newspapers that made their way to the colonies in the nineteenth century provided vital connections with familiar social values, serving for many to organize an otherwise unpredictable environment into recognizable patterns."[15] Travelers' accounts written in the nineteenth century confirm this. In *Australia and New Zealand* (1873), Anthony Trollope records:

> I have been at very many bush houses,—at over thirty different stations in the different colonies,—but at not one . . . in which I have not found a fair provision of books. It is universally recognised among squatters that a man who settles down in the bush without books is preparing for himself a miserable future life. . . . [He] has no other recreation to entice him. He has no club, no billiard table, no public-house which he can frequent. Balls and festivities are very rare. . . . I think that reading is at least as customary as it is with young men in London. The authors I found most popular were certainly Shakespeare, Dickens, and Macaulay. I would back the chance of finding Macaulay's *Essays* at a station against that of any book in the language except Shakespeare. To have a Shakespeare is a point of honour with every man who owns a book . . . whether he reads it or leaves it unread.[16]

As British emigrants settled abroad in increasing numbers throughout the nineteenth century, the colonial settlers established semi-autonomous communities with varying degrees of dependency and levels of cultural and economic ties to Britain. They maintained these ties through expanding networks of trade, transportation, and communication, and the "thousands of books, tracts, letters and newspapers" that circulated in the colonies and wherever the English language was read.

On the most basic material level, the late-Victorian boom in books and printed media was made possible by imperial processes of expansion and centralization. For instance, the massive production of books, magazines, and newspapers required raw materials from around the world, such as copper and gutta-percha for the Empire's hundreds of thousands of miles of trans-oceanic telegraph cables;[17] steel, rubber, cloth, copper, and iron ore for manufacturing rotary presses;[18] cotton rags, wood pulp, wool, and grass fibers for making paper;[19] and ink, resins, and linseed oil for printing on it. In the 1880s and 1890s, as the expansion of the periodical press "exploded into cacophony,"[20] newspapers and magazines also spread widely and rapidly along the same colonial trade routes—which also served as the world's mail delivery routes—developed and maintained by private companies heavily subsidized by the British during the previous four centuries.

According to Robert Lee: "[T]hat the railway age and era of the new imperialism coincided was not accidental, because the railway and imperialism were interdependent."[21] Lee explains:

> During the second half of the nineteenth century, the horizons of railway engineers widened dramatically. From being conquerors of the relatively tame environment of northern England ... they went to bring safe, economical and fast travel ... to some of the remotest parts of the globe. ... [T]he technological changes of the mid-nineteenth century gave [Britain] the means to develop large territorial empires in previously unhospitable lands. Railways were foremost among these innovations, but not alone. Beside them were quinine ... the steamship ... and the electric telegraph, which in the 1870s was extended across the world.[22]

The interdependence of the popular periodical press and British imperial expansion was a factor in these sweeping transformations in distribution and transportation. This interdependence might be mapped and statistically determined through data tables in annual yearbooks and colonial lists of the period, but it was never on more ostentatious display than at the Imperial Press Conference of 1909. In the following section, I describe how British publishers repositioned themselves with respect to both the politics of Empire and their own expanding foreign and colonial markets. The influence they had as "arbiters of public opinion" helped them broker an informal arrangement to align the concerns of Empire with the operations of colonial publishers. The formation of an Empire Press Union (EPU) was one direct result of this meeting and, in 1909, signaled that more substantive changes were to come, while building on developments in colonial publishing of the past half century.[23]

Figure 1.1 The Illinois, U.S. Mail Steamer (1906); U.S. Mail Railway Post Office (1930); Workers on a Telegraph Line (circa 1890); Post Office, Mombasa, Kenya (1905); Railway Workers Unloading Mail (circa 1930); UK Bicycle Postmen (1900); Post Office, Nairobi, Kenya (1905); and U.S. Postmen (1915).

The Imperial Press Conference of 1909

Organized by Harry Brittain (*The Standard*), the first Imperial Press Conference gathered populist press barons Edward Levy-Lawson (*Daily Telegraph*), Alfred Harmsworth (*Daily Mail*), C. Arthur Pearson (*Daily Express*), and W.T. Stead (*Pall Mall Gazette, Review of Reviews*); 55 press representatives from Canada, Australia, New Zealand, South Africa, Burma, Ceylon, the Straits Settlements of Malaya, and India; and "[s]ix hundred newspapermen from the United Kingdom."[24] It convened Saturday evening, June 5, at the Imperial International Exhibition Halls in Shepherd's Bush, London, where many of the journalists from around the world received their first direct impressions of the colonial and imperial exhibition movement in Europe of the period 1886–1914.[25] British hospitality was at a premium, however, and the newspapermen were treated like foreign dignitaries. In his opening remarks, former prime minister Lord Rosebery instructed that newspapers "should be eternal; and the power of a great newspaper, with the double function of guiding and embodying the public opinion of the province over which it exerts an influence is immeasurably greater than that of any statesmen could be."[26] Much of the rhetoric was directed to impress upon delegates the historic position of the newspapers, their influence on readers, and their responsibility to defend the Empire. According to

Figure 1.2 Australian and New Zealand Delegates at the Imperial Press Conference; Members in Front of Hollow Tree in Stanley Park (June 4, 1909).

Rosebery, the conference "stands out by itself, and marks a distinct epoch in the history of our Empire."[27] Stead remarked that it was the first time that, "the keepers of the eyes and ears of King Demos had been gathered together from Britain and from Britain's dominions overseas."[28]

Harmsworth called it "one of the most important gatherings that has ever taken place in England."[29]

Over the course of three highly choreographed weeks, they discussed international cable rates, news wire services, improved press communication, and literature and journalism.[30] Other "vital topics on the agenda" included Germany's impending military threat, the Royal Navy, and expectations regarding colonial contributions to the Empire's defenses.[31] The representative for the *Halifax Daily Echo*, A.F. MacDonald, claimed that the meeting demonstrated for him "Unity of the Empire, and the solidarity of the race which spreads its roots and branches to the far ends of the earth."[32] Representing *The Times of India*, Stanley Reed claimed that more important work would be accomplished later by the "fifty-one missionaries of empire which will be diffused over the globe."[33] P.D. Ross of the *Ottawa Evening Journal* reflected on his return to Canada, "every man of us has come back a stronger imperialist than he was before, if he was one—and if he was not, he was probably converted."[34] If these "overseas newspapermen" ever suspected Fleet Street of having less than disinterested motives, public statements from 1909 suggest otherwise.[35] Their prestigious reception at the "heart of the Empire" was, for journalists in Canada, India, Australia, New Zealand, and South Africa, a source of political capital and brought opportunities for public relations at home.[36] For G. Fenwick's readers of the *Otago Daily Times* (Dunedin, NZ): "[I]t was a striking gathering called for memorable reasons, at a portentous time, and held in the place of great associations. It was a strange and significant meeting which, surely, will make history."[37] The *Sydney Daily Telegraph* and *Evening Post* (Wellington, NZ) claimed that it "could not fail to have a far-reaching and time-enduring influence for good on the overseas Dominions."[38] Lee Thompson suggests that: "[T]here is little doubt that press delegates returned home with a greater awareness of their ties to each other and the mother country."[39] And, as Andrew Thompson notes:

> [I]t is impossible not to be struck by the large number who identified their careers with the cause of imperial unity[,] wrote extensively on the reconstruction of the Empire[, and] shared a profound belief in the importance of the press in forming and directing public opinion. . . . They were not so much spectators as participators in the drama of imperial politics, and they regarded their papers as instruments.[40]

They arrived as the representatives of 55 home newspapers spread throughout the Empire, and they returned to their separate markets in due course. For many of these journalists, however, the experience had impressed upon them the significance and urgency of their historical moment. In expressions of brotherhood and camaraderie, they were reminded of values and interests they shared. Bound by common language and professional print culture—a theme of talks throughout the conference—and charged to proclaim Imperial interdependence to constituencies back home, the recognized arbiters of public opinion thus became potential nodes in a larger, more powerful print communications network of news, information, and culture.

Colonial presses had expanded and consolidated operations throughout the nineteenth and early twentieth centuries. In major cities such as Bombay, Ottawa, and Cape Town, they developed the infrastructures for printing, publishing, and distributing works based on European models. In New Zealand, the number of POs increased 186 percent between 1892 (1,263) and 1912 (2,350). In the same period, the number of books received and dispatched by POs in New Zealand grew 1,760 percent (3,342,781 received in 1891–92; 58,828,436 received in 1911–12) and 1,600 percent (3,827,980 dispatched in 1891–92; 61,364,917 dispatched in 1911–12). Statistics regarding newspapers are much higher, although percentage increases are lower: 448 percent (9,768,226 received in 1891–92; 43,801,719 received in 1911–12) and 498 percent (8,733,686 dispatched in 1891–92; 43,460,016 dispatched in 1911–12).[41] From 1841 to 1911, the number of POs in Australia grew 5,600 percent (from 101 to 5,664),[42] and the statistics for letters, packets, and newspapers in Australia are astonishing. In 1911, Australian POs handled 139,603,000 newspapers, including newspapers received from (11,691,000) and dispatched to (7,926,000) overseas locations. This is an 11,200 percent increase over the 1,247,099 newspapers handled in 1841.[43] In India, the number of printing presses in 1890 (1,465) compared with 1904 (2,139) shows a 146 percent increase, and the growth of newspaper and magazine publishing in that period is 163 percent (1890: 526 newspapers, 302 magazines: 828 total vs. 1904: 709 newspapers, 640 magazines: 1,349 total).[44] Of course, they were importing and exporting books, magazines, and newspapers as well.

In 1909–10, even the Territory of Papua (British New Guinea, pop. 879) received 52,178 and dispatched 21,104 newspapers for the year[45] (see Appendix E).

Although based on exported British and European models, print cultures in English had also diversified, developed independently, and differentiated through the rapid expansion of their markets. Practices of publishers and printers respond to different sets of concerns, and ultimately their fortunes depend on book and periodical buyers' expectations. Although Indian and colonial readers had literary tastes in common, publishers and printers met their demands under a variety of conditions.[46] By 1909, British journalism had also reached its capacity to expand under current cable rates and regulations across the Empire. The strain this placed on press infrastructures was leading to breakdowns in their communications beyond national borders. With the emergence of a global scope in the operations of colonial

Figure 1.3 Four Colonial Newspaper Wrappers, Including "The Australian Stamp
Collector" (Addressed to Chicago, USA [1895]); and "The Daily
Chronicle" (Addressed to Paramaribo, Surinam, Bearing 1889 1c
[1890, 12 December printed]).

publishing, concerns of the Empire were imbricated, shared concerns had
become international, and this is certainly a telling portrait of the confluence
of print media and Empire in the early decades of the twentieth century.[47]
The first Imperial Press Conference marks an important turning point in
the globalization of publishing, and its year, 1909, divides Chapters 3
and 4 in this chronological study. By 1909, the mobilization of domestic
mass markets for newspapers and magazines had virtually run the course.
Dramatic leaps in circulation year after year had slowed, and to expand
further into foreign markets required some significant shifting, politically
and commercially, of the British world. The role of the EPU, a partnership
of newspapermen formed at the 1909 conference, was to be a mouthpiece
or forum for newspapers throughout the Empire, and, throughout the first
half of the twentieth century, the EPU conducted regular conferences and
lobbied governments and private companies for looser regulations and lower
cable rates.[48] It was at this time that new copyright legislation was passed
on both sides of the Atlantic (see Appendix D).[49] Further revisions to the
postal codes of Great Britain and the US were also enacted. These affected

literary authorship, agency, publishing, and the professional business of selling popular fiction to large international readerships in particular.

Alfred Harmsworth's production of the *Daily Mail* in 1896 was a milestone in the history of popular British journalism. The paper achieved sales of nearly 1 million by 1900 and ushered in an unprecedented era of national mass-circulation dailies based in London, "involving a vast increase in readership, but a considerable reduction in the number of titles."[50] Although this was "genuinely innovative," the *Daily Mail* "did not spring from nothing." As John Feather notes, its "immediate predecessors included several magazines ... notably *Tit-bits*. ... Indeed, it was the success of *Tit-bits*, and his own similar magazine *Answers*, which persuaded Harmsworth that there was a gap in the market."[51] In terms of relative numbers, enormous leaps in the circulations of British and American periodicals had also been characteristic of many titles in the middle of the nineteenth century. The introduction of popular shilling monthlies, most notably *Macmillan's* (1859) and *The Cornhill Magazine* (1860), had brought a high degree of intellectual, literary, and cultural entertainment within the economic reach of hundreds of thousands of readers,[52] and the penny bloods, and other fiction papers of the penny press, had phenomenally higher circulations than these.[53]

As with any complex social and historical event, the factors contributing to the industry's material expansion at the end of the nineteenth century were numerous, accumulative, and often contradictory. Literacy rates for Victorian men and women certainly rose in the wake of Forster's Education Act (1870),[54] for instance, but that does not acknowledge the critical distinction—one recognized by the Victorians themselves—between literacy, or an ability to read, and Literacy, as an ability to not only read but also appreciate certain forms of approved and uplifting material—as in the Bible, religious tracts, and other forms of "wholesome reading" promoted by "evangelical and utilitarian literary reformers."[55] As Richard D. Altick, Jonathan Rose, and others argue,[56] the facts are more complicated, as Victorian educators did not posit a simple relationship between reading and literacy education. Taking into account contemporary definitions of literacy, nearly 90 percent of Victorian men and women were already literate by the mid-century. Education, in the fullest Victorian sense, signified more than that. It was both instruction in elementary skills, such as basic reading and writing, and instruction in the proper use of those skills, intended to form character.[57] It was not sufficient to read: reading had to involve the proper texts.

In R.W. Rawson's report on British and Welsh prison inmates in 1841, the men who were recorded as having at least the basic ability to read and write still "had not received that amount of instruction which would be worthy of the title of education."[58] And, as Brantlinger suggests, the question of adult literacy rates in the nineteenth century becomes "not one of literacy versus illiteracy, but of two kinds of literacy, dividing those who read books from those who read only, at best, newspapers."[59] Regarding connections between compulsory education and the expansion of the American periodical press, moreover, Richard Ohmann has noted the creative chronology. Ohmann writes:

> To be sure, there can be no print culture for millions unless millions can read. Yet the spread of literacy cannot explain why the magazines of the 1890s grew so fast. It is enough to note that the timing is wrong . . . most women and almost all men could read at the beginning of the nineteenth century. . . . [In the United States] . . . basic literacy among white people reached nearly 90 percent in 1850.[60]

Recent historians of reading have further interpreted the education Acts and reading programs of the nineteenth century in light of culture clashes, highlighting the ultimate failure of empowered classes to impose their values on those below.[61] Educational efforts directed toward working-class children were supposed to combat the dangers of reading penny bloods, fiction papers, and other pernicious texts, but they often achieved the opposite effect.[62]

Technological improvements in printing, ink, and paper production, rising literacy rates, and advertising subsidies are routinely cited as being among the primary factors leading to the massive sales and circulations recorded for American mass-market magazines in the 1890s.[63] According to Theodore Peterson:

> [Frank A. Munsey] vividly demonstrated a basic economic principle of twentieth-century magazine publishing—a principle which McClure, Walker, Curtis, and others were discovering in the late nineteenth century. It was simply this: one could achieve a large circulation by selling his magazine for much less than its cost of production and could take his profits from the high volume of advertising that a large circulation attracted. For not only did Munsey, like McClure and the others, make his appeal to a large mass of hitherto ignored readers; he also made his appeal to a large and untapped class of advertisers, advertisers as eager for inexpensive space rates as readers were for inexpensive magazines.[64]

This decision to rely on advertising revenues, rather than subscription rates or single-issue prices, might explain how many publishers financed expanding circulations, but not why they wanted to in the first place. As advertisers paid only for net paid circulation, and not the total print run, large-scale productions subsidized by advertising revenues were a monumental risk. In *Scientific Circulation Management for Newspapers* (1915), William Scott argues, "there is little incentive to building excessively large circulations . . . because advertising rates cannot be made to advance commensurately with circulation." To illustrate this point, Scott offers the following example:

When the European War began, some metropolitan papers doubled their circulations almost overnight. The *New York Evening Telegram*, for example, leaped from 200,000 to 400,000 daily, and this was a dead loss, because advertisers refused to pay, even if they were asked, any higher advertising rate, and the cost of print paper made the gain a business calamity.[65]

If a print order was too high, and advertisers paid for page space based on number of copies sold, the publisher bore the loss "of all that wasted white paper, and the cost of handling it both ways." Scott writes that, "the cost of white paper makes the waste in returns and overprint economically disastrous."[66] S.S. McClure, editor of *McClure's Magazine* and Newspaper Syndicate, observed in *My Autobiography* (1913) that large circulations often meant large numbers of unsold copies. McClure explains:

> In our excess of confidence, we overstepped ourselves. For our January number, 1896, we overprinted so far that we had about 60,000 returned copies on our hands. ... We were losing money, moreover, on account of our enormous increase in circulation. Most of our advertising contracts were made on a basis of 40,000 to 80,000 circulation. We had taken on an unprecedented body of advertising at a low rate, and now we were printing 250,000 magazines a month, with the enormously increased cost of manufacture which such a large printing entailed, and we were getting no more for our advertising than if we were printing only 80,000 copies a month. ... [W]ith our low-rate advertising contracts and increasing circulation, the magazine was losing $4000 a month.[67]

When periodical publishing entered the world of Victorian industrialized mass production in the second half of the nineteenth century, the level of risk involved—by virtue of sheer numbers and volume sizes made possible—became enormously high.[68]

In the absence of new markets, networks of newsagents and dealers, and ultimately more readers of magazines, print run totals in the hundreds of thousands could precipitate a publisher's financial ruin. "Scientific circulation management" would become the question of managing, and more importantly enabling and building, the wider distribution networks needed for shipping and moving those enormous print runs, as Munsey's 1907 memoir suggests:

> I covered the country with traveling men from Maine to Nebraska, and from New Orleans to St. Paul. Beyond Nebraska I used the mails. I kept fifteen to twenty men on the road, and each man employed from one to a dozen helpers ... I laid out routes for the men ... and sent every man a daily letter ... I not only wrote to these men, but I wrote to

newsdealers everywhere, and saw that they were amply supplied . . .
I attended to the shipping, and to freight-bills . . . The expenses of
men on the road, of freights, expressage, shipping, printing, and binding
. . . literally chewed up money.[69]

From 1893 to 1895, *Munsey's Magazine* increased its monthly circulation
from 40,000 to 500,000. By March 1906, Munsey claimed a combined
monthly circulation of 2,100,000: *Munsey's Magazine* 800,000, *The Argosy*
500,000, *The Scrap Book* 500,000, and *The All-Story* 300,000.[70]

Two magazines on Munsey's list, *The Argosy* (1896) and *The All-Story*
(1905), devoted not more than 10–15 percent of their page counts to
advertising.[71] By the start of the First World War, this figure had fallen below
10 percent. And still these magazines became market leaders, and they
retained the position for three decades or more, all this without the significant presence of advertising or advertising revenues (see Appendix F).

In Britain, the "first phase" of expansion in the nineteenth-century
periodical press—from 716 to 1,787 titles annually between 1846 and
1864[72]—involved a similar dynamic. Circulation was then also a matter of
smart distribution, and, from this phase, "the name of W.H. Smith would
be identified in the popular mind with the world's first great railway system."
History of the firm shows that, by 1830–39, "the growth of cheaper and
more regular forms of transport . . . carried out a growing supply of London
newspapers, journals, and books."[73] Charles Wilson asserts, "Here in the
making was a market for news and literature. London had both the news
and the literature: the task was to bridge the gaps in transport and
communications."[74]

Periodical Expansion, Publishing Networks

Several key international events of the late 1880s facilitated the continuation
of this trend, and the volumes of material involved would increase at an
astonishing rate. Dramatic expansions of publishers' horizons in the final
decades of the nineteenth century correspond to Simon Eliot's "second
phase" of British periodical expansion, representing a return to the growth
experienced from 1830 to 1855, but on a scale much larger than before.
From 1875 to 1903, the number of periodical titles published annually in
the UK increased from 2,252 to 4,943, and the circulations of some of these
titles, most notably *The Strand Magazine* (1891) and the *Daily Mail* (1896),
climbed to levels in the neighborhood of half a million to one million
copies.[75] The introduction of overseas markets, networks of newsagents and
dealers, and increasing volumes of magazines transported and distributed
globally is an expansion underscored by technological advances in late-
Victorian trade, shipping, travel, and communication. The development of
the infrastructure—the ability to move volumes of magazines *en masse*,
to be sold on newsstands and by news dealers around the world—helps to

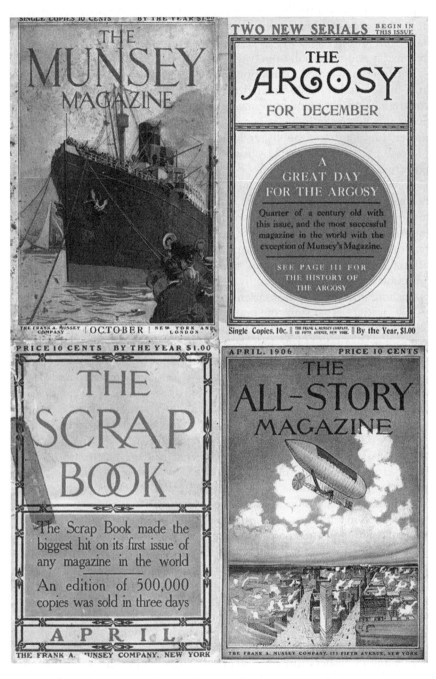

Figure 1.4 Four Covers: *Munsey's Magazine* (October 1907); *The Argosy* (December 1907); *The Scrap Book* (April 1906); and *The All-Story Magazine* (April 1906).

explain more fully a willingness on the part of many publishers at the turn of the century to embrace operations on such behemoth scales, and contextualizes an industry's resolve to accept risks imposed by seemingly unbridled expansion and potentially runaway circulations.

The long-anticipated ratification of the International Copyright Convention in September 1886 created an unprecedented system of automatic copyright between member states. Signatory nations included four of the five major European industrial countries and their colonies.[76] Eight months earlier, London-based publisher Macmillan & Co. had launched the first successful series of affordable reprints for overseas distribution, the Colonial Library of Copyright Books.

In 1891, the U.S. International Copyright Act was linked to events in Europe and the Empire and extended its own limited system of copyright for foreign nationals into large North American markets. Requirements of the Act expanded operations between British and American publishers and reinforced the development of transatlantic print networks.[77] These events offered powerful incentives to expand sales and circulations beyond domestic markets and profoundly influenced decisions shaping the British publishing industry and transatlantic print cultures for decades.

The initial expansion of book sales and circulations beyond the United Kingdom involved some of the most prestigious publishing firms in London and Edinburgh, but also had immediate effects on the production and distribution of popular and mass-market books and periodicals. The expansion taking place on the heels of the Berlin Conference (1885) was no coincidence either.[78] Berlin occasioned the imperial powers' division of physical geographies of the world (Africa); those same countries met again a year later, in Berne, to divide the world's intellectual geography.

British publishers had been trying to expand their book and periodical operations beyond domestic markets for much of the nineteenth century. Early efforts were continually frustrated by the ready availability of American pirated editions and the prohibitive cost of transporting books and printed material thousands of miles away—with enough regularity and reliability to maintain a secure, steady profit. During the 1840s, the firm of Wiley & Putnam attempted to sell British periodicals on the American market,[79] but the absence of reciprocal copyright laws between the two nations, and logistical difficulties of meeting demands before much cheaper pirated editions were produced, undermined these early efforts.[80] Attempts to supply the large colonial markets beyond the African Cape—readerships in India, Australia, and New Zealand, for example—were particularly sensitive to the prohibitive cost of shipping the material, sluggish delivery schedules, and unreliable distribution networks. Combined, these factors cut deeply into publishers' already slim profit margins. After the British Imperial Copyright Act of 1842, John Murray attempted the first series of Colonial reprints for India, Australia, and Canada,[81] but complications with shipping schedules, distribution networks, and loopholes in the Act itself precipitated

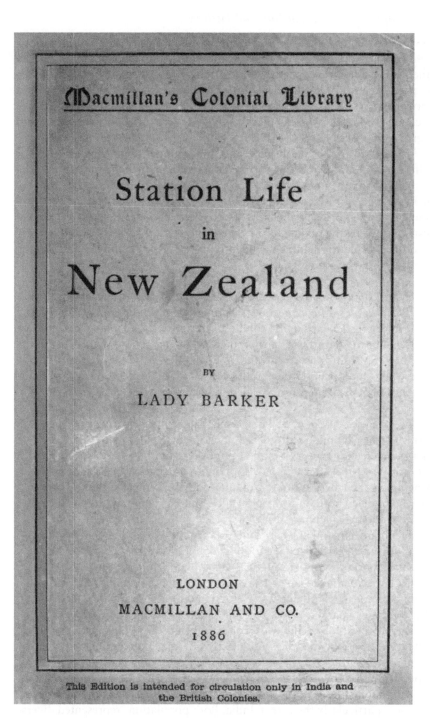

Figure 1.5 Lady Barker, *Station Life in New Zealand*. London: Macmillan & Co.,
1886. Macmillan's Colonial Library, Number 1.

the library's demise (1843–49). Despite William Blackwood's "connections with retailers and publishers in Australia, India, Canada, and South Africa, [the firm] made little concerted effort to market aggressively in these areas, in part because of difficulties in establishing transport and distribution networks."[82] Other firms, such as Smith, Elder & Co. and Oliver & Boyd, declined to pursue overseas markets aggressively for these same legal and logistical reasons.[83]

For years, British publishers had maintained significant exports of different types of book and printed material, including magazines. The virtual monopoly on textbook sales to schools in India was a reliably lucrative trade for Macmillan, Cambridge, Longmans, and Oxford.[84] Laurel Brake notes that British publishers of books and periodicals had international distributions by the middle of the nineteenth century at least, and that their recorded circulation figures included both domestic shipments and foreign exports. Brake explains:

> *The* [London] *Times* was the most widely read newspaper [and] both *Blackwood's Magazine* and *Chamber's Edinburgh Journal* achieved healthy readerships in the colonies. The latter . . . adapted its publishing schedule to fit patterns of shipping, producing a monthly number in the mid-1840s in order to cater for the colonies. Mudie's offered a service . . . by ship to subscribers in the colonies, and it seems highly probable that periodical literature formed a part of this consignment.[85]

The large-scale export of books and magazines to foreign markets—in terms of the volumes, and on the phenomenal scale, realized by the end of the nineteenth century—eluded publishers until 1886. That year, with ratification of the International Copyright Convention in Berne imminent, Macmillan launched another Colonial copyright reprint series. This was closely modeled both on Murray's failed 1843 attempt and recent successes of the German Tauchnitz series.

Macmillan and others had laid the groundwork, lobbying for British approval of the 1886 convention and exploring the potential for new colonial markets.[87] In 1884–85, Macmillan's junior partner, Maurice Macmillan, conducted an extended railway tour of India and Australia, in an attempt to scope out ways of expanding the firm's business beyond the textbook market. This reconnaissance demonstrated that markets abounded there for quality, affordable reprints of popular-fiction titles.[88] Potential sales extended beyond strictly colonial populations supplied by large numbers of expatriates each year. There were native populations, especially those involved in government, agencies, religious organizations, educational institutions, the system of libraries, and various public services. This was particularly the case in India. Both populations represented diverse and rapidly growing markets of colonial readers eager for many different kinds of printed matter, but especially low-priced novels written in English.

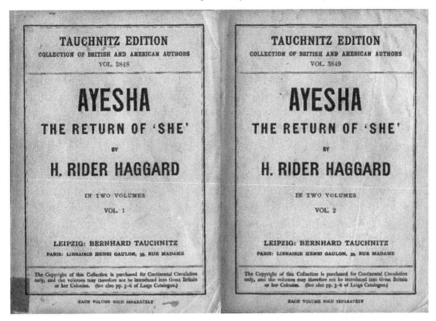

Figure 1.6 H. Rider Haggard, *Ayesha: The Return of 'She'*, Vols. 1 & 2. Leipzig: Bernard Tauchnitz, 1905.[86]

Macmillan also hired translators, and its Indian catalogue would feature "hundreds of books in twenty-one of the chief vernaculars."[89]

Launched the next year, Macmillan's Colonial Library of Copyright Books saw its firm's annual profits on the investment begin to climb, and steadily. Within just a few years, markets in India, Australasia, and the colonies became major sources of revenue. According to Priya Joshi, the realignment of resources influenced the firm's long-term marketing strategies and publishing practices, both at home and abroad.[90] By the beginning of the First World War, exports to India had increased to such volumes that Macmillan established permanent supply depots in Bombay (1901), Calcutta (1907), and Madras (1913). Before Imperial German submarines patrolling the coasts of the Atlantic made international shipping too dangerous,[91] Macmillan introduced a new title—printed, bound, and shipped from England, onto the colonial market—every 2 weeks.[92]

Macmillan's success might have seemed an unlikely gamble, if not for critical innovations in shipping and transportation, improved communication technologies, and the 1869 opening of the Suez Canal. These and the international trade infrastructure they helped develop dramatically decreased the time, effort, and cost necessary for steady, long-term supplies of periodical exports to overseas markets several thousands of miles away. The combination of international copyright legislation and Macmillan's successful series shows that, by the mid-1880s, large-scale publishing operations overseas had become possible, and it proved an irresistibly attractive commercial risk.

The firms Kegan Paul, Sampson & Low, and George Robertson (Melbourne)[93] followed Macmillan's lead into the Indian and colonial markets in 1887; Richard Bentley & Son launched a successful Australian Series that same year. Longmans entered the field with Rider Haggard's latest novel, a wild Zulu romance, *Nada, the Lily* (1892), and Blackwood arrived in 1894.[94] By the turn of the twentieth century, Murray (1900), Methuen (1895), Cassell & Co. (1895), Bell & Sons (1894), Heinemann (1892), and 12 other leading UK publishers had established house imprints of Colonial library copyright books, and they issued sequentially numbered paperback titles at regularly scheduled intervals of 2–4 weeks. This anonymous editorial, published in *The Bookseller* (November 6, 1895), captures some sense of urgency in regards to the future of the Colonial Library:

> We are convinced that it is worth the while of every publisher to follow the successful lead that has been set, and that is, not to waste valuable time, but, *simultaneously with the English edition*, to issue one for the Colonies in paper covers.[95]

Australia and New Zealand became the single largest overseas market for exports of books, newspapers, and magazines from Britain. This accounted for nearly one-third of all shipments, while native-born colonial writers[96] contributed some of the most popular titles included on publishers' lists.[97] In 1901, George Bell's Indian and Colonial Library had 35 agents operating in New Zealand alone.[98]

The publishers not only exported large shipments of cheap books, paperback reprints, and a host of periodicals, but also print culture. *Blackwood's* (Blackwood & Son), *Edinburgh Review* (Archibald Constable), *Macmillan's Magazine* (Macmillan), *The Cornhill* (Smith, Elder), *All the Year Round* (Chapman & Hall), and *Longmans'* (Longmans, Green) were all "house" journals of major publishers. Their advertising pages included extensive monthly lists of book publications, and scholars of Victorian periodicals have long viewed them as promotional organs for the book lists. David Finkelstein shows that magazines were "used both as a showcase for new talent and as a method for attracting potential contributors to [the firms'] book lists,"[99] and Brake notes that publishers "Macmillan and George Smith . . . created periodicals to bolster book publication."[100] Brake explains, not only that, "house periodicals supplied free publicity for house book lists," but also that, "the non-serialised or non-series book title . . . was a commercial risk." For these reasons, Victorian "authors and publishers of books . . . came to view the periodical press as an extension of their sphere."[101] Publishing houses brought out magazines during the 1860s and 1870s if they did not already have one, many of which bore the names of the house itself.[102] *Tinsley's Magazine* lost £25 a month, but, as William Tinsley declared: "What cheaper advertisement can I have for twenty-five pounds a month? It advertises my name and publications; and it keeps my authors together."[103]

The expansion of colonial library series, and the authors they published together beyond the UK in the 1880s and 1890s, cannot be viewed separately from the production and distribution of periodicals, because, by that time, "the spheres of the book and the serial inhabited one and the same galaxy."[104] The two were synergistically linked and they shared the same rhythm for the most prestigious London and Edinburgh publishers. A "system of pre-volume publication in the magazine" culminating in "the appearance of the book edition" were two integral parts of doing business.[105] *Macmillan's Magazine*, *The Cornhill*, *Blackwood's*, *Edinburgh Review*, *All the Year Round*, and *Longmans'* were among the house periodicals that streamed into colonial markets, along with their publishers' books, after 1886. American magazines such as the *Atlantic Monthly* and *Harper's Monthly Magazine* were not far behind.

Figure 1.7 Eight Covers: *The Cornhill Magazine* (January 1897); *Blackwood's Magazine* (July 1885); *All the Year Round* (January 1891); *Longman's Magazine* (November 1887); *The Atlantic Monthly* (November 1880); *Harper's New Monthly Magazine* (March 1886); *Scribner's Magazine* (January 1887); and *The English Illustrated Magazine* (January 1886).

Martyn Lyons asserts:

> *Blackwood's Magazine* and the *Illustrated London News* linked readers
> all over the [world]. Melbourne readers ... were little different from
> their counterparts in Birmingham, Boston or the Cape. They were ...
> supplied by the same publishers, informed by similar journals [and]
> distinguished by a very high rate of newspaper consumption.[106]

During the 1880s and 1890s, markets for periodical exports to the
colonies also extended beyond adult readers of *The Times*, *Illustrated
London News*, *Chamber's*, *Macmillan's*, *Longmans'*, and *Blackwood's
Magazine*. Australian boys grew up on English comic papers such as *Gem*,
Magnet, and *Boy's Own Paper*;[107] so did teenage girls in South Africa,
India, and the Caribbean.[108] When Macmillan, Methuen, Blackwood, and
Bentley expanded distributions into colonial markets with copyright
reprints, journals, and literary reviews, the transatlantic publishing empires
of George Newnes, Harmsworth, Stead, and Pearson seized those same
opportunities presented overseas.

Periodical Expansion and the Media Empire

The great media empires of Harmsworth, Stead, Newnes, and Pearson were
flourishing by the mid-1890s.[109] American publishing magnates such as
Cyrus Curtis, William Randolph Hearst, Frank A. Munsey, and S.S.
McClure were also expanding interests abroad and diversifying and
reinforcing empires at home.[110] The mass-market giants of the 1890s were
no more aggressive than old-established, nineteenth-century firms such as
Macmillan, Murray, and Blackwood, but they were engaged in the business
of low-cost publishing for massive profits on much greater scales. They were
not adverse to major contracts with agencies handling retail or commodity
advertising either. As E.S. Turner notes in his study, *The Shocking History
of Advertising* (1953), the middle of the 1890s was "the period when modern
advertising began, the scale of advertising expanded [and the ...] tempo
quickened."[111]

What industrious firms such as Macmillan and Munsey had in common,
however, were new markets of English-speaking readers overseas, not just
across the ocean, but thousands of miles away on the other side of the world.
And, by the middle of the 1890s, the prohibitive cost of supplying these
markets in bulk and consistently on time had fallen precipitously. In 1891,
Blackwood signed an agreement with Leonard Scott & Co. of New York
to begin producing the U.S. edition of *Blackwood's Magazine*; American
sales of *Blackwood's* increased the publisher's circulations by 20 percent
within the year.[112] In 1896, the July issue of *The Strand Magazine* sold more
than 300,000 copies in Britain and 60,000 more in the US, with many of
them purchased by news dealers and bound, in bulk, for export markets

overseas. By 1900, the monthly circulation of *The Strand*'s American edition had nearly tripled to 178,000 copies, and the American edition of the *London Illustrated News* (1889) sold an average of 28,000 copies per week the same year.[113]

Though just one of the principal developments contributing to a phenomenal expansion in titles, sheer volume, and sales of British and American magazines at the turn of the century, the exploitation of global infrastructures and international markets made possible from 1880 to 1900 was a critical[114] and now, surprisingly often, overlooked one. The enormous vertical expansion of print and periodical industries in Britain and the United States throughout the 1890s owes as much to these global, horizontal developments as it does to innovations in printing technologies such as the rotary press and Linotype machine, a domestic "explosion of literacy," the cheap cost of paper and ink, or the "conceptual breakthrough" in mass-market advertising "that pumped vast amounts of capital into the publishing business."[115]

British and anglophone print cultures, publishers, and audiences of readers at the turn of the twentieth century became increasingly integrated through a global crisscrossing of the world by print and periodical exports, and modern publishing became intricately tied to "problems of credit, of exchange rates, of transport and of competing [global] interests."[116] Packed into the holds of mail steamers, cargo ships, freight trains, and delivery trucks, these crates and pallets of copyright reprints from London, scientific journals from Calcutta, newspapers from Melbourne, monthly reviews, cheap yellow paperbacks, American pulps, and mass-market glossy magazines were all measured in terms of their tonnage, container size, and freight load. They mapped lines of global distribution by degrees of latitude and longitude and flowed outward to all parts of the world through an expanding infrastructure of seaways, shipping lanes, canals, tropical belts, inland roads, and iron railways. According to Eliot:

> [S]tarting in 1869 and concentrating on the period of late-Victorian expansion the rate of growth in the postal distribution of printed materials such as newspapers, books and circulars is quite extraordinary: in 1869 109 million such packets were delivered; by 1913–14 this figure had risen to 1,379.4 million packets. In other words, in the space of forty-six years the communication of printed material by mail had increased more than twelve-fold.[117]

These shipments of news, fiction, and literary culture traced the outlines of postal delivery routes and undersea cables of the electric telegraph, which had been established by imperial armies and commercial trading companies of Europe and North America. The range, frequency, and volume of the shipments became inextricably bound to these very same systems of trade, transportation, and communication infrastructures. This burgeoning global culture of modern print media also became tightly linked with concerns about speed, risk, mobility, technology, contact, and control. Thus, by the end of the nineteenth century, British and American magazines and the print cultures they represented had been folded squarely into the major concerns of empire. Twenty-five years later, the London publisher Hodder & Stoughton appropriated the notion of an imperial conquest in the firm's advertisements for a successful series of popular paperback novels: "The 1000-title list that spans the Empire: the List upon which the sun never sets."[118]

As the nineteenth century drew to a close, Walter Besant looked back over the course of the last 100 years of British publishing, and he noted: "Largely as a result of British colonial policies, the readership of the English-speaking world has expanded from 50,000 in 1830 to 120 million by the late 1890s."[119] Writing to his literary agent, James B. Pinker, in 1911, Conrad thus recalled his own relationship with the "readership of the English-speaking world" a decade before: "There isn't a single club and messroom and man-of-war in the British Seas and Dominions which hasn't its copy of Maga—not to mention all the Scots in all parts of the world."[120]

By the beginning of the First World War, British and American publishers had permanent agents and representatives all over the world. Berlin, Leipzig, Paris, Pretoria, Bombay, Calcutta, Toronto, Melbourne, and Tokyo became major nodes of supply and distribution. Global readers' tastes, preferences, and buying habits were of course influenced by particular class, cultural, and geographic prejudices, but, in terms of the material commodity—the simple and elegant fact that books and magazines are still objects, and, as objects, they must first be delivered into the hands of their readers—these factors are often secondary to choices made by publishers that determined the range and availability of reading materials at hand.[121]

Noting that Australian readers certainly responded to novels, newspapers, and magazines in a variety of ways, Lyons nonetheless maintains that, "common literary preferences persisted ... throughout the Empire."[122] But, as Joshi demonstrates, British publishing also became embedded in conditions of global marketing to Indian and colonial readers, and these markets soon directly shaped and determined their publishing practices and long-term marketing strategies. Paul Eggert suggests that at least one reason for Mudie and Smith's campaign against the three-decker novel, which ultimately succeeded in 1894, was the increasing popularity and traffic of cheap periodical exports overseas. The round-trip trafficking of heavy borrowed book freight to Australia and New Zealand could not compete.[123] Joshi also contends that the dominance of literary romance (vs. realism) in Britain at the turn of the century was influenced largely by the literary tastes and preferences of Indian readers. Based on her research in the Macmillan archives, Joshi maintains that:

Readers of the 'nineties and of the following years had an anti-realistic bias [that] blended nicely with the firm's already established practice toward fiction, especially in the Colonial Library . . . pursued because it found . . . repeated approval among Indian readers who made Macmillan their firm of choice . . . for the novels they consumed voraciously. . . . The firm's willingness to please this audience through "anti-realistic" fiction may in fact have cost it some of the "young lions" of the new century . . ., but it appeared to be a price the firm was willing to pay, as it clearly cost it nothing in profits or prestige in an overseas market that was increasingly central to the firm's fiscal health.[124]

Finkelstein uncovers a similar dynamic informing the decisions of the publishers of *Blackwood's Magazine*. Imperial imagery pervaded the magazine's pages at the end of the nineteenth century, and Blackwood drew heavily from an extensive network of foreign and colonial authors.[125] In 1888, J.E.C. Bodley remarked on the magazine's importance, not only for readers in Capetown, Kimberley, and Pretoria, "but also in remote stations and solitary Magistrates' residences"[126] of the African interior. Blackwood's colonial readers were not taken for granted either, but directly helped shape editorial decisions made by the old-established Edinburgh firm, as Finkelstein cites in the following two examples.

In 1881, William Blackwood warned one writer to tone down the wording of an article on military reforms in India, noting that, "[t]he Magazine in India is very popular," and Blackwood meant to avoid material "that might be prejudicial to them & destroy the influence of the 'old ship' out there."[127] Colonial readers exercised their own agency and increasing influence over Blackwood's editorial decisions that same year, when the publication of George Chesney's *The Private Secretary*—which featured its male protagonist seducing an unmarried heroine and making her his mistress—prompted a sharp decline in the magazine's sales overseas.[128] Such degeneracy, according to readers, "had no place in the comfortable drawing rooms of the British Empire."[129] Stories such as these are not uncommon and suggest that the arch conservatism of *Blackwood's Magazine*, particularly at the turn of the twentieth century, was not necessarily a product of domestic readers' views on British imperialism overseas. Rather, the magazine reflected the views of colonial readers in markets across India, Australia, South Africa, and the West Indies. Their personal investment in the issues and concerns of a strong and viable British Empire was no simple matter of conservative political prejudice and abstract jingoism, but rather of complex regional issues affecting the safety and economic stability of their own communities, their families, and the livelihoods of their friends and neighbors.[130]

The expansion and development of the periodical industry at the turn of the twentieth century were firmly embedded in this modern imperial cultural space[131] of increasingly integrated global communities of readers.[132]

During the 1890s and years leading up to the First World War, when popular literary tastes in Britain and America were shifting,[133] the preferences of readers in India, Australia, South Africa, and the West Indies were shifting as well, toward "anti-realistic" forms of serialized popular fiction, including romance, western, crime, mystery, and fantastic "adventure."[134] Some of the most popular items checked out from Indian public libraries in the 1880s and 1890s, for example, were novels written by R.L. Stevenson, Captain Frederick Marryat, R.M. Ballantyne, Conan Doyle, Rider Haggard, and Walter Scott.[135] In the records of Australian public libraries, these same names appear consistently as well. Stevenson, Doyle, Haggard, Rudyard Kipling, and the popular crime-fiction writer Edgar Wallace all topped readers' lists in Australia at the turn of the twentieth century. According to Mowbray Morris—who, as general reader for Macmillan from 1891 to 1911, helped shape and direct the publisher's phenomenally successful Colonial Library series—works displaying "unreal" formal qualities and a "good, brisk, stirring tale" could sell even better in India, Australia, and the colonies than in Britain.[136] Fantastic adventures, crime, sensational romances, melodramas, and ghost stories were perennial favorites for British and American readers at the turn of the twentieth century, but they were also the preferences of English-speaking readers the world over. Preferences toward popular stories, fantasies, and thrilling tales of romance, crime, and adventure are part of the much older history of the common reader.

Part II: Popular Adventure Fiction and the Nineteenth-Century Periodical Form

The globalization of popular literary fiction launched a diffusion of print and paper exports throughout the Empire and the world. The final two decades of the nineteenth century were also, importantly, critical years in which paradigms of adventure fiction noticeably began to change. Richard Fulton has observed that, "[t]oward the end of the '70s the [boys'] magazines . . . added a strong dose of Britishness, patriotism, and British racial superiority to their texts,"[137] and David Reed remarks that, in the 1880s and 1890s, contributors to popular boys' periodicals such as *Boy's Own Paper* (*BOP*; 1879–1967), *Chums* (1892–1934), and *The Halfpenny Marvel* (1893–1922) helped channel the discourses of:

> adventure away from heroes who operated outside the law or on its margins, as in the 'bloods,' and . . . towards the outposts of empire, the possibilities of technology and, above all, the playing fields of minor public schools. . . . Conan Doyle and Jules Verne began to appear.[138]

These were significant changes in the ideological content of boys' adventure fiction. And they became increasingly critical for a historical development of the adventure genre, just when scores of British publishers

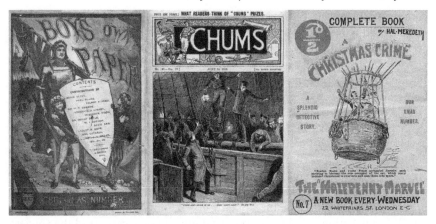

Figure 1.8 Boy's Own Paper (December 1887); *Chums* (June 24, 1896); and *The Halfpenny Marvel* (December 20, 1893).

began exporting cheap paperbacks and popular periodicals to foreign and colonial markets overseas. The wholesome fiction papers of the Religious Tract Society and similarly Empire-minded organizations were not without their detractors, however; nor were they alone in the expanding field of periodical production at the end of the nineteenth century. In the 1880s and 1890s, when "Conan Doyle and Jules Verne began to appear" in boys' magazines and fiction papers such as the *BOP*, a new generation of "transitional" authors—starting with Stevenson, and continuing on through Haggard, Doyle, Kipling, Wells, and Anthony Hope—brought a tide of adult novels written in the vein of classic boys' adventure fiction to the attention of growing audiences of readers and literary critics alike.[139] Roger Lancelyn Green has dubbed this period and the generation's rise to literary prominence in the British popular-fiction magazines "the Age of the Story Tellers."[140]

John Peck notes that, "[a]fter 1880 the adventure story acquired fresh energy, reached out in new directions and began to appeal to a much broader audience than just boys."[141] Haggard's first major commercial success, *King Solomon's Mines* (1885), sold 31,000 copies (UK editions) in its first 12 months of publication. In the US, at least 13 different U.S. editions also appeared that year[142] through Cassell & Co.'s New York offices. Later editions were printed in London, but bound in Paris, Toronto, and Melbourne for the European, Canadian, and Australian markets, and they sold just as well.[143] In 1886, the German firm Tauchnitz issued a paperback copyright edition for sale on the colonial market. In November 1887, Cassell's UK printed its 53,000th copy of the widely read novel, which included nine illustrations by Walter Paget, elder brother of the artist and illustrator Sidney Paget.[144] In addition, piracy of *King Solomon's Mines* was rampant, especially in the United States, although it paled in comparison with the scads of U.S. pirated copies of *She: A History of Adventure* (1886). Transcribed from the novel's serialized version in *The Graphic* (UK)—this popular British illustrated weekly ran the novel in 14 installments between October 2, 1886 and January 8, 1887—there were some American pirated editions of *She* that even predated the first British edition issued by Longmans, Green on New Year's Day 1887.[145]

This organized transatlantic system of American piracy was condemned by Haggard, who warned of its consequences for American readers and the development of a national literature[146] in "About Fiction," an essay published in the February 1887 issue of *The Contemporary Review*.[147] Haggard's essay tellingly presents his arguments in the context of a much wider set of concerns. These include an overproduction of new books in Britain, the public's insatiable appetite for reading material, its preference for "inferior fiction . . . the reports of famous divorce cases and the spiciest paragraphs in Society papers,"[148] and the Grundyism of the British press.[149] According to Haggard, who had only just recently become a best-selling and widely pirated author: "If three-fourths of [these books] were never put into print the world would scarcely lose a single valuable idea, aspiration, or amusement."[150] Despite a "crude mass of fiction . . . poured from the press into the market" every year,[151] however, Haggard regards this situation as a unique opportunity for writers of romance to renew and reinvigorate English fiction. The author writes:

> Day by day the mental area open to the operations of the English-speaking writer grows larger. . . . Abroad the colonies are filling up with English-speaking people, who, as they grow refined and find leisure to read, will make a considerable call upon the literature of their day.[152]

Acknowledging that, "by far the largest demand for books in the English tongue comes from America, with its reading population of some forty millions," Haggard goes on:

> In the face of this constant and ever-growing demand at home and abroad writers of romance must often find themselves questioning their inner consciousness as to what style of art it is best for them to adopt, not only with the view of pleasing their readers, but in the interests of art itself.[153]

He concludes by stating: "[W]hat is wanted in English fiction is a higher ideal and more freedom to work it out."[154] And, to the challenge, he offers the following aesthetic prescription: "There [is] a refuge, and it lies in the paths . . . of pure imagination." Haggard continues:

> Here we may weave our humble tale . . . without being mercilessly bound down to the prose of a . . . dreary age. Here we may even cross

the bounds of the known [and] gaze with curious eyes into the great profound beyond. There are still subjects that may be handled *there* if the man can be found bold enough to handle them.[155]

Haggard's challenge found a number of male authors "bold enough to handle them," because the transatlantic market for romance and adventure fiction was never in short supply following his 1887 essay. According to Green:

> The "age of the Story Tellers", initiated by Stevenson with *Treasure Island* in 1883 and ushered in by Rider Haggard with *King Solomon's Mines* two years later, was already becoming rather overblown by the end of the century. A host of followers . . . were pouring out romances and adventure stories in an ever thickening stream.[156]

In retrospect, Haggard's 1887 essay suggests that the "ever thickening stream" of romance and adventure fiction at the end of the nineteenth century developed in response to overproductions of the British press—and in opposition to *too many* books produced of "effeminate" or morally questionable character. Regarding romance—or "works of fancy which appeal, not to a class, or a nation, or even to an age, but to all time and humanity at large"[157]—as the antidote to this overproduction of "unreal, namby-pamby nonsense with which the market is flooded,"[158] Haggard views the exportation and domestic supply of a masculine literary fiction as two corresponding fronts in the romance writers' war on "three-volumed novels of an inferior order."[159]

Boys' magazines and single-volume "shilling shockers" were not the only publications in which late-Victorian readers encountered stirring narratives of far-off adventure. They had fierce competition from the penny and halfpenny papers, or bloods, such as *Black Bess*[160] and *The Red Revenge*,[161] and other down-market titles such as Edwin J. Brett's *Boys of England* (1866–99), "the leading boys' periodical of the nineteenth century."[162] In the 1890s, their market positions were further challenged by the flood of new magazines issued by Harmsworth, Newnes, Pearson, and others. Such competition within the field was just one of the many parallel developments in the wider, much more complicated tradition of British literary adventure in the nineteenth century.[163]

From 1800 to 1900, the adventure story manifested countless new, popular configurations. Modeled on epic formulas, and updated in the historical romances of Walter Scott, it was drafted into the service of Empire by the works of R.M. Ballantyne and G.A. Henty in the 1850s and 1860s.[164] In the 1880s and 1890s, Haggard wrote several competing versions of it himself: the Stevenson-inspired tongue-in-cheek boyishness of *King Solomon's Mines* (1885)[165] was quickly surpassed by the dark and suggestive psychological uncertainties of *She: A History of Adventure* (1886).[166] The profound disillusionment of *Allan Quatermain* (1887) found its nadir in *The World's Desire* (1890),[167] wherein Haggard and Andrew Lang rewrote the heroic ending of Homer's *Odyssey* and thereby seemed to undermine the very tradition in which Haggard had made his literary fame and fortune. More explicitly, the comically futile antiheroes of Kipling's "The Man Who Would Be King" (1888), Stevenson's *The Ebb-Tide* (1894; co-written by Lloyd Osbourne), and Joseph Conrad's "An Outpost of Progress" (1896) established a decidedly anti-romantic strain, locating a series of Empire-bound colonial adventure stories at a critical impasse by the turn of the century. Bram Stoker's *Dracula* (1898) turned the traditions of Ballantyne and Henty on their heads, and Conrad's literary output over the next several years—comprising his so-called "major phase" of novels: *Heart of Darkness* (1899), *Lord Jim* (1900), and *Nostromo* (1904)—sounded the death-knell of Empire's heroic adventure repeatedly. Many of these writers adopted the end of geographical adventure and the demise of heroic idealism as central organizing themes in their writings at the fin de siècle. Their works make reference repeatedly to vanishing regions of unexplored territory in the world and a parallel rise of modern, European bureaucratic states. Though this crisis of confidence would not stop serial writers for *Chums* (1892–1934), *The Halfpenny Marvel* (1893–1922), and *The Captain* (1899–1924) from celebrating the bright future of the British Empire, writers such as Stevenson, Conrad, Doyle, and Olive Schreiner would scrutinize and condemn European involvement in Africa, the South Pacific, Asia, and elsewhere.

That the prominent, hotly contested official foreign policy of British expansion at the end of the nineteenth century produced such a complicated late-Victorian genealogy—and within a literary tradition that had historically, and directly, engaged its concerns—should come as no surprise. Although it generated a complex range and versatility of romantic adventure fiction by the early twentieth century, the dynamic mobility of the adventure form had already, in fact, been well-trod ground by the middle of the nineteenth century.

In the 1860s and 1870s, combined weekly circulations of notorious fiction papers such as *Wild Boys of London* (1864–66) and *Tales of Highwaymen* (1865–66) reached some estimated figures of 3 million copies in London alone.[168] The fortunes being made with these tales of cowboys, vampires, pirates, and criminals—by publishers such as Edward Lloyd, Edwin J. Brett, Charles Fox, Samuel Beeton, and others—induced some upscale publishers and religious societies to augment the burgeoning market for cheap, thrilling fiction. They introduced "healthy," "inspiring" weekly periodicals, including *Boys of England* (1866–99), *Young Folks* (1871–97), and *Boy's Own Paper* (1879–1967). Circulations of these new titles never approached those of the former, despite their publishers' special summer and Christmas annuals and serializations of new works by Stevenson, Jules Verne, and Talbot Baines Reed. But, the competition they inspired continued to expand the range of available variations on the adventure form.[169] There were cowboy stories, jungle stories, historical romances, Navy stories, school stories, detective serials, scientific romances, and more. Most of the major genres of popular periodical fiction in the early twentieth century, in fact, had their beginnings in the pages of American "dime novels" and the Victorian boys' magazines.[170]

By the mid-1880s, this first wave of boys' magazines had swelled the lists of newsagents' catalogues by inspiring a host of equally successful imitators, such as W.H.G. Kingston's *Union Jack* (1880–93) and the Sunday School Union's *Young England* (1880–1937). London boys "of all ages" could choose between 46[171] (although figures run as high as 95[172]) different weekly and monthly fiction papers, featuring serials ranging from the "rattling good yarns"[173] of jungle explorers, cowboys, Mounties, soldiers, missionaries, Navy men, and the detective Sexton Blake to the "highly immoral fictions" of the paranormal, pirates, Indians, and the outlaws Robin Hood and Dick Turpin. Before the arrival of the mass-market illustrated monthlies such as *The Strand* (1891), *Pall Mall* (1893), *Windsor* (1895), and *Pearson's Magazine* (1896) introduced middle-class family audiences to works of Stevenson, Doyle, Haggard, Kipling, and Wells, much of the invention and experimentation in the adventure form was carried out by authors of fiction papers, penny bloods, and the boys' magazines.[174]

In addition to the large number of titles dominating the racks of W.H. Smith & Sons at railway stations, sidewalk bookstalls, and newsstands, even some prestigious and sober-minded periodicals such as *Blackwood's* (1817), *The Illustrated London News* (1842), the *British Journal of Photography* (1854), and W.E. Henley's *The New Review* (1889) routinely published romance or fast-action adventure stories of their own, and these stories were often indistinguishable from the reports, editorials, and informative articles surrounding them. In a September 1879 article in *The Atlantic Monthly*, W.H. Bishop calls attention to a prominence of "story-paper literature" in both America, which "leads in this form of publication," and Europe, while noting that such literature is also not confined to the story papers themselves:

> It is an enormous field of mental activity, the greatest literary move-
> ment, in bulk, of the age . . . [R]omances that do not appear to be of a
> greatly higher order are almost as profuse with the vendors of reading
> matter at Paris, Turin, or Cologne . . . and not a daily paper on the
> continent of Europe, in any language, but has its scrap of a continued
> story, its *feuilletton*, in every issue.[175]

The most reputable mid-century publishers—and adroit literary advisors —were not immune to the lure of big sales and profits to be made from stories of romance, adventure, and sensationalism. John Lane and William Blackwood, for example, applied increasing pressure, and larger advance payments, on celebrity explorers David Livingstone and John Speke to

THE MISSIONARY'S ESCAPE FROM THE LION.

Figure 1.9 "The Missionary's Escape from the Lion," *Missionary Travels* (1857) and "He Strode Quickly Forward, with Revolver Pointed at the Lion," Cover of *Chums* (October 18, 1905).

incorporate the popular conventions of romance and adventure into their travel writings.[176] Livingstone complained that "liberties" taken by John Murray with the manuscript of *Missionary Travels* (1857) had made the book resemble a "penny primer" in character. Regarding a particularly "abominable" illustration, "The Missionary's Escape from the Lion," Livingstone wrote unhappily to his publisher to inform him that "Every one [*sic*] who knows what a lion is will die with laughing at it."[177]

The practice continued on steadily, largely unabated, nonetheless. And alongside the jingoism of popular boys' books by Captains Frederick Marryat and Mayne Reid, the pessimism of works by Stevenson, Haggard, Kipling, and Conrad, and the subversive cultural anarchism of thrillers, detective serials, pirates' yarns, and Wild West tales of the disreputable penny papers, the larger-than-life persona of the Victorian adventurer achieved legendary status in the mass-circulation dailies. Henry Morton Stanley (1841–1904) was among the world's most recognizable public personalities; with his African adventures generously financed by the *New York Herald*, *The Times*, and *Daily Telegraph*, the world-famous explorer delivered his editors a regular flow of exciting new copy, ensured huge profits and circulations for his publishers, and ultimately helped to create a powerful myth, and cult of celebrity, around himself.

Livingstone had realized nearly half a century before that, in order to secure funding for prohibitively expensive expeditions, publishers and readers had to be satisfied. Stanley was more than willing to comply with this economic reality. In his African narratives, he adheres to a classic adventure formula as strictly as any romance novelist. In 1899, when he was made a Knight Grand Cross of the Order of Bath, Sir Henry Morton Stanley, it only reinforced the rags-to-riches story that he had helped create, and the transatlantic press had helped nurture, for three decades.[178] By that time, Stanley had so blurred the lines between fact and fiction that even Stanley would believe his own myth.[179]

"My Empire is of the Imagination"

At the turn of the twentieth century, the adventure story, sailor's yarn, or traveler's tale had been writ large in the transatlantic imagination by its consistent appeal to popular audiences, its influence on editorial policies, countless variations on its form, and the anonymity, instability, and sheer power of mass mediation. New media had presented romantic possibilities for writers of adventure in some often unforeseen ways. In 1885, Doyle's "J. Habakuk Jephson's Statement" was reprinted by the editors of the *Boston Herald*. First published anonymously in *The Cornhill Magazine* (January 1884), the self-consciously stylized "eye-witness" account, which purported to have been written by a passenger aboard the doomed *Mary Celeste*, was so convincing that the newspaper's readers accepted it as fact.

An ensuing uproar persuaded Solly Flood, Her Majesty's Advocate-General in Gibraltar, to issue a spate of telegrams to major newspapers denouncing the statement as "fabrication from beginning to end." Flood then filed an official complaint with the British Admiralty, charging "Mr. Jephson" with perpetrating the hoax.[180] That same year, the public convergence of mass media and adventure also informed the London advertising campaign for Haggard's *King Solomon's Mines*. During the night of September 29, runners hired by Cassell & Co. plastered leaflets, posters, and banners throughout the city proclaiming: "King Solomon's Mines—The Most Amazing Book Ever Written." The next day, Londoners on their way to work were talking about it, and the book sold 31,000 copies within the first 12 months.[181]

In *She: A History of Adventure* (1886), Haggard's Ayesha proclaims, "My empire is of the imagination," and whether pirated by penny bloods, serialized on the cheap by boys' papers, at more elevated prices in the general fiction magazines, or published in gilt-edged volumes by the leading firms of the day, adventure fiction dominated the public's imagination with an empire of its own, throughout the pages of the expanding press and in the global spread of new media.[182]

Wendy Katz demonstrates that romance at the turn of the twentieth century was a mobile literary form, characterized by freedom and expansiveness. As a genre opposed to realism, it was immune from ties with actuality but was also immune from the mediating contexts that shaped readers' responses to it. Characters in romantic adventure fiction could be loosed free from time, place, and history. In Haggard's writings, real time is continually subverted by rebirths, doubles, reincarnations, and returns to former lives.[183] Adventure could be rebellious, sometimes criminal, and explicitly anarchic for both the established literary authors of the day and the professional writers from the fringes of Grub Street. It could also be a source of despair, a site of intense self-exploration, and a context for political, explicitly imperial, critique.[184] This complicates any view of the adventure story as simply a vehicle for imperialist ideologies at the turn of the twentieth century. Many adventure authors subscribed to the ideals and prejudices of Empire, to be sure, but one-dimensional, uncritical pro-imperial stances were always in the minority.

Breaking news reports of celebrated explorers, action-packed serials with intrepid heroes, detective novels, gothic thrillers, and tales of courage and conquest in the far-flung undiscovered regions of the world—or farthest reaches of space, for fans of science fiction—remained a steady and disproportionately influential facet of new media beyond the pages of the nineteenth-century periodical press.[185] Adventure fiction helped contextualize and shape popular responses to the emergence of alien technologies, such as film, radio, and high-speed modes of travel, well into the twentieth century. New media offered books, newspapers, and magazines a host of new subjects in which to specialize. And a burgeoning range of periodicals was devoted, not only to a dizzying variety of romance and adventure, but also to film, photography, electricity, radio, advertising, spiritualism, aviation, physical improvement, sport, celebrity culture, authorship, and publishing.

This is the rich and complicated background against which the following chapters of this study are situated. The changing dynamic of adventure in the early twentieth century is firmly rooted in both a rapidly expanding periodical press and a robust, multifaceted literary tradition. From the uneven, shifting development of the adventure genre in the first decade of the twentieth century to the renewal of possibilities for adventure through technologies of the modern world, adventure's engagement with the threats and promises of global modernity looked to adventure's past in order to chart its way forward.

Notes

1　Simon Eliot, "Section E: Periodical Publication," *Some Patterns and Trends in British Publishing 1800–1919*, Occasional Papers of the Bibliographical Society, No. 8 (1994), p. 88.

2　Ibid., p. 79.

3　The brief "plateau of production" that occurred between 1858 and 1872 in the British periodical industry was repeated in 1903. In the American industry, a similar plateau occurred 3 years later in 1906. These figures suggest a familiar commercial cycle, where dynamics in the market are determined by the laws of supply and demand. As new markets become available, demand increases production. When markets become saturated, demand bottoms out. Production levels retract in due course, and supplies adjust accordingly.

4　David Reed, *The Popular Magazine in Britain and the United States 1880–1960*, Toronto and Buffalo, NY: University of Toronto Press, 1997, p. 18.

5　Ibid., p. 23.

6　Eliot, p. 107.

7　Reed, p. 19.

8　Eliot, p. 101.

9　This study does not attempt to account for all popular genres of periodical publishing or their audiences. In fact, it purposefully elides the most successful mass-market periodicals of the time: the national newspapers and women's magazines such as *Ladies' Home Journal* (1883). Of the two major publications of the Religious Tract Society from 1880–1900, for example, the *Girl's Own Paper* was the more successful. And though the masculine romances of Conan Doyle, Rider Haggard, and Rudyard Kipling were popular at the turn of the century, the sensational melodramas of Ellen Wood, Wilkie Collins, Mary Elizabeth Braddon, and Marie Corelli were far more popular still. On a per-title basis, the best-selling author of the nineteenth century was not Sir Walter Scott, but Harriet Beecher Stowe: *Uncle Tom's Cabin* (1852) holds the record for the greatest short-term sale of any book published that century. To put things in perspective, the more than six *billion* copies of Agatha Christie novels sold around the world to date easily dwarfs the combined sales figures of the entire lifetime literary output of Edgar Allan Poe, R.L. Stevenson, Haggard, Doyle, Kipling, and H.G. Wells, plus the combined circulations of *every* monthly issue of the *Strand Magazine* published during its 60-year existence.

Global sales of Jules Verne's novels to date, however, are second only to Christie's, at four-and-a-half billion, whereas Doyle's two billion are a distant, but respectable, third.

10 John Feather, *A History of British Publishing*, 2nd Ed., Oxford and New York: Routledge, 2006, p. 94.

11 Wellington is the capital city and second most populous urban area of New Zealand; Victoria is the capital city of British Columbia, Canada. These former colonial capitals were established c. 1840 and 1862, respectively.

12 Janet C. Myers, *Antipodal England: Emigration and Portable Domesticity in the Victorian Imagination*, Albany, NY: The State University of New York Press, 2009.

13 Ibid., p. 12.

14 The author references *Chamber's Edinburgh Journal* as an example.

15 Bill Bell, cited in John Plotz, *Portable Property: Victorian Culture on the Move*, Princeton, NJ: Princeton University Press, 2008, p. 6.

16 Anthony Trollope, *Australia and New Zealand*, 2 vols., London: Chapman & Hall, 1873–74, Vol. 1, p. 85.

17 Major exporters of copper included Australia; gutta-percha came from Southeast Asia and the South Pacific.

18 British manufacturers relied on major shipments of these raw materials from Canada, Brazil, Egypt, Australia, and South Africa, respectively.

19 The majority of wood pulp used by British paper mills came from the Scandinavian countries; India was a major producer of various vegetable fibers, and esparto grass was grown in Spain and North Africa.

20 Edward Beasley, *Empire as the Triumph of Theory*, p. 23.

21 Robert Lee, "Potential Railway World Heritage Sites in Asia and the Pacific," York, UK: Institute of Railways Studies, University of York, 2003, p. 2.

22 Ibid., pp. 1–2.

23 See a number of the papers presented at Australian Media Traditions Conference: Politics Media History, and the University of Canberra, November 24–25, 2005, including Denis Cryle, "The Ebb and Flow of the Tasman Mediasphere: A Century of Australian and New Zealand Print Media Development, 1840–1940"; Ross Harvey, "When Media Histories Collide: Researching the Development of Print Media in Australia and New Zealand, 1840–1940"; and Peter Putnis and Kerry McCallum, "The Role of Reuters in the Distribution of Propaganda News in Australia in WW I." See also Glen O'Hara, "New Histories of British Imperial Communication and the 'Networked World' of the 19th and Early 20th Centuries," *History Compass* Vol. 8, No. 7, 2010, pp. 609–25. For a detailed discussion of the Imperial Press Conference from a contemporary Canadian perspective, see J.C. Hopkins, "The Imperial Press Conference and the Australian Delegates' Visit to Canada," "Empire Defence and Proceedings of the Imperial Press Conference," and "Results of the Imperial Press Conference; and Canadian Opinion," *The Canadian Annual Review of Public Affairs* 9. Toronto: Annual Review Publishing Company, 1910, pp. 61–76.

24 Andrew S. Thompson, *Imperial Britain: The Empire in British Politics, c. 1880–1932*, London: Routledge, 2014, p. 76.

25 The location chosen for the conference's opening reception had also been the site of the Franco-British Exhibition the summer before. Eight times larger than the Great Exhibition of 1851, its grounds encompassed 140 acres, 20 palaces, and eight exhibition halls. There were French and British Palaces of Industry, a 3,000-seat open-air Indian Arena, and Irish and French Senegalese villages arranged around spaces with names such as the Court of Honour, Court of

Arts, Court of Progress, and Elite Garden. Constructed as an Empire in miniature, the Great White City—so-called because of its brightly painted stucco walls—was advertised by *The Times* as an "Oriental fantasy" and "a veritable City of Pleasure" that would be "the most popular and delightful Pleasure Resort in the United Kingdom." In 1908, Britain had also staged the third Olympic Games here, with a stadium added to the exhibition complex. For more on imperial exhibitions, see Alexander Geppert, *Fleeting Cities: Imperial Expositions in Fin-de-Siècle Europe*, Basingstoke, UK: Palgrave Macmillan, 2010; Daniel Stephen, *The Empire of Progress: West Africans, Indians, and Britons at the British Empire Exhibition, 1924–25*, Basingstoke, UK: Palgrave Macmillan, 2013; and David Cannadine, *Orientalism: How the British Saw Their Empire*, Oxford, UK: Oxford University Press, 2000. In contemporary accounts, see "The Franco-British Exhibition, Shepherd's Bush, London, W. to Be Opened on May 14th by T.R.H. The Prince and Princess of Wales," *The Times*, May 8, 1908, p. 20; "The Franco-British Exhibition," *The Times*, November 16, 1908, p. 12; *A Pictorial and Descriptive Guide to London and the Franco-British Exhibition*, London: Ward Lock, 1908; and *The Franco-British Exhibition Illustrated Review*, Ed. F.G. Dumas, London: Chatto & Windus, 1908.

26 J. Lee Thompson, "Selling the Mother Country to the Empire: The Imperial Press Conference of June 1909," *Imperial Co-Histories: National Identities and the British and Colonial Press*, Ed. Julie F. Codell, Cranbury, NJ and London: Associated University Presses, 2003, p. 113.

27 Thomas Hardman, *A Parliament of the Press: The First Imperial Press Conference*, with preface by the Rt. Hon. the Earl of Rosebery, London: Constable, 1909.

28 W.T. Stead, "The Editors of the Empire at Home," *The Contemporary Review* (July 1909), p. 48. The phrase "His Majesty King Demos" was often used by Stead in reference to modern democracy's mass public, as in "the people." For context, see Stead's article "The Wasted Wealth of *King Demos*," *Review of Reviews* (July 15, 1893), pp. 83–87.

29 Reginald Pound and Geoffrey Harmsworth, *Northcliffe*, London: Cassell, 1959, p. 369.

30 J. Lee Thompson, pp. 109–24.

31 Ibid., pp. 114–15.

32 Ibid., p. 120.

33 Ibid., pp. 120–21.

34 Ibid., p. 121.

35 P.D. Ross, "Some Deductions from the Imperial Press Conference: An Address by Mr. P.D. Ross, Chief Editor of the *Ottawa Journal*, before the Empire Club of Canada," *The Empire Club of Canada Addresses* (Toronto, Canada), February 17, 1910, p. 149–60.

36 For a complete listing of the names of the delegates and publications represented at the Imperial Press Conference, see Hardman, pp. 4–5.

37 "The Press Conference," *Otago Daily Times*, Issue 14570 (July 8, 1909), p. 7.

38 "Imperial Press Conference," *Evening Post*, LXXVIII, Issue 58 (September 6, 1909), p. 7.

39 J. Lee Thompson, p. 120.

40 Andrew S. Thompson, p. 76.

41 *The New Zealand Official Year-Book*, Vols. 2, 22. Wellington, NZ: John Mackay Government Printer, 1893, 1913.

42 *The Official Year Book of the Commonwealth of Australia, 1901–1912,*
No. 6, Melbourne, VIC: McCarron, Bird, 1913, p. 746.

43 *The Official Year Book of the Commonwealth of Australia* (1901–07, –1912),
No. 1, 6. Melbourne, VIC: McCarron, Bird, 1908, 1913; pp. 601, 747. See
also "The Number of Letters, Packets, and Newspapers Despatched and
Received by the Various Ocean Mail Routes during the Year 1897, as
Compared with Similar Information for the Year 1896," *The Annual Report
of the Post-master General for the Year 1897*, Legislative Assembly, New South
Wales. Sydney: William Applegate Gullick Government Printer, 1898, p. 12;
and "The Number of Letters, Packets, and Newspapers Despatched and
Received by the Various Ocean Mail Routes during the Year 1900, as
Compared with Similar Information for the Year 1899," *The Annual Report
of the Post-master General for the Year 1900*, Legislative Council, New South
Wales. Sydney: William Applegate Gullick Government Printer, 1901, p. 13.

44 "Number of Printing Presses at Work, and Number of Newspapers,
Periodicals, and Books Published," *East India Statistical Abstract: Statistical
Abstract Relating to British India*, Vols. 41–44, London: India Office,
1907–10.

45 "Postal Statistics of Papua, 1905–06 and 1909–10," *The Official Year Book
of the Commonwealth of Australia*, No. 4, Melbourne, VIC: McCarron, Bird,
1911, p. 1110.

46 See *Book & Print in New Zealand: A Guide to Print Culture in New Zealand*,
Penny Griffith, Keith Maslen, and Ross Harvey, Wellington, NZ: Victoria
University Press, 1997, especially Harvey's essay, "Newspapers," where he
cites the difference in the British and colonial press regarding their relationship
to the book: "unlike the situation in Britain where book publishers were established well over a century before newspapers were produced, in its New Zealand
colony, newspapers came first" (128). Cryle confirms that, "Harvey's observa-
tion applies equally to colonial Australia" (9).

47 On the relationship between empire and modern print media, Cryle, J.
Hartley, and Chandrika Kaul note that rule by force gave way increasingly to
rule by information, at a time when concentration of ownership was becoming
a feature of the English-speaking daily press and modern media organizations
were assuming their recognizable form. See Hartley, *Popular Reality:
Journalism, Modernity and Popular Culture*, London: Arnold, 1996; and Kaul,
Reporting the Raj: The British Press and India, c. 1880–1922, Manchester,
UK: Manchester University Press, 2003. Also see G. Osborne, and G. Lewis,
Communication Traditions in Twentieth-Century Australia, Melbourne, VIC,
and Oxford, UK: Oxford University Press, 2001.

48 The stated purpose of the Empire Press Union was "bringing a vast and
scattered Commonwealth closer together by providing cheaper, quicker, and
better means of communication." According to Robert Donald, Chairman of
the EPU in 1920: "Although much has already been done in this direction, the
union considers that its work has only begun. Distant parts of the Empire must
be brought into yet closer contact with the centre by quicker and cheaper cables,
and what is of equal importance, all the dominions and overseas territories must
have improved means of communication with each other. A complete system
of rapid communication is the surest bond of Empire" (Robert Donald, "Story
of the First Imperial Press Conference," *Vancouver Daily World* (August 23,
1920), p. 9. See also Cryle, "A British Legacy? The Empire Press Union and
Freedom of the Press, 1940–1950," *History of Intellectual Culture* Vol. 4,
No. 1 (2004), p. 1.

49 This was a significant period of evolution for international copyright law. In 1908, the Berne Convention had been revised for the second time. This Berlin Act of the Convention introduced broad prohibitions against "formalities" concerning the "exercise and enjoyment" of copyright. The U.S. Copyright Act (first introduced in 1906) was ratified in 1909, just 1 year before a new copyright bill was brought before the British parliament. The Imperial Copyright Act of 1911 (in effect as of July 1, 1912) greatly influenced laws in many countries of the British Empire, including Australia, Canada, Israel, New Zealand, Nigeria, and South Africa. See Daniel J. Gervais, "The 1909 Copyright Act in International Context," Vanderbilt Public Law Research Paper No. 10–23: 2010.

50 "Daily Mail (1896–)," *Dictionary of Nineteenth-Century Journalism in Great Britain and Ireland*, Laurel Brake and Marysa Demoor, Eds., Ghent, Belgium: Academia Press, 2009, pp. 157–58; and Graham Murdock and Peter Golding, "The Structure, Ownership and Control of the Press," *Newspaper History: From the 17th Century to the Present Day*, G. Boyce, J. Curran, and P. Wingate, Eds., London: Constable, 1978, p. 130.

51 Feather, *A History of British Publishing*, p. 149.

52 Laurel Brake records sales of the two journals at "120,000 for early numbers of *Cornhill* and 8,000 to 9,000 for early issues of *Macmillan's.*" See Brake, "Maga, the Shilling Monthlies, and the New Journalism," *Print Culture and the Blackwood Tradition 1805–1930*, Ed. David Finkelstein, Toronto: University of Toronto Press, 2006, pp. 184–211.

53 See Reed, pp. 81–86.

54 The Elementary Education Act of 1870, more commonly known as the Forster Education Act, set the framework for schooling all children between 5 and 12 in England and Wales. See Thomas Preston, *The Elementary Education Act, 1870: Being the Act to Provide Public Elementary Education in England and Wales*, London: William Amer, 1870.

55 Patrick Brantlinger, *The Reading Lesson: The Threat of Mass Literacy in Nineteenth-Century British Fiction*, Bloomington and Indianapolis, IN: Indiana University Press, 1998, pp. 5–6.

56 See also Simon Eliot, "The Reading Experience Database: Or, What Are We to do about the History of Reading?" at www.open.ac.uk/Arts/RED/redback.htm (accessed May 15, 2012); Rosalind Crone, "The Dimensions of Literacy in Victorian England: A Reappraisal," *Journal of Victorian Culture* (forthcoming); and Rosalind Crone, Katie Halsey, and Shafquat Towheed, "Examining the Evidence of Reading: Three Examples from the Reading Experience Database, 1450–1945," *Reading in History: New Methodologies from the Anglo-American Tradition*, Ed. Bonnie Ciunzenhauser, London: Pickering & Chatto, 2010, pp. 29–45.

57 Richard D. Altick, *The English Common Reader*, Chicago, IL: University of Chicago Press, 1957, *passim*; Brantlinger, *The Reading Lesson*, *passim*; Jonathan Rose, *The Intellectual Life of the British Working Classes*, 2nd Ed., New Haven, CT, and New York: Yale University Press, 2010, *passim*; and Beth Palmer and Adelene Buckland, Eds., *A Return to the Common Reader: Print Culture and the Novel, 1850–1900*, Farnham, UK: Ashgate, 2011, *passim*.

58 Rawson W. Rawson, "An Inquiry into the Condition of Criminal Offenders in England and Wales with Respect to Education," *Journal of the Statistical Society of London* 3 (January 1841), p. 334.

59 Brantlinger, *The Reading Lesson*, p. 182.

60 Richard Ohmann, *Selling Culture: Magazines, Markets and Class at the Turn of the Century*, London and New York: Verso, 1996, p. 34.

61 See Rosalind Crone, "Attempts to (Re)shape Common Reading Habits: Bible Reading on the Nineteenth-century Convict Ship," and Sharon Murphy, " 'Quite Incapable of Appreciating Books Written for Educated Readers': the Mid-nineteenth-century British Soldier," in *A Return to the Common Reader: Print Culture and the Novel, 1850–1900*, Eds. Beth Palmer and Adelene Buckland, Farnham, UK: Ashgate, 2011, pp. 103–20, 121–32.

62 Regarding the success of the Forster Education Act (1870) in combating the "penny blood" peril of the nineteenth century, Altick not only makes a compelling case against the Act's effectiveness, but also suggests that it might have achieved the opposite of its intended effect. Altick cites crowded conditions, poorly-lit rooms, incompetent teachers, and a basic lack of reading materials.

63 See Reed, Feather, Ohmann, and Theodore Peterson, *Magazines in the Twentieth Century*, Urbana, IL: University of Illinois Press, 1964; Mark Morrison, *The Public Face of Modernism*, Madison, WI: University of Wisconsin Press, 2001; Patrick Collier, *Modernism on Fleet Street*, Farnham, UK: Ashgate, 2006; David Earle, *Re-Covering Modernism*, Farnham: Ashgate, 2009; and Robert Scholes and Cliff Wulfman, *Modernism in the Magazines: An Introduction*, New Haven, CT: Yale University Press, 2011.

64 Peterson, p. 7.

65 William R. Scott, *Scientific Circulation Management for Newspapers*, New York: The Ronald Press Company, 1915, p. 78.

66 Ibid., 82–83.

67 S.S. McClure, *My Autobiography*, New York: Frederick A. Stokes Company, 1913, pp. 222–23.

68 This situation had not changed much by the 1930s; Harold Hersey, *Pulpwood Editor*, Westport, CT: Greenwood Press, 1974, pp. 41–42.

69 Frank A. Munsey, *The Story of the Founding and Development of the Munsey Publishing-House*, New York: The Frank A. Munsey Company, 1907, pp. 25–26.

70 George Brett, *Forty Years—Forty Millions: The Career of Frank A. Munsey*, New York: Farrar & Rinehart, 1935, p. 87.

71 For full-text digital editions of both magazines, and others from the Frank A. Munsey publishing company, see the Pulp Magazines Project, at www.pulp mags.org (accessed May 15, 2012).

72 Eliot, pp. 82, 148.

73 Charles Wilson, *First with the News: The History of W.H. Smith 1792–1972*, Garden City, NY: Doubleday, 1986, pp. 28–29.

74 Ibid., p. 36.

75 Eliot, p. 148.

76 Formally proposed by Victor Hugo as president of the Association Littéraire et Artistique Internationale in Paris, the International Copyright Convention of 1886 followed in the footsteps of other protective international rights agreements in Europe in the 1870s and 1880s (covering trade, transportation, communications, even concerns with diseases). Augmented in 1891 by the U.S. International Copyright Act—also known as the Chace Act—and revised in Paris in 1896, the convention would be adopted by representatives of four of the major world empires—Britain, France, Holland, and Germany—most of the European countries, the British Dominions of Canada, Australia, New Zealand, and South Africa, Tunisia, Haiti, Liberia, and the United States. The agreements obligated member nations to recognize the copyright laws of other member nations. There were numerous complications and exceptions, and nations' representatives would spend the next several decades attempting to hammer out major points of contention.

77 American copyright included a "manufacturing" clause, for example, that required the type for new novels to be set in the United States. It also required that foreign authors, or their legal representatives, deposit a type-set copy of the first edition in the Library of Congress, on or before the date of first publication in their own country.

78 As Olufunmilayo Arewa writes: "The Berlin Conference of 1884–85 formalized the partitioning of Africa among European powers, in a process . . . akin to a form of Imperial Monopoly. . . . The hierarchical assumptions underlying Imperial Monopoly carried over to other spheres of international relations and international lawmaking as well, and were reflected in the constitution and process of adoption and implementation of international intellectual property agreements such as the Paris and Berne Conventions. The Berne Convention, for example, permitted colonial powers to bind their colonial possessions on their accession." See Arewa's paper, "Culture as Property: Intellectual Property, Local Norms, and Global Rights," *Northwestern Public Law Research Paper No. 07–13* (April 2007), pp. 39–40.

79 By 1840, Wiley and Putnam had already cornered the modest British market for American periodicals. Of course, the business of publishing magazines on a transatlantic model had existed informally, in one way or another, since the arrival of English colonists in the sixteenth century.

80 See Ezra Greenspan, *George Palmer Putnam*, p. 119.

81 Murray's 1843 prospectus referred to potential audiences in both "the backwoods of America" and the "remotest cantonment of our Indian dominions."

82 David Finkelstein, *The House of Blackwood: Author-Publisher Relations in the Victorian Era*, University Park, PA: Pennsylvania State University Press, 2002, pp. 101–02.

83 Ibid.

84 Feather, pp. 187–88.

85 Laurel Brake, *Dictionary of Nineteenth-Century Journalism in Great Britain and Ireland*, Laurel Brake and Marysa Demoor, Eds., Ghent, Belgium, and London: Academia Press, 2009, p. 172.

86 The launch of Macmillan's Colonial Library series in 1886 was partly a strategic move, in fact, to get the jump on American publishers' threats of a Colonial series of pirated editions. The Berne Convention–Chace Act nonetheless consolidated, between 1886 and 1896, the implementation of the strongest legal framework to date by which British, American, European, and Colonial publishers—aided by growing armies of copyright lawyers—could seek recourse from the murky trade conditions that had helped derail efforts in past decades to globalize the business of printed media. The Berne Convention (1886–94) protected the rights, not only of authors, but also of artists, photographers, and even cinematographers, which, in retrospect, seems amazingly prescient.

87 For a history of Macmillan & Company in India, see Priya Joshi, *In Another Country: Colonialism, Culture, and the English Novel in India*, New York: Columbia University Press, 2002, pp. 93–138.

88 Booksellers, librarians, retailers, journalists, and readers questioned during Macmillan's tour confirmed this fact. Again, see Joshi, pp. 98–101.

89 Thomas Mark's unpublished notes, Morgan Source Files, Macmillan Archives, British Library, box M75d, as qtd. in Joshi, p. 98.

90 Joshi, pp. 115–38.

91 Macmillan's Colonial Library resumed operations after the war and continued profitably into the 1960s.

92 New shipments left London every 2 weeks, though they still left far in advance of the date of issue for each new installment. Regarding shipping times, the Bentley archive at the University of Illinois includes a printed list of days to various ports, in a trade pamphlet issued by the firm: "Foreign and Colonial List: Corrected to March 25, 1885" (London: R.B.& S., 1885). Adelaide was 38 days, Melbourne 40, Sydney 43 (pp. 8–9).

93 Unsigned editorial, "Cheap Editions for the Colonies," *The Colonial Book Circular and Bibliographical Record* Vol. 1, No. 1 (September 1887), p. 3.

94 See Finkelstein, *The House of Blackwood*, pp. 101–02.

95 Anonymous editorial, "The Colonial Library", *The Bookseller*, No. CCCCLVI (November 6, 1895), p. 1073.

96 These writers included Rudyard Kipling (India), Rolf Bolderwood (Australia), and Jagadananda Roy (Bengal).

97 John Spiers, 'Must Not Be Sold or Imported. . .': British Colonial Editions, 1843–1972, *The Colonial and Postcolonial History of the Book, 1765–2005*, London: Open University, 2005, p. 8.

98 Ibid., pp. 7–19. See also Luke Trainor's "Colonial Editions," New Zealand Electronic Text Centre, at www.nzetc.org/tm/scholarly/tei-GriBook-_div3-N11A1D.html (accessed January 20, 2011).

99 Finkelstein, p. 9.

100 Brake, *Print in Transition 1850–1910*, Basingstoke and New York: Palgrave, 2001, p. 14.

101 Ibid., p. 13. Here, Brake goes on to explain in more detail: "Publishers and authors preferred to rely on a system of pre-volume publication in the magazine or in part-issue, in which system book publication then 'culminated' the serial rhythm, often with the appearance of the book edition simultaneous with the last number in part-issue or in the magazine."

102 Barbara Quinn Schmidt, "Novelists, Publishers, and Fiction in Middle-Class Magazines: 1860–1880," *Victorian Periodicals Review* Vol. 17, No. 4 (Winter 1984), p. 143.

103 Qtd. in Royal Gettman, *A Victorian Publisher: A Study of the Bentley Papers*, Cambridge, UK: Cambridge University Press, 1960, p. 148.

104 Brake, p. 26.

105 Ibid., p. 13.

106 Martyn Lyons, "Reading Practices in Australia," *A History of the Book in Australia, 1891–1945*, Marton Lyons and John Arnold, Eds., Brisbane: QLD: University of Queensland Press, 2001, pp. 269, 335–36.

107 Ibid., p. 340.

108 Constance Barnicoat, "What Did the 'Colonial Girl' Read?" *The Nineteenth Century* (1906), as qtd. in Lyons, pp. 337–38.

109 Publications of these media giants include the *Daily Mail* (1896), *Tit-Bits* (1881), *Review of Reviews* (1890), *The Strand* (1891), and *Pearson's Magazine* (1896).

110 The publications of these magnates included the *Ladies' Home Journal* (1883), *Cosmopolitan* (1886), *Munsey's* (1889), and *McClure's* (1893). See Morrison, *The Public Face of Modernism*, p. 3.

111 E.S. Turner, *The Shocking History of Advertising*, 1953, p. 132.

112 See Finkelstein, pp. 165–66.

113 Several leading U.S. illustrated monthlies had penetrated the British market by 1890, including *Harper's Monthly* (1880), *Century Illustrated* (1881), *Ladies' Home Journal* (1883), *Cosmopolitan* (1886), *Scribner's Monthly* (1887), *Munsey's* (1889), *Lippincott's* (1890), and *McClure's* (1893). In 1866, Cassell's launched an American edition of the *Quiver* (1900 U.S. circ.,

monthly: 27,000). In 1889, the *Illustrated London News* established its American edition, sold through the International News Company of New York (1900 U.S. circ., weekly: 28,000). Requirements of the U.S. International Copyright Act of 1891 led other British publishers to follow suit, and, throughout the 1890s, many opened offices and contracted agents in New York and Chicago. Established on three continents, in London (1891), New York (1892), and Melbourne (1893), W.T. Stead's *Review of Reviews, American Review of Reviews*, and *Australasian Review of Reviews* represented a global publishing empire for this "foremost publisher of paperbacks in the Victorian Age." Three years after the launch of *Pearson's Magazine* (1896) in Britain, Arthur Pearson also signed an agreement with an American publisher and printer, J.J. Little & Co., to produce an American edition of *Pearson's* (1899). By 1900, there were American editions of *Pall Mall Magazine* (UK 1893, U.S. 1896: 1900 U.S. circ., monthly: 15,875) and *The English Illustrated Magazine* (1883), retitled *The New Illustrated Magazine* (1884) for the American market (1900 U.S. circ., monthly: 57,000). Transatlantic contracts and operations like these would become common for many other leading British and American publishers in decades to come. All figures are taken from *N.W. Ayer & Son's American Newspaper Annual and Directory*, Philadelphia, PA: N.W. Ayer, 1880–1915.

114 If, as Paul Eggert suggests, the success of the various colonial libraries from major publishers led to Mudie's decision in 1894 to finally abandon the three-decker novel, then the events of 1886 changed British literary history in truly profound ways. See Eggert's "Robbery Under Arms: The Colonial Market, Imperial Publishers, and the Demise of the Three-Decker Novel," *Book History*, Vol. 6, Ezra Greenspan and Jonathan Rose, Eds., University Park, PA: Pennsylvania State University Press, 2003.

115 Sean Latham and Mark Morrison, "Introduction," *Journal of Modern Periodical Studies* Vol. 1, No. 1, University Park, PA: Penn State University Press, 2010, p. iii.

116 David McKitterick, *A History of Cambridge University Press: New Worlds for Learning, 1873–1972*, Cambridge, UK, and London: Cambridge University Press, 2004, p. 139.

117 Eliot, p. 101.

118 Hodder & Stoughton launched its yellowjacket series of popular novels in 1923–24. Priced affordably, and bound in distinctive yellow covers, the series became a worldwide commercial success. The novels of Edgar Wallace alone sold 9.5 million copies in 20 years (1923–41). In their second season, the yellowjackets were advertised as "The 1000-title list that spans the Empire: the List upon which the sun never sets" (Marton Lyons, "Britain's Largest Export Market," *A History of the Book in Australia, 1891–1945*, Marton Lyons and John Arnold, Eds., Brisbane: QLD: University of Queensland Press, 2001, p. 21).

119 Quoted by Finklestein from Margaret Diane Stetz, "Sex, Lies, and Printed Cloth: Bookselling at the Bodley Head in the Eighteen-Nineties," *Victorian Studies* 35 (Autumn 1991), pp. 80–81.

120 Frederick R. Karl & Laurence Davies, Eds., *The Collected Letters of Joseph Conrad, Volume 4: 1908–1911*, Cambridge, UK: Cambridge University Press, 1990, p. 130.

121 See both Joshi (on India) and Lyons (on Australia), as cited above. In fact, the differences are surprising. Indian readers across the subcontinent as a whole, Joshi argues, preferred sensational melodrama, but, in the port city of Calcutta, science fiction was more popular. Bengalese science fiction developed into a major periodical publishing industry in itself. Lyons writes that Australian

readers preferred British and American adventure fiction and enjoyed a vibrant tradition of Australian frontier literature as well. Readers in New Zealand, though they shared a common market with Australia, demonstrated a clear preference for poetry and literary criticism imitative of British models.

122   Lyons, *A History of the Book in Australia*, pp. 336–43.
123   Eggert, "Robbery Under Arms," *Book History* 6, p. 142.
124   Priya Joshi, *Print Areas: Book History in India*, Abhijit Gupta and Swapan Chakravorty, Eds., Delhi: Permanent Black, 2004, p. 118. Joshi further notes: "In the decade or so between 1890 and 1902, Macmillan's sales to India more than doubled, from between £15,000 to £16,000 in 1890 to £36,852 in 1902."
125   David Finkelstein, "Imperial Self-Representation: Constructions of Empire in *Blackwood's Magazine*, 1880–1900," *Imperial Co-Histories: National Identities and the British and Colonial Press*, Ed. Julie F. Codell, London: Associated University Presses, 2003, pp. 95–108.
126   Ibid., p. 105.
127   Ibid.
128   Ibid., p. 106.
129   Ibid.
130   Ibid., *passim*.
131   Lyons, *A History of the Book in Australia*, p. 22.
132   In one form or another, English-speaking readers throughout the world had long been connected by transportation and telecommunications, but they had remained scattered in terms of an organized literary culture.
133   This was, in fact, far from a recent downturn in public taste, as critics would then complain; Priya Joshi contends that Murray's Colonial Library failed in the 1840s, partly because, despite the fact that half the series were travel books, what readers in the remote corners of the Empire really wanted were copies of the latest *Waverly* novel or a juicy Gothic romance (*Print Areas*, p. 29).
134   Lyons, pp. 336–38.
135   Membership to public libraries in India, moreover, was reserved for Indian readers exclusively. Joshi, "Trading Places: The Novel, the Colonial Library, and India," *Print Areas*, pp. 33–34.
136   Ibid., p. 40.
137   Richard Fulton, "Boys' Adventure Magazines and the Discourse of Adventure, 1860–1885," *Australasian Journal of Victorian Studies* Vol. 15, No. 1 (2010), p. 5.
138   Ibid.
139   Janice Radway has utilized the concept of "literary planes" in her work on middlebrow culture, and particularly in her work on the activities of the U.S. Book-of-the-Month Club from the 1920s and later; see *An Introduction to Book History*, David Finkelstein and Alistair McCleery, Eds. New York and London: Routledge, 2005, pp. 23–24.
140   Roger Lancelyn Green, "Introduction," *The Prisoner of Zenda* (1894), Anthony Hope, London: J.M. Dent, 1966, qtd. by Mike Ashley, *The Age of the Storytellers: British Popular Fiction Magazines 1880–1950*, London: The British Library, 2006, p. 1.
141   John Peck, *Maritime Fiction: Sailors and the Sea in British and American Novels, 1719–1917*. Basingstoke, UK, and New York: Palgrave, 2001, p. 151.
142   Dennis Butts, "Introduction", *King Solomon's Mines*, Rider Haggard, Oxford, UK, and New York: Oxford University Press, 1989, p. vii.
143   Cassell & Co.'s first printing of the novel consisted of 2,000 copies, half of which were bound in September 1885 (constituting the first issue); 500 were bound the next month, and 500 were sent to New York (bound in November

for the American issue). The book was reprinted in October, November, and December. Subsequent editions were issued by Cassell's Paris and Melbourne offices.

144 Sidney Paget was the artist and illustrator of the Sherlock Holmes series, published in *The Strand* (1891–1927).

145 See Jessica Amanda Salmonson, "An Annotated Bibliography of H. Rider Haggard's Fantasies in 1st Editions, Alphabetically Arranged; *She: A History of Adventure*, at www.violetbooks.com/haggard-bib.html (last accessed December 27, 2011; no longer available). According to Salmonson: "The US 1st edition includes 14 full-page illustrations by E.K. Johnson. There were also scads of pirated editions in the US as early as 1887 & 1888 (including from Ivers, F.F. Lovell, J.W. Lovell, George Munro, N.L. Munro, Ogilvie, Rand McNally), but none others predate the UK 1st."

146 Regarding American piracy, and its consequences for American readers and on the development of a national literature, Haggard writes: "Most of the books patronized by this enormous population are stolen from English authors, who, according to American law, are outcasts, unentitled to that protection to the work of their brains and the labour of their hands which is one of the foundations of common morality. Putting aside this copyright question, however . . . [T]he Americans are destroying their own literature, that cannot live in the face of the unfair competition to which it is subjected . . . [and] the whole of the American population . . . must be in course of thorough impregnation with English ideas and modes of thought. . . . [I]t would be difficult to overrate the effect that must be from year to year produced upon the national character of America by the constant perusal of books born in England" (pp. 174–75).

147 Rider Haggard, "About Fiction," *The Contemporary Review* 51 (February 1887), pp. 172–80.

148 Ibid., pp. 173–74.

149 Ibid., pp. 178–80.

150 Ibid., p. 172.

151 Ibid.

152 Ibid., p. 174.

153 Ibid., p. 175.

154 Ibid., p. 178.

155 Ibid., p. 180. The full text of the paragraph reads: "There is indeed a refuge for the less ambitious among us, and it lies in the paths and calm retreats of pure imagination. Here we may weave our humble tale, and point our harmless moral without being mercilessly bound down to the prose of a somewhat dreary age. Here we may even—if we feel that our wings are strong enough to bear us in that thin air—cross the bounds of the known, and, hanging between earth and heaven, gaze with curious eyes into the great profound beyond. There are still subjects that may be handled *there* if the man can be found bold enough to handle them. And, although some there be who consider this a lower walk in the realms of fiction, and who would probably scorn to become a 'mere writer of romances,' it may be urged in defence of the school that many of the most lasting triumphs of literary art belong to the producers of purely romantic fiction, witness the 'Arabian Nights,' 'Gulliver's Travels,' 'The Pilgrim's Progress,' 'Robinson Crusoe,' and other immortal works. If the present writer may be allowed to hazard an opinion, it is that, when Naturalism has had its day, when Mr. Howells ceases to charm, and the Society novel is utterly played out, the kindly race of men in their latter as in their earlier developments will still take pleasure in those works of fancy which appeal, not to a class, or a nation, or even to an age, but to all time and humanity at large" (180).

156 Green, as qtd. by Ashley, p. 1.
157 Haggard, "About Fiction," p. 180.
158 Ibid., p. 177.
159 Ibid., p. 174.
160 Edward Viles's *Black Bess; or, the Knight of the Road* concerns the imaginary exploits of real-life highwayman Dick Turpin. It ran for 254 weekly episodes (c. 1863–68), and was reprinted many times in the following decades.
161 G.K. Chesterton refers to this title in his essay "A Defense of Penny Dreadfuls," published in *The Speaker*, New Series, III, No. 76 (March 16, 1901), pp. 648–49. He writes: "It might at least cross our minds that for whatever other reason the errand-boy reads 'The Red Revenge,' it really is not because he is sated with the gore of his own friends and relatives" (649).
162 Christopher Banham, " 'England and America Against the World': Empire and the USE in Edwin J. Brett's *Boys of England*, 1866–99", *Victorian Periodicals Review* Vol. 40, No. 2 (2007), pp. 151–71.
163 See Radway, *An Introduction to Book History*, pp. 23–24.
164 Some of the more notable adventure writers in the nineteenth century include Walter Scott (1771–1832), James Fenimore Cooper (1789–1851), Captain Frederick Marryat (1792–1848), Alexandre Dumas (1802–70), W.H.G. Kingston (1814–80), Captain Mayne Reid (1818–83), R.M. Ballantyne (1825–94), Jules Verne (1828–1905), and G.A. Henty (1832–1902). Largely ignored today, but amazingly prolific and widely read in their time, were the professional writers of serialized fiction for the British bloods, penny dreadfuls, and boys' papers, such as J.M. Rymer, Thomas Prest, Malcolm Merry, George Reynolds, Samuel Hemyng, Percy and Vane St. John, Walter Viles, E.H. Burrage, James Greenwood, and scores of other Victorian "fiction factory" workers, and the American dime novelists Colonel Prentiss Ingraham, Ned Buntline, Frederic Dey, George Lippard, Burt Standish, and many more.
165 As is well known, Haggard's first commercial success was inspired by a dare from his brother that Haggard could write a better boys' book than R.L. Stevenson's best-selling *Treasure Island* (1883).
166 Decades later, in the early twentieth century, *She* (1886) would attain the ultimate modernist credentials, when this classic of imaginative literature was cited as a direct and crucial influence on Sigmund Freud's dream writings.
167 Written in collaboration with Andrew Lang, *The World's Desire* was first serialized in *The New Review*, April to December 1890, and published by Harper's (US) in October and Longman's (UK) that November. After the success of *King Solomon's Mines*, all of Haggard's novels were also extensively pirated in both the US and UK. With *Allan Quatermain*, two pirated American editions even preceded the authorized first editions of both countries by a month.
168 Unsigned editorial, "How Best to Promote the Sale of Pure Literature in Our Schools," from *The Sunday School Chronicle: A Weekly Journal of Help and Intelligence for Sunday School Workers* (January 19, 1877), p. 36. In 1887, B.G. Johns reported sales of "sensational novels in serial form" in excess of "two million copies a week, with individual titles selling from ten to sixty thousand each" (Altick, p. 308).
169 See Fulton, *passim*; Kelly Boyd, *Manliness and the Boys' Story Paper in Britain: A Cultural History, 1855–1940*, London: Palgrave Macmillan, 2003, *passim*; and also Richard Noakes, "The *Boy's Own Paper* and late-Victorian juvenile magazines," *Science in the Nineteenth-Century Periodical*, Cambridge, UK: Cambridge University Press, 2007, pp. 151–283, *passim*.
170 Ibid.

171 See Victor E. Neuberg's *Popular Literature: A History and Guide*, London: The Woburn Press, 1977.

172 Kelly Boyd's *Manliness and the Boys' Story Paper in Britain* includes a bibliography of 95 titles, 34 of which begin with *Boy's*, *Boys*, or *Boys'*.

173 This narrative form was perfected by Kingston, publisher and contributor to *The Union Jack*; Ballantyne, contributor to *BOP*; and Henty, editor of *The Union Jack* and contributor to both papers.

174 Models for changing the adventure story's dynamic can be indentified in periodicals from the mid-nineteenth century. In 1879, the Religious Tract Society established the *BOP*. W.H.G. Kingston, an accomplished adventure writer himself, launched the *Union Jack* as a "Library of high class fiction" the following year (1880). In his premier editorial, Kingston states: "[T]here will be nothing of the 'dreadful' type in our stories. No tales of boys rifling their employers' cash-boxes and making off to foreign lands, or other such highly immoral fiction products". When the Paris-based *Magazine of Education and Recreation* began serializing Jules Verne's "extraordinary voyages" in 1863, the magazine's publisher, Jules Hertzel, advertised his intent to "outline all the geographical, geological, physical, and astronomical knowledge amassed by modern science and to recount, in an entertaining and picturesque format ... the history of the universe" (A.B. Evans, *Jules Verne Rediscovered: Didacticism and the Scientific Novel*, Westport, CT: Greenwood Press, 1988, p. 30). Part of a social movement that made education a collective ideal and cure for social injustice, such magazines promised a better life and contributed to the spread of knowledge, but their audiences were small by comparison, and readers were drawn largely from the middle classes.

175 W.H. Bishop, "Story-Paper Literature," *The Atlantic Monthly* 44, Issue 263 (September 1879), p. 383.

176 More travel narratives were written in the nineteenth century than in all preceding years: see the *Encyclopedia of Exploration, 1800–1850: A Comprehensive Reference Guide to the History and Literature of Exploration, Travel, and Colonization between the years 1800 and 1850*, by Raymond John Howgego (Raymond John Howgego, Ed., Potts Point, NSW: Horden House, 2004). Publishing and periodical markets for first-person accounts by celebrity explorers became highly competitive, and the serialization of these narratives could spike a newspaper's circulation figures dramatically. For a discussion of the competition between publishers for Victorian explorers' first-person accounts, see Louise Henderson's " 'Everyone will die laughing': John Murray and the Publication of David Livingstone's Missionary Travels" at Livingstone Online, at www.livingstoneonline.ucl.ac.uk/companion.php?id=HIST2 (last accessed December 27, 2011; no longer available). Also see Chapter 3 in Finkelstein's *The House of Blackwood*. Regarding influences of romance on true explorers' accounts, most critics take the opposite view, that adventure writers adopted the conventions of best-selling travel narratives, which, of course, is also true. See pp. 44–46 in Andrea White's *Joseph Conrad and the Adventure Tradition*, Cambridge, UK: Cambridge University Press, 1993.

177 National Library of Scotland: Blackwood Papers, MS 42420, Letter from Livingstone to Murray, May 31; May 22, 1857.

178 The romance of Henry Morton Stanley's life is striking. He was an illegitimate boy from the north of Wales, born John Rowlands. He spent his formative years beaten and starved in a workhouse. He escaped to America to fight on both sides of the Civil War. He then became a journalist, explorer, best-selling author, and Member of Parliament.

179 See, for example, Tim Jeal's biography, *Stanley: The Impossible Life of Africa's Greatest Explorer*, New Haven, CT: Yale University Press, 2007. The author wishes to thank Dr. John Barnett (of Dallas, TX) for introducing him to this entertaining, well-researched, and highly engaging work. Jeal's book proved a crucial resource in the early stages of drafting this chapter.

180 It was reprinted as a news item on April 3, 1885, under the heading "Strange Tale of the Sea. Remarkable Voyage of the Brig Marie Celeste. A Missing Crew and What Became of Them. A Mystery Explained After Many Years." The *Herald*'s mailroom was swamped by readers' letters pouring in from all over the country. Not every reader took this position, of course. It was attributed by several to R.L. Stevenson, and the *Illustrated London News* compared it to Edgar Allan Poe. In 1844, Poe had achieved similar success with his purportedly true "The Balloon Hoax," which itself had been inspired by the 1835 "Great Moon Hoax." Both appeared in the same newspaper, *The New York Sun*.

181 Gerald Monsman, *H. Rider Haggard on the imperial frontier: the political and literary contexts of his African romances*, Greensboro, NC: ELT Press, 2006, p. 79.

182 Henty's jingoism, Haggard's high late-Victorian fantasy, and Conrad's proto-modernism all register their mediation in the spread of a global print media ecology in sometimes profound and subtle ways.

183 Wendy Katz, *Rider Haggard and the Fiction of Empire: A Critical Study of British Imperial Fiction*, Cambridge, UK: Cambridge University Press, 1987, pp. 30–57.

184 See, for example, Joseph A. Kestner, *Masculinities in British Adventure Fiction 1880–1915*, Farnham, UK: Ashgate, 2010.

185 See Tim DeForest, *Storytelling in the Pulps, Comics, and Radio: How Technology Changed Popular Fiction in America*, Jefferson, NC: McFarland, 2004; and Adam Roberts, "Late Twentieth-Century Science Fiction: Multimedia, Visual Science Fiction and Others," *The History of Science Fiction*, Basingstoke, UK: Palgrave Macmillan, 2005, pp. 326–40.

2 Imperial Technologies

Adventure and the Threat of New Media in Conrad's *Lord Jim* (1899)

In *Lord Jim*, the fictional South Seas district of Patusan is located "three hundred miles beyond the end of telegraph cables and mail-boat lines,"[1] meaning that it is a place outside the reach of nineteenth-century systems of transportation and communication. It is a perfect location, in other words, to which to escape and not be found.

Conrad's narrator, Marlow, couches this description of Patusan in the form of a question, moreover, asking his audience and readers:

> But do you notice how, three hundred miles beyond the end of telegraph cables and mail-boat lines, the haggard utilitarian lies of our civilization

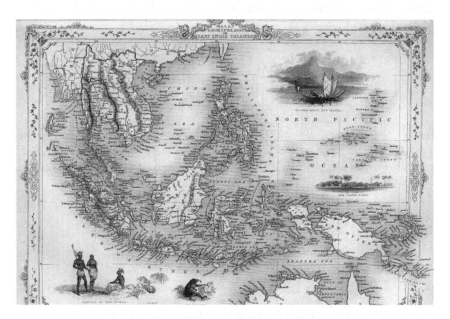

Figure 2.1 Malay Archipelago or East India Islands, J. and F. Tallis, from the *Illustrated Atlas of the World*, 1851.

wither and die, to be replaced by pure exercises of imagination, that
have the futility, often the charm, and sometimes the deep hidden
truthfulness, of works of art?[2]

This question raises a familiar specter of an imaginary dividing line between
civilization and the spaces of imperial fantasy beyond its frontiers. This
romantic convention was deeply embedded in imperialist rhetoric at the
turn of the century,[3] but here it is put forward in order to be ultimately
discredited. Framed in such terms, Patusan's distinction as a space of imaginative possibilities is temporary, as it is dependent on its physical and
geographical location outside the aggressive reach of modern telegraph and
imperial postal systems. Thus, Marlow's division of the world is defined
by technologies that would have threatened Patusan at the end of the
nineteenth century. By 1900, there were few places left on Earth that
remained beyond the reach of the telegraph.[4]

This chapter examines the original periodical context of Conrad's *Lord
Jim*, which was first serialized in *Blackwood's Magazine* from October 1899
to November 1900.

It shows how the novel anticipates a displacement of much older, heroic,
and mythic literary traditions by the spread of worldwide information
networks. This displacement is registered on four interrelated subgenres of
late nineteenth-century adventure fiction featured in the novel: imperial
encounter, pirate tale, exotic love story, and lost-world romance. The novel
draws upon conventions of sea stories, travel books, and discoverers'

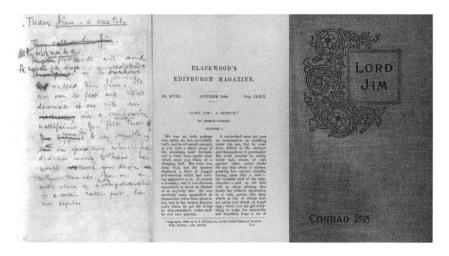

Figure 2.2 "Tuan Jim: A Sketch" Manuscript Page; First Page of *Lord Jim:
A Sketch*, in *Blackwood's Magazine* (October 1899); and First UK
Edition of *Lord Jim* (Edinburgh: Blackwood & Sons, 1900).

journals of the past two centuries, even as it interrogates the adventure tradition's contingency and diminishing possibilities in an increasingly integrated, more mobile world. I suggest that this position poses complications for Conrad, an author of sea stories and adventures whose career depended heavily on expanding new markets for periodical publication. It also marks the creative tension between *Lord Jim*'s Patusan section and its material context in a magazine such as *Blackwood's*, which not only "took [Conrad's] name wherever the English language is read,"[5] but also aimed to develop new and growing markets of those readers worldwide. I show how reading *Lord Jim* through its first periodical contexts adds an important dimension to the novel's notoriously complex composition history, and how *Blackwood's* own transitional identity offers a cogent explanation for the novel's "structural rift,"[6] or what Conrad called its "plague spot . . . [the] division of the book into two parts."[7] Jim's embrace of the pre-modern, pre-industrial Patusan emerges from my reading as a sign of the novel's modernity, its "advocacy of the past," which was a "peculiarly twentieth-century form of reaction."[8] It is both an imaginary solution to *Blackwood's* difficult transition to the twentieth century and a literary exploration of the themes expressed in Charles Whibley's monthly column, "Musings Without Method," which debuted in February 1900 and ran in the magazine for almost 30 years.[9]

Conrad as a *Blackwood's* Author

Serialized in *Blackwood's* from October 1899 to November 1900,[10] *Lord Jim* was by far Conrad's longest contribution to the Edinburgh periodical with which his name is today most closely associated.[11] By the summer of 1900, the protracted manuscript had grown to 45 chapters that totaled 249 printed pages. It spread across 14 installments and, at more than 120,000 words, it easily dwarfed the 38,000-word novella "(The) Heart of Darkness"—which had been serialized in just three issues the previous year (February–April 1899).[12] For the first UK serial rights to *Lord Jim*, Conrad was paid £300, or nearly twice the amount earned by the author from three previous appearances in *Blackwood's* combined. This was also Conrad's only contribution to the magazine issued separately by its publisher in book form (*Lord Jim: A Tale*, 1900).[13]

Blackwood's arguably played a greater role than any other magazine in Conrad's literary career. The magazine's cultural prestige, Tory politics, and global circulation were key factors in establishing the author's early reputation as a "writer of consequence."[14] Over a 5-year period from 1897 to 1902,[15] Conrad wrote some of his most important works expressly for it—three of the four Marlow narratives: "Youth," "Heart of Darkness," and *Lord Jim*—and through its pages he was guaranteed a wide, international readership. As Conrad remarked to his agent J.B. Pinker in February 1908, *Blackwood's* "took my name wherever the English language is read."[16] And, in 1911, he famously wrote: "There isn't a single club and messroom and man-of-war in the British Seas and Dominions which hasn't its copy of Maga—not to mention all the Scots in all parts of the world."[17] These statements are fully confirmed by Conrad's contemporary observers. In an April 1900 letter to William Blackwood, for example, Hugh Clifford wrote, from his governor's residence in North Borneo:[18] "I must thank you again for the copies of Maga which have reached us so regularly."[19] Anthony J. Stockwell observes about expatriate life in early twentieth-century colonial Malaysia, moreover, that, "culturally, as so many visitors remarked, the range was small: Savoy Operas and *Blackwood's Magazine* were characteristic fare."[20] As a transnational medium through which his works would be disseminated far and wide, *Blackwood's* had provided Conrad with an enviable publishing situation.

Knowing the author's own peripatetic, colonial, and cosmopolitan history, there is little surprise he would appreciate *Blackwood's* for that very reason.[21] By the time *Lord Jim* began its serialization in October 1899, Conrad's fiction had already appeared in a number of respectable London literary magazines, including *The Savoy, Cornhill, Cosmopolis*, and W.E. Henley's *New Review*.[22]

These four monthlies had international distributions at the time, but only *Cosmopolis* styled itself as an international journal and touted its international readership. Printed in London from January 1896 to November 1898, *Cosmopolis* subtitled itself "*An International Review*" and was offered "as a forum for European culture and international understanding in a time of escalating nationalism and militarism."[23] It printed essays on history, international politics, the arts, and contemporary journalism by contributors from a wide range of national and political backgrounds. Combining social and political commentary, reviews, biography, and new fiction, the magazine also appeared in several local editions, each with a different cover, in Paris, Berlin, and (starting January 1897) St. Petersburg. Edited by Fernand Ortmans, the Baron de Senechal,[24] issues featured separate literary sections in English, French, German, and (in the St. Petersburg edition from January 1897) Russian. After 35 issues and with a monthly circulation that hovered at around 20,000 issues, however, *Cosmopolis* ceased publication at the end of Volume XII. If not for the unexpected demise of the magazine, Conrad would have certainly continued to publish material in it. Although scornful of its politics, which were liberal and internationalist, he could appreciate the magazine's pay rates and cultural cachet. Stephen Donovan writes:

> [In 1897] Conrad . . . told a correspondent in private: "That Magazine [*Cosmopolis*] pays me very well . . . and I intend to sell them more of my work" (*CL* 1:350). Although he opposed the . . . division [of "An Outpost of Progress"] into two parts, complaining that "The sting of the thing is in its tail—so that the first installment, by itself will appear

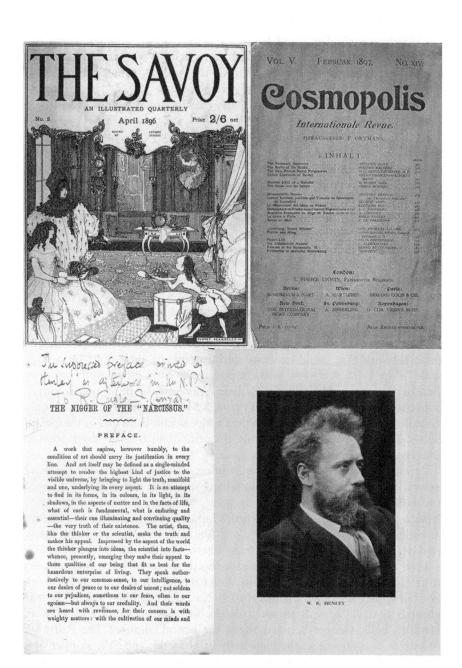

Figure 2.3 The Savoy (April 1896); Cosmopolis (February 1897); Page from First
         UK Edition of The Nigger of the "Narcissus," with a Note from
         Conrad: "The suppressed preface printed by Henley as afterword in his
         N.R. (New Review). To R. Curle—J. Conrad"; and Photograph
         Portrait of William Ernest Henley.

utterly meaningless—and by the time the second number comes out people would have forgotten all about it and would wonder at my sudden ferocity," he did not fail to see the publicity value of serialization in this remarkable periodical, observing in June 1897: "The *Sat[urday] Review* notices my story in the *Cosmo[polis]* with great discrimination" (*CL* 1:335, 363).[25]

Blackwood's offered Conrad a significantly smaller monthly circulation, but the magazine was distributed on a much wider scale. Although the publisher's ledgers record that annual sales of the magazine were just below 60,000 issues in 1898,[26] there were other, obvious advantages to *Blackwood's* truly global distribution. To be published in *Blackwood's* at the turn of the century was—as Conrad's remarks to Pinker from 1908 and 1911 indicate—the opportunity to be read, reviewed, and talked about "over there" in the colonial clubrooms, in the legal and medical offices of expatriate professionals,[27] aboard Her Majesty's Ships, and by a dispersed audience of "linked colonial, military, and political circles and networks"[28] throughout the Empire and the English-speaking world. The magazine's circulation, in terms of numbers of copies alone, does not reveal everything. David Finkelstein reminds us that the firm had access to "an efficient and localized print network that could generate and disseminate their texts on a wide scale."[29] In 1902, it cost 60 cents in postage to carry 12 monthly issues of *Blackwood's* to a subscriber in Canada, Australia, or the Cape Colony.[30] Subscriptions to secondhand issues through Mudie's Select Library cost only 15 shillings per year for readers on the European continent and in the United States. Through W.H. Smith & Sons, the price of an annual subscription to *Blackwood's* was just 13 shillings.[31]

At what point Conrad first became impressed with *Blackwood's* far-flung network of imperial and international subscribers is not known.[32] One of the earliest indications to appear in print, however, is from a May 1900 letter to David Storr Meldrum, the firm's London office manager and literary advisor. Here, Conrad remarks: "*Lord Jim* brings me letters. From Spain to day! They take in *Maga* in Madrid. Where is it they don't take *Maga*!"[33]

Over the next 20 years, he returned to this theme several times in his letters to friends and other correspondents. For Conrad, the desire that his work be read widely became a mantra. In 1902, he defended his "talent" on the grounds that it "appeals to such widely different personalities" as W.E. Henley, Wells, George Bernard Shaw, the fiction editor of *The Pall Mall Magazine*, a professor at the University of Helsinki, and "the skipper of a Persian Gulf steamer who wrote to the papers of my 'Typhoon'."[34] Conrad later bragged in a letter to Edward Garnett that the 1906 publication of "The Informer" in the Christmas issue of *Harper's* had brought him letters from both French and American readers.[35] In 1908, he quoted a correspondent from South America who had written to the author that *Nostromo* (1904): "met with no end of appreciation on the seaboard where the scene is laid, and from people in the know."[36] In 1909, Conrad claimed that a sailor and ship's master on leave from Penang[37] had recently confided to him while visiting: "We are all reading your books out there" in the Archipelago.[38] The audience constructed by these claims is not confined to the UK market, but reaches around the world. That Conrad himself hoped to be regarded by editors and peers as an author able to reach, and sustain, this widely dispersed global audience is equally on display. Writing to F.N. Doubleday in 1918, Conrad famously remarked: "I want to be read by many eyes and all kinds of them."[39] The fact that Conrad first acknowledges *Blackwood's* far-flung readership during the summer of 1900, in connection with *Lord Jim*'s ongoing serialization, is made all the more remarkable by his remarks a decade later. Despite having published with several houses, and in a variety of periodicals, which circulated his name as far afield as the Persian Gulf, South America, and the Malay Archipelago, Conrad continued to associate the period of his greatest achievement and most widespread global readership with the 5 years he had spent as a *Blackwood's* author at the turn of the century.

As Andrea White has argued,[40] Conrad's works "were initially read within and against" a tradition of romantic adventure fiction enjoying a popular resurgence with late-Victorian readers. The author's deeply pessimistic romances "challenged to greater or lesser extents the ways in which that form had constituted the imperial subject."[41] Marlow describes how Jim, for example:

> would forget himself, and beforehand live in his mind the sea-life of light literature … saving people from sinking ships, cutting away masts in a hurricane, swimming through a surf with a line; or as a lonely castaway, barefoot and half naked, walking on uncovered reefs in search of shellfish to stave off starvation. He confronted savages on tropical shores, quelled mutinies on the high seas, and in a small boat upon the ocean kept up the hearts of despairing men—always an example of devotion to duty, and as unflinching as a hero in a book.[42]

Marlow is not only referencing a familiar form and tradition of nineteenth-century adventure, but also revisiting this field as a textual source that later precipitates Jim's romantic disillusionment. Chapter II of the novel thus begins: "After two years of training [Jim] went to sea, and entering the regions so well known to his imagination, found them strangely barren of adventure."[43]

In two previous explorations of failed romantic idealism at the frontier, "An Outpost of Progress" and "Heart of Darkness,"[44] Conrad's heroes are similarly primed for disappointment by having internalized the romantic illusions of "light holiday literature."[45] Kayerts and Carlier are moved to tears by stories of "Richelieu and of d'Artagnon, of Hawk's Eye and of Father Goriot,"[46] and Marlow recounts his boyhood fascination with maps and the "many blank spaces on the earth,"[47] a fascination well subscribed in the pages of late-Victorian boys' periodicals. A challenge to the adventure romance is registered explicitly by both texts. Kayerts and Carlier go mad from sheer boredom and the futility of their service in the tropics. Though briefly they may have entertained heroic pretentions to exciting lives of romance and swashbuckling adventure, these dreams are violently dismissed by the duo's grotesque murder-suicide. Anticipating some paragon of the European Enlightenment in the heart of central Africa, Marlow instead discovers the savage and criminal Colonel Kurtz. And, in "Youth,"[48] Marlow recounts another experience of romantic disillusionment. The narrative recalls how, 22 years earlier, when he was second mate on board the *Judea*, his first voyage to the Far East was postponed, and almost cut short, by one interminable series of disasters and technical steamship malfunctions after another.

Figure 2.4 The *Torrens*, on which Conrad Served as First Mate from London to Adelaide, Australia (November 21, 1891–July 26, 1893); the *Otago*, of which Conrad Was Appointed Captain (January 19, 1888); the *S.S. Somerset*, which Towed Conrad's Ship, the *Palestine* (March 15, 1883); and the *Roi des Belges*, in which Conrad Sailed up the Congo River (1890).

The tragedies of these would-be adventure romance heroes are framed by their respective failures to achieve what, in the second part of *Lord Jim*, is a successful, but brief, negotiation of "fantasy" and "actualization"[49] at the disappearing frontiers of empire. Having failed himself in the *Patna* debacle, Jim pursues a second opportunity in the remote South Seas setting of Patusan. Marlow's descriptions of this faraway location, "shut . . . off from the sight of an indifferent world" by "[t]hirty miles of forest,"[50] collapses Jim's actualization of former adventure fantasies and the reparation of his lost romantic idealism[51] with Patusan's geographical setting. It is this setting, in fact, that elicits his spiritual transformation. Remote, isolated, and full of romantic possibilities, Patusan suggests the influence of lost-world stories. The exotic setting of Jim's redemption is conditioned by "pure exercises of imagination,"[52] because Patusan is geographically remote. And, Patusan is geographically remote precisely because it remains outside the nineteenth century's expanding networks of global and technological integration. Jim's Patusan fantasy unfolds in the gaps or interstices that persisted between overlapping fields of nineteenth-century information systems well into the twentieth century—until radio, aviation, electricity, and aerial photography had conceptually altered the imaginative possibilities of such fissures.[53]

In 1923, Conrad remarked on the diminishment of these fissures in global mapping, in the face of advancing, modern travel technologies. He writes:

> These basic facts of geography having been ascertained . . . the modern traveler contemplating the much-surveyed earth beholds in fact a world in a state of transition; very different in this from the writers of travel-books of Marco Polo's time, who in their conscientious narratives seem to progress among immutable wonders, to feed their curiosity on a consistency of the splendid and the bizarre, presented to their eyes to stare at, to their minds to moralize upon.[54]

Elsewhere in the essay, Conrad concludes:

> [T]he time for such books of travel is past on this earth girt about with cables . . . lighted by that sun of the twentieth century under which there is nothing new left now, and but very little of what may still be called obscure.[55]

The spread of the telegraph, wireless, and electricity was well underway in late March to April 1900,[56] however. Although the novel is set roughly a quarter of a century earlier, in 1886–89,[57] as a rent or gap in global mapping, Patusan is already temporary. The arrival of Gentleman Brown's pirates, who locate Patusan 3 years after Jim's own arrival, precipitates the fantasy's final destruction and the hero's anticlimactic fall from power.

Regarding the sudden arrival of Brown and his pirates, Marlow can only surmise:

> Perhaps he had heard of Patusan—or perhaps he just only happened to see the name written in small letters on the chart—probably that of a largish village up a river in a native state, perfectly defenseless, far from the beaten tracks of the sea and from the ends of submarine cables. He had done that kind of thing before—in the way of business; and this now was an absolute necessity, a question of life and death—or rather of liberty. Of liberty![58]

Only, Patusan no longer remains hidden or cut off from the outside world, as Marlow explains: "These were the emissaries with whom the world he had renounced was pursuing him . . .—white men from 'out there.' . . . This was all that came to him—a menace, a shock, a danger."[59]

That this menace to Jim's adventure fantasy arrives in the form of Brown, the "latter-day buccaneer," pits one series of popular late nineteenth-century adventure tropes against another.[60] The narrator describes Brown as "the most reckless of desperadoes," a leader of "bloodthirsty" pirates, "men without a country," and a "horde of wandering cutthroats" in search of "loot" who use stock phrases such as "Hands off my plunder!"[61] The opposition is also shared by the novel's frustrated, exotic love story theme. In his cynical description of Jim's "love story," Marlow hints at the inevitable failure of fantasy to measure up to expectations, framing the event in terms of a wealth of similar stories pervading periodical literature at the time. He declares:

> I suppose you think it is a story that you can imagine for yourselves. We have heard so many such stories, and the majority of us don't believe them to be stories of love at all. For the most part we look upon them as stories of opportunity: episodes of passion at best. . . . This view is mostly right. . . . Yet I don't know.[62]

Drawing upon the tropes of late nineteenth-century adventure fiction, Conrad refuses to dismiss them. Hence, Marlow equivocally concludes: "This view is mostly right. . . . Yet I don't know."[63] Rather than a critical subversion of this tradition, *Lord Jim* registers Conrad's investment in the tensions and contradictions of late-Victorian romance and adventure fiction.[64]

Like the lost-world novels of Rider Haggard and Conan Doyle, *Lord Jim*'s bifurcation of the world is threatened by the encroaching presence of a grid-like global modernity. The novel advances a frequently recurring thesis from the turn of the twentieth century: that an increasingly blurred division between civilization and the frontier was vanishing, owing to modern expansions of media, transportation, and communication networks.

An "end of romance" was a synecdoche of this idea. In critical debates between realism and romance, literary aesthetics, and predictions of literature's future, a specter of global technological integration is present and pronounced. In Haggard's 1894 article "Elephant Smashing and Lion Shooting," the author predicts that, "soon the ancient mystery of Africa will have vanished," and he wonders: "[Where] will the romance writers of future generations find a safe and secret place, unknown to the pestilent accuracy of the geographer, in which to lay their plots?"[65] In 1911, Doyle posed the question to his audience at the Royal Geographical Society dinner.[66] He asked: What will writers do, now that the "blank spaces, in which a man of imagination might be able to give free scope to his fancy . . . are rapidly being filled up?"[67] It was this inexorable progress of exploration and mapping that represented, for John Buchan, a "drawing back of that curtain which had meant so much to the imagination."[68] Conrad agreed: "Presently there will be no back-yard left in the heart of Central Africa that has not been peeped into by some person more or less commissioned for the purpose."[69]

The invasion of these "commissioned" representatives—variously charged by state and private companies to carry out the colonial processes of the late nineteenth century—displaced an officially sanctioned need for "the heroic figure of the day, the explorer-adventurer."[70] The romance surrounding the explorer-adventurers' discovery and exploration of the last remaining pockets of uncharted territory on Earth was stimulated by the anticipation and postponement of the gratification of geographical knowledge, not by its more prosaic attainment. It was rather for bureaucrats to conduct the much less glamorous tasks of extending colonial industry and control: the surveying, ordering, classifying, and otherwise domesticating of the world's frontier areas for integration into an emergent world economy.[71]

Read this way, *Lord Jim* registers its author's profound turn-of-the-century nostalgia for a waning global license, whereby a series of improbable but thrilling adventures in "the impossible world of romantic achievements"[72] might still—be believed to—flourish in the corners, crevices, and just beyond the margins of empires. For Conrad, as a latecomer to sea stories and adventure literature, the turn of the century's mechanized travel, steam and electricity, mass media, and communication technologies menaced the very postulation of this imperial frontier, the requisite borderland for adventure's transgressive fantasies of escape and renewal—setting out for "distant parts of the world," leaving behind no "precise address," and vanishing "into space like a witch on a broomstick."[73] This position reiterates Frederick Jackson Turner's 1893 thesis about the closing of the American frontier,[74] but on the global scale of world empires. It poses implications for an author of sea stories and adventure fiction, however, because Conrad's second career[75] depended on expanding new markets for the distribution and circulation of books and periodicals. It also marks the creative tension between *Lord Jim*'s Patusan section and the material context of its serialization in a magazine such as

Blackwood's, which not only "took [Conrad's] name wherever the English language is read,"[76] but also aimed, throughout this period, to develop new and larger markets of those readers worldwide. Re-embedding *Lord Jim* in the context of its first serialization in *Blackwood's* (October 1899–November 1900) requires a broader understanding of these developments. It is necessary to locate the magazine's place in the culture of transatlantic publishing at the turn of the century, and especially within a rapidly changing popular market for books and periodicals at home and abroad. That is the subject of this chapter's following section.

Blackwood's at the Turn of the Century

Conrad's 5-year creative association with *Blackwood's* coincided with an important period of transition for the magazine.[77] From 1880 to 1890, annual circulations had declined nearly 20 percent, from 65,937 to 54,328—or from about 5,500 to 4,500 copies per month. Sales of an American edition—produced by *Blackwood's* after 1891[78]—increased the magazine's annual circulation by 12,000 copies. Its sales in the United States remained steady over the next decade, but overall figures continued to decline, from 66,028 (1890–91) to 60,713 (1900–01). By 1900, *Blackwood's* annual sales in the UK had fallen to 49,047—or 4,100 copies per month. This was a 25 percent decrease from 1880.[79] On average, it was 1,400 fewer sales per issue.[80] Faced with this steadily shrinking readership, the growth of a "brighter, racier" new journalism,[81] "multiplication and . . . fractionalization of niche markets in middle class periodical consumption," and direct competition from new publishers such as William Heinemann (1890), Methuen & Co. (1892), and *The National Review* (1883),[82] Blackwood's began looking into other opportunities that opened farther afield, while "aiming more directly at its steadiest customer base: the colonial audience."[83]

Blackwood's profitable 1890–91 expansion into the North American market had provided a logistical model for its other large-scale expansion into India, Australia, New Zealand, and the colonies starting in 1894. The firm had contemplated new marketing strategies involving foreign and colonial markets before,[84] but the establishment that year of Blackwood's Colonial Library series was its first major step in that direction.[85] Sales of new books to colonial markets grew, as did their influence on publishers' lists, and, as firms geared increasingly toward colonial markets, a shift in target audiences for book sales made an indelible mark on the firm and its magazine.[86]

Blackwood's account ledgers do not record any marked improvement in the firm's annual profits until 1902–03, but, in that fiscal year—and through the period of prosperity that continued on into the First World War—its fortunes began to rise steadily, although not dramatically. An improved financial standing becomes noticeable in the first few years of the twentieth century. A recorded annual profit of £2,488.7s.8d, in 1889–90, increases to £3,160.5s.7d in 1902–03.[87] The result of a variety of decisions made over a period of years throughout the 1880s and 1890s, it was also, in large part, a return on investments made in new, expanding markets overseas. By 1903, however, Conrad had effectively parted ways with Blackwood & Sons. His last major commission for their magazine was *The End of the Tether* (July–December 1902). Two minor essays did follow—"Her Captivity" (September 1905) and "Initiation" (January 1906)—but they were arranged by Pinker. In 1901, he had assumed charge of Conrad's literary affairs.[88] In a letter to Ford Maddox Hueffer, Conrad made only a slight reference to their recent sale: "Two for B'wood to pay off an old debt."[89]

Conrad's literary career had taken a decidedly different turn in the meantime,[90] but, in the 5 years that he published with Blackwood, works such as "Youth,"[91] "Heart of Darkness,"[92] and *Lord Jim: A Sketch*[93] were dispersed throughout the world thanks to that very encroachment of global modernity from which, in *Lord Jim*, his protagonist flees. It is also the encroachment of which, eventually, Jim becomes a victim. But, as my previous chapter has shown, the nineteenth-century periodical industry developed in tandem with the increasing centrality of industrialized, metropolitan cities, while it radiated outwards, alongside "the evolution of the railway system"[94] and through the combined efforts of organized and "efficient long-distance services ... [which] also meant regular and faster postal and small package services."[95] As David Reed notes, the same transport networks were "important for both business communication and the distribution of magazines."[96] Although *Blackwood's*, at the turn of the century, became an icon of Victorian tradition, consistency, and uncompromising literary quality in an ever-changing popular market, it was also quintessentially modern. The magazine could not have maintained this image without its publisher's highly regulated system of shipping agents, distributors, and retailers worldwide. Linda Dryden observes that:

> [b]y the turn of the twentieth century, the colonial markets ... were becoming lucrative ones for British publishers, and [so in 1894] Blackwood joined the ranks of [London and Edinburgh] publishing houses issuing novels in Colonial Libraries for consumption only in the British colonies.[97]

The increasingly global coverage of a modern telegraph system, faster and more reliable mail boats and cargo steamers, and other advances in communication and transport technologies were essential to this emergent world economy. Global modernity had made a new scale of periodical publishing possible, and magazines with dynamic, interconnected cultural networks on such a global scale—as *Blackwood's* had—were always more modern than

Figure 2.5 Six Covers: *Blackwood's Magazine* from November 1825; July 1885; February 1899; July 1915; September 1948; and December 1958.

their appearance might suggest.[98] *Blackwood's* maintained a comparatively sober, level-minded attitude in its approach to new technologies, modernity, and the coming century.[99] It was no less concerned or directly involved with modern developments in the world, although it avoided the celebratory effusions of the popular press. Opting for an old-fashioned skepticism and skillfully crafted position of critical detachment, the magazine's complex and often ironic attitudes toward modern social and technological changes masked its material embodiment in the highly efficient, state-of-the-art system of production, distribution, and circulation.

Against this wider context of *Blackwood's* global dissemination and its state of transition at the turn of the twentieth century, the following section locates Conrad's abrupt decision during the spring of 1900 in the pages of the magazine's serialization itself.

Serializing *Lord Jim*'s Patusan Section

Conrad's decision to fully develop the story of Jim's adventures in Patusan extended the novel's already protracted serialization an additional 6 months; it also dramatically shifted the novel's narrative and thematic focus. What Conrad imaginatively achieves in Jim's desperate act, a flight beyond imperial modernity, is a provocative evasion of imperial modernity's information and communication infrastructure. Patusan becomes an opportunity, not only to escape, but also to repudiate "the spiritual and ethical malaise of modernity."[100] Jim's embrace of the pre-modern, pre-industrial society of Patusan carves out an imaginary geographical space that serves as the novel's critique of expanding systems of global trade and technology. According to Thomas C. Moser's timeline for *Lord Jim*'s composition, the decision to develop this aspect of the novel's complicated plot was made sometime between mid-February and April 1900. Correspondence also indicates that this was a crucial 6–8 weeks in his tortuous development of the novel.[101] Not completed until July, the manuscript at this time did not include the second section, which fully develops the story of Jim's life and death in Patusan. A dramatic and unpremeditated shift in the direction of *Lord Jim*'s narrative, it was most likely not envisioned until late February or March at the earliest. Moser writes:

> Conrad originally intended [*Lord Jim*] to be a story of twenty thousand words . . . three or four installments in the magazine. Even in November . . . when Conrad had been planning and working . . . on "Lord Jim: A Sketch" for eighteen months and when the second installment was already on sale, he envisioned only four or five installments. . . . Perhaps the crucial moment in the writing occurred shortly after a letter of February 12, 1900, in which Conrad states flatly that, with twenty chapters finished, he will need only two more to complete the story.[102]

According to Moser's reckoning:

> Since Chapter XX concerns Marlow's visit to Stein, Conrad must still, at so late a date, not have decided to develop fully Jim's life in Patusan. It is hard to imagine how there could have been a Gentleman Brown, or even Jim's death.[103]

In Conrad's letter to Blackwood dated February 12, 1900—3 months and 20 chapters into *Lord Jim*'s serialization—he assures his editor that only "another two" chapters are needed to finish it.[104] Zdzisław Najder suggests that Conrad decided to extend the novel in late March.[105] These dates assume that the Patusan story evolved in manuscript form sometime between mid-February and the end of March 1900. In a letter to Meldrum of April 3, Conrad confirms that, "[the editors] have already . . . enough matter for *two* numbers."[106] If this estimation is correct, Blackwood had received the May and June installments by late March, or in early April. These two installments include the narrative's dramatic shift, which occurs between Chapters XVI–XX and XXI–XXIII, representing the May and June installments, respectively.

Marlow first announces the author's intention to extend *Lord Jim* at the start of Chapter XX. This chapter appeared in *Blackwood's* June installment, where Marlow poses the rhetorical question: "I don't suppose any of you have heard of Patusan?" He continues: "It does not matter; there's many a heavenly body in the lot crowding upon us of a night that mankind has never heard of."[107] In this late installment, Marlow thus introduces Patusan as a remote "region of another planet."[108] It is "outside the sphere of [man's] activities" and "of no earthly importance to anybody but ... astronomers who are paid to talk learnedly about its composition, weight, [and] path." Regarding even astronomers' interest in such a remote, isolated, and insignificant place, Marlow qualifies that as "a sort of scientific scandal-mongering."[109] The narrator continues:

> Thus with Patusan. . . . However, neither heavenly bodies nor astronomers have anything to do with Patusan. It was Jim who went there. I only meant you to understand that had Stein arranged to send him into a star of the fifth magnitude the change could not have been greater. He left his earthly failings behind him and what sort of reputation he had, and there was a totally new set of conditions for his imaginative faculty to work upon. Entirely new, entirely remarkable.[110]

In *Blackwood's* July 1900 number, Chapter XXIV opens with a further disquisition on Patusan's sublime exoticism and the profound mystery of its landscape. The connection between Patusan's remote geographical location and Jim's renewal is immediately drawn.[111] According to Marlow:

> The coast of Patusan . . . is straight and somber, and faces a misty ocean. Red trails are seen . . . streaming under the dark-green foliage of bushes and creepers clothing the low cliffs. Swampy plains open out at the mouth of rivers, with a view of jagged blue peaks beyond the vast forests. . . . [A] chain of islands . . . stand out in the everlasting sunlit haze like the remnants of a wall breached by the sea.[112]

Regarding Jim's arrival in Patusan, Marlow continues:

> [A]nd thus entered the land [Jim] was destined to fill with the fame of his virtues. . . . At the first bend he lost sight of the sea . . . and faced the immovable forests . . . everlasting in the shadowy might of their tradition. . . . Such was the way in which [he] was approaching greatness as genuine as any man ever achieved.[113]

Conrad spends several pages on Patusan's location, and the author goes out of his way to stress the geographical remoteness of it. The site of Jim's renewal is an outpost at the farthest edges of the galaxy. According to Padmini Mongia, it is "reminiscent of aspects of imperial Gothic, [and it] *reminds* us of the appeal of regions beyond earthly boundaries, an appeal that stemmed from the sense that the world had become too small to allow for 'genuine' adventure any longer."[114] This "sense that the world had become . . . small" is also reflected much earlier in the novel by the transnational composition of its broad cast of characters, a point especially evident in Marlow's description of the *Patna*.

Marlow first introduces the *Patna* in the context of its motley crew of nations and races. It is "owned by a Chinaman, chartered by an Arab, and commanded by a sort of renegade New South Wales German, [who is] very anxious to curse publicly his native country."[115] The *Patna* employs an Englishman, Jim, as its first mate, two Malay helmsmen, and 800 Muslim pilgrims of various nationalities compose the ship's passenger list. Gerard Barrett thus describes the *Patna* "as a ship of babel."[116] Stephen Ross extends this transnational context further:

> [T]he *Patna* is damaged when it runs over a Norwegian derelict, after which it is salvaged by a French gunboat and towed to the British-administered port of Aden. Finally, when the trial is over, Jim finds himself (thanks to the intervention of the German Stein) meting out justice in a Dutch colonial region that is subject to . . . various tribes (some of which are indigenous, some of which are immigrants) of Bugis, Dyaks, Muslims, and Arabs [who] strive to dominate the region's trade.[117]

Ross argues that, in *Lord Jim*, "Conrad was becoming aware of . . . the emergence of a qualitatively different world order" characterized by "radical uncertainty and contingency . . . surrounding Jim with a . . . specifically international cast."[118] Barrett draws attention to the connection in *Lord Jim* between a new international world order and diminishing possibilities for adventure: "When we see Jim on board the training-ship in the first chapter, the narrator informs us that 'in the babel of two hundred voices he would forget himself, and beforehand live in his mind the sea-life of light literature.'"[119] Jim's disenchantment with the realities of imperial modernity is anticipated by the social and linguistic babel on board the *Patna*. From this "babel of two hundred voices," he seeks an imaginary refuge in forms of popular romance that still privilege the mythic and heroic world. Jim escapes to this older, romantic literary tradition of sea stories and adventures and, through its fiction, into a world of excitement and danger, as the world it constructs remains purposefully, and forever, "starkly divided, partially wild and mysterious, [and] dramatically dangerous."[120]

Readers early on recognized the novel's division into two distinct narrative sections.[121] First, there is the proto-modernist account of the *Patna* disaster and Jim's subsequent trial, which is narrated through multiple perspectives and makes use of a complex chronology. It constitutes Chapters I–XX of the serialized version of *Lord Jim* in *Blackwood's* (October 1899–May 1900). Then, there is the story of Jim's Patusan adventure, which is more linear and rigorous in its narrative and employs recognizable subgenres of late nineteenth-century adventure romance. It constitutes Chapters XX–XLV of the *Blackwood's* serialization (June–November 1900). From the "searching method … of the first part to the … action-oriented account of the second"[122] spans an 8-week period that marked the radical departure in Conrad's plans for completing *Lord Jim*. In his letter to Blackwood dated April 12, Conrad finally makes the following unexpected confession:

> I feel the need of telling you that I've done something anyway and to assure you that *Lord Jim has* an end, which last I am afraid you may be beginning to doubt. It has though—and I am now trying to write it out.[123]

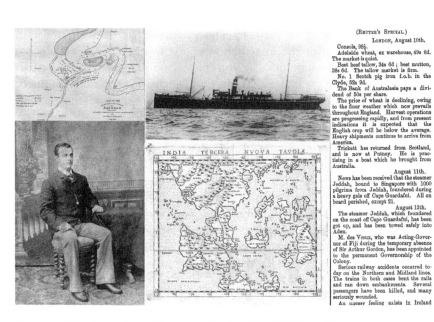

Figure 2.6 Reader's Map of Patusan; *The Jeddah*; "British and Foreign" Telegraph Reports, *Otago Witness*, Issue 1501, August 21, 1880, Page 11; Girolamo Ruscelli, *India Tercera Nuova Tavola*, One of the First Maps of Southeast Asia (Venice, 1561); and Photograph Portrait of Jim Lingard (1861–1921), who May Have Partially Inspired the Character of Conrad's Lord Jim.

In the meantime, Conrad had "decided to develop fully" the second part of the novel, dealing with Jim's brief adventurous life in Patusan.[124]

In the subsequent chapters of *Lord Jim* (Chapters XX–XLV, serialized from June to November 1900), a romantic cultural and artistic worldview predominates. Jim is pursued, for example, by "that rotten old *Patna* racket"[125] and its "scandalous gossip"[126] for years. The insidious notoriety of the court proceedings spreads so quickly that Egström warns him: "[I]f you keep up this game you'll very soon find that the earth ain't big enough to hold you."[127] From one short-term menial employment to the next, "adorned version[s] of the story"[128] threaten to unmask Jim's "secret," and trail his reputation throughout the whole South Pacific, a geographical "circle . . . which had a diameter of . . . three thousand miles."[129] Prior to Jim's disappearance "up country"[130] and into the remote jungles of Patusan, the hero's endless pursuit "find[s] the nature of his burden as well known to everybody as though he had gone about all that time carrying it on his shoulders."[131]

Marlow's narration of the final verdict in Jim's public trial describes "the passionless and definite phraseology" of the French magistrate's judgment, which is handed down publicly in the "phraseology a machine would use, if machines could speak."[132] Marlow's critique rests on the inadequacy of "official language,"[133] the reduction of reality to "mere surfaces,"[134] and an over-determination of "facts."[135] This is doubly a critique of the rhetorical models that privilege using such disguises. The rhetoric common to newspaper reports, court and legal documents, and even some advertisements supposedly elides charges of persuasion by the sheer force of the message's direct address and its unadorned delivery of facts. Marlow suggests instead that, "there will be no message, [but] such as each of us can interpret for himself from the language of facts, that are so often more enigmatic than the craftiest arrangement of words."[136] He protests famously: "They wanted facts. Facts! They demanded facts from him, as if facts could explain anything!"[137]

Lord Jim's Patusan section develops Conrad's imaginary solution to this spread of global modernity, an extension of a European modernity already contaminated by its public obsession with spectacle, a social and intellectual failure of modern journalism, and the homogenization of cultural experience. Monthly installments of *Lord Jim*, beyond Chapter XX (June 1900), develop Jim's own desperate experience of a counter-fidelity to the more romantic past. This complicated and anachronistic worldview renders Jim out of step with, and wholly unprepared for, the rupture of tradition through technology that is characteristic of the novel's modern present. Although a thoroughly modern protagonist, Jim is not a man of the modern world. Rather, Jim is one of the world's dislocated romantics. He is out of step with the present, because he remains devoted to "the past,"[138] "an old unreasoning tradition."[139]

At the turn of the twentieth century, Conrad's critique of modernity was entirely at home in *Blackwood's*. It is symptomatic of the same aesthetic and technological concerns explored, for example, by Charles Whibley in his monthly *Blackwood's* column, "Musings Without Method," which ran in the magazine for almost 30 years.[140] *Blackwood's* own transition from respected nineteenth-century cultural institution to just one of the twentieth century's lingering survivals of the old Victorian monthly involved a similarly complicated set of simultaneous positions. In this context, finally, *Lord Jim*'s embrace of the pre-modern and pre-industrial Patusan is a sign of the novel's modernity, its "advocacy of the past," which became a "peculiarly twentieth-century form of reaction."[141] It is both an imaginary solution to *Blackwood's* transitional identity in 1900 and an extended exploration in literary fiction of the "over-arching theme" of Whibley's column, the modern "journalization of public discourse."[142]

In February 1900, Whibley proposed the sabotage of journalists' lines of communication, provocatively suggesting: "[I]t will be fortunate for us if we conduct our next war with the wires cut behind us, and all the correspondents kicking their heels at the coast."[143] This act of sabotage theoretically assures an evasion of a hostile information infrastructure. This premise also informs Jim's escape into the pre-industrial Patusan.

In March 1900, Whibley wrote:

> The dark ages . . . have passed away, and are succeeded (maybe) by a too general intelligence. The old times were more entertaining and less meritorious. . . . For all that, they still attract us; and . . . we pray that in some corner . . . [someone] will preserve the few eccentricities of the last decades.[144]

Such attitudes would have been familiar to many of *Blackwood's* conservative readers, if only on a general level.[145] *Blackwood's* writers also shared values, and the magazine's editors aimed much of the new material directly at their conservative readership. Conrad's abrupt determination to develop more fully the story of Jim's adventures in Patusan is thus indicative of *Blackwood's* complicated literary value system, and during a period in which Whibley's dire pronouncements on technology became a "resounding success."[146] This coherent set of concerns registers these authors' shared social and political conservatism and the anachronism inherent in *Blackwood's* romantic cultural and artistic worldview.

The uneven, shifting development of the adventure romance in the first decade of the twentieth century continued to dominate Conrad's creative attention. These aesthetic concerns framed an attitude of contempt toward adventure's modern variation, tourism, and occupied the writing of Conrad's first best-seller, *Chance*.[147] According to Lawrence Graver, demand for the novel was extraordinary. It sold 20,194 copies in the United

States in 5 months, and another 13,200 copies in England in the first 2 years. By contrast, total British sales for first editions of *Lord Jim, Nostromo, The Secret Agent,* and *Under Western Eyes* was little more than 10,000.[148] The author's abiding preoccupation with adventure's anachronistic place in the world finally made good in the modern marketplace, but in a subtler, greatly diminished form.

Notes

1 Joseph Conrad, *Lord Jim* (1900), Ed. Thomas C. Moser, Norton Critical Edition, New York: W.W. Norton, 2006, p. 168.

2 Ibid.

3 See John McClure, *Late Imperial Romance,* London and New York: Verso Books, 1994, pp. 1–7.

4 In 1901, the British cable ship *Colonia* set out from Bamfield, British Columbia, to lay 4,000 kilometers of undersea cable to Fanning Island (1,600 kilometers south of Hawaii). The trans-Pacific telegraph line between Bamfield and Fanning Island was finished October 31, 1902. The next day, the first telegraph messages to circle the globe were relayed along this line, known as the All Red Cable Route. See Daniel R. Headrick, *The Tentacles of Progress: Technology Transfer in the Age of Imperialism, 1850–1940,* Oxford, UK: Oxford University Press, 1988, pp. 104–10.

5 Joseph Conrad, Letter to J.B. Pinker (February 1908), *The Collected Letters of Joseph Conrad, Volume 4: 1908–1911,* Eds. Frederick R. Karl and Laurence Davies, Cambridge, UK: Cambridge University Press, 1990, p. 49.

6 Daphna Erdinast-Vulcan, "The Failure of Myth: *Lord Jim,*" *Lord Jim* (1900), Joseph Conrad, Ed. Thomas Moser, Second Norton Critical Edition, New York and London: W.W. Norton, 1996, p. 493.

7 Conrad, Letter to Edward Garnett (12 November 1900), *The Collected Letters of Joseph Conrad, Volume 2: 1898–1902,* Eds. Frederick R. Karl and Laurence Davies, Cambridge, UK: Cambridge University Press, 1986, p. 302.

8 Stephen Donovan, "The Muse of *Blackwood's*: Charles Whibley and Literary Criticism in the World," *Print Culture and the Blackwood Tradition, 1805–1930,* Ed. David Finkelstein, Toronto: University of Toronto Press, 2006, p. 263.

9 From February 1900 to December 1929, Whibley's monthly review column, "Musings Without Method," engaged its readers in a virtually uninterrupted 30-year-long diatribe against the modern world. This ultra-conservative's opinions on art and literature were equally uncompromising, and, as Donovan notes, the column was a "resounding success" (Donovan, "The Muse of *Blackwood's*," p. 276).

10 *Lord Jim: A Sketch* was originally serialized in 14 installments, as follows: Chaps. I–IV, Vol. 166 (October 1899): pp. 441–59; Chap. V (November 1899): pp. 644–57; Chaps. VI–VII (December 1899): pp. 807–28; Chaps. VIII–IX, Vol. 167 (January 1900): pp. 60–73; Chaps. X–XI (February 1900): pp. 234–46; Chaps. XII–XIII (March 1900): pp. 406–19; Chaps. XIV–XV (April 1900): pp. 511–26; Chaps. XVI–XX (May 1900): pp. 666–87; Chaps. XXI–XXIII (June 1900): pp. 803–17; Chaps. XXIV–XXVII, Vol. 168 (July 1900): pp. 88–106; Chaps. XXVIII–XXX (August 1900): pp. 251–63; Chaps. XXXI–XXXV (September 1900): pp. 358–83; Chaps. XXXVI–XL (October 1900): pp. 547–72; and Chaps. XLI–XLV (November 1900): pp. 688–710.

11   See Donovan, "Serialization of Lord Jim; A Sketch in Blackwood's Magazine (Oct 1899–Nov 1900)," Conrad First, at www.conradfirst.net/view/serialisa tion?id=93 (accessed February 3, 2012); and Moser, Ed., "The Division, by Chapters, of the Monthly Installments of *Lord Jim: A Sketch in Blackwood's Edinburgh Magazine,*" *Lord Jim* (1900), Second Norton Critical Edition, New York and London: W.W. Norton, 2006, p. 308.

12   Philip V. Allingham, "The Initial Publication Context of Joseph Conrad's *Heart of Darkness* in *Blackwood's Edinburgh Magazine,*" The Victorian Web, at www.victorianweb.org/authors/conrad/pva46.html (accessed February 3, 2012).

13   Three versions of the first book edition appeared subsequently: the first was published in London and Edinburgh on October 15, 1900, as *Lord Jim: A Tale* (Blackwood & Sons); the second was published before the end of the year as *Lord Jim: A Romance* (Doubleday & Co.); and a third was published in Toronto as *Lord Jim: A Tale of the Sea* (Gage). The shorter works—"Youth" (10,500 words; September 1898), "The Heart of Darkness" (38,000 words; February–April 1899), and "The End of the Tether" (53,500 words; July–December 1902)—were issued together as a single volume, *Youth: a Narrative; and Two Other Stories* (1902).

14   Donovan, *Joseph Conrad and Popular Culture*, Basingstoke, UK, and New York: Palgrave Macmillan, 2005, p. 6; and "Blackwood's Magazine," Conrad First, at www.conradfirst.net/view/periodical?id=35 (accessed February 6, 2012).

15   Under the guidance and direction of *Blackwood's* editor, William Blackwood, and London literary advisor David Storr Meldrum, Conrad experienced one of the "most bewildering but fruitful periods" of his literary career (William Blackburn, Ed., *Joseph Conrad: Letters to William Blackwood and David S. Meldrum*, Durham, NC: Duke University Press, 1958, p. xxix).

16   Conrad, Letter to J.B. Pinker, *Collected Letters, Volume 4*, p. 49.

17   Ibid. (November 12 or 19, 1911), p. 506.

18   Sir Hugh Charles Clifford, GCMG, GBE (1866–1941) was a British author and colonial administrator. He served as British Resident at Pahang (1896–1900; 1901–03) and governor of North Borneo (1900–01). In 1903, he was made colonial secretary of Trinidad. Later, he was appointed governor of the Gold Coast (1912–19), Nigeria (1919–25), and Ceylon (1925–27). He wrote *Farther India*, a chronicle of European exploration and discovery in Southeast Asia, and stories and novels about Malayan life. He was governor of the Straits Settlements and British high commissioner in Malaya from 1927 until 1930.

19   National Library of Scotland: Blackwood Papers, MS 4686, fol. 105.

20   Anthony J. Stockwell, "The White Man's Burden and Brown Humanity: Colonialism and Ethnicity in British Malaya," *Journal of the Malaysian Branch of the Royal Asiatic Society* Vol. 10, No. 1 (1982), p. 49.

21   Conrad's letters are also full of praise for the magazine's quality and cultural status. In 1902, he wrote to David Meldrum: "To appear in P[all] M[all] M[agazine] and the Ill[ustrated] Lond[on] News is advantageous no doubt, but I only care for *Maga*, my first and only Love!" (CL 2:368). As Donovan writes: "For all their obvious flattery, statements like these gave voice to Conrad's genuine affection for what he saw as a traditional periodical that, in an era of cultural debasement, had continued to put literary quality above commercial appeal" (Donovan, *Blackwood's Magazine*, Conrad First, at www.conradfirst. net/view/periodical?id=35 (accessed July 5, 2012). Again, in 1902, Conrad declared: "It is an unspeakable relief to write for *Maga* instead of for the market—confound it and all its snippetty works. I had much rather work for

Maga and the House than for the market: were the market stuffed with solid gold throughout" (2:375, 376). The author was also a "regular reader of *Blackwood's*—'the only monthly I care to read' (CL 2:129)—[and] he identified closely with its conservatism in politics and culture" (Donovan, *Blackwood's Magazine*, Conrad First). He told a correspondent during the Spanish–American War (1898): "I do like the attitude of the *Maga* on the Spanish business" (CL 2:81), and confessed after the magazine changed its typeface: "I am 'plus royaliste que le roi'—more conservative than *Maga*" (CL 2:81, 162).

22 Conrad's "The Idiots" first appeared in *The Savoy* (October 1896); "The Lagoon" was published in *The Cornhill Magazine* (January 1897); "An Outpost of Progress" was published in two parts in *Cosmopolis* (June and July 1897); and *The Nigger of the "Narcissus"; a Tale of the Forecastle* was serialized in five parts in *The New Review* (August–December 1897).

23 Donovan, "Cosmopolis," Conrad First, at www.conradfirst.net/view/period ical?id=73 (accessed June 18, 2012).

24 In October 1900, Fernand Ortmans, the Baron de Senechal, was described by *The New York Times* as "a linguist of note and a member of all the prominent politico-literary clubs of London and Paris" ("Mrs. P.F. Baring Engaged to be Married to Baron F. Ortmans of Paris by Mayor Van Wyck," *New York Times*, October 8, 1900).

25 Donovan, "Cosmopolis," Conrad First.

26 This figure includes both regular sales (46,074) and American sales (12,050) of the magazine. Tallies for the year cover the period from June 1897 to June 1898. See David Finkelstein, "Appendix 2: Blackwood's Magazine Sales, 1856–1915," *The House of Blackwood: Author-Publisher Relations in the Victorian Era*, University Park, PA: Pennsylvania State University Press, 2002, pp. 165–66.

27 In 1889, for example, Robert Louis Stevenson had discovered copies of the magazine, containing reviews of his most recent work, in a lawyer's office in the capital city of Apia, on the island of Samoa. Ironically, just 3 years later, Stevenson's friend and legal advisor, Charles Baxter, remarked on a very different image of *Blackwood's*. On hearing that its editor had refused to pay Stevenson £2,000 for the serial rights to *Weir of Hermiston* (1896), Baxter wrote to Stevenson: "You see, an old humdrum house has no machinery for selling these [magazines] all over the world" (Robert Louis Stevenson, Letter to Charles Baxter [December 1892], DeLancey Ferguson and Marshall Waingrow, Eds., *RLS: Stevenson's Letters to Charles Baxter*, New Haven, CT: Yale University Press, 1956, p. 314).

28 David Finkelstein, "Imperial Self-Representation: Constructions of Empire in Blackwood's Magazine, 1880–1900," *Imperial Co-Histories: National Identities and the British and Colonial Press*, Ed. Julie F. Codell, Madison, NJ: Farleigh Dickinson University Press, 2003, p. 104.

29 Finkelstein, "Introduction," *Print Culture and the Blackwood Tradition 1805–1930*, Toronto: University of Toronto Press, 2006, p. 6.

30 This is based on the Imperial rate of postage for second-class matter, which, in 1902, was 8 cents per pound. Many still considered this a "prohibitory rate" for carrying newspapers and magazines within the Empire. The U.S. Post Office, in contrast, charged only 1 cent per pound postage on newspapers, periodicals, and certain classes of book. See John A. Cooper, "A Heavy Handicap. A Canadian Outlook. Imperial Rates on Newspapers and Magazines," *The Author* Vol. XII, No. 10 (May 1, 1902), p. 190.

31 Subscription prices are taken from an 1890 advertisement for Mudie's Catalogue and another for W.H. Smith & Son from the same decade (Laurel

Brake, *Print in Transition, 1850–1910*, Basingstoke, UK: Palgrave, 2001, pp. 12, 17).

32 Conrad's subject matter had made him an obvious attraction to readers overseas and in the colonies. From the start of his career, Conrad had targeted these overseas markets. But, readers and reviewers did not always respond in kind. His first novel, *Almayer's Folly* (1895), received mixed reviews from *The Straits Times*, a Singapore newspaper, and prompted indignant reactions from one of the paper's subscribers. Just 4 months later, *The Straits Budget*, another Singapore paper, criticized *An Outcast of the Islands*. See the unsigned review, "Almayer's Folly. A Romance of the Indian Archipelago" *The Straits Times* (January 16, 1896); " 'Almayer's Folly': To the Editor of the 'Straits Times' " (January 17, 1896); and "Review of *An Outcast of the Islands,*" *The Straits Budget* (May 19, 1896).

33 Conrad, Letter to David S. Meldrum (May 19, 1900), *The Collected Letters of Joseph Conrad, Volume 2: 1898–1902*, Eds. Frederick R. Karl and Laurence Davies, Cambridge, UK: Cambridge University Press, 1986, p. 272.

34 Conrad, Letter to William Blackwood (May 31, 1902), *Joseph Conrad: Letters to William Blackwood and David S. Meldrum*, p. 153.

35 Conrad, Letter to Edward Garnett (August 21, 1908).

36 Ibid. (November 15, 1908).

37 Penang is a state in present-day Malaysia and the name of its constituent island. It is located on the northwest coast of Peninsular Malaysia by the Strait of Malacca.

38 See Robert Hampson, *Cross-Cultural Encounters in Joseph Conrad's Malay Fiction*, New York and Basingstoke, UK: Palgrave Macmillan, 2001, pp. 11–12. Conrad relates the news of his meeting with Captain Marris in a letter to Edward Garnett (August 4, 1911).

39 Conrad, Letter to F.N. Doubleday (December 21, 1918), *The Collected Letters of Joseph Conrad, Volume 6: 1917–1919*, Eds. Frederick R. Karl, Laurence Davies, and Owen Knowles, Cambridge, UK: Cambridge University Press, 2003, p. 333.

40 Andrea White, *Joseph Conrad and the Adventure Tradition*, Cambridge, UK: Cambridge University Press, 1993.

41 Ibid., p. 7.

42 Conrad, *Lord Jim*, p. 9.

43 Ibid., p. 11.

44 "An Outpost of Progress" was first published in *Cosmopolis* (June–July 1897), and "The Heart of Darkness" in *Blackwood's Magazine* (February–April 1899).

45 Conrad, *Lord Jim* (1900), p. 8.

46 Conrad, "An Outpost of Progress," *Tales of Unrest*, New York: Doubleday, Page, 1920, p. 159.

47 Conrad, *Heart of Darkness* (1902), Ed. Paul B. Armstrong, Fourth Norton Critical Edition, New York and London: W.W. Norton, 2006, p. 8.

48 "Youth" was Conrad's first published story for *Blackwood's*. It appeared in the magazine's September 1898 issue.

49 Joseph Kestner, *Masculinities in British Adventure Fiction, 1880–1915*, Farnham, UK: Ashgate, 2010, p. 1.

50 Conrad, *Lord Jim*, p. 136.

51 Again, Jim's romantic idealism was a product "absorbed" from his reading "a course in light holiday literature" and subsequently compromised by circumstances aboard the sinking steamship.

52 Conrad, *Lord Jim*, p. 168.

53 An article in *Popular Science Monthly* from 1925, for example, offered readers—who felt perhaps that they "were born too late for adventure"—a map of the remaining pockets of unexplored territory on Earth, while it quipped: "Aerial travel and photography will make exploration of the future a much quicker process than in the past" (see "Earth's Unknown Lands Beckon Explorers," *Popular Science Monthly* [December 1925], p. 24).

54 Conrad, preface to Richard Curle's *Into the East: Notes on Burma and Malaya*, reprinted in *Last Essays*, London: J.M. Dent, p. 130.

55 Ibid., pp. 128–31.

56 It was at this time, writing to Blackwood in a letter dated April 12, 1900, that Conrad first expressed his intention to extend the story of Jim's life in Patusan, a decision that effectively quadrupled the novel's originally projected length of 15,000–20,000 words.

57 See Dwight H. Purdy, "The Chronology of *Lord Jim*," *Lord Jim* (1900), Joseph Conrad, Ed. Thomas Moser, Second Norton Critical Edition, New York and London: W.W. Norton, 1996, p. 385.

58 Conrad, *Lord Jim*, p. 212.

59 Ibid., p. 228.

60 The two most obvious examples from contemporary British popular fiction—upon which Conrad draws for this fictional clash between bloodthirsty pirates and an English adventurer who becomes the king of a remote part of the world—are Robert Louis Stevenson's *Treasure Island* (1883) and Rudyard Kipling's "The Man Who Would Be King" (1888). Like the Patusan section of Conrad's *Lord Jim*, Kipling's 1888 story (first published in Vol. 5 of the *Indian Railway Library: The Phantom Rickshaw and other Eerie Tales* [Allahabad: A.H. Wheeler, 1888]) was also partially inspired by the exploits of Sir James Brooke, an Englishman who, in 1841, became the governor—or White Rajah—of Sarawak in Borneo. Brooke ruled Sarawak until his death in 1868.

61 Ibid., pp. 228, 209, 215, 217, 219–20, 218, and 204.

62 Conrad, *Lord Jim*, p. 168.

63 Ibid.

64 For an excellent survey of the history of scholarly dispute on this point, see White, "Travel Writing and Adventure Fiction as Shaping Discourses for Conrad," *Joseph Conrad and the Adventure Tradition*, pp. 100–15.

65 Rider Haggard, "'Elephant Smashing' and 'Lion Shooting,'" *The African Review* (June 9, 1894), pp. 762–63.

66 The dinner was held in honor of the American explorer Admiral Robert Peary.

67 Doyle, *The Times*, May 4, 1910, quoted by Roy Pilot and Alvin E. Rodin, "Introduction," *The Annotated Lost World*, Indianapolis, IN: Wessex Press, 1996, pp. ix–x; and Rosamund Dalziell, "The Curious Case of Sir Everard im Thurn and Sir Arthur Conan Doyle: Exploration and the Imperial Adventure Novel, *The Lost World*," *English Literature in Transition, 1880–1920* Vol. 45, No. 2 (2002), p. 132.

68 John Buchan, *The Last Secrets: The Final Mysteries of Exploration*, London, Edinburgh, and New York: Thomas Nelson, 1923, p. 18.

69 Conrad, *Last Essays*, pp. 128–29.

70 White, *Joseph Conrad and the Adventure Tradition*, p. 2.

71 As White observes, "adventure fiction derived its authority not only from its popular appeal but also from societal approval of its basic, and rather non-fictional, claims. . . . So closely allied with travel writing, a genre that aspired to fact, after all, adventure fiction came to be viewed as a special case, demanding more credibility than other fictions." She observes that, "both

appeared not only in such . . . important publication[s] as *Blackwood's* . . . but also side by side in . . . popular periodicals [like] *The Graphic*, the *Illustrated London News, Cassell's, Cosmopolis, Cornhill, Fraser's, Longman's*, and *T.P.'s Weekly*" and argues that the genres' print ubiquity "earned for both a special status, marking them as part of the factual, workaday world of newsprint, not fanciful but part of the informational machinery of the day" (*Joseph Conrad and the Adventure Tradition*, pp. 40–41).

72   Conrad, *Lord Jim*, p. 53.

73   Ibid., pp. 24, 32–33.

74   See Frederick Jackson Turner, "The Significance of the Frontier in American History," *A Report of the American Historical Association* (1893), pp. 199–227. This paper was first delivered at the meeting of the American Historical Association in Chicago, July 12, 1893.

75   According to Cedric Watts, "In the early eighteen-nineties it must sometimes have seemed to [Conrad] that he had gambled and lost as a seaman. As steam gradually superseded sail, and as ships became larger and more efficient, it had become harder for him to find appointments that matched his qualifications." Watts explains that Conrad, "[i]n abandoning the sea for a writer's career . . . was gambling again." He writes: "Conrad had needed one kind of courage when he persevered in his maritime career. . . . He needed courage of another kind when he embarked on his second career, as a professional novelist; [Conrad] was working ambitiously and uncompromisingly in a foreign language . . . possessed . . . literary ambitions" and "English was becoming an international currency" (Watts, "Introduction," *Lord Jim*, New York: Penguin, 1986, p. 15).

76   Conrad, Letter to J.B. Pinker, *Collected Letters, Volume 4*, p. 49.

77   For one thing, the readership of the magazine seemed to be changing. *Blackwood's* was courting new subscribers, while reaching out to other large markets overseas. According to Laurel Brake, "Looking at Maga of the 1890s, one sees that its market niche appears increasingly to engage with a new cultural and physical geography—the framework of Empire and readers in the colonies, rather than its mid-century readership base in Edinburgh/Scotland and English parishes[. Although] some of the latter reader groups are retained, the expanding readership seems to be elsewhere" (Brake, "Maga, the Shilling Monthlies, and the New Journalism," *Print Culture and the Blackwood Tradition, 1805–1930*, Ed. David Finkelstein, Toronto: University of Toronto Press, 2006, p. 186).

78   In order to comply with rules and stipulations imposed by the U.S. Copyright Act (better known as the Chase Act; 1891), Blackwood's began producing its second edition in New York, for exclusive distribution in the United States through Leonard Scott & Company. From 1891 to 1893, the circulation of *Blackwood's* U.S. edition totaled 11,700 (1890–91), 15,600 (1891–92), and 14,700 (1892–93) copies per year, and contributed to the annual profits of the firm that were 5–15 percent higher than in previous years.

79   Finkelstein, "Appendix 2," pp. 165–66.

80   *Blackwood's* repackaged itself in terms that took advantage of this dwindling readership. The magazine's smaller market share became an asset, an indicator of its good taste, sound judgment, and exclusivity. Its appeal to a smaller audience promoted the image of an intimate, pre-industrial familiarity between the magazine and a more discerning, less hurried, higher class of readers it solicited and evoked. This rhetoric was a central feature in the playbook used by small publishing houses such as John Lane's The Bodley Head (1887), and

would later be adopted by modernist promoters such as Ezra Pound, Ford Maddox Hueffer, and Virginia Woolf.

81 Brake, "Maga, the Shilling Monthlies, and the New Journalism," p. 205.

82 *The National Review* (1883–1960) was a Tory monthly published in London; Leopold Manxse edited it from 1893 to 1932.

83 Finkelstein, *The House of Blackwood: Author–Publisher Relations in the Victorian Era*, p. 101.

84 This resolve to finally expand operations into India, the colonies, and foreign markets was strengthened, of course, by the international copyright laws passed in 1886 and 1891.

85 The firm hired David S. Meldrum in late 1893, and with him came new networks of readers and contributors, new developments in the publisher's lists, and a new image for *Blackwood's*. He was appointed Blackwood's London office manager and literary advisor in 1896, and soon thereafter brought Conrad into the fold.

86 Brake, "Maga, the Shilling Monthlies, and the New Journalism," p. 186.

87 Finkelstein, "Appendix 2," p. 166.

88 Donovan suggests that, "[a]lthough Conrad's unwelcome requests for advances, failure to supply copy on time, and hiring of . . . Pinker resulted in a cooling of his friendship with the Blackwoods, the publication of [these] two short essays in *Blackwood's* in 1905–06 may have given him hopes of reestablishing the relationship." He then notes, however, that it was just not to be: "[I]n April 1906, he submitted 'The Brute' . . . for consideration . . . [but] the story, which went on to become one of Conrad's most widely reprinted magazine tales, was rejected by Blackwood as insufficiently original" (Donovan, "Blackwood's Magazine," Conrad First [accessed June 26, 2012]).

89 Conrad, Letter to Ford Maddox Hueffer (October 15, 1904), *Collected Letters, Volume 3: 1903–1907* (1988), p. 170.

90 Conrad's recent work had appeared in a range of popular periodicals. They included *The Illustrated London News*, *The Pall Mall Magazine*, *T.P.'s Weekly*, and *The Daily Mail*, and these were examples of the "brighter, racier" new journalism (Brake, "Maga, the Shilling Monthlies, and the New Journalism," p. 205) against which *Blackwood's* had come to define its own uncompromising brand. "Amy Foster" was serialized in *The Illustrated London News* (December 14–28, 1901); *Typhoon* first appeared in *The Pall Mall Magazine* (January–March 1902); "To-morrow" in *The Pall Mall Magazine* (August 1902); *Nostromo; a Tale of the Seaboard* in *T.P.'s Weekly* (January 29–October 7, 1904); " 'Missing'! The Passing of a Ship at Sea" was published in *The Daily Mail* (March 8, 1904), as were "Overdue" (November 16, 1904) and "Stranded" (December 2, 1904). Donovan, "Main Index: Chronological," Conrad First (accessed June 26, 2012).

91 *Blackwood's* (September 1898).

92 Ibid. (February–April 1899).

93 Ibid. (October 1899–November 1900).

94 Simon Eliot, "Section E: Periodical Publication," *Some Patterns and Trends in British Publishing 1800–1919*, Occasional Papers of the Bibliographical Society, No. 8 (1994), p. 107.

95 David Reed, *The Popular Magazine in Britain and the United States 1880–1960*, Toronto and Buffalo, NY: University of Toronto Press, 1997, p. 19.

96 Ibid.

97 Linda Dryden, "At the Court of *Blackwood's*," *Print Culture and the Blackwood Tradition, 1805–1930*, Ed. David Finkelstein, Toronto: University of Toronto Press, 2006, p. 226.

98   Outwardly, the magazine had changed very little since 1817; its covers would indeed vary only slightly from one decade to the next throughout the magazine's 163-year history (1817–1980).

99   The Blackwood firm was nonetheless engaged at the time with its own centennial prediction-making. In 1896, the firm commemorated 83 years in publishing by commissioning Margaret Oliphant's history, *Annals of a Publishing House: William Blackwood and His Sons, Their Magazine and Friends* (2 vols., London and Edinburgh: Blackwood, 1897; 3 vols., New York: Scribner's Sons, 1897–98). Oliphant's history effectively closed a chapter on the first half of the firm's history; the firm's shift to new overseas markets opened a chapter on the second half.

100 Erdinast-Vulcan, "The Failure of Myth: *Lord Jim*," p. 494.

101 Thomas C. Moser, "Editor's Note on the Composition of *Lord Jim*," *Lord Jim* (1900), Joseph Conrad, Second Norton Critical Edition, New York and London: W.W. Norton, 2006, p. 277.

102 Ibid.

103 Ibid.

104 Conrad, Letter to William Blackwood (February 12, 1900), *Joseph Conrad: Letters to William Blackwood and David S. Meldrum*, p. 84.

105 Zdzisław Najder, *Joseph Conrad: a Life*, Rochester, NY: Camden House, 2007, p. 303.

106 Conrad, Letter to David Meldrum (April 3, 1900), *Joseph Conrad: Letters to William Blackwood and David S. Meldrum*, p. 89.

107 Conrad, *Lord Jim*, p. 132.

108 Padmini Mongia, " 'Ghosts of the Gothic': Spectral Women and Colonized Spaces in *Lord Jim*," *Conrad and Gender*, Ed. Andrew Michael Roberts, Amsterdam and Atlanta, GA: Rodopi, 1993, p. 6.

109 Conrad, *Lord Jim*, p. 132.

110 Ibid.

111 As Michiel Heyns suggests, "Patusan is almost explicitly acknowledged as a creation of the artistic imagination" (Michiel Heyns, "Like People in a Book," *Under Postcolonial Eyes: Joseph Conrad after Empire*, Eds. Gail Fincham and Myrtle Hooper, Capetown: Juta, 1996, p. 85.

112 Conrad, *Lord Jim*, pp. 146–47.

113 Ibid.

114 Mongia, p. 6.

115 Conrad, *Lord Jim*, p. 13.

116 Gerard Barrett, "The Ghost of Doubt: Writing, Speech, and Language in *Lord Jim*," *Master Narratives: Tellers and Telling in the English Novel*, Ed. Richard Gravil, Aldershot, UK, and Burlington, VT: Ashgate, 2001, p. 246.

117 Stephen Ross, *Conrad and Empire*, Columbia, MO: University of Missouri Press, 2004, pp. 66–67.

118 Ibid., p. 66.

119 Conrad, *Lord Jim*, p. 9, quoted in Barrett, p. 246.

120 McClure, *Late Imperial Romance*, p. 3.

121 Early readers dismissed the novel's narrative disjunction as a stylistic failure. Fredric Jameson's reading of *Lord Jim* suggested, however, that the romance plot is, in fact, integral to the novel, as a "Utopian compensation" (266) for the reification of modern life. According to Jameson, it allows Jim to escape from a world dominated by capitalism into a world of "precapitalist social forms on the imperialist periphery" where traditional "communities and ways of life ... still, for another moment yet, exist" (253–54). Romance in *Lord Jim* is a "wish-fulfilling" fantasy that attempts to evade certain realities of

modernity (255). See Fredric Jameson, "Romance and Reification," *The Political Unconscious: Narrative as a Socially Symbolic Act*, Ithaca, NY: Cornell University Press, 1981, pp. 194–270.

122 Jakob Lothe, *Conrad's Narrative Method*, Oxford, UK: Clarendon Press, 1989, p. 165.

123 Conrad, Letter to William Blackwood (April 12, 1900), *Joseph Conrad: Letters to William Blackwood and David S. Meldrum*, p. 90.

124 Moser, "Editor's Note on the Composition of *Lord Jim*," p. 277.

125 Conrad, *Lord Jim*, p. 114.

126 Ibid., p. 119.

127 Ibid., p. 118.

128 Ibid., p. 119.

129 Ibid.

130 Ibid.

131 Ibid., p. 120.

132 Ibid., p. 97.

133 Ibid., p. 98.

134 Ibid., p. 157.

135 Ibid., p. 201.

136 Ibid.

137 Ibid., p. 22.

138 Charles Whibley, "Musings Without Method," *Blackwood's Magazine* 167 (March 1900), p. 426.

139 Ibid.

140 See Note 9.

141 Ibid., p. 263.

142 Ibid., p. 270.

143 Whibley, "Musings Without Method," pp. 285–86.

144 Ibid. (March 1900), p. 430.

145 *Blackwood's* other major, long-running column appeared under the pseudonym "The Looker-On," and reviewed social, cultural, political, and world events from a similar perspective. For nearly a century (from 1894 to 1980), "The Looker-On" was written by a revolving cast of contributors, including Margaret Oliphant, Neil Munro, and Charles Chenevix Trench. A majority of Whibley's arguments against the forces of modern social and technological change may seem intellectually reactionary now, but neither he nor Conrad was peculiar in these opinions.

146 Donovan, "The Muse of *Blackwood's*," p. 276.

147 Despite its more domestic and typically English topics, *Chance* marked Conrad's first full-length novel treating life at sea since *Lord Jim* (1900). The novel was first serialized in *The New York Herald* from January to June 1912. Methuen (UK) and Doubleday (US) published *Chance* in book form in 1914.

148 See Lawrence Graver, *Conrad's Short Fiction*, Berkeley and Los Angeles, CA: University of California Press, 1969, p. 170. Graver cautions that, "one should remember that another Doubleday product, Gene Stratton Porter's *Laddie*, sold 300,000 copies during the same five month period. *Chance* was [21] on American best-seller lists for 1914; *Victory* [42] in 1916; *The Arrow of Gold* [2] in 1919; and *The Rover* [3] in 1923 ... none of Conrad's books was successful enough to be included among the one hundred best-selling books for ... 1895–1925, a group headed by *Quo Vadis*, *Beside the Bonnie Briar Bush*, *The Four Horsemen of the Apocalypse*, *Main Street*, and *If Winter Comes*" (170).

3   Transatlantic Crossings

The Technological Scene of H.G. Wells's *Tono-Bungay* (1909)

Serialized in *The Popular Magazine* (US; September 1908–January 1909) and *The English Review* (UK; December 1908–March 1909),[1] H.G. Wells's *Tono-Bungay: A Romance of Commerce* first appeared in book form through its American publisher, Duffield & Co., New York. The publisher registered for copyright on "October 31, 1908",[2] depositing two copies of the red, cloth-covered first North American edition, issued January 15, 1909. Coordinating subscription, retail, and mail-order sales along with the final installment of the novel's four-part serialization in *The Popular Magazine*, Duffield organized a promotional run-up that included complimentary bottles of "Tono-Bungay," given away as incentives to early trade orders.[3] *Tono-Bungay* appeared in bookstores at the start of the post-season January book sales[4] and debuted at No. 1 on *The Bookman* "Sales of Books During the Month."[5] New editions were announced for April, July, and October.[6] Toronto-based Macmillan Company of Canada[7] bought 500 copies in January to distribute simultaneously with the Duffield edition;[8] in July, the Canadian firm ordered 500 additional copies.[9] The first English edition was published a month later—on February 15, 1909—by Macmillan & Co., London,[10] and it too sold out in just a matter of weeks.[11] Copies of both editions may still be found today in good to very good condition, with slightly higher prices fetched for the Macmillan light-green, cloth-covered volumes. This reflects a commonly held assumption that the British first edition of *Tono-Bungay* represents what book dealers, collectors, and bibliographers term the book's "true first edition," or the first edition printing that supersedes all other editions chronologically. Other editions, such as the two-volume continental paperback issued by Bernhard Tauchnitz, in Leipzig,[12] also deserve our attention, however, in order to provide a more complete publishing history, and as a basis for further study. As Roger Osbourne suggests, "readers need to be alert to the material multiplicity of published versions . . . and its implications for their interpretation" of text.[13] This chapter argues that, although he was not unique in pursuing simultaneous serialization in magazines followed by book publication on both sides of the Atlantic,[14] Wells was particularly attuned to its role in the innovation and development of a transnational, globalized literary marketplace.

As the range of opportunities for best-selling writers of popular fiction expanded in the early twentieth century, however, complications arose when publishers' international expansion met with differences between national copyrights. The production of multiple witnesses satisfied these legal constraints; the practice could introduce errors as well. In Wells's case, simultaneous transatlantic serialization was an opportunity both to address multiple readerships, and to address them differently through multiple witnesses of the text. For this reason, *Tono-Bungay* offers us a particularly compelling case study for the kinds of version-based research made possible by the proliferation of these multiple witnesses.[15]

Immersed in the kaleidoscopic print culture of the modern media society, *Tono-Bungay* is very much about global flows of information, expanding technologies, news, and transformations in commerce and industry. In other words, it is a novel *about* the business of book and periodical publishing. The novel's narrator, George Ponderevo, asks readers to consider the many available forms of modern textual media vying for their attention, while he references books, newspapers, magazines, illustrated crime sheets,[16] and pamphlets repeatedly throughout. There are references to letters, telegrams, and various forms of visual medium as well, such as advertisements, posters, and billboards.

The practice of simultaneous serialization in magazines followed by volume publication on both sides of the Atlantic was a standard feature of late nineteenth- and early twentieth-century literary publishing. It developed in response to international copyright requirements, in particular the U.S. mandatory requirement for the "legal deposit of an American manufactured (i.e., type-set *and* printed) first edition by a British author on or before the day of first publication in the United Kingdom."[17] This was known as the "manufacturing clause." It was one of the "copyright formalities" of the International Copyright Act, or Chase Act,[18] which, according to Robert Spoo, "effectively made first or simultaneous manufacture and publication in the United States a condition of American copyright for any book published abroad," and replaced an established nineteenth-century practice of "self-restraint among American publishers that came to be called *the courtesy of the trade*."[19] Spoo writes:

> As a way of regulating . . . competition for unprotected titles, and to give themselves an aura of respectability and fairness, major publishers adopted trade courtesy whereby . . . the first publisher to announce plans to issue an American edition of an unprotected foreign work acquired informal title to [it]—a kind of makeshift copyright grounded on tacit trade agreements and community-based norms. . . . [N]ineteenth-century courtesy and its regime of entitlements, exceptions, and penalties . . . permitt[ed] . . . publishers and authors to benefit . . . [from] wholly informal exclusive rights recognized by this self-interested chivalry.[20]

With the passage of the Chace Act on March 3, 1891,[21] these "wholly informal exclusive rights" were formalized into law. Spoo describes the concomitant demise of "trade courtesy" within the following three decades. This was the period from 1890 to 1922, when the "transformation of a media ecology already undergoing rapid change under the pressure of new media and increasing flows of information"[22] led to the expansion of publishing opportunities despite the constraints posed by differences and complications in international copyright laws (see Appendix D). Spoo continues:

> [In] the twentieth century, trade courtesy had become difficult to practice openly. The climate of trust-busting . . . made the proud collusiveness of . . . genteel publishers an antiquated and suspect chivalry . . . ministrations of literary agents revealed the faithful monogamy of author and publisher to be dispensable[; c]ompetition [and] an expanding literary marketplace, awakened an entrepreneurial spirit in authors. [U]ncontrolled competition and piracy . . . made courtesy seem fusty and ineffective.
>
> Gentlemanly honoraria gave way to up-front sums and backend royalties, paid . . . as a matter of law. No longer were advance sheets rushed across the ocean in order to steal a few days' march on competitors; such first-to-market strategies belonged to a world [of] unprotected materials from abroad, and the race and the profits were to the swift. . . . The pressures generated by the law's manufacturing requirements ensured that authors and publishers would still be racing against time, but the compulsions were now legal ones, not fueled by contests with pirates or subject to a code of honor . . .
>
> . . . The Chace Act was a bureaucratization of honor . . . Although American publishers continued to preserve an ideal of fairness . . . [t]he old paternalistic spirit had been diminished and . . . the sense of professional camaraderie and joint pursuit of honorable ends.[23]

These complex shifts and transformations influenced authorship in profound and multiple ways; Towheed argues, "multiple, involved, and sometimes determining exigencies of specific changes in national and international copyright law" also influence "our reading and interpretation" of the authors' individual works.[24] The formal attribution of copyright laws—and changes to those laws throughout this period—thus poses questions for scholarship and research into this period's print culture on some important and fundamental levels. As a term defined geographically, rather than chronologically,[25] all four parallel published versions of *Tono-Bungay*[26] remarked on above were technically "first appearances" in their respective markets. Situated within this densely integrated modern media environment,[27] Wells's transatlantic serialization of his novel, in both an English literary magazine (circ. 1,000) and large-circulation popular American pulp-paper magazine (circ. 300,000), affords research opportunities and rich territory to explore. These opportunities include comparative studies of the multiple witnesses, and issues of textual production and transmission. As Roger Osbourne argues:

> [T]he physical and mechanical process of textual production . . . [has] a significant effect on the way an author transmits a text to readers. Behind the stability of the text . . . [that is] familiar to readers is a complex network of transmission that poses many interpretative challenges; challenges that, when . . . engaged, will offer a better understanding.[28]

They also involve examinations of the role of authors' agents, control and engagement with their markets, and the institution of literary agency in the placement of best-selling works of wide and popular appeal. As quantitative studies of book sales figures show, the publication of books and periodicals was scheduled and expertly organized to coincide with well-defined, "substantial" seasons.[29]

This study combines both comparative and quantitative approaches to literary studies in the context of the period's most influential commercial and technological changes. From 1880 to 1914, Western nations of Europe —along with the British Empire and the United States—built faster, more reliable, and ever more efficient shipping, industry, and mechanical luxuries. Together, they introduced the promise of affordable travel and brought that promise within reach of the middle classes. The dependability of the transatlantic telegraph system facilitated copyright compliance, which made the legal requirement and a "30-day window for deposit" possible. The practice of simultaneous transatlantic serialization required speed, efficiency, and connection. Modern transportation and communication systems provided them—as book and periodical publishers' negotiations passed, moreover, through the telegraph and postal systems.

This chapter investigates Wells's response to the constraints and opportunities presented by the contemporary press and its transatlantic periodical fiction markets. *Tono-Bungay*'s spoof on the popular late-Victorian adventure romance, "How I Stole the Heaps of Quap from Mordet Island,"[30] draws sustained attention to Conrad's territory and style of literary impressionism; the Polish author's eccentric style of dress, thick foreign accent, and other signature features are also attacked.[31] It was a very different period in Wells's professional life, when, in 1895–98, the world-famous author of popular scientific romances—including *The Time Machine* (1895),[32] *The Island of Doctor Moreau* (1896),[33] *The Invisible Man* (1897),[34] and *The War of the Worlds* (1898)[35]—at least partially modeled his own "new" literary genre, the forerunner of early science fiction,[36] on the conventions of late-Victorian romance, a genre that was modeled quite consciously on the boys' adventure book, penny papers, and the current revival of Jonathan Swift, Mary Shelley, Sir Walter Scott, and James Fennimore Cooper.[37] Paul A. Cantor and Peter Hufnagel write:

It is [. . .] understandable that when [Wells] was trying to imagine a journey into the future, he ended up modeling it on something more familiar, a journey to the imperial frontier. Imperialist narratives—either factual or fictional—became very popular in Britain in the nineteenth century, and had reached the level of a fad in the mid-1880s with the publication of H. Rider Haggard's bestsellers, *King Solomon's Mines* and *She*. Drawing upon [R.L.] Stevenson's *Treasure Island*, Haggard crystallized the form of the imperialist romance as a journey to a remote corner of European dominion, where a group of intrepid British explorers encounter an exotic civilization, with strange and often bizarre customs that seem the antithesis of the European way of life. This formula would in itself have been useful to Wells, preparing as he was to create a new form of exoticism in his first science fiction novel.[38]

In response to Conrad's aesthetic valuing of, and literary preoccupations with, fading nineteenth-century forms of romance, Wells evokes a more oppositional spirit. This chapter argues further that Conrad's fundamental aesthetic functions as a clear but partial palimpsest for Wells's spoof and, returning *Tono-Bungay* to its first periodical contexts, examines "Mordet Island" as Wells's modern, critical response to Patusan. In the context of the simultaneous transatlantic serialization of *Tono-Bungay*, this chapter shows how he rewrote Conrad's imaginary solution to the contradictions and aesthetic limitations of the global marketplace, commercial publishers' expansions, and the global gridding of imperial modernity.

The momentous technological changes that took place in the last quarter of the nineteenth century continued apace throughout the first quarter of the twentieth. In just the 24-year period separating *Lord Jim*'s serialization in *Blackwood's Magazine*, in which Conrad imagines Patusan located "three hundred miles beyond the end of telegraph cables and mail-boat lines,"[39] and Conrad's preface to Richard Curle's travelogue *Into the East: Notes on Burma and Malaya* (1923), the world had witnessed dramatic advances in aviation, broadcast radio, and technologies of industry and war. Later reprinted as "Travel,"[40] its assessment of a world in 1923 describes an Earth so connected and utterly familiar that the "time for such books of travel [as those written by Marco Polo or Mungo Park] is past," because "there is nothing new left now, and but very little of what may be called obscure."[41] As the spread of global capitalism advanced across the world, the net of commercial exchanges and transactions grew denser, and shipping and trade networks found faster, more reliable ways to expand, consolidate, and stay connected. Through telegraph cables, telephone, and the wireless, the international press played a prominent role in the process of expanding commercial interest throughout the Empire. The rhetoric of adventure and romance was inevitably altered, and "the registration in romance of anxieties produced by anticipations of global gridding"[42] became a consequence of the romance writers' conflicted loyalties. Plumbing the imagined mysteries and otherness of the remote corners of the world, the adventure romance was materially embedded—through its publication in books, newspapers, and magazines—in this wider media landscape and ever-expanding global grid.

In October 1902, the first trans-Pacific telegraph cable began operation between the west coast of Canada and the Fanning Islands, 1,100 miles north of American Samoa. This completed a network of around 100,000 miles of under-sea cables referred to as the British "All Red Line," which now fully encircled the Earth.[43]

Just 10 months earlier, in December 1901, Guglielmo Marconi's team had reported the first successful transatlantic wireless transmission from the east coast of Newfoundland to Cornwall, England.[44] Throughout the nineteenth century, traveling to a faraway, foreign country simply for pleasure was an uncommon event in the lives of the middle and professional classes in England, the Colonies, and the US. In 1863, the New Zealand Post-Master General submitted the following assessment:

> Perhaps the present Government may be disposed to inaugurate a new era, and in endowing a company for the conveyance of mails, will look to a provision for the middle and less wealthy residents of our immense possessions in the Pacific. [I]n past days the estrangement of colonies may fairly be attributable to the difficulties of free communication with the parent State. [T]he commerce of this country cannot fail to

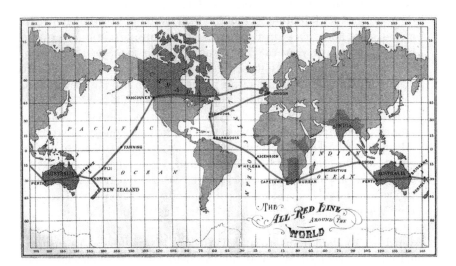

Figure 3.1 Map of the "British All Red Line" (1902), from George Johnson's *The All Red Line: The Annals and Aims of the Pacific Cable Project* (1903).

profit by the passing to and fro of the middle class of colonists, whilst many members of our commercial community will avail themselves of moderate rates to visit the sphere of their operations.[45]

This call for the establishment of improved services between England and Australia is indicative of similar efforts underway in Sydney, New York, and Cape Town during that time. By the early twentieth century, the popular illustrated magazines on both sides of the Atlantic featured entire sections of advertising devoted to the growing culture and institution of accessible and affordable travel tourism. In 1902, Frank Presbrey observed, in his address before the Atlas Club (Chicago), "Transportation and Advertising":

> As a nation of travellers . . . eighty thousand of us cross the Atlantic every year to view the sights of Europe. [T]his annual migration . . . is largely responsible for the magnificent fleet of ocean liners . . . which is growing rapidly year by year. [T]o the citizens of the US is due the honor of having created by demand the luxurious and swift floating palaces of the Atlantic and Pacific which to-day . . . bring the Old and New Worlds, both to the East and West of us, within a few days of our shores.[46]

Presbrey then noted the rapid increase of travel advertising pages in six magazines from 1887 to 1902:

> For the purpose of securing a fitting illustration of the development and growth of transportation advertising, I asked the advertising managers of six magazines (all of importance, which were published fifteen years ago) to give me a record of the amount of transportation advertising carried during the year 1887 as compared with the eleven months of 1902. . . . Fifteen years ago these six magazines carried, during the entire year, but thirty-two and a quarter pages of steamship advertising. For the eleven months of 1902, not counting December, the same magazines have carried three hundred and eighty-five pages of railroad advertising and eighty-five pages of steamship advertising. . . . Compared with the advertisements which are being put out to-day many of these earlier efforts appear crude, but bear in mind that we have been making great strides not only in the art of illustrating but in the various mechanical processes, and advertisements of ten years ago can be properly criticised only when compared with other advertisements [from] that time.[47]

From 1887 to 1903, fares from New York to Liverpool via Queenstown (Cunard Line) averaged $60–100 (in 1887) to $90–150, first class; and $40–50, second class (in 1903). From 1853 to 1903, the average price of a first-class, single-fare steamer ticket from London to Sydney on the Peninsular and Oriental Steamship Co. Line had fallen 22 percent (from

£84 to £66); from 1853 to 1913, the price fell one-third (from £84 to £60).[48] By the start of the First World War, traveling quickly, cheaply, reliably, and comfortably had become familiar slogans for these advertisements in the American general monthly, popular illustrated, and pulp-paper magazines.

The August 1910 issue of *Harper's Magazine*—a general-interest, quality-paper monthly established in 1850—includes four advertisements for "around-the-world" tours on page 15 of its back matter. Thomas "Cook's 39th Annual Series of Tours leave August 23, September 13, 27, November 5, 24, 1910; January 7, 1911, for the Grand Tour of the World. Six months' leisurely travel *de luxe.*"

From Oelrichs & Co., General Agents, 5 Broadway, NY: "Around the World Trips" to Egypt and India, China, Japan, Siam, Burma, Australia, The Philippines, Ceylon, Java, and the South Sea Islands "[c]ost from $617.70 up" and feature "Fast, Comfortable, Modern Steamers." Clark's Orient Cruises, Times Bldg., NY, offers "3 high-class 6 mos. Round World Tours" on the S.S. Arabic for only "$400 up, including shore excursions; 71 enchanting days. Stop-over privileges."

Figure 3.2 "Cook's, Clark's, etc. Travel Advertisements," Back Matter. *Harper's Magazine* Vol. 121 (August 1910), New York and London: Harper & Brothers, p. 15.

De Potter Tours, 32 Broadway, NY, offers their "World Tour—Orient" and "Also: Tour Spain, Sicily, Italy (Christmas in Rome), and France, sailing November, December, January, [and] February"[49]

The February 1910 issue of *Scribner's Magazine* carries an advertisement for the Oceanic Steamship Co. of San Francisco, which offers "rest, recreation, and pleasure" on OSC's regularly scheduled "tropic isles" tours to the South Seas and New Zealand. The price is just "$375" round-trip.[50] The magazine also features an advertisement for the Hamburg-American Line. It offers a weekly service from New York to Jamaica that is "modern in every way" for "$85.50" round-trip.[51] In a simple five-line advertising insert for a personal "Travelling Companion," one man of "22 years of age" offers his companionship to any "party travelling abroad . . . for expenses only, no salary asked."[52] On the following page, a more sophisticated advertisement is for *Terry's Mexico*, the first installment in a popular series of *Terry's* tourist guides published by Houghton Mifflin.[53] In this advertisement, *Terry's Mexico* claims to be "[m]odelled after the celebrated Baedeker Guide Books," and to be "[i]mmensely useful to the traveler who wishes to see all there is worth seeing in Mexico . . . fully described." Along with the convenience of having a "complete" guide with "26 maps and plans," the advertisement promises continuing value as well. It assures readers that the traveler buying a copy of *Terry's Mexico* will see all this "in the most expeditious, satisfactory, and economical way." The 595-page illustrated guide can be purchased by mail for "$2.50 net, postpaid."[54] Another Hamburg-American Line advertisement follows 4 pages later, featuring the announcement "A Winter Vacation in a Summer Land." This half-page illustrated advertisement reinforces its message, "modern in every way," with a similar claim: "Most modern vessels." In addition to having "modern vessels," the advertisement promises its readers "cruises to all parts of the world."[55] Established (in 1887) as a $.25 general magazine in "standard format to compete with *The Century* and *Harper's* as a magazine for people of quality rather than with *Leslie's* [popular monthly] as a popular magazine,"[56] *Scribner's* subsequently became the model for George Newnes's *The Strand Magazine* (1891), which combined the format of the American "quality illustrated magazines with the low-price level of *Longman's* [*Magazine*]," also priced at 6 pence and devoted to serial fiction since its launch in 1882. *The Strand's* American emulators were "three magazines which established their success during a price-war in 1893–94, . . . which resulted in the ten-cent American magazine (previously the usual price for a standard illustrated monthly had been 25 or even 35 cents)": *McClure's Magazine* (1893), *The Cosmopolitan* (1886; price halved to $.12 in 1893), and *Munsey's Magazine* (1891; price lowered to $.10 in 1893).[57] In this way, *Scribner's* occupies that large middle ground of standard quality monthly magazines, which, from 1892 to 1911, "all look[ed] very much alike . . . [t]he same authors contribute to all [of them, and] merchandise advertised in the slick-paper sections . . . is again virtually the same."[58]

Advertisements such as these appeared, not only in a burgeoning number of quality-paper monthly and popular illustrated magazines, but also in books, pamphlets, train and steamship schedules, travel guides, brochures, and newspapers. They were found in the glossy advertising sections of literary publications[59] and in pulp-paper magazines as well.[60] From 1906 to 1908, three pulp-paper magazines were established by the Frank Munsey Co. that can help to demonstrate the kinds of change in textual matter "occurring in the magazine field" and the period's "decline of the standard magazine"[61] in which these new forms of popular reading, magazines, and global technologies came together. Technically catering to specialist audiences in the US, *The Railroad Man's Magazine* (1906), *The Ocean* (1907), and *The Live-Wire* (1908) also enjoyed significantly large circulations outside the country. In the May 1911 issue of *The Railroad Man's Magazine*, the publishers reprinted the following letter sent "[f]rom Darkest Africa," in which "Dr. Revis . . . stated that he had visited one of the [African] tribes far removed from the [American] missionary station, and from civilization." The letter declares:

> The people were very ignorant concerning all the arts of civilization and had never seen but one specimen of printing. The specimen was carefully cherished by the chief, and on rare occasions he would bring it out and let his subjects get a glimpse of it. It was a copy of *MUNSEY'S MAGAZINE*. I thought you might be interested in knowing what a wide circulation your publication had reached.[62]

Claiming this "emphasizes a remarkable phase of *The Munsey's* distribution," the advertisement then adds the following context:

> One advertiser . . . in *The Munsey* has just turned over to us inquiries from China and Germany; another, an inquiry from Greece; another from South Australia. Our records contain instances . . . from virtually every habitable country on the globe. A financial advertiser received a query from a mountain fastness of India . . .—a periodical of such worldwide influence must be powerful through the length and breadth of its own land.[63]

Along with many other popular titles from major publishing companies of the period, magazines of the Munsey Co. shared advertising pages, so that "From Darkest Africa" would have appeared, not only in *The Railroad Man's Magazine*, but also in *Munsey's* (1889–93), *The Argosy* (1896), *The All-Story* (1905), *The Scrap-Book* (1906), and *The Cavalier* (1908).[64] In the same May 1911 issue of *The Railroad Man's Magazine*, another advertisement warns readers: "Don't have your vacation marred by the spectres of old-fashioned heating methods. . . . The savings in fuel, repairs, doctor bills, labor, etc. [from using American Radiators & Ideal Boilers] will pay for your annual vacation."[65] In addition to celebrating the new or exotic, travel advertisements in the magazines of the early twentieth century could also appeal to the mundane and be supremely level-headed.

Advertisements like these were also printed on banners, posters, leaflets, and fliers. Their familiar slogan of "rest, recreation, and pleasure"[66] in the "most expeditious, satisfactory, and economical way"[67] was trumpeted across virtually every channel of print and visual media of the period. But, modern tourism's message of swift, comfortable, and economical access to all distant parts of the world paradoxically collapsed the very qualities—such as distance, otherness, and the sublime[68]—that travel advertisements simultaneously claimed to offer.

Conrad was generally less sympathetic to the tourists who bought into the fraud than to the commercial industry involved in perpetuating it. As he writes in "Travel" (1923):

> That category of travelers with their parrot-like remarks ... do not appear as travelers even to the most naïve minds and perhaps even to their own minds. They are simply an enormous company of people who go round the world for a change and rest, either suffering from overwork (whatever that may mean) or from neurasthenia. And I am

Figure 3.3 Cook's Oriental Travellers' Gazette (January 1892) and "Around the World," Hamburg-American Line Poster (October 1912).

sure my best wishes go with them for an easy and radical recovery. Steamship companies love them.[69]

Wells's spoof on the Conradian adventure, however, launches this critique of travel-tourism and "[t]he inanity of the mass of travel-books the Suez Canal is responsible for"[70] with an almost equal measure of contempt against Conrad's own adventure romances. His caricature of Conrad as the "cowardly and financially corrupt"[71] captain of a doomed ship suggests that Conradian adventure fiction may perform the same rhetorical fraud as both modern travel advertisements and a "mass of travel-books."[72] In the context of this densely integrated modern media environment, the next section of this chapter performs close readings of several key passages in "How I Stole the Heaps of Quap From Mordet Island." It pays critical attention to the novel's transatlantic serialization in both a British literary magazine and popular American pulp magazine, moreover, and shows how important editorial changes to the two different versions of the episode's "first" serial appearance could dramatically alter readers' receptions of essentially the same text. Dramatic reorganization of the publishing industries of Great Britain and the United States between 1880 and 1914 forms another important background for this chapter, which finally links Wells's critique to particular changes in periodical publishing, regarding the development of agency, advertising, and literary authorship.

The Materiality of Texts and Simultaneous Transatlantic Serialization

Simultaneous transatlantic serialization of new novels was a defining feature of early twentieth-century British popular fiction. As a pre-publication practice, serializing novels in magazines and newspapers developed on both sides of the Atlantic in response to the "manufacturing" clause of the 1891 U.S. Copyright Act. In short, the "manufacturing" clause required that the type for new novels be set and the plates for printing them be made in the United States, in order to extend copyright to foreign authors. The measure was implicitly protectionist and, at first, extended only to authors from Great Britain, France, Belgium, and Switzerland.[73] The Act required that foreign authors, or their legal representatives, deposit a type-set copy of the first edition in the Library of Congress, in Washington, D.C., on or before the date of first publication in the home country. A challenge to British authors was whether to publish first in Britain—thus securing copyright in European and Colonial markets—or arrange first publication in the United States— thus risking copyright everywhere else. The solution was simultaneous transatlantic publication, which, as James West observes, only benefited publishers such as Macmillan, Blackwood, and John Lane, who "had offices on both sides of the Atlantic."[74] For others, the logistics of planning and organizing—and at the same time conducting negotiations between multiple parties on different continents over a period of several months, and then finalizing the process on the same day in both countries—proved too unrealistic a demand.

Transatlantic serialization did more than secure American copyright for works by British authors, however: it increased their readership abroad, provided valuable marketing of upcoming publications, and ultimately expanded book sales in both the US and Britain. Authors were being paid twice for the same work, moreover, at least in theory. In 1908, the American serial rights to Wells's new novel, *Tono-Bungay*, were purchased by the S&S Corp.'s editor, Charles Agnew Maclean, for the publisher's flagship title, *The Popular Magazine*, and this earned Wells the tidy sum of £100, which at the time was twice the annual salary of a British laborer employed in the printing trade.[75] Wells's contract with *The English Review*, on the other hand, was based on 20 percent profit share on the magazine's first four issues. When sales of *The English Review* failed to live up to Ford Maddox Hueffer's early expectations, Wells was not paid. This case illustrates another important benefit of transatlantic serialization: it minimized authors' risks by multiplying their markets and spreading the risks between them.

The requirement of first U.S. publication was abandoned by the U.S. Copyright Act (1909). The 1909 Act also revised the definition of "simultaneous" publication, allowing 30 days between the first publication abroad and the deposit of a copy in the Library of Congress—regardless of which came first. The deposit of a copy in the Library of Congress was followed by a provisional copyright period of 30 days, during which time foreign publishers had to organize an American "manufacture" of the edition. It was not only a complex and time-consuming process, but also an extra expense for the publisher. It was mostly reserved for authors who had commercial viability and the potential to return a profit on the publisher's investment–such as Wells, Arnold Bennett, Conan Doyle, Baroness Orczy, or John Buchan, for example. Popular British authors who took advantage of the risk management that simultaneous transatlantic serializations offered included many of the most important, best-selling literary professionals of the period. Rudyard Kipling's *Captains Courageous* was serialized both in *McClure's Magazine* (US; November 1896–March 1897) and in *Pearson's Magazine* (UK; December 1896–April 1897). *The Strand Magazine* serialized Wells's *First Men on the Moon* (November 1900–August 1901) in 10 parts; in *The Cosmopolitan*, Wells's novel ran (November 1900–June 1901) in eight parts. In 1904–05, Rider Haggard's *Ayesha*—a sequel to the best-selling *She: A History of Adventure* (1886–87)—appeared in *The Windsor Magazine* (UK; December 1904–October 1905) and *The Popular Magazine* (US; January–August 1905). A sign of the author's rising fortunes, Conrad's first simultaneous transatlantic serialization was *Under Western Eyes*, which appeared in 11 parts in *The English Review* and *North American Review* (both from December 1910 to October 1911). During the First World War, Sax Rohmer's early Fu Manchu stories (1912–17) were simultaneously published through *Collier's Weekly* (US) and Cassell & Co.'s all-fiction pulp-paper magazine, *The Story-Teller* (UK).[76] In 1919–20, Conrad's *The Rescue: A Romance of the Shallows* was serialized in Hilaire Belloc's sixpenny military broadsheet *Land & Water* (UK; January 30–July 31, 1919; 27 weekly parts) and in the first seven issues of *Romance* (US; November 1919–May 1920; seven monthly parts),[77] the Ridgway Co.'s latest addition to the burgeoning post-war pulp market and their companion title to *Adventure*. For these authors, a multiple-market mediation of simultaneous transatlantic serialization became the rule.

Works serialized simultaneously on both sides of the Atlantic Ocean were offered to two different sets of readers—with different expectations and often competing interpretations—who were reading substantially the same narrative at the same time.[78] The range of first publication contexts framing new publications of commercially viable and aggressively marketed works also extended to differences between periodical formats and their frequencies of publication. Wells's *Mr. Britling Sees It Through* (1916), for example, was simultaneously serialized in the American *Collier's Weekly* (US; April 29–July 29, 1916; national weekly) and, in Britain, by *The Nation* (UK; May 20–October 2, 1916; sixpenny weekly). In an anonymous review of the novel printed in *The Dial* (Chicago; October 5, 1915), a London reviewer noted:

> [The novel] has, I believe, been serialized on your side; here, it is still running in 'The Nation,' which, being an ordinary sixpenny weekly, cannot give up a great deal of space to each instalment, and has been issuing it for some considerable time. But the announcement of the volume shows that Mr. Britling's efforts to see things through are doomed to failure this journey. When Mr. Wells began the book he may have thought that its termination could be neatly arranged to co-incide with the end of Armageddon. But though the French general who said that the first five years of the war would be the worst was perhaps unduly pessimistic, it still promises to tax Mr. Britling's endurance for some time longer.[79]

As the *Dial* reviewer suggests, with simultaneous transatlantic serializations, the staggered rates of delivery, publication schedule, and even periodicity itself can often alter readers' perceptions of the same text.

Collating and Comparing Two "First" Appearances: Title-Level[80]

Serialized across five issues of S&S's *The Popular Magazine* (September 1908–January 1909) and in four issues of Ford Maddox Hueffer's *The English Review* (December 1908–March 1909), *Tono-Bungay* provides an exemplary case study for these sorts of comparison, mediating two very different sets of implied audiences and their expectations. In fact, some differences between the two magazines—and their respective editorial decisions that framed *Tono-Bungay* for first-time readers—could hardly be more pronounced. When published in New York, *Tono-Bungay*'s readers first encountered the novel's "Mordet Island" episode through one of America's biggest, best-selling fiction magazines of the time. Established in 1903 as a 96-page monthly "for Boys and 'Old Boys'," *The Popular Magazine* transitioned to the standard 128-page format, dropping "for Boys and 'Old Boys' " from its masthead, with issue no. 2 (December). Four more signatures were added with issue no. 3 (January), bringing the total page count to 192, and, in February, the magazine's cover bore the new masthead: "The Biggest Magazine in the World."[81] By 1906, *The Popular* claimed a monthly circulation of 265,000, owing largely to its serialization of Haggard's *Ayesha* in 1905.[82] In 1908, circulation was 300,000. Single issues cost $.15 on newsstands, with annual subscriptions at $1.50. The December 1908 issue ran 264 two-columned pages (181,079 words), and it included 36 pages of slick-paper advertisements—with six pages of front matter, and 30 pages of back matter. Although publishing hundreds of books, dime novels, and story papers every year, in addition to magazines, the S&S Corporation was primarily known for these latter. The publisher Ormond Smith's 1908 Harvard class record lists his parents, date of birth, preparation, admittance date (June 1879), and role as a magazine publisher of "large proportions." It then notes that: "In 1900 he started *Ainslee's Magazine*; in November, 1903, *The Popular Magazine*; in April, 1905, *Smith's Magazine*; and in July, 1906, *The People's Magazine*,—all of which are successful."[83] Owing to the poor quality of wood-pulp paper, the magazine is lightweight, despite being 264 pages. Power O'Malley's cover illustration depicts two hunters from Herbert Quick's *The Stalking of Pauguk*, a tale of "modern commercialism," in brilliant orange, yellow, and green inks.[84]

In marked contrast, Duckworth & Co.'s high-quality, heavy book-paper production of the March 1909 issue of *The English Review* reminds readers of how the Duckworth firm specialized in first editions and "large factual books for universities." Sold in London bookshops for 2/6 net, with annual subscriptions for 1 guinea,[85] the magazine ran 244 single-columned pages (103,558 words), included 16 un-illustrated book-paper pages of publishers' advertisements—eight pages each of front and back matter—and featured a plain, dark-blue cardboard-paper cover. Throughout Hueffer's brief tenure as editor (1908–09), monthly circulation of *The English Review* would not exceed 1,000. Wells's disappointment might have been at least partially conciliated, then, by the roughly 1 million readers of *The Popular*, who had only recently finished *Tono-Bungay*'s serialization on the other side of the Atlantic[86] (see Figure I.5).

British authors during the early twentieth century—especially British popular-fiction writers who were clients of A.P. Watt—routinely sold first North American serial rights to pulp-paper magazines such as *The Argosy*, *The Popular*, *All-Story*, *Blue Book*, and *Adventure*—reaping significant financial rewards from those large and dedicated readerships, at a time when coverage of small-town America following the sale of second, third, and sometimes fourth serial, reprint, and syndication rights often meant higher U.S. first edition book sales. In the common journalistic parlance of the day, this low-paying, but guaranteed form of publicity was referred to by writers as "boom."

Collating and Comparing Two "First" Appearances: Issue and Constituent-Level

Relative to the considerable length of monthly installments appearing in England through the four-part serialization for *The English Review*, which range from 56 to 97 pages per installment (or 25,000–45,000 words), *Tono-Bungay*'s five-part American serialization is quite severely truncated.[87] Installments are much shorter, ranging from 14 to 32 pages (or 10,000–20,000 words), and this allows much less material to be published per issue. At 75,038 total words, the full text of the American serialization is just over half the length of the original manuscript,[88] which Wells serialized fully in the four issues of *The English Review*.[89] With 264 pages, 181,079 words, and 12 works of original new fiction—including one complete novel, one novelette, and three serials—featured in the table of contents that month,[90] *The Popular Magazine* for December 1908 was a behemoth compared with most other American fiction magazines on newsstands at the time. In the context of such a magazine, which was resolutely and unabashedly middle-brow—American readers could depend on 224 pages of good, quality fiction delivered once a month, at an affordable price—the irony of the novel's subtitle "A Romance of Commerce" seems subdued, if not altogether lost. In 1908, S&S's general manager, C.C. Vernon, claimed that "The Popular Trio" reached the "greatest number of buyers of advertised goods at the lowest comparative cost" among other magazines.[91] *The Popular* lived up to its name.[92]

Owing to the truncated length of installments, characters in the novel develop more quickly, or else not at all. Entire scenes have been cut, such as George's stay in Chatham with his cousin Nicodemus Frapp.[93] Dialogue is pared down. Names of places, specifically old and English locations, and connections to them are abstracted. In the second sentence of the first long paragraph of Part 2 in *The English Review*'s serialization, for example, the address of the PO reads: "Bampton, S.O., Oxon,"[94] whereas, in the American serialization, this reads simply: "Bampton."[95] George Ponderevo engages less frequently with his doubts in the American serialization, and his reference to "the contemporary state" is excised from the December 1908 issue. The English serialization reads in full:

> I realised that I was a modern and a civilised man. I found the food filthy and the coffee horrible; the whole town stank in my nostrils . . .

and the bedroom I slept in was infested by a quantity of exotic but voracious flat parasites . . . I fought them with insect powder, and found them comatose in the morning. I was dipping down into the dingy underworld of the contemporary state.[96]

Much of Wells's critique of modern commercialism is expressed through George's inner voice, or conscience. In the novel's American serialization, this anxiety of conscience has been excised, along with the opportunities for self-awareness those moments provide. Long passages of tender, comic dialogue between George and his uncle Edward have been foreshortened; social activities are minimized. Meanwhile, their plots advance quickly, as the novel's action unfolds at ripping speed.[97]

Professional magazine editors such as S&S's Maclean made difficult decisions on a regular basis. Their potential egos and reputations aside, authors' careers and livelihoods were at stake, but Maclean's choices indicate that Wells's novel would be presented to the readers of *The Popular* as a more straightforward adventure story. The manuscript was edited to emphasize this adventure plot and to bring elements of action to the foreground. Reflection and characterization were minimized or edited out. In the December 1908 installment, for example, as the *Maud Mary* sits idly off the coast of Mordet Island, George scans the African landscape and speculates on the quap's "primary influence": an "increase [in] the conductivity of . . . nerves" producing irritability, languor, and impatience in the ship's crew. Chapter IX, Part 5, in *The Popular Magazine*, begins:

> I can witness that the beach and mud for two miles or more either way were lifeless—lifeless as I could have imagined no tropical mud could ever be, and all the dead branches and leaves and rotting dead fish and so forth that drifted ashore became presently shriveled and white. Sometimes crocodiles would come up out of the water and bask, and now and then water-birds would explore the mud and rocky ribs that rose out of it, in a mood of transitory speculation. That was its utmost animation.
>
> I believe that the primary influence of the quap upon us was to increase the conductivity of our nerves, but that is a mere unjustifiable speculation on my part. At any rate it gave a sort of east-wind effect to life. We all became irritable, clumsy, languid and disposed to be impatient with our languor.[98]

In *The English Review* serialization, however, the same scene is preceded by two paragraphs that describe George's scientific theories on the nature and origins of quap; thoughts on radioactivity; and prediction that many more, and much bigger, heaps of the "cancerous" stuff will someday be discovered in other parts of the world. Referencing an article he has published in the *Geological Magazine* (October 1905), George's thoughts finally turn to ruminations on the potential dangers imposed by quap, including the effects of this "incalculably maleficent and strange" substance on human evolution, and its role in the ultimate destruction of this planet. Chapter 4, Part 5, of *The English Review* serialization begins:

> Sooner or later the ridiculous embargo that now lies upon all the coast eastward of Mordet Island will be lifted and the reality of the deposits of quap ascertained. I am sure myself that we were merely taking the outcrop of a stratum of nodulated deposits . . . merely the crumbled-out contents of two irregular cavities in the rock . . . the mud along the edge of the water for miles is . . . radio-active and lifeless and faintly phosphorescent at night. But the reader will find the full particulars of all this . . . in the *Geological Magazine* for October 1905. . . . There too he will find my unconfirmed theories of its nature . . . there is something . . . *cancerous* . . . something that . . . lives as a disease lives by destroying . . . incalculably maleficent and strange.

In the next paragraph, several lines down from the top of the next one-columned, book-paper page of *The English Review*, George continues:

> When I think of these inexplicable dissolvent centres that have come into being in our globe . . . I am haunted by a grotesque fancy of the ultimate eating away and dry-rotting and dispersal of all our world. So that while man still struggles and dreams his very substance will change and crumble from beneath him. . . . Suppose indeed that is to be the end of our planet; no splendid climax and finale . . . just—atomic decay! I add that to the ideas of the suffocating comet, the dark body out of space, the burning out of the sun, the distorted orbit, as a new and far more possible end . . . to this strange by-play of matter that we call human life. . . . These are questions I have never answered . . . but the thought of quap and its mysteries brings them back to me.[99]

Moments like these reveal the book's darker and more serious dimensions. The moral and ethical framework acts upon the center, and it pushes against George's impulses to adventure throughout the novel. In the pared-down version for American serialization, however, *Tono-Bungay*'s adventure story is highlighted. The action scenes are moved to the center, and George's ruminations expressing ideas to the contrary, questioning adventure's place in the modern world—which comprise long sections of the original manu-script—have been excised. *Tono-Bungay*'s "romance of commerce" is thus re-presented to be less at odds with this adventure plot without the novel's accompanying moral and ethical framework. Crimes are more often, and more easily, committed when men cannot be pestered by inner voices.[100]

His heavily edited version of *Tono-Bungay* as a more straightforward adventure story was neither a runaway success, nor a failure for Maclean's readers.[101] As serializations in *The Popular Magazine* wore on, hundreds of writers saw final installments pushed to the back pages, in order to make room for Maclean's newer prospects coming up the pike. In all likelihood, *Tono-Bungay* ran its course like the majority of fiction that passed through Maclean's hands each month. In the competition between pulp-paper magazines for the title of "The Largest Magazine in the World," American editors such as Maclean at *The Popular*, Karl Edwin Harriman at *The Blue Book*, Robert H. Davis at *The All-Story*, and Matthew White, Jr. at *The Argosy* were publishing some of the top British fiction writers of the time in fairly quick rotation, and on a fairly regular basis. Maclean had competition from Harriman's *The Blue Book*, starting in June 1905, when its second issue ran Eden Phillpotts's *Letters from Algiers* as the lead story. This was the start of a popular trend, and, over the next few years, *The Blue Book* ran stories by Robert Hichens, W. Pett Ridge, William Hope Hodgson, Coulson Kernahan, Max Pemberton, E. Phillips Oppenheim, and Guy Boothby. According to Mike Ashley, some of these were reprinted from *The Windsor Magazine* (UK), but most of them were original submissions "following an announcement . . . in the British magazine *The Author* . . . [and a] later editorial announcement suggested that stories by British authors were amongst the most popular published in the magazine's first couple of years."[102] Other authors in *The Blue Book* during that time include Crittenden Marriott and Johnston McCulley. Davis's *The All-Story* for January 1909 features Part 1 of the six-part serialization of Garrett P. Serviss's *A Columbus of Space*, and in *The Argosy* that month are both Part 1 of a four-part serialization of McCulley's *Shipmates with Horror* and Part 2 of a four-part serialization of Albert Paysun Terhune's *From Flag to Flag*. In the high-stakes business of selling popular fiction for a profit, a professional editor at the turn of the twentieth century was expected to understand both readers and authors. They followed their careers, knew their work habits and temperaments, and learned to marshal their reputations most effectively. Editors such as Maclean—who determined the content of every issue of S&S's flagship title for nearly a quarter of a century (1904–28)— maintained their positions because they were talented in making those decisions. Editors framed, juxtaposed, even manipulated, texts. They also orchestrated authors' appearances alongside other authors. In doing so, editors could achieve desired effects and make the impressions they wanted to make, and, each year, their readers witnessed virtually uninterrupted growth in the number and variety of choices available to them to buy on growing numbers of newsstands (see Appendices A, F).

Although George himself claims that the expedition to Mordet Island lacks any relevance to the central themes of the novel, stating in the opening paragraph of Part 3 that it "stands apart from all the rest of my life, detached, a piece by itself with an atmosphere of its own,"[103] Edward Mendelson and others argue that, "Wells gives the whole African episode far greater significance than George understands in narrating it,"[104] that in fact his expedition to Mordet Island forms "the imaginative and moral centre" of the novel.[105] In the American serialization, the centrality of this episode is reinforced by the editorial deletion of a single sentence. In Part 3 of both the original manuscript and *The English Review*'s serialization of it, George's narration continues: "It would, I suppose, make a book by itself—it has made a fairly voluminous official report—but so far as this novel of mine goes it is merely an episode, a contributory experience, and I mean to keep it at that."[106]

Contrary to this claim, the dramatic episode is at the center of the narrative figuratively. It represents George's last-ditch attempt to rescue his uncle's collapsing commercial empire, and, as the expedition is unsuccessful, it also marks the boundary between Edward Ponderevo's rise and fall. In the American serialization, the episode is at the center of the novel literally, in terms of page count. As an aficionado of British popular adventure fiction, Maclean would have scrutinized the installment closely and considered options, opportunities, and ways to maximize its effect on readers of the magazine. Maclean's readers had reason to expect a high concentration of action in British popular fiction, moreover, and the episode is published practically stand-alone in the December 1908 issue. We can be certain that a controlled orchestration has been performed editorially here. Part 7 of Chapter VIII, "Soaring," and Parts 1–5 of Chapter IX, "How I Stole the Heaps of Quap from Mordet Island," comprise 15 pages of two-columned text (or 10,422 words). That is 5.7 percent of the total word count of the December 1908 issue of *The Popular* (181,079 words). The "Mordet Island" episode alone is 12.25 pages (or 8,424 words), which is 11.2 percent of the five-part serial's total word count (75,038 words).[107]

By contrast, in *The English Review* issue of March 1909, Parts 2–5 of Chapter the Third (Cont.), "Soaring," Parts 1–7 of Chapter the Fourth, "How I Stole the Heaps of Quap from Mordet Island" (Book the Third: The Great Days of Tono-Bungay), Parts 1–9 of Chapter the First, "The Stick of the Rocket," Parts 1–4 of Chapter the Second, "Love Among the Wreckage," and Parts 1–4 of Chapter the Third, "Night and the Open Sea" (Book the Fourth: The Aftermath of Tono-Bungay), comprise 91 pages (or 41,383 words)—and this represents a full 40 percent of the issue's total word count (103,558 words). The "Mordet Island" episode is 21.5 pages (or 9,530 words) in *The English Review*, and comprises just 6.7 percent of the four-part serial's total word count (142,140 words). In this extant version, *Tono-Bungay*'s moral and ethical superstructure is left intact; its critique frames the Mordet Island episode as an absurd, appalling adventure, and this reinforces Wells's complicated relationship to popular fiction in a way the American serialization attempts to repair or elide.[108] By 1908, Wells was both a famous writer and a public intellectual, whose persistent desire to improve and reform humanity could not conceal his ambivalent attitudes toward them. Maclean's heavily edited version of *Tono-Bungay* encourages us to form a distinctly different impression, however, and these are two distinctly different impressions based on two equally viable "first" appearances of the same novel. Simultaneous transatlantic serialization in Hueffer's *The English Review* and S&S's *The Popular Magazine* requires that we explore, and take seriously, this novel's multiple material, aesthetic, historical, and first periodical contexts—and take into full account this expanded field of modern literary production and the transatlantic print cultures through which the novel was first produced, twice.

Modern copyright legislation began in 1886 with the convention at Berne and evolved in tandem with the increasing difficulty of authors, editors, and publishers to protect their investments abroad. It also established a complicated legal framework and set the stage for a rising class of literary agents. Like global tourism, the travel advertisements described early in this chapter, and the magazines themselves, the Conradian adventure valorizes those very places that its conditions of possibility must eventually eradicate. Adventure romance's nostalgia for those imaginary, isolated worlds at the margins of imperial modernity is complicated by the dependency of magazines on expanding lines of popular print and publishing networks, multiplying outlets for international distribution after 1886,[109] and growing markets of new readers worldwide. As Munsey's advertisement "From Darkest Africa" suggests, Conrad's serial publications in popular magazines reached "virtually every habitable country on the globe."[110] This densely integrated modern media environment is an especially important context for transatlantic serializations of popular fiction. When cast within the dramatic expansions and reorganization of the publishing industries in Britain and the United States in 1880–1914, the "pervasive anxiety about value and authenticity"[111] characterizing Wells's spoof on imperial romances, "How I Stole the Heaps of Quap from Mordet Island,"[112] is a critique, not only of advertising, but also of the modern commercial romance of professional literary authors, agency, publishing, and readerships.

Considered alongside the contemporary travel advertisements for holiday cruises, express tour packages, and discount resort destinations as far afield as Egypt, Jamaica, the tropical South Seas, Australia, and New Zealand, Wells's parody of the Conradian adventure and his "vicious attack on Conrad" suggest rather more than just a settling of old scores.[113] The episode's absurdist spin on the themes explored in both Conrad's "Author's Note" to *The Nigger of the "Narcissus"* and *Lord Jim* suggests that Wells repurposes Jim's flight to Patusan[114]—the geographical location beyond the reach of modern "civilization" with its intrusive journalistic "gossip"— challenges the author's aesthetic solutions, and ultimately overwrites him on terms of acquiescence to tourism's changing representation of foreign and faraway places. Wells's parody inscribes a world that has become more disenchanted, because increasingly familiar, but also more connected, controlled, and tightly policed.

The botched expedition at the episode's center is framed by direct allusions to Conrad's work, and the allusions particularly recall the author's

Figure 3.4 "Weltverkehrs-Karte," Bibliographical Institute: Leipzig, 6th Edition
Prepared for *Meyers Encyclopedia* (1907).

description of Patusan. They reiterate the episode's sense of imitation, but
direct its critique especially toward *Lord Jim*. In 1909, almost a full decade
after its first serialization in *Blackwood's Magazine*,[115] *Lord Jim* was
Conrad's most iconic, and certainly his best-selling, novel to date. *Tono-
Bungay*'s narrator, George Ponderevo, describes his experience like this:

> That expedition to Mordet Island stands apart from all the rest of my
> life. . . . [It is] detached, a piece by itself with an atmosphere of its own.
> It would, I suppose, make a book by itself—it has made a fairly volum-
> inous official report—but so far as this novel of mine goes it is merely
> an episode, a contributory experience, and I mean to keep it at that.[116]

This sense of "detach[ment]" accorded to an "atmosphere" and "experience" that "stands apart" from the narrator's life is reproduced several
paragraphs later, but in a way that explicitly locates its more imaginary
effects—what Conrad terms "pure exercises of imagination"[117]—beyond the
reach of "civilization." The narrator continues:

> All these African memories stand by themselves. It was for me an
> expedition into the realms of undisciplined nature out of the world
> that is ruled by men, my first bout with that hot side of our mother
> that gives you the jungle. . . . They are memories woven upon a fabric
> of sunshine and heat and a constant warm smell of decay . . . our first
> slow passage through the channels behind Mordet's Island was in
> incandescent sunshine.[118]

Ponderevo attempts to act out this imperial fantasy in the jungles of a fictional Mordet Island, in which he and the rest of the crew of the *Maud Mary* ultimately fail to recover a mysterious and radioactive material called "quap." This chapter begins and ends, moreover, with references to the ubiquitous medium of the daily newspapers. At the start, Ponderevo's aging uncle, Edward, expresses a keen awareness of his own "impending calamity" and predicts the downfall of his commercial empire. He rails against his long-time business competitor, Lord Boom—who, with "placard[s]" and "his damned newspapers," is, according to Edward, "trying to fight me down. Ever since I offered to buy the *Daily Decorator* he's been at me. . . . He wants everything[!]"[119] When Ponderevo returns to England after his failed Mordet Island expedition, he discovers the most recent misfortunes of his uncle's commercial empire through placards and newspapers. In the chapter's final paragraph, Ponderevo recalls: "The newspapers I bought, the placards I saw, all England indeed resounded to my uncle's bankruptcy."[120] These frames of shock and control in the form of menacing information— the narrator's knowledge and its dramatic discovery via signs and the newspapers—then bracket the violent, surreal, and impressionistic scenes of heat and decay associated in Ponderevo's memory with the failed expedition to Mordet Island. These frames heighten the suspense that already pervades this episode, with its wild and desperate last-ditch measure to rescue Uncle Edward's lucrative and proportionally fraudulent business empire. They also allude to the threatened division of the world explored in *Lord Jim*, wherein Conrad's narrator identifies imperial civilization by the web of geographical areas already integrated with its telegraph cables, shipping lanes, and mail-boats. Beyond the reach of these systems—where Marlow has suggested that "the haggard lies of our civilization" are "replaced by pure exercises of imagination"[121]—Ponderevo situates the failed Mordet Island expedition. But the expedition fails, partly, because it is also an illicit one. Mordet Island is not off the map, and the expedition to it takes place on the fringes of potential and, finally, confirmed surveillance.

The muckraking newspapers back home in England seem to know everything, but news and information travel quickly in a world connected. In the penultimate scene at Mordet Island, when the "gunboat . . . sent down the coast to look"[122] for them confronts the captain and crew of the *Maud Mary*, Ponderevo's narrative stipulates that a menacing reach—and conse-quent power to surveil and control—effected by the electric "telegraph" is at the center of this dangerous new development. He writes:

> People had been reconnoitering us, the telegraph had been at work, and we were not four hours at sea before we ran against the gunboat that had been sent down the coast to look for us and that would have caught us behind the island like a beast in a trap. . . . The gunboat came out as a long dark shape wallowing on the water to the east. She sighted the *Maud Mary* at once, and fired some sort of popgun to arrest us.[123]

The menacing presence of an information system employed as an agent of policing and control here at the imperial periphery effectively collapses Marlow's distinctions between "civilization" and the spaces of fantasy accorded to geographical areas beyond its frontiers. The Mordet Island episode leaves no room in the world for sites effectively beyond the pale of imperial modernity, because it reorganizes Conrad's exploration into that same imaginary dichotomy through *Lord Jim*. This dichotomy, Conrad himself suggested, was on the verge of collapse by the late 1880s.[124] Wells attributes the Ponderevos' misfortunes to the scheming machinations of "Lord Boom," a modern journalism magnate, and the muckraking power of his daily newspapers. But here, Lord Boom's newspapers—which have militaristic, mechanized, and violent overtones already—are given the obvious and imperialistic extension, in the increasingly aggressive global reach of the electric telegraph. In comparison, a ship's cannon is just "some sort of popgun."[125]

In the next chapter of Wells's novel, "The Stick of the Rocket," the uncanny power of new media and communication technologies to locate and control activities, even at the world's periphery, is reintroduced more explicitly. When Ponderevo escapes with his uncle to a remote village in the south of France, described as "that queer corner of refuge out of the world [that] was destined to be my uncle's deathbed,"[126] it is yet again the ubiquity of the newspapers that leads to a profound discovery on which the narrative dramatically turns. Ponderevo recalls:

> Towards the end it became evident our identity was discovered. I found the press, and especially Boom's section of it, had made a sort of hue and cry for us, sent special commissioners to hunt for us, and though none of these emissaries reached us until my uncle was dead, one felt the forewash of that storm of energy. The thing got into the popular French press.[127]

Like Conrad's fictional Patusan, Mordet Island and the obscure village in the south of France are Wells's versions of the foreign setting located beyond the pale of surveillance. More significant for the novel's renegotiation of Conrad's imaginary dividing line are Ponderevo's descriptions of his abrupt discovery. In both instances, his discovery takes place via the global extensions of imperial modernity, the electric telegraph and the newspapers. The expedition to Mordet Island is reported to the authorities via "the telegraph . . . at work."[128] As a technology of surveillance, it is reintroduced and reinforced when Ponderevo and his uncle Edward are discovered hiding in a remote French village, because the newspapers have tipped the villagers off to their real identity. Ponderevo is aware, in this episode near the end of the novel, that, in order for his Uncle Edward to even die peacefully, they must escape the grid-like system of new media and communications. Their desperate flight to the south of France becomes, however, only a brief, and illusory, means of escape, because even this "queer corner of refuge out of the world"[129] is connected through an expanding system of control. The telegraph and newspapers connect all places everywhere to the center of the modern information infrastructure, and thus nowhere is really foreign at all.[130]

In the early decades of the twentieth century, the romance of travel, adventure, discovery, and exploration, of exotic destinations untouched by contact with modern industrial progress and enterprise, was rapidly giving way. New media technologies, magazines, newspapers, the electric telegraph, and telephone meant that all places now had the potential to be known, accessible, and connected. Benefits of the new technologies were the abilities to erase distance, connect continents, and shed "light" on the formerly "dark" areas of the world. This power had profound, sometimes imaginary, consequences. "How I Stole the Heaps of Quap from Mordet Island" registers a wider system of media and global communication, and it invites readers to participate in various extratextual investigations that highlight its own intertextuality. Drawing attention to the strategies by which genres mediate readers' receptions of a text, it also shows how genres are simultaneously re-mediated by readers and popular reception.[131]

Further on, Ponderevo invites readers to pursue a secondary source outside the text for "the full particulars." Regarding "the reality of the deposits of quap," their "stratum of nodulated . . . irregular cavities," and his "uncon-firmed theories of its nature," Ponderevo addresses readers directly, stating: "But the reader will find the full particulars of my impression of all this in the *Geological Magazine* for October, 1905, and to that I must refer him."[132] This explicit reference to a supplementary source outside the text occurs, aptly enough, in a chapter marked by dashed hopes, frustrated expectations, and a failed quest for material. No surprise, then, that the October 1905 issue of *Geological Magazine*, published by Cambridge University, makes no mention at all of any material that resembles quap, or any geographical area similar to Mordet Island. There is no description of phosphorescent deposits or West Africa of any kind. Wells's explicit invitation to this archival adventure proves futile, just as it points readers outside the text, toward scientific periodical literature of the day. Wells directs his readers away, momentarily at least, from the set of rhetorical and discursive practices normally associated with the genre of his fictional novel, and he appropriates, albeit tongue-in-cheek, the culture of modern scientific discourse. It reinforces Ponderevo's authority as the narrator, an explorer, and, most importantly, a man of science. This factual, scientific dimension to the chapter not only contrasts with the chapter's own violent and absurd narrative, but also serves to implicate factual and scientific discourses in this enterprise. Geology, geography, and anthropology routinely dealt with the imaginative realm of the unverifiable.[133]

Conclusion

In new media's emergent global culture, unverifiable representations of the foreign and faraway could be reinforced by the authority and influence of the medium. An archival adventure into the October 1905 number of *Geological Magazine* turned up nothing more relevant to quap or West Africa than a report on the proceedings of the annual meeting of the "British Association for the Advancement of Science in Cape Town, South Africa, August 16th, 1905."[134] And yet, articles in *Geological Magazine*, travel ads in *Scribner's*, and *Blackwood's* serialization of *Lord Jim* all register one or several concerns in Wells's novel. If these disparate texts are juxtaposed, they all deal in highly mediated representations of the foreign and faraway places of the world. These representations situate *Tono-Bungay*'s Conradian adventure episode, "How I Stole the Heaps of Quap from Mordet Island," thematically closer to the central preoccupations it explores than the contemporary book reviews, literary histories, or other rhetorical and discursive practices that are usually associated with the cultural context of novel writing. The novel's cultural and intellectual environment is defined in these modern travel advertisements, periodicals, patent medicines, and information technologies at the turn of the century, while it also looks forward to a period further advanced in technology and its global media expansion

Locating Wells's spoof on the Conradian adventure within this wider media ecology, its seemingly straightforward caricature of the Polish exile and former master mariner[135]—Conrad was also a consummate European traveler and a global citizen—registers more than professional jealousy.[136] It registers the transition from late-Victorian discovery to imperial modernity's "grid of the rational and the known,"[137] from the Baedeker travel tour of

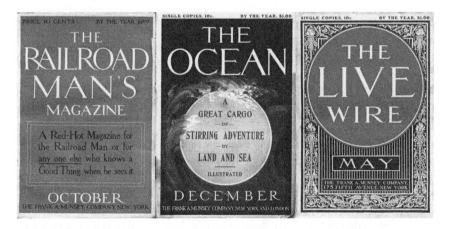

Figure 3.5 Three Covers: *The Railroad Man's Magazine* (October 1906); *The Ocean* (December 1907); and *The Live Wire* (May 1908).

Egypt to the "Pleasure Pirate Christmas"[138] in Jamaica. The episode is a clear disavowal of the adventure romance novelist of an anachronistic, late-Victorian tradition. For Wells, this tradition had already begun to represent the fraudulent pose of a bankrupt aesthetic by the end of the twentieth century's first decade. The "balmy isles,"[139] "strange lands,"[140] and "mysterious cities"[141] of foreign and faraway travel ads offered "many a gay buccaneer"[142] throughout this period the rhetoric, not the experience, of real travel. These were places that existed only in the travel ads in magazines, posters, and steamship company brochures. They were brighter, more colorful, and more thoroughly exotic than the real world. They were located in the travel ads' ideal world, a world full of romantic possibilities, but a world not found on any map, or off any beaten track.[143]

Chapter 4 examines the first UK publication of Doyle's *The Lost World* (1912), which was serialized in *The Strand Magazine* from April to November 1912. It shows how new media and illustrated magazines could also be used to reinstate the visual evidence of lost geographical frontiers beyond civilization. Recalling Ponderevo's appropriation of the familiar discourses of modern scientific materialism—his suggestion that readers should "find the full particulars . . . of all this in the *Geological Magazine* for October, 1905"[144]—Doyle appropriates late-Victorian photography's claims to objective proof and documentary evidence. Manipulating photography's illustrated representation in the popular illustrated monthly magazines, the author postulates new imaginary avenues for artistic escape and transgression in the modern world. As this next chapter shows, the Mordet Island episode represents just one solution to the aesthetic limitations imposed upon the adventure romance by imperial modernity's global mapping. Doyle's *The Lost World* represents another, far more imaginative, solution to these same aesthetic preoccupations.

Notes

1 The novel was first serialized in four parts in both *The Popular Magazine* (September 1908–January 1909) and *The English Review* (December 1908–March 1909).

2 This entry is recorded in the Library of Congress Copyright Office, *Catalog of Copyright Entries*, Pt. 1, Vol. 5, No. 22 (November 25, 1908). Washington, D.C.: U.S. Government Printing Office, p. 754.

3 See "To be published January 16th: Tono-Bungay by H.G. Wells," *The Bookseller, Newsdealer & Stationer* Vol. 30, No. 1 (January 1, 1909), p. 32.

4 "January Book Sales", *The Publisher's Weekly: The American Book Trade Journal* Vol. XCV, No. I (January 4, 1919). New York: R.R. Bowker, p. 12.

5 "Sales of Books During the Month [. . .] as sold between the 1st of January and the 1st of February," *The Bookman* (March 1909), p. 108.

6 Trade-journal advertisements from 1909 reference the second, third, and fourth "editions" of *Tono-Bungay*; edition here probably means impression, the additional printing based on a publisher's original plates. See John Carter, *ABC for Book Collectors*, 8th Ed., London: Oak Knoll Press, 2004. For a

contemporary perspective, see "What Makes an Edition?", *The Publisher's Weekly* Vol. 84, No. 9 (August 30, 1913), pp. 575–76. In April, for example, *The Literary Digest* ran this half-page ad: "A hit in two countries. H.G. Wells's big novel (3rd Edition) TONO-BUNGAY" ("A hit in two countries," advertisement, *The Literary Digest* Vol. 38, No. 15 (April 10, 1909), p. 00d.)

7 Macmillan Company of Canada (Toronto) was established in December 1905 as the Canadian branch office for the London home office of Macmillan Company, London, with a mandate to market Macmillan's English and American publications in Canada. Read Ruth Panofsky's *The Literary Legacy of the Macmillan Company of Canada*, Toronto: University of Toronto Press, 2012.

8 The Duffield & Co. contract granted first North American rights, so the American firm had control of the Canadian market as well. Macmillan Co. of Canada purchased 500 copies of the Duffield edition and imported them, "bound, with a cancel title" (Bruce Whiteman, "The Early History of the Macmillan Co. of Canada, 1905–21", *Papers of the Bibliographical Society of Canada* 23 [1984], pp. 68–80; 75).

9 In mid-July, the *New York Times* reported that a "fourth edition of H.G. Wells's *Tono-Bungay* is announced for this country and a second edition for Canada by Duffield & Co." (*The New York Times*, Saturday Ed. [July 17, 1909], p. 26).

10 According to Norman and Jeanne MacKenzie's biography: "By 14 May 1908, Wells had settled with Macmillan for an advance of £1,500 on *Tono-Bungay* ... and he was thinking about plans for serialisation" (*H.G. Wells: A Biography*, New York: Simon & Schuster, 1973, p. 234). It is unlikely that Wells involved his literary agent, Charles Cazenove, in negotiations with Macmillan (he would not have needed to), but, for American rights to *Tono-Bungay*, he retained two agents, Paul Reynolds and Curtis Brown, who could coordinate copyright registration and deposit of copies in New York and arrange North American and even South American reprint, translation, and dramatic rights.

11 In England, the first printing of the first edition was of 7,500 copies; these copies include an eight-page publisher's catalog in rear, dated "1.09." The second printing was bound in February for sale in March; these copies will have the same advertisements, dated "2.09". Also see "Tono-Bungay," *Time Literary Supplement* (February 11, 1909), p. 52.

12 *Tono-Bungay* was introduced in Europe through the Tauchnitz "Collection of British Authors" series, Vols. 4122 and 4123. This long-running series (est. 1841) would eventually include 5,372 works of British and American fiction, with hundreds of titles in related series. Peter Davison notes: "Of all the attempts in the nineteenth-century to create popular reprint series ... Tauchnitz paperbacks were the most successful ... and, since the Tauchnitz firm attempted to publish its volumes on the Continent simultaneously with the English first editions, they often had to be typeset from unrevised English proofs, thus preserving important textual variants" (*The Review of English Studies* 41.164 [1990], pp. 540–41).

13 Quoted from Shafquat Towheed's essay, "Geneva v. Saint Petersburg: Two Concepts of Literary Property and the Material Lives of Books in *Under Western Eyes*," *Book History* 10 (2007), p. 183.

14 In Chapter 5, I discuss the growing importance of the practice for British publishers and authors of popular fiction at the turn of the century. In March 1909, for example, Conrad expressed "in a letter to Norman Douglas the need to secure American copyright on all his future publications there, which he was

now determined to achieve by means of simultaneous serialization and volume publication" (letter of March 6, 1909, quoted by Towheed, 170).

15 Scholars interested in the version-based research of multiple witnesses should see the Modernist Versions Project, co-founded by Stephen Ross and Matt Huculak in 2011, and based at the University of Victoria, in Victoria, B.C., at http://web.uvic.ca/~mvp1922/ (accessed December 15, 2016).

16 *The Illustrated Police News* (1843) was a weekly tabloid newspaper focusing on sensational crimes and mysteries. In 1886, it was voted "worst English newspaper" by readers of *The Pall Mall Gazette* (see " 'The Worst Newspaper in England': an Interview with the Proprietor of the 'Police News,' " *The Pall Mall Gazette* [23 Nov 1886]). Ponderevo recalls reading the paper: "The news shops appealed to me particularly. One saw there smudgy illustrated sheets, the *Police News* in particular, in which vilely drawn pictures brought home to the dullest intelligence an interminable succession of squalid crimes, women murdered and put into boxes, buried under floors, old men bludgeoned at midnight by robbers, people thrust suddenly out of trains, happy lovers shot, vitrioled and so forth by rivals" (Wells, "Book the First, Chapter the Second: Of My Launch Into the World and the Last I Saw of Bladesover," Part I, *Tono-Bungay*, *The English Review* Vol. I, No. 1 [December 1908], p. 113).

17 Towheed, Ibid., p. 171.

18 The full text of the Chace Act is published as Chap. 565 in *The Statutes at Large of the United States of America, from December, 1889 to March, 1891* (1891), 26, pp. 1106–10. The manufacturing clause is contained in Sect. 4952 of the law. For an introduction to the Act and its effects on Anglo-American literary relations, see Robert Spoo, *Without Copyrights: Piracy, Publishing, and the Public Domain*, Oxford, UK: Oxford University Press, 2015, pp. 59–64. For the more detailed discussion consulted for this chapter, read James West, "The Chace Act and Anglo-American Literary Relations," *Studies in Bibliography* 45 (1992), pp. 303–11.

19 Spoo, *Without Copyrights*, p. 5. Italics are mine.

20 Ibid.

21 West, p. 303.

22 Mark Wollaeger, *Modernism, Media, and Propaganda: British Narrative from 1900–1945*, Princeton, NJ: Princeton University Press, 2006, p. xvii.

23 Spoo, pp. 62–64.

24 Towheed, Ibid., p. 169.

25 Chronologically speaking, the novel's four-part serialization in *The Popular Magazine* (which commenced with the September 1908 issue) and first hardcover issue by Duffield & Co. (available in bookstores mid-January 1909) are jointly "true first" appearances.

26 My own research has suggested the following timeline for *Tono-Bungay*'s multiple first publications: a first North American serialization appeared in *The Popular Magazine*; a first U.S. hardcover edition was published by Duffield & Co.; this appeared simultaneously with a first Canadian hardcover edition issued by the Macmillan Co. of Canada; the first U.K. hardcover edition was then published by Macmillan Co. Ltd.; and finally, the first U.K. serialization in *The English Review* appeared.

27 See Wollaeger, *Modernism, Media, and Propaganda*.

28 Roger Osborne, "Joseph Conrad's Under Western Eyes: The Serials and First Editions," *Studies in Bibliography: Papers of the Bibliographical Society of the University of Virginia* 54 (2001), pp. 301–16.

29 Sales periods for new copyright works of literary fiction followed traditional monthly patterns that aligned with seasons. According to Simon Eliot, English

book sales "consisted of a substantial spring season spanning March to May" that declined "through July and August . . . reaching a minimum in September." It was followed by an "increase in October and November . . . peaking in December" (Eliot, *Literature in the Marketplace: Nineteenth-Century British Publishing and Reading Practices*, Eds. John O. Jordan and Robert L. Patten, Cambridge, UK: Cambridge University Press, 2003, pp. 32–33).

30   "Chapter IX: How I Stole the Heaps of Quap from Mordet Island," *Tono-Bungay*, Part 3, *The Popular Magazine* Vol. 12, No. 2 (December 1908), pp. 125–39, and "Book the Third, Chapter the Fourth: How I Stole the Heaps of Quap from Mordet Island," *Tono-Bungay*, Part 3, *The English Review* Vol. I, No. 4 (March 1909), pp. 723–49.

31   Several scholars have noted the similarities between the Polish author and Wells's Romanian captain of the *Maud Mary* over the years. For examples, see Bernard Bergonzi, *The Turn of a Century: Essays on Victorian and Modern English Literature*, London: Macmillan, 1973; Frederick R. Karl, "Conrad, Wells, and the Two Voices," *PMLA* Vol. 88, No. 5 (October 1973), pp. 1049–65; R.G. Hampson, "The Physical Presence of Conrad in Certain Works by H.G. Wells," *The Conradian* Vol. 6, No. 2 (June 1981), pp. 16–19; Martin Ray, "Conrad, Wells, and 'The Secret Agent': Paying Old Debts and Settling Old Scores," *The Modern Language Review* Vol. 81, No. 3 (July, 1986), pp. 560–73; William Kupinse, "Wasted Value: The Serial Logic of H. G. Wells's 'Tono-Bungay,'" *NOVEL: A Forum on Fiction* Vol. 33, No. 1 (Autumn, 1999), pp. 51–72; and Linda Dryden, " 'The Difference Between Us': Conrad, Wells, and the English Novel," *Studies in the Novel* Vol. 45, No. 2 (Summer 2013), pp. 214–33.

32   First UK serial rights for *The Time Machine* were sold to W.E. Henley, who then serialized Wells's novel in *The New Review* from January to May 1895. The first U.S. hardcover edition was published by Henry Holt & Co. (N.Y.) on May 7, 1895. Three weeks later, on the morning of May 29, 1895, William Heinemann published the English first hardcover edition in London.

33   It is noted that Wells's second scientific romance, *The Island of Doctor Moreau*, did not appear in serialized form.

34   *The Invisible Man* was first published in *Pearson's Weekly* in two parts (June and July, 1897).

35   *The War of the Worlds* was serialized in the UK by *Pearson's Magazine* (April–December, 1897), for which Wells was paid £200 (non-exclusive; first UK serial rights, national domestic market). The novel appeared simultaneously through an identical nine-part American serialization in John Brisben Walker's *The Cosmopolitan* (April–December, 1897). It was first published in hardcover by William Heinemann (London) in January, 1898; although "1st Edition: 1st State" copies of this volume have a 16-page publisher's catalog dated "Autumn MDCCCXCVII" (1897) in back.

36   The term "scientifiction" was first coined by Hugo Gernsback in his debut editorial, "A New Kind of Fiction," for *Amazing Stories* (April 1926). During the first 3 years of this magazine, Gernsback reprinted nearly 30 works by Wells, including his major novels *The First Men in the Moon*, *The Invisible Man*, *The Island of Dr. Moreau*, *The Time Machine*, *The War of the Worlds*, and *When the Sleeper Wakes*.

37   Swift, Shelley, Scott, and Cooper are most notably the authors of *Gulliver's Travels* (1726), *Frankenstein* (1818), *Ivanhoe* (1820), and *The Leatherstocking Tales* (1827–41), respectively.

38   Paul Cantor and Peter Hufnagel, "The Empire of the Future: Imperialism and Modernism in H.G. Wells," *Studies in the Novel* Vol. 38, No. 1 (Spring 2006), pp. 36–37.

39   Conrad, *Lord Jim* (1900), Ed. Thomas C. Moser, Norton Critical Edition, NY: W.W. Norton, 2006, p. 168.
40   Conrad, "Travel," *Last Essays*, Ed. Richard Curle, London: J.M. Dent, 1926, pp. 121–34.
41   Ibid., p. 128.
42   John McClure, *Late Imperial Romance*, London: Verso, 1994, p. 3.
43   Sir Sanford Fleming, "Our Empire Cables," *The Empire Club of Canada Speeches 1903-1904*, Ed. William Clark, Toronto: William Briggs, 1904, p. 84. In 1911, with the possibility of a war in Europe looming, the Committee of Imperial Defense analyzed the All Red Line and concluded that it would be essentially impossible for Britain to be isolated from her telegraph network owing to the redundancy built into the network: 49 cables would need to be cut for Britain to be cut off, 15 for Canada, and 5 for South Africa. Furthermore, Britain and British telegraph companies owned and controlled most of the apparatus needed to cut or repair telegraph cables.
44   Alvin F. Harlow, *Old Wires and New Waves: The History of the Telegraph, Telephone, and Wireless*, New York: Appleton-Century, 1936, p. 446. See also Robert L. Thompson, *Wiring a Continent: The History of the Telegraph Industry in the United States, 1832–1866*, Princeton, NJ: Princeton University Press, 1947, *passim*.
45   "Section D—No. 7, Correspondence Relative to the Establishment of a Mail Service Between England and the Australian Colonies," *Appendix to the Journals of the House of Representatives of New Zealand*, Auckland, NZ: Robert J. Creighton, 1863, p. 16.
46   "Frank Presbrey's Address, Transportation and Advertising," delivered at the annual dinner of the Atlas Club, Chicago (November 1902). *Printers' Ink: A Journal for Advertisers* Vol. XLII, No. 2 (January 14, 1903). New York: Geo. P. Rowell, 1903, p. 25.
47   Ibid.
48   In 1853, fares (via the Peninsular & Oriental Steamship Co.) from London to Sydney were £84 6s (first class) and £42 12s 6d (second class); including wine, etc., £106 and £63. A limited number of third-class fares were also available at 26 guineas. In 1893, *Cook's Australasian Travellers' Gazette and Tourist Advertiser* lists the following fares from Sydney to London: £70 (first class) and £37 (second class); return £105 (first class) and £65 (second class). In 1903, London to Sydney (Freemantle, Adelaide, and Melbourne) fares were £66–77 (first class, single berth, exclusive of wine, etc.), and £38–44 (second class, single berth, exclusive of wine, etc.); with child (3–12 yr) fares at half price. Through fares to New Zealand were £71–80 (first class) and £43–46 (second class); via Brindisi: £11 15s extra (first class); and to Brisbane: £1 and £2 extra (first class). In 1913, fares from London to Sydney (first class, single berth, exclusive of wines, etc.) were £60–70. Prices increased in the First World War: in 1917, the P. & O. steamers left London every 2 weeks for Sydney—touching at Gibraltar, Marseilles, Port Said, Aden, and Colombo en route—for £76–88 (first class) and £48–52 (second class). See *The American and European Railway and Steamship Guide*, New York: J. Disturnell, 1853, p. 204; *Cook's Australasian Travellers' Gazette and Tourist Advertiser*, London: Thomas Cook, 1892, p. 17; *Bradshaw's Through Routes to the Capitals of the World and Overland Guide to India, Persia, and the Far East*, London: Henry Blacklock, 1903, p. 339; Hubert Bancroft, *The New Pacific*, New York: Bancroft, 1914, p. 331; and *Australia To-day*, Sydney: United Commercial Travellers' Association of Australia, 1917, p. 32.

49 "Cook's, Clark's, etc. Travel Adverts, *Harper's Magazine Advertiser*," back matter, *Harper's Magazine* 121 (August 1910), New York and London: Harper, p. 15.

50 "Oceanic Steamship Co.," advertisement, *Scribner's Magazine* Vol. 47, No. 2 (February 1910), p. 58.

51 "Hamburg-American Line," advertisement, *Scribner's Magazine* Vol. 47, No. 2 (February 1910), p. 58.

52 "Travelling Companion," advertisement, *Scribner's Magazine* Vol. 47, No. 2 (February 1910), p. 58.

53 T. Philip Terry, *Terry's Mexico: Handbook for Travellers*, Sonora, CA: Sonora News Company, 1909.

54 "Terry's Mexico," advertisement, *Scribner's Magazine* Vol. 47, No. 2 (February 1910), p. 59.

55 "Hamburg-American Line," advertisement, *Scribner's*, p. 63.

56 R.D. Mullen, "From Standard Magazines to Pulps and Big Slicks: A Note on the History of US General and Fiction Magazines," *Science Fiction Studies* Vol. 22, No. 1 (March 1995), p. 146.

57 Mike Ashley, *The Age of the Storytellers: British Popular Fiction Magazines 1880–1950*, London: British Library, p. 197–98.

58 Mullen, p. 146.

59 See, for example, "Egypt and How To See It," advertisement, *The English Review* Vol. I, No. 4 (March 1909), p. iii. This ad, which appears in the same issue as Wells's "Book the Third, Chapter the Fourth: How I Stole the Heaps of Quap from Mordet Island," suggests that, "It is as well to secure a passage early, as, especially in the late autumn, the boats may be crowded."

60 See, for example, "Where Are You Going This Summer?" advertisement for *Munsey's* "Special Summer Resort Number," in *All-Story Weekly* Vol. XLV, No. 4 (June 5, 1915), p. iii.

61 Mullen, p. 144.

62 "From Darkest Africa, *The Railroad Man's Magazine—Advertising Section*," back matter, *The Railroad Man's Magazine* Vol. XIV, No. 4 (May 1911), p. 18.

63 Ibid.

64 In 1911, these six Munsey magazines claimed an aggregate circulation of 1,476,000 issues per month. Circulation claims for individual titles are listed in *N.W. Ayer & Son's American Newspaper Annual and Directory*, 1911, Vol. 2. Philadelphia, PA: N.W. Ayer, 1911 as: Munsey's 500,000; Argosy 450,000; All-Story 250,000; Scrap-Book 100,000; Railroad Man's 150,000 (from figures released in 1913); and Cavalier 26,000 (from figures released in 1912).

65 "Vacation Thoughts on Heating, *The Railroad Man's Magazine—Advertising Section*," back matter, p. 1.

66 "Oceanic Steamship Co.," advertisement, *Scribner's*, p. 58.

67 "Terry's Mexico," advertisement, *Scribner's*, p. 59.

68 See Ann C. Colley, *Victorians in the Mountains: Sinking the Sublime*, Farnham, UK: Ashgate, 2010.

69 Conrad, "Travel," *Last Essays*, pp. 124–25.

70 Ibid.

71 Bergonzi argues: "It is hardly possible that Conrad should have remained unaware of [Wells's] caricature, which is not merely ludicrous but malicious (the captain is cowardly and financially corrupt)." Bergonzi adds that, "given his notorious sensitivity, it is certain that [Conrad] would have been outraged by it" (*The Turn of a Century*, p. 98).

72 Conrad, "Travel," *Last Essays*, pp. 124–25.

73 This was the case on July 1, 1891, when the Act first came into effect.
74 James L. West, "The Chace Act and Anglo-American Relations," *Studies in Bibliography* 45 (1992), p. 306.
75 *Hazell's Annual for 1910*, Ed. Hammond Hall, London: Hazell, Watson, & Viney, 1910, p. 435.
76 For details of Sax Rohmer's transatlantic serializations in *Collier's Weekly* and *The Story-Teller* from 1912 to 1917, see Lawrence Knapp and R.E. Briney's excellent bibliographical resource, The Page of Fu Manchu, which is located online at http://njedge.net/~knapp/FuFrames.htm (accessed July 5, 2015).
77 Data are derived from The FictionMags Index, my own collection of 500+ periodicals, and Mike Ashley's *The Age of the Storytellers*.
78 See Shafquat Towheed, "Geneva vs. St. Petersburg: Two Concepts of Literary Property and the Material Lives of Books in 'Under Western Eyes,'" *Book History* 10 (2007), pp. 169–91.
79 Anonymous, "Literary Affairs in London," *The Dial* Vol. 61, No. 726 (October 5, 1915), p. 251.
80 Research for sections of this chapter used Juxta v1.7, an open-source collation/comparison program developed by Applied Research in Patacriticism (University of Virginia) and supported by NINES (Networked Infrastructure for 19th-Century Electronic Scholarship). Site for download was last accessed June 5, 2016, at www.juxtasoftware.org/.
81 *The Popular* claimed the title "The Biggest Magazine in the World" by printing on its February 1904 cover, "194 Pages Adventure Fiction." The magazine has in fact 192 pulp-paper pages in twelve 16-page signatures, and two slick-paper pages; that is, "the first leaf of the rear slick-paper section is used for text rather than advertising." For more on the competition between early U.S. pulp magazines for "Largest Magazine in the World" (1903–14), see Mullen, pp. 149–50.
82 According to Sam Moskowitz: "Before [*Ayesha*] began, the magazine had little more than 70,000 circulation. By its conclusion, it was well on its way to the quarter-million mark" (Moskowitz, *Under the Moons of Mars: A History and Anthology of "The Scientific Romance" in the Munsey Magazines, 1912–1920*, New York: Holt, Rinehart, 1970, p. 311).
83 "Ormond Gerald Smith, Class of 1883," *Records of the Class, 1883–1908*. Harvard College, 1908, p. 132.
84 Power O'Malley (1877–1946) was an accomplished Irish-American painter, graphic artist, and illustrator of books and magazine covers for *Harper's Monthly*, *Pearson's* (US), Street & Smith Corp., *Puck*, *Literary Digest*, and *Life*.
85 1 guinea is equivalent to 21 shillings, or £1.05. Professional fees, livestock, and luxury items were often quoted in guineas before the decimalization of the British currency system in 1971. Withdrawn from circulation in 1816 by the British Crown in an attempt to restabilize Great Britain's economy after the French Revolutionary Wars, the guinea carried aristocratic overtones. Old-established magazines such as *Blackwood's* set annual subscriptions at 30 shillings.
86 According to the publishing industry's standards of the day, *The Popular Magazine* reached 900,000–1,500,000 readers each month, determined by monthly circulation (300,000) × 3–5 = 900,000–1,500,000 (projected readership).
87 For comparison, I have included the total number of parts; total, mean, and median page counts of representative serializations published in *The Popular Magazine* from 1905 to 1909, alongside the same statistics for *Tono-Bungay* in both *The Popular* and *The English Review*: Rider Haggard, *Ayesha* (PM;

1905): 8 parts (12–36 pp.); mean: 19; median: 17. Wells, *Tono-Bungay* (PM; 1908–9): 5 parts (14–32 pp.); mean: 22; median: 20. Wells, *Tono-Bungay* (ER; 1908–9): 4 parts (56–92 pp.); mean: 79; median: 82. Anna Katharine Green, *The House of the Whispering Pines* (PM; 1909): 5 parts (18–37 pp.); mean: 26; median: 23.

88 For reference, I have included the issue date; TOC position; starting page number; total page count; and total word count for each of the five installments of *Tono-Bungay* in *The Popular Magazine*: September 1908; 3/12; starts on p. 71; 32 pp.; 22,240; October 1908; 5/12; starts on p. 97; 27 pp.; 18,765; November 1908; 3/12; starts on p. 83; 20 pp.; 13,900; December 1908; 6/12; starts on p.125; 15 pp.; 10,422; and January 1909; 12/12; starts on p. 210; 14 pp.; 9,730.

89 For reference, I have included the issue date; TOC position; starting page number; total page count; and total word count for each of the four installments of *Tono-Bungay* in *The English Review*: December 1908; 7/16; starts on p. 81; 71 pp.; 31,950; January 1909; 8/20; starts on p. 261; 56 pp.; 25,200; February 1909; 11/18; starts on p. 466; 97 pp.; 43,650; March 1909; 9/13; starts on p. 700; 92 pp.; 41,383.

90 They include Craig Middleton, *Stocky Brown* (a complete novel); Ralph D. Paine, "A Case of Professionalism" (short story); Louis Joseph Vance, "Shadow Reef" (two-part story); Herbert Quick, "The Stalking of Paugijk" (short story); F. Goron, "The Rue Montera Mystery" (short story); H. G. Wells, *Tono-Bungay* (serial); A.M. Chisholm, *The Come-On* (novelette); B.M. Bower, *Jack Bellamy, Lawbreaker* (series); J. Kenilworth Egerton, *The Mafia and the Contessa* (two-part story); Author of "The Black Barque," "A Keg of Ambergris" (short story); Frederick Niven, *Lost Cabin Mine* (serial story); and Walter Hackett, "Mr. Garfield's Matrimonial Experiment" (short story).

91 "What Influenced the N.K. Fairbank Company," Street & Smith advert, *Life* 51 (March 19, 1908), front pps.

92 For national advertising rates, "The Popular Trio" included *The Popular Magazine*, Street & Smith's flagship title, and companion titles *Ainslee's* (1897) and *Smith's Magazine* (1905).

93 This episode appears in *The English Review*'s serialization as "The Second of My Launch Into the World and the Last I Saw of Bladesover," Book the First: Chapter the Second, Parts 1–4, *Tono-Bungay*, *The English Review* (December 1908), pp. 110–19.

94 Wells, "Book the Third, Chapter the Fourth: How I Stole the Heaps of Quap from Mordet Island," pp. 726–27. It is also an official PO. See the "List of Provincial Offices in the United Kingdom," *Post Office Guide*, Great Britain, 200 (April 1–June 30, 1906), London: Wyman & Sons Printers, 1906, p. 335.

95 Wells, "Chapter IX: How I Stole the Heaps of Quap from Mordet Island," p. 129.

96 Wells, "Book the Third, Chapter the Fourth: How I Stole the Heaps of Quap from Mordet Island," pp. 727–28.

97 It is clear from Maclean's edits that his motives were primarily to quicken the novel's narrative pace. Always with an eye toward a broad audience and pass-along readership, Maclean's editorials on writing, reading, and authorship show a predilection for good stories and especially fast-paced adventure fiction. The majority of the magazine's content consisted of it. According to MacLean: "[F]or our part we choose the chronicles of these restless ones whose joy is in accomplishment. Much of it is not literature. Little of it is great literature. It comes so straight and fresh from the loom of life that it may well be imperfect in spots and lacking in that finish which a more meticulous taste may provide.

But for all that . . . it is the primal stuff out of which all great art and all great literature is made" (*Charles Agnew Maclean: Editor of the Popular Magazine, 1904–1928*, New York: Bartlett Orr Press, 1928, p. 12).

98   Wells, "Chapter IX: How I Stole the Heaps of Quap from Mordet Island," p. 138.

99   Ibid., "Book the Third, Chapter the Fourth: How I Stole the Heaps of Quap from Mordet Island," pp. 741–42.

100   Wells's anti-imperialism is only one part of that larger ideological apparatus that contains the story.

101   *Tono-Bungay* debuted on page 71 of the September 1908 issue, positioned third of twelve on the table of contents; later installments, including the installments for December and January, are less prominently positioned; by the end of its 5-month run, the novel dropped to final position, where it ended on page 210, positioned 12th of 12.

102   Mike Ashley, "Blue Book—The Slick in Pulp Clothing," *Pulp Vault* No. 14. Barrington Hills, IL: Tattered Pages Press, 2011, pp. 210–53; p. 212.

103   Wells, "Chapter IX: How I Stole the Heaps of Quap from Mordet Island," p. 133.

104   Edward Mendelson, "Introduction," *Tono-Bungay*. H.G. Wells (1909). London: Penguin, 2005, pp. xiii–xxviii; p. xviii.

105   Ibid., p. xvii.

106   Wells, "Book the Third, Chapter the Fourth: How I Stole the Heaps of Quap from Mordet Island," p. 733.

107   *Tono-Bungay* (PM; 1908–9), Parts 1–5, word count per part: Part 1 (September): 32 pp., 22,240 words; Part 2 (October): 27 pp., 18,765 words; Part 3 (November): 20 pp., 13,900 words; Part 4 (December): 15 pp., 10,422 words; Part 5 (January): 14 pp., 9,730 words.

108   As his earlier works—*The Time Machine* (1895), *The Island of Dr. Moreau* (1896), *The Invisible Man* (1897), and *The War of the Worlds* (1897)—attest, Wells's fiction was firmly rooted in the author's ambivalent attitudes toward humanity. Victorian crusader turned scientific romancer, for essentially the same reasons.

109   The year 1886 was the year of the International Copyright Convention at Berne, and the launch of Macmillan's successful Colonial Library series. See Chapter 1, "An Imperial History of Late Nineteenth-Century Periodical Expansion."

110   "From Darkest Africa, *The Railroad Man's Magazine—Advertising Section*," back matter, p. 18.

111   Ruth Hoberman, *Museum Trouble: Edwardian Fiction and the Emergence of Modernism*, Charlottesville, VA: University of Virginia Press, 2011, p. 21.

112   Wells, "Chapter IX: How I Stole the Heaps of Quap from Mordet Island," pp. 125–39, and "Book the Third, Chapter the Fourth: How I Stole the Heaps of Quap from Mordet Island," pp. 723–49.

113   See, for example, Ray, "Conrad, Wells, and 'The Secret Agent,'" pp. 560–73.

114   Previous scholars have fixated on geographical and biographical clues that would identify the "real" location of the setting for Conrad's "imaginary" Patusan. But, it is more important where Patusan isn't—namely, within the reach of intrusive journalistic "gossip"—than where it is on the globe. I want to thank Stephen Donovan for crystallizing this point for me in the early stages of writing this chapter.

115   Conrad, "Lord Jim: A Sketch," *Blackwood's Magazine* 166–68 (October 1899–November 1900).

116   Wells, "Chapter IX: How I Stole the Heaps of Quap from Mordet Island," pp. 133–34; "Book the Third, Chapter the Fourth: How I Stole the Heaps of Quap from Mordet Island," p. 733.

117 Conrad, *Lord Jim*, p. 168.
118 Wells, "Chapter IX: How I Stole the Heaps of Quap from Mordet Island," p. 136; "Book the Third, Chapter the Fourth: How I Stole the Heaps of Quap from Mordet Island," p. 738.
119 Ibid., pp. 128, 723.
120 Ibid., *The Popular Magazine* Vol. 12, No. 3 (January 1909), pp. 210–24, 749.
121 Conrad, *Lord Jim*, p. 168.
122 Wells, *The Popular Magazine* Vol. 12, No. 3 (January 1909), pp. 210–24; "Book the Third, Chapter the Fourth: How I Stole the Heaps of Quap from Mordet Island," p. 747.
123 Ibid.
124 The fictional events in *Lord Jim* are set approximately from 1886 to 1889.
125 Wells, *The Popular Magazine* Vol. 12, No. 3 (January 1909), pp. 210–24; "Book the Fourth, Chapter the First: The Stick of the Rocket," p. 747.
126 Ibid., pp. 210–24, 765.
127 Ibid.
128 Ibid., pp. 210–24, 747.
129 Ibid., pp. 210–24, 765.
130 This scene prefigures a famous event from July 1910, when Dr. Harvey Crippen, a London patent medicine man, and Ethel Le Neve attempted to escape to Canada after murdering Crippen's wife. Their capture by wireless became international news. With the aid of the new technology, the authorities of Scotland Yard arrested the couple on board the SS Montrose the moment it entered the St. Lawrence River, between Ontario and New York. See Julie English Early, "Technology, Modernity, and 'The Little Man': Crippen's Capture by Wireless," *Victorian Studies* Vol. 39, No. 3 (Spring 1996), pp. 309–37.
131 The novel's Mordet Island episode, a parody of adventure romances such as *Lord Jim*, is of course centrally concerned with the plunder of a mysterious ingredient to forestall the demise of a financial empire, an empire predicated on the marketing of a wildly popular but fraudulent patent medicine, Tono-Bungay: the title of the novel.
132 Wells, "Book the Third, Chapter the Fourth: How I Stole the Heaps of Quap from Mordet Island," p. 741.
133 See, for example, George W. Stocking, Jr., *Victorian Anthropology*, New York: Simon & Schuster, 1991.
134 H.A. Miers, *Geological Magazine*, New Series, II, No. X (October 1905), pp. 473–78.
135 Bergonzi, *The Turn of a Century*, p. 98.
136 Ray, "Conrad, Wells, and 'The Secret Agent,'" pp. 560–73.
137 Wollaeger, *Modernism, Media and Propaganda*, p. 34.
138 "Pleasure Pirate Pilgrimages," advertisement, *Time* magazine Vol. 7, No. 26 (June 28, 1926), p. 22.
139 Ibid.
140 "Around the World," advertisement, *Time Magazine* Vol. 7, No. 26 (June 28, 1926), p. 3.
141 Ibid.
142 "Pleasure Pirate Pilgrimages," advertisement, *Time*, p. 22.
143 In the 1920s, famous ads of the "Round-the-World Society" featured color illustrations and photographs of exotic places around the world, promoting "A Unique Plan that Brings You the Thrills, Adventure and Romance of Travel Without Its Discomforts or Expense in Time and Money." The ads offered "A Six Months' Trip Around the World—*for less than 5 cents a day!*"

asking: "If your dreams came true tonight; if you could forget work, pack your grips and start on a trip around the world; where would you go? To the usual places where everybody goes on tame, staid, 'personally conducted tours'? Or would you visit strange lands; the countries where travelers are seldom seen; the mysterious cities of inner Asia; every place off the beaten track of tourists!" ("Around the World," ad, *Time*, p. 3).

144   Wells, "Book the Third, Chapter the Fourth: How I Stole the Heaps of Quap from Mordet Island," p. 741.

4 Spectacular Texts

Conan Doyle's Essays on Photography and *The Lost World* (1912)

On the afternoon of Friday June 2, 1922, Conan Doyle took the stage before a crowded audience of the American Club of Magicians at the McAlpin Hotel on Herald Square, corner of Broadway and 34th Street, in New York City. The 63-year-old, world-famous spiritualist, historian, and author of the Sherlock Holmes stories announced that he would present them with a "strange exhibition." Doyle carefully explained to the expectant crowd:

> These pictures are not occult, but . . . psychic because everything that emanates from the human spirit or human brain is psychic. It is not supernatural; nothing is. It is preternatural in the sense that it is not known to our ordinary senses. It is the effect of . . . joining . . . imagination, and . . . some power of materialization. The imagination . . . comes from me—the materializing power from elsewhere.[1]

Following a moment of calculated suspense, the lights of the auditorium were turned down, and Doyle's audience was amazed to see actual film footage of dinosaurs. Reportedly, one skeptical member of the American press was even persuaded by these "extraordinarily life-like" creatures pictured on the projector screen. The following morning, *The New York Times* ran an intriguing front-page headline that was partially printed in bold, block capital letters. The headline read: "DINOSAURS CAVORT ON FILM FOR DOYLE: Spiritist Mystifies World-Famed Magicians With Pictures of Prehistoric Beasts: KEEPS ORIGIN A SECRET . . ." According to this article's eye-witness reporter, Doyle's "Monsters of Other Ages Shown, Some Fighting, Some at Play, in Their Native Jungles" were seemingly "genuine." They may also have been intended "as a joke." Unable to decide whether "the sober-faced Englishman was making merry with them" or "lifting the veil" on some previously undiscovered world in the ether, the reporter explained:

> Whether these pictures were intended by the famous author as a joke on the magicians or genuine pictures, like his photographs of fairies, was not revealed. . . . His monsters of the ancient world, or of the new

world which he has discovered in the ether, were *extraordinarily lifelike.* If fakes, they were masterpieces.[2]

Doyle revealed later that evening[3]—in a public letter sent to Harry Houdini and members of the American press—that his amazingly life-like pictures were in fact test sequences from a not-yet-released film adaptation of *The Lost World* (1912).[4] Directed by Harry O. Hoyt,[5] the film version from 1925 featured the pioneering stop–motion and model animation work of Willis O'Brien.[6]

It was the cutting edge of cinema technology in 1922, employing painstakingly crafted miniature clay and wire models designed to merge with live-action footage—scenes featuring Hollywood actors Bessie Love and Wallace Beery—in order to create the fantastic illusion of "DINOSAURS CAVORT[ING]."[7] These film stills were some of the earliest examples of stop–motion animation to appear in cinematic history, and the most sophisticated examples to date. As *The New York Times* reporter had observed, these "fakes" were certainly "masterpieces."[8] Doyle had been forwarded the test footage for his approval by the studio only days before.

Although seemingly an extra-literary episode in the author's high-profile public career,[9] this choreographed event from June 1922 foregrounds the important kinds of relationship that existed, commercially and professionally, between popular print publishing and complementary forms of new mediation on which publishers drew in the early decades of the twentieth century. Taking this event as its starting point, this chapter examines Doyle's expert command of modern publicity methods, knowledge of innovative film and photography techniques, and programmatic use of the "spectacular texts" of modern romance for the re-enchantment of modernity's "Society of the Spectacle."[10] Through that circuit, I show how Doyle mobilized celebrity, new media, and the unstable representation of photographic evidence in the popular illustrated monthlies in order to extend the diminishing horizons of adventure in the modern world. This furthered the author's lifetime campaign against scientific materialism. As John M. Lynch has noted:

> Like many in the early twentieth century, Doyle saw a world destroyed not only by human violence but also by scientific materialism. The success of science . . . appeared to have stripped nature of its magic [and it had] left traditional religion reeling. . . . —spiritualism was advocated by many who, like Doyle, sought . . . a re-enchantment with nature.[11]

In my second chapter, I argued that Joseph Conrad's *Lord Jim* (1900)[12] had advanced a similar thesis on the cusp of the new century. The trope was expressed in terms of an expansion of the new media, high-speed transportation, and instant communication systems, and held that such systems threatened to erase the structural divisions separating imperial

Figure 4.1 Promotional Poster and Four Film Stills from *The Lost World*
(First National Pictures, 1925).

modernity from its vanishing global frontiers. Conrad's response in *Lord Jim* was a rejection of this encroachment of grid-like global modernity, which inspired an abrupt decision to extend *Lord Jim*'s narrative, and develop the full account of Jim's desperate flight into a pre-modern, pre-industrial Patusan. This "advocacy of the past" was a "peculiarly twentieth-century form of reaction"[13] and also a sign of the novel's modernity. H.G. Wells's *Tono-Bungay* (1909)[14] was then situated within the same set of concerns, but here I argued that Wells's own Conradian adventure episode,[15] "How I Stole the Heaps of Quap from Mordet Island,"[16] was a riposte to literary debates that took place in *Blackwood's Magazine* at the turn of the twentieth century: it puts an absurdist spin on *Lord Jim*'s themes of romantic flight and renewal. Although published just a decade later, this novel illustrates a rapid decline in adventure fiction's cultural cachet, even at the time its market share was steadily increasing.[17] Between 1899 and 1909—a decade separating Conrad's nostalgia for unexplored places and Wells's smug dismissal of the Conradian romance as *"Boy's Own Paper* stuff"[18]—modern attitudes toward adventure in the real world had become increasingly skeptical, ironic, and even hostile. According to Wells's protagonist, a "general discomfort and humiliating self-revelation are the master values of these memories."[19]

This chapter revisits the same concerns, but examines them through an ironic perspective, which is offered by Doyle's spectacular performance in New York in June 1922. For Doyle, new media, film, and the popular illustrated press could also be used to reinstate the visual evidence of lost frontiers and geographical mysteries. In *Tono-Bungay*, George Ponderevo appropriates as a signifier of authenticity the familiar discourse of modern scientific materialism, suggesting that readers "find the full particulars . . . of all this in the *Geological Magazine* for October, 1905."[20] A cursory examination of the issue recovers nothing of relevance and exposes the author's gag. In similar fashion, Doyle's tongue-in-cheek performance at the McAlpin Hotel in 1922 appropriates film and photography's claims to indexical proof and documentary evidence. As this chapter will show, however, Doyle's creative solution to the aesthetic limitations imposed by the spread of global modernity involved, not only the very latest Hollywood film technologies, but also the expanding volumes of popular, illustrated media: slick-paper magazines, posters, and glossy advertisements of modern society. Doyle's more imaginative solution to the same aesthetic preoccupations that troubled Wells's notion of modern adventure exploited diminishing possibilities for adventure at the turn of the century, which had underwritten Conrad's creation of a pre-modern, pre-industrial Patusan. As a romance of lost geographical survival that extended adventure's imagined horizons into the modern world, Patusan joined a long literary tradition of adventure romances mocked by Wells as a fraudulent pose. Drawing on the rhetoric of modern advertising, newsprint, and patent medicines, Wells also situated his critique against the multicolored backdrop of new media, with its brighter, more colorful, and more exotic representation of modern tourism. Against this same backdrop, however, Doyle postulates new imaginary avenues for escape and transgression in the modern world through an expert manipulation of film, photography, new typographies, and half-tone reproduction processes in the popular illustrated press.

In 1923, Conrad noted the confluence between romance's decline in the modern world and a burgeoning field of photographs and other mass-produced, publicly disseminated visual media. He wrote:

> The Nigeria of Barth ... Denham ... Clapperton ... Mungo Park, of other infinitely curious and profoundly inspired men, will be bristling with police posts, colleges, tramway poles, and all those improving things ... the great cloud of fatuous daily photographs and even more fatuous descriptive chatter, under whose shadow no traveler could live, will brood over those seldom-visited places of the world that, despoiled of their old black soul of mystery, have not yet acquired its substitute, which will be marvelously piebald when it comes.[21]

Conrad was referring to the jungles of the Belgian Congo, but he would have sympathized with John Buchan's attitudes toward the arrival of explorers in Lhasa, Tibet, high up in the heart of the Himalayas, nearly 4,800 miles away on the other side of the world, in 1905. Regarding this event, and its effects on romance, Buchan remarked: "The shrinkage of the world goes on so fast, our horizon grows so painfully clear, that the old untiring wonder which cast its glamour over the ways of our predecessors is vanishing from the lives of their descendants."[22]

This chapter shows, however, that, although photography's representation of faraway places, published in the pages of popular illustrated magazines, destroyed much of the modern world's former sense of mystery, romance, and glamour,[23] the aura that surrounded this technology was also a source of new possibilities. Techniques and mechanics associated with photography could unlock powerful new imaginary avenues for extending adventure into the modern world.

This chapter is divided into two parts. Part I retraces the author's lifelong fascination with amateur photography, early participation in the British photographic "outing," and knowledge of innovative photography manipulation. Part II examines the first serialization of Doyle's *The Lost World* (1912), which appeared in *The Strand Magazine* from April to November 1912. This first appearance of *The Lost World*, "especially when it has the trimmings of faked photos, maps, and plans,"[24] demonstrates how Doyle appropriated photography and its illustrated reproduction in a popular British monthly magazine as both a seemingly objective form of proof and documentary evidence, and an ironic hoax; however, his experience with photography in the 30 years leading up to the performance presents the more intriguing motive, or reasoning, for it.

For Doyle, photographs could reinstate the visual evidence of lost geo-graphical frontiers beyond civilization, as the technology positioned itself already at the edge of the unknown. In the photographic process, modernity was not a threat, but rather an opportunity to reveal hidden avenues and unlock other worlds. This chapter emphasizes that paper, printer's ink, and the new media were all complementary forms of a "new mass entertainment culture."[25] The performance of *The Lost World* in the pages of *The Strand Magazine* in 1912 would not have worked without the novel's serialization, and illustration, alongside "indexical idioms of scientific objectivity."[26] Evidence and proof of discovering lost worlds, "important for establishing the imaginary world as a virtual space consistent in all its details,"[27] required the glossy, slick paper of an illustrated monthly such as *The Strand Magazine,* or the fine-toned book-quality paper of an illustrated weekly paper such as *The Graphic.*[28]

These would reproduce the faked photographs, maps, charts, and plans in enough fine detail for the performance to be effective.

In Doyle's screen-test sequences from *The Lost World,* hand-painted miniature dinosaur models were photographed one frame at a time and repositioned between each exposure. When the processed film was projected

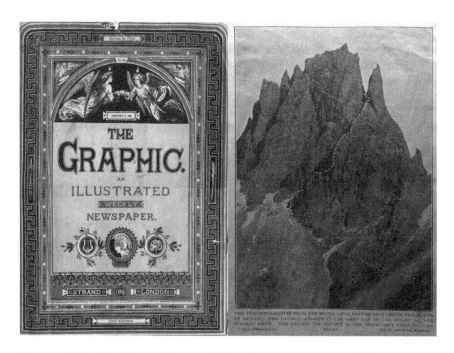

Figure 4.2 The Graphic: An Illustrated Weekly Paper (January 8, 1887) and
"The Funffingerspitze from the South," from a Photograph by
George P. Abraham, "A Night Adventure on the Funffingerspitze,"
The Strand Magazine (October 1912), p. 256.

in sequence, the inanimate models appeared to move as though alive. In common with the trick cinematography of Georges Méliès from the turn of the century, these scenes sharpen a contrast between the most basic illusions of cinema and the more prosaic technical realities behind them. They highlight the fact that moving pictures do not really move. They are composed rather of 16–24 individual frames per second. Fed rapidly across the interior shutter of an electrical projector, however, 100,000 transparent photographs give the powerful appearance of movement. These apparently continuous flows of sequential photographs fool the optical senses and test the credulity of unsuspecting audiences. Thus, threatening moon-men disappear amid great puffs of smoke,[29] and dinosaurs seemingly "cavort" across the screen. The medium is less spectacular, but the effect is equally illusory, with the detailed reproduction of photographs in glossy, slick-paper magazines at the turn of the century.

Michael Saler observes that, "[w]riters of the New Romance were assisted in their efforts at fantastic realism by new printing technologies of the 1880s, such as half-tone lithography."[30] According to Neil Harris, "with [half-tone], a photomechanical reproduction of a photochemical image, *the illusion of seeing an actual scene*, or receiving an objective record of such a scene, was *immeasurably enhanced*."[31] It made the more accurate reproduction of photographic detail, intricately illustrated with fine gradations of shadow and tone, possible. Half-tone processes also seemed more objective than earlier forms of printing, which had used woodcuts or metal plates, as hand-driven etching had invariably left traces of individual artists' and engravers' idiosyncratic styles. The more mechanical processes of the new print technologies—which were indicative of changes taking place across the modern print publishing industry as a whole—also provided the necessary "illusion of objectivity" to the "spectacular texts" of the New Romance. According to Saler, they "added to the rational glamour [readers] were seeking." He adds:

> The illusion of objectivity was also induced [by] other paratextual elements traditionally associated with scholarship, such as footnotes, glossaries, and appendices. [T]he New Romance ... combined these diverse elements ... [and through them presented] empirically detailed imaginary worlds.[32]

But, Doyle's performance that afternoon was more than a clever hoax. His preoccupation with psychic phenomena and "the preternatural" world had similarly informed public campaigns in support of spirit photography, the Cottingley fairy photographs, and other forms of modern photographic manipulation. Parceled together, these events describe a sophisticated and calculated operation. Doyle's mobilization of celebrity, new media, and photography in order to cast doubt on science and materialism was a program. For nearly half a century, Doyle had been fascinated with the potential of photographic technology to reveal and document new worlds. By 1922, his appropriation of photography's claims to objective proof and documentary evidence, to unlock new avenues for the imagination, had already developed a long and dynamic genealogy.

Part I: Essays on Photography

Before Professor Challenger, before Holmes and Dr. Watson, even before J. Habakuk Jephson,[33] there was the nameless narrator of 13 semi-autobiographical, first-person essays by Dr. A. Conan Doyle, M.B., for *The British Journal of Photography*, from 1881 to 1885. The author had submitted his first article, "After Cormorants with a Camera" (1881),[34] at the behest of a family friend, William Burton.[35] The article proved auspicious. The editor of *Anthony's Photographic Bulletin* in New York reprinted it,[36] and "After Cormorants with a Camera" became Doyle's first magazine publication in the United States. When reprinted, it was juxtaposed with the American editor's note that British photography journals have "well-written and entertaining descriptions of what, in their peculiar way, they call *outings*." The editor added, "[W]e do not see why some of our serious amateurs do not occasionally treat themselves to an outing."[37] This note provides one of the earliest indications of the convergence of interests— photography, popular forms of adventure,[38] and a pattern of publication in magazines—that would continue to dominate Doyle's developing literary and artistic imagination well into the twentieth century.

The British photographic "outing" entailed a group of amateur photographers striking out from the suburbs or city into the surrounding countryside with cameras, tripods, chemicals, and other necessary equipment. These short holidays, usually scheduled for the weekends, became a popular pastime in the 1880s and 1890s. They dated back to the earliest days of portable cameras in England and on the Continent, and quickly spread to the United States as well.[39] Doyle's first essay, "After Cormorants with a Camera," describes one of these outings.

The essay was written for a new series in *The British Journal of Photography*, "Where to Go with the Camera," launched by its editor in 1880. It describes an outing taken by the narrator and his two memorable companions in summer, featuring a walking tour on the Isle of May, just off the eastern coast of Scotland. Curiously anticipating the opening scene of Erskine Childers's *The Riddle of the Sands* (1903),[40] the essay begins:

> It was about the end of July that my old friend "Chawles" . . . endeav-
> ouring to vary the humdrum monotony . . . disclosed his latest
> project[:] "The Isle of May, my boy! . . . None of your tame rabbits and
> semi-civilised pheasants over there; but fine, old, pre-Adamite
> cormorants. . . . That's where a fellow can knock the cobwebs out of
> him . . .!" . . . The University session was over, my friends out of town,

Princes-street a howling wilderness, and I in need of a change. The Isle of May seemed to offer "fresh fields and pastures new" both for myself and to my camera.[41]

With his two companions—"Chawles," described as being "unshackled by a profession, and a keen shot," and the Doctor, whose "one fault of hatching vile puns and incubating over-abstruse riddles was rather agreeable"—the narrator strikes out on a 4-day journey with his camera, a "folding, bellows-body, half-plate camera, by Meagher, with half-a-dozen double backs."[42] The article exhorts its readers to venture out into the open air, into the countryside or further afield, and take their cameras and dry plates with them.[43] Doyle commanded an impressive knowledge of the equipment, techniques, and skills required in outdoor amateur photography. This becomes apparent through detailed descriptions at the essay's outset, such as when the narrator describes his own inventions:

> I had two stands—one a short ash tripod, the other an invention of my own, which I have found of great service in working the moorlands of Scotland ... advantages ... for this simple arrangement are not only its lightness (a consideration which will have weight with every practical worker in the open air) but also ... cheapness. ... I selected from among my lenses a single achromatic for ordinary use, and a rapid rectilinear with drop shutter for instantaneous work. The plates were of my own manufacture ... and, being exquisitely sensitive, they enabled me to get many instantaneous exposures.[44]

Doyle's technical knowledge is complemented by an artist's eye for natural detail and landscape. On the group's first morning out with the camera, for example, the unnamed narrator of the essay remarks on how the day's:

> weather was of that clear, breezy character which warms the heart of a photographer. Our light craft danced like a cork upon a heavy swell setting up channel from the North Sea ... [and we] ... proceeded to haul down the sheet as we glided into the little rocky cove which served as a harbor to the Isle of May.[45]

When they "commence operations,"[46] however, photographs described by the essay become an opportunity for displaying, not only the narrator's technical skills, but also a skillful manipulation and objectification of the surrounding landscape. Subjected to the mechanical gaze of his camera, the cliffs are "got"[47] and beaches are "taken,"[48] such as when the narrator describes his first plate:

> It had been arranged that we were to commence operations upon the cliffs. As there are no inhabitants upon the island, except the keeps ...

we had only our own convenience to consult. Springing ashore we made our way up the rough pathway which leads past the lighthouse. It was here that I got my first plate, including the rocky cliff and the boat lying snugly moored among the rocks below.[49]

The narrator's second photograph is taken from the height of the cliffs, directly before returning to the southern side of the island. The narrator pauses to remark, "[A] beautiful spectacle met my eyes. Nine fine yachts . . . were rounding the point of the island, each under a cloud of canvas and lying well over, for the breeze was beginning to freshen."[50] Impressed by such a "spectacle," he describes nine yachts, "like some great flock of seabirds as they rose and fell on the crests of the waves."[51] But, alerted to his role as photographer—which also reminds him that his camera is the recording device, and that he is charged with documenting the exquisite views around him—the narrator abruptly shifts his focus and returns to narrating the technical requirements demanded of his recording device: "The appearance of these tempted me to bring out my own patent stand and fix to my camera the rapid lens and shutter. The light was exceedingly brilliant."[52] And the narrator continues:

> I reduced the aperture to about f 1/3. The distance of the nearest yacht was such that the lens being focussed for "the distance" did not require to be further adjusted. I took care that the iron spike was driven deep in the sand, so as to ensure steadiness. After once fixing the camera I did not use the focussing glass, but trusted to my eye to judge when the yacht would cross the axis of the lens.[53]

The narrator follows this with a lengthy disquisition on the comparative "advantage of having the aperture in the shutter several times the diameter of the lens in the direction in which the shutter moves."[54]

As Roger Lancelyn Green has observed, "After Cormorants with a Camera" reveals that the author, as early as 1881, "already had a firm grasp of the principles of photography and of the contents of recent numbers of the journal."[55] It is surprising that few of Doyle's own photographs survive, but the considerable degree of technical skill and talent on display in these early essays is evidence of a true aficionado. The article's appearance in *The British Journal of Photography*, published in two parts on October 14 and 21, 1881, also coincided with the author's departure for the African west coast. Doyle's second article for the journal was titled "On the Slave Coast with a Camera" (1882).[56] It would not only confirm the author's adroit sense of, and familiarity with, the various effects, advantages, and deficiencies of several different types of camera lens, but also draw the convergence of photography, forms of adventure, and Doyle's developing literary imagination into closer proximity with the site most commonly associated with the traditions and conditions of the late nineteenth-century adventure romances—Africa, with its "brilliant tropical sunlight." According to the narrator:

> The lenses which I took were the following: First, a wide-angle "landscape" lens, which I used whenever I could, always bearing in mind that this form is comparatively slow and the angle limited. I find that the so-called "single" lens gives, *coeteris paribus*, a more brilliant picture than is given by any other. Secondly, I took a "symmetrical," to be used where a large angle was desirable. Thirdly, a "rapid rectilinear" of long focus, which would come useful where instantaneous effects were needed.[57]

In the last article that Doyle ever wrote for *The British Journal of Photography*, "With a Camera on an African River" (1885),[58] his narrator registers a skillful aesthetic individualized to account for the peculiar conditions of photographing on the African coast, sacrificing a stricter clarity of image for the sake of a softer, more artistic effect:

> Opposite us in the town of Old Calabar, a confused assemblage of brown thatched native huts, and just along the water's edge a row of whitewashed factories in which the European agents do their business. Hills, all clad in feathery foliage, rise up behind the town. It is worth a plate now, for at this early hour there is some hope of a soft effect. A little later and the glaring sun will admit only those chalky and hard effects which mar so many tropical pictures.[59]

As these passages suggest, the most coveted photograph throughout Doyle's 13 essays is the perfect landscape shot. For Doyle, this is the holy grail of a particularly successful photographic outing. None of these essays focuses on the preeminent Victorian art of photographic portraiture,[60] which had enjoyed an "explosive popularity [after 1851] ... especially as manifested in the carte-de-visite."[61] The popularity of Victorian portraiture increased exponentially as advances in dry-plate processes, from the 1870s on, made the technology accessible to virtually anyone, despite social class.[62] Also absent—from the author who, in 1887, would "depict the squalor and anomie of modern urban existence"[63] as the necessary moral and social background to the world's most famous detective—are the crowded city streets and gritty urban vistas of photographers such as Thomas Annan, Willie Swift, or, across the English Channel, Eugène Atget.[64]

Camera equipment in tow, the wind at his back, and photographing just off the beaten path, Doyle's narrator seeks out "that delicious physical awakening that pulses through the nerve-sick townsman when city airs and bald routine are left behind him."[65] Doyle promotes the benefits of fresh air and healthy exercise, the broadening of a first-hand experience of the world and nature, and developing technical expertise. These essays portray Doyle's narrator less as an adventurer, however, than as a tourist on holiday. The destinations chosen are not always conducive to those adventures either. In "Easter Monday with the Camera" (1884),[66] for example, he remarks at one point: "Both views, to the north and to the south," would have made "splendid photographs, but we had already done them justice and were in quest of rarer game."[67] This quest for "rarer game" leads to an unexpected disappointment:

> [The] crowd was so dense ... photography was not only out of the question, but it was absolutely necessary for us to abandon our apparatus if we wished to see anything. . . . We elbowed our way through the crowd . . . there must have been more than a hundred thousand people on the hill.[68]

This experience reflects the growing popularity of Victorian amateur photography outings. By the end of the nineteenth century, advances in the gelatino-bromide dry-plate process and cheaper, lighter-weight portable cameras, such as the Eastman Kodak Co.'s "Brownie,"[69] led amateur photographers to abandon the cities and escape to the countryside at the weekend in growing numbers. In July 1871, as the pioneer of the gelatino-bromide process, Thomas Sutton was already offering these enthusiastic remarks to *The British Journal of Photography*:

> A tourist, employing [my] process, would have his bromide of silver emulsion ready ... in a semi-solid state. . . . [H]e would melt it by putting the bottle ... into boiling water; he would then coat his plates at night for the next day, and put them at once into the plate-box to get dry. . . . He would have no dangerous, explosive, strong-smelling, unhealthy collodion to carry about with him on his travels, and he might pack in a very small compass enough chemicals in a dry state to last him for a tour of the world. What a blessing it would be to be independent of collodion![70]

The independence and mobility Sutton celebrated in 1871 was increasingly available to growing numbers of wide-ranging, camera-toting world travelers as well. Decreasing the size, weight, and complexity of the portable camera gave droves of world-traveling amateur photographers a wider discretion for wandering farther afield, for longer periods of time, burdened by less baggage and equipment. Innovation followed innovation. When the George Eastman Co. introduced its light-weight film to replace the photographic dry plate, photographers no longer had the cumbersome boxes of heavy plates or toxic chemicals to transport. Eastman's new technology was introduced in London during the summer at the 1885 Inventions Exhibition. According to *The Times*, it was "a revolution in out-of-door photography . . . [and] near approach to complete triumph." Its August 11, 1885 report on the Exhibition continued:

> [The film] promises . . . the complete attainment of the long-sought-for desideratum in a flexible substance for the glass plate, which . . . has been indispensable to the best results in landscape photography. The weight and the risk of fracture when the route of the photographer lies through countries difficult in communications make the use of even dry plates in all out-of-the-way places an impediment with which no enterprising amateur is unfamiliar.[71]

Three years later, the Kodak camera[72] came pre-loaded with a full roll of film, with 100 exposures. Its advertising campaign invited amateurs to mail away their cameras when the roll was finished. Advertisements touted the slogan: "You Press the Button. We Do the Rest." With its original $25.00 sticker price, the Kodak No. 1 was not exactly the universal access to a vernacular photography that it claimed to be, but it offered a level of affordability and simplicity that was unprecedented for its time. Although not available to everyone, even the most unskilled novice on a travelling holiday could work it.

In his guidebook, *Photography Indoors and Out: A Book for Amateurs* (1894), Alexander Black declared amateur photography was the "most popular," "general," and "universal" pastime in Britain.[73] In an address to the UK Photographic Convention in 1898, M. John Stuart remarked: "[T]he amateur has become ubiquitous, there is scarcely a home now which does not harbor an amateur photographer."[74] In 1907, the editor of *The Amateur Photographer* claimed that amateur photography was "*the* popular hobby of the day."[75] Photographers at the turn of the century had access to an expanding world through transportation improvements, and the most out-of-the-way places now had the potential to be "got" and transformed into exquisite moments of panorama.

A worldwide industry developed around amateur photography at the turn of the century. It included networks of retailers and manufacturers of cameras, plates, canisters, carrying cases, developing agents, chemical processers, tripods, labels, lenses, brushes, guidebooks, and other equipment. Photography exhibitions, formal societies, and amateur camera clubs cropped up in towns and cities from Galesburg, IL, to Calcutta.[76] Ads promoted the photographic holiday, with appeals of clean air, vigorous exercise, and no prior skills needed. Speed and flexibility became catchwords: R. Kennett's "rapid pellicle plates" offered a "greater latitude of exposure . . . with their now universally acknowledged wonderful and unprecedented rapidity"[77]; the cover of *The Photographer's World* (1886) featured Morgan & Kidd's ad for a "Special Instantaneous" plate that was "Guaranteed to be the Quickest"[78]; the Stereoscopic Co. offered "Free Lessons in Photography"[79] in 1891; and Kodak featured its popular slogan:

"You Press the Button. We Do the Rest."[80] In an ad for Meagher's Improved Portable Camera in *The Year-Book of Photography* (1893), the caption "Light, Portable, and Rigid" is placed in large, bold capital type.[81] In *The Photographic Times-Bulletin* (January 1902), a Bausch & Lomb advert touts the Plastigmat f 6.8 "Perfect Photo Lens" for "greater speed"; it is designed to be the "most compact, fitting it for the smallest folding cameras"; and it is easy to use, as it "take[s] any shutter [and] will fit any camera."[82] Amateur photography was developed across an industry, advertised in a growing number of popular-specialist periodicals, and promoted as an easy and affordable hobby for virtually anyone.

Through the convergence of their respective audiences, the culture of amateur photography also dovetailed with the modern tourist industry. According to a correspondent for *The Photographer's World* (1886):

> I have been out West on a visit to my married sister—way out where there isn't much but prairie and wind, you know. Well, there's a photographer there—I'd like to know where you can go in this country and not find one.[83]

The Photographic News for Amateur Photographers referenced an article from the Melbourne Argus in 1888:

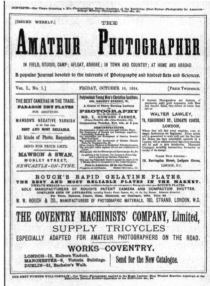

Figure 4.3 Conan Doyle, "After Cormorants with a Camera," *The British Journal of Photography* (October 14, 1881), p. 533; and Cover of *The Amateur Photographer* (October 10, 1884).

To judge by an article in the *Melbourne Argus*, the amateur photographer has overrun Australia, and is as much dreaded as the terrible rabbit. The amateur photographer, we are told, is "rampant in the land." He excites the jealousy of rivals, who complain that he takes a mean advantage of his brief authority.[84]

The Victorian amateur photographer enjoying a seaside summer holiday joined the ranks of scientists, geographers, anthropologists, and ethnographers, along with other travelers and explorers in the visual documentation and mapping of nearly every known corner of the world.[85]

The explosive growth of an image-making culture produced a field of books and magazines inundated by photographs of the world. Every part of it became the potential subject matter for a camera's recording gaze. The most difficult heights of the world's tallest mountains or "the most southerly point ever reached by man"[86] could now be accessed by just flipping a page. Strange lands were represented through the pages of books, periodicals, and government reports. A secluded stretch of tropical coastline one day was an illustration on a perfume box, a cigar advertisement, or a faded travel poster the next. In the visual panoply of the national press, these representations of mysterious places were often juxtaposed with the mundane advertisements for soup, soap, and flavored cigarettes. Photo-realism's impact on the Victorian imagination was decisive. As Paul Martin's 1939 memoir *Victorian Snapshots* describes it, an omnipresence of photographs at the turn of the century was an invisible, because all-pervasive, power. Martin writes:

[A]ccurate and uncompromising supply of photographic knowledge is continually poured into our minds. We are fed on photographs daily until we die. They meet us on hoardings, in shops, in newspapers, in books, in our work and in many of our amusements. Behind the scenes of everyday life they have spread in their applications until there is scarcely a department of science and industry that does not employ them. Photography has not only helped the modern eclipse of time and space, but brought about a revolution in thinking and (for good or evil) transported the world to our doorstep.[87]

In addition to the numerous theories of the photographic image, developed in response to literary and artistic modernism in the twentieth century,[88] the photograph could also act as an exhilarating, if sometimes unsettling, threshold. Its technology associated formerly dissociable objects and worlds. Separated by geographical distances, which photography often seemed to collapse, all places were potentially conceivable within its singular, and uncanny, visual imagination. The technology of Victorian photography "transported the world to our doorstep,"[89] if only in still, silent forms.

The popular geographical journal of the day, the *National Geographic*, is an obvious case in point. The first issue of the *National Geographic* was published in 1888, 9 months after the Society was founded at the Cosmos Club in Washington, D.C. for "the increase and diffusion of geographical knowledge."[90] The *National Geographic* would eventually become one of the most innovative and recognizable periodicals in the world. Offering readers "what they want to know" about "the world and all that is in it," the magazine introduced its realistic, albeit highly stylized, aesthetic of documentary photography in 1896. These first photographs published in its pages, through the process of steel engraving, were expensive and slow to produce, but photoengraving techniques developed after the turn of the century reduced costs and production time significantly. In 1905, the magazine's editor, Gilbert Hovey Grosvenor, published "eleven full pages of photographs of Lhasa, Tibet, mailed in to the magazine by two Russian explorers."[91] The Society's membership and subscription lists increased dramatically, from 3,400 to 11,000 by the end of the year. Grosvenor's editorially decisive "move and this response served to establish photographs as the mainstay and distinctive feature of the magazine."[92] Its 11-page photographic spread of the "forbidden city" exposed thousands of armchair explorers and geography buffs to what John Buchan later described as, "[t]ill the summer of 1904 . . . the most mysterious spot on the earth's surface."[93]

The visual representation of the "city among the clouds about which no tale was too strange for belief"[94] was material for popular entertainment. It was disseminated as information, signified a march of Western technology, and was ultimately a knowable object of exploration's desire. An editorial for *The British Journal of Photography* in 1880 declared that subscribers to the journal "valued photography because it brought within their reach the choicest landscapes of the earth."[95] Local spaces at the turn of the century were inundated with photographic images of a world outside the one most people would ever see. The familiar was brought into closer contact with an exhilarating, but seemingly antagonistic, unknown.

Images of foreign and faraway places were printed in books, magazines, newspapers, and popular science–travel journals such as the *National Geographic.* They were also rendered powerful commodities and lent their aura of mystery and romance to products such as perfumes, fabrics, cigarettes, furniture, and shuffleboards. They were marketable products in their own right too.[96] Buchan's comments on Lhasa, Tibet do not directly reference photography's role in the process of romance's decline, but photography's visual possession of "the final mysteries of exploration" pivotally effected "the drawing back of that curtain which had meant so much to the imagination of mankind."[97] The dissemination of those "final mysteries" as images in books, magazines, and the popular press effectively brought about the decline of romance's aura. The documents made by official functionaries of insular organizations for non-commercial purposes had far less of an influence, as they accrued little attention outside the organization. Buchan wrote nostalgically that, "[w]ith the unveiling of Lhasa fell the last

THE "SOUTHERN CROSS" AT MOUNT MELBOURNE, NEAR NEWNES LAND.

The Palace of the Dalai-Lama at Lhasa

The palace of the Dalai-Lama, Potala, is about two-thirds of a mile west of the city, and built upon a rocky height. The foundation of the palace, tradition says, was laid by Srongzang Khan during the seventh century. The main central portion, called the "red palace," was added some time later. Ths palace and additions were planned to serve as a means of defense

Figure 4.4 "The Southern Cross Antarctic Expedition" (*The Strand Magazine*, September 1900); and "The Palace of the Dalai-Lama at Lhasa" (*National Geographic Magazine*, January 1905).

stronghold of the older romance,"[98] but the blame might lie more economically on the immense popularity of the 11-page photographic spread of Lhasa published in the January 1905 *National Geographic*. The photos so thrilled readers that Grosvenor ran 32 pages of photographs of the Philippines in the magazine's February issue.

Drawing on the public's reception of photography and photographs during the last half of the nineteenth century, Doyle organized his fantastic representation as a threshold, able to bridge the actual geographical here and imagined, other, faraway worlds. The status of the photograph as persuasive, but highly unstable, signifier of proof and objectivity lent powerful support to Doyle's imaginative transformation. His research into sophisticated developing techniques also exposed the photograph as a threshold technology. The photograph had become our eyes on a world and, in the process, it had robbed that world of its hidden and unknown places, but Doyle channeled a wonder associated with adventure into a reinvigorated source of provocative uncertainty. Visual indexes of an imaginary unknown geography were located in both images and the image-making process itself. Conrad's pejorative use of the term "piebald" to describe a "great cloud of . . . daily photographs"[99] published in the newspapers notes an incongruity between the mass media and a commodity use of the aura of geographical mysteries. The *National Geographic*'s "geographical knowledge"[100] was diffused through its thousands of photographs printed monthly. It transported foreign and faraway places home, in a magazine that was eagerly subscribed to by readers. Doyle appropriated and radically transformed this popular articulation of visual media that flooded the late-Victorian world with images of exotic lands, cultures, and adventure from all over the globe.

Part II: Picturing the Lost World

Seeing firsthand, in order to verify the unbelievable and often unimaginable, was crucial to early Western exploration. This emphasis on the faculty of unmediated sight became a characteristic of explorers' narratives. Mary Louis Pratt demonstrates how "the act of discovery itself, for which all the untold lives were sacrificed and miseries endured, consisted of . . . [simply] seeing."[101] Itself a "passive experience," Pratt argues that seeing becomes an act of discovery when brought "into being by texts: a name on a map, a report to the Royal Geographical Society . . . a diary, a lecture, a travel book."[102] These texts give an act its supplemental "rhetoric of presence."[103] Photographs perform a truncated version of Pratt's thesis. By the turn of the twentieth century, it was not only the naked human eye's acts of discovery that were brought "into being" by printed texts, but also the photograph's act of recording the discovery. The photograph is its own persuasively mimetic text, because it records the proof of its own discovery, conquest, and visual possession. When it is mobilized beyond the frontiers of the Empire, it can both capture the event of discovering the faraway geography and record the capturing of that event. Preserving those images for transport, it reproduces them for dissemination. The photograph enacts its "monarch-of-all-I-survey" scene in each version.

The scene that Pratt describes was a common feature of the explorers' narratives since the early fifteenth century, but, in photographs, this scene is given a modern, ambiguously persuasive, and technological dimension. The legal and epistemological status of the photograph continued to be contested in legal courts throughout the nineteenth and twentieth centuries. The photograph's status as proof in the court of public opinion, however, made it a powerful register of authenticity and fact. Evidence was contained in the photograph, without recourse to a supplementary text. It had its own powerful rhetoric, and Doyle exploited this rhetoric in response to the scientific and geographical mapping of the world's last frontiers at the turn of the twentieth century. Drawings, photographs, and illustrations of foreign and faraway places reproduced en masse by the popular press and in illustrated magazines diminished the romantic associations once attributed to places that, by the turn of the twentieth century, were no longer remote and unexplored. Reconstituting this lost imaginary separation between civilization and the spaces of imperial fantasy beyond its frontier, Doyle appropriated the rhetorical proof of the photograph.

In his speech at The Royal Society Club in London in 1910—in honor of Admiral Robert Peary as the first man to have reached the geographic North Pole a year before—Doyle pitted the great weight of scientific facts and evidence about the known geography of the world against the powerful desire to preserve the romance writer's literary imagination, "[un]hampered by facts."[104] He begrudgingly acknowledged Peary's success and the success of other explorers like him, but defended the romance writer's need to maintain the mystery associated with remote, unexplored places of the world. Mystery was needed "to give free scope to his fancy,"[105] and to people those mysterious places with all manner of adventures, miracles, and monsters. Despite the knowledge that miracles and monsters did not exist, he defended the readers' right to believe that they did. Doyle spoke:

> The writers of romance have always a certain amount of grievance against explorers. It is the grievance that explorers are continually encroaching on the domain of the romance-writer. There has been a time when the world was full of blank spaces, in which a man of imagination might be able to give free scope to his fancy. But owing to the ill-directed energy of our guest and other gentlemen of similar tendencies, these spaces are rapidly being filled up; and the question is where the romance-writer is to turn when he wants to draw any vague and not too clearly defined region. Romance-writers are a class of people who very much dislike being hampered by facts.[106]

In the speech, subsequently printed in *The Times*, Doyle complained of the loss of undiscovered places as potential settings for romantic adventure. Two years later, in his novel *The Lost World* (1912), he located another, entirely overlooked geography for limitless exploration, one existing simultaneously alongside our own world, but cut off, or lost, from civilization. Doyle's interest in photography, knowledge of its technology, and manipulation informed his arrangements for the novel's first serialization in *The Strand Magazine*. Installments ran monthly throughout the summer holiday months of 1912 (April–November), alongside faked, but realistic, photographs and illustrations presented as though they were factual, documentary evidence. Photography was visual proof of the imaginary existence of this lost world and one of the primary means by which its existence was brought into productive being.

Doyle's 1912 novel recounts an expedition taken by an intrepid band of British explorers to a remote plateau hidden deep inside the South American jungle. Populated by dinosaurs, long-extinct flora, and two warring tribes, one human and the other humanoid, the geological survival has been cut off from the surrounding forests and has developed along radically different, much older, evolutionary lines. Adopting a pseudo-scientific posture—which many of his readers would have recognized—Doyle explains the geological and evolutionary anachronism in this way:

> South America is . . . a granite continent. At this single point in the interior there has been, in some far distant age, a great, sudden volcanic upheaval. . . . An area, as large perhaps as Sussex, has been lifted up *en bloc* with all its living contents, and cut off by perpendicular precipices of a hardness which defies erosion from all the rest of the continent . . . the ordinary laws of nature are suspended. The various checks which influence the struggle for existence are all neutralized or altered. Creatures survive which would otherwise disappear.[107]

The party of adventurers includes "Professor George E. Challenger, Lord John Roxton, Professor Summerlee, and Mr. E. D. Malone of the *London Gazette*,"[108] who embark on a mission to verify or dispute the veracity of Professor Challenger's claim about a lost world. Challenger's evidence includes a recovered sketchbook, a damaged photograph, and several uncertain archaeological remains. Rosamund Dalziell has observed that "Doyle himself created a deliberate mystification as to the geographical setting of his novel,"[109] and this "deliberate mystification" is paralleled by Challenger's refusal to divulge the secret whereabouts of the hidden world. Malone, Roxton, and Summerlee may accompany him on the expedition to verify the existence of the hidden Jurassic-age plateau, but Challenger demands that they keep its exact location a secret. Malone reports:

> [T]he Professor . . . made each of us give our word of honor that we would publish or say nothing which would give any exact clue as to the

whereabouts of our travels. . . . It is for this reason that I am compelled
to be vague in my narrative, and I would warn my readers that in any
map or diagram which I may give the relation of places to each other
may be correct, but the points of the compass are carefully confused,
so that in no way can it be taken as an actual guide to the country.[110]

Narrated in the first person by a skeptical representative of the daily press,
Malone's reports give the story its sense of authenticity and believability.
The novel playfully questions its status as a purely fictional representation.
This same provocative instability is registered throughout the lost-world
novels of Rider Haggard.[111] It is further emphasized in Doyle's novel by the
addition of false maps, topographical charts, and the manipulated portrait
and landscape photographs. One of the photographs depicts Doyle himself,
disguised in a big fake red beard and bushy eyebrows, seated at his desk as
Professor Challenger, along with the members of his exploring party. The
photograph was staged with friends at Doyle's home toward the end of 1911,
and the prints were prepared later by William Ransford and Doyle.[112]

However, the most curious photographs arranged by the author for *The
Strand* serialization of *The Lost World* involved a traditional process of
developing called multiple exposures. Multiple exposures are created by
exposing a photographic dry plate to obtain a single negative image. Second,
third, and sometimes fourth exposures are then produced on the same plate.
This impresses multiple images over the original negative. The negative
retains the traces of all earlier negatives, and, when done correctly, the
resulting photograph gives the appearance of an image created by a single
exposure of the camera. Each element appears to the human eye as coher-
ently situated and temporally concurrent. In Chapter Four of the novel, a
landscape photograph is titled "A Distant View of the Plateau." Supposedly
taken by Challenger on an earlier expedition, the photograph depicts the
sheer walls of the hidden world rising above a mist-filled jungle. In fact,
the photograph was developed by Doyle himself using the technique of
multiple exposures, by which he superimposed multiple images in order
to produce the single, skillfully accomplished visual depiction of what Pratt
has termed the quintessential "monarch-of-all-I-survey" scene. The recurring element in explorers' narratives of more than 400 years, the scene is
repeated when Malone describes the photograph:

> [It was] very off-coloured. An unkind critic might easily have misinter-
> preted that dim surface. It was a dull grey landscape, and as I gradually
> deciphered the details of it I realized that it represented a long and
> enormously high line of cliffs exactly like an immense cataract seen in
> the distance, with a sloping, treeclad plain in the foreground.[113]

When Malone is shown "a nearer view of the same scene, though the
photograph was extremely defective," he declares: "I have no doubt of it

E. D. Malone, "Daily Gazette."   Prof. Summerlee, F.R.S.   Prof. G. E. Challenger, F.R.S., F.R.G.S.   Lord John Roxton.

THE MEMBERS OF THE EXPLORING PARTY.

Copyright. From a Photograph by William Ransford.

A DISTANT VIEW OF THE PLATEAU. (From a photograph by Professor Challenger).

Facing p. 55.

Figure 4.5 "The Members of the Exploring Party" and "A Distant View of the Plateau" (*The Strand Magazine*, April 1912).

at all."[114] In the reporter's case, the damage to the photographs adds a measure of provenance, which only reinforces the already powerful sense of authenticity. According to the popular maxim, "seeing is believing."

The readers of *The Strand Magazine* had been thrilled by Doyle's master storytelling for more than two decades, but the magazine's serialization of *The Lost World* gave them something else: this was not only a master storyteller, but also a sophisticated photographer and master magician at work. The photographs were supplemented by illustrations from Harry Rountree, which were based on hypothetical zoological drawings of Jurassic-age dinosaurs in Edwin Ray Lankester's 1905 *Prehistoric Animals*. Doyle's arrangement for serializing *The Lost World* in this "spectacular package"[115] guaranteed his narrative at least a modicum of credibility. Saler explores how it also situated Doyle in "a tradition going back to [Edgar Allan] Poe,"[116] noting:

> [Doyle] took care that the photographs and illustrations for the book appeared realistic ... [and] scrupulously supervised the creation and placement of other photographs, sketches, and illustrations of the Lost World and its ... inhabitants. Several of the illustrations were captioned [as though they had come] from the sketchbook of one of the novel's characters, and others were photographs of the Lost World these characters discovered in South America. ... [Doyle] created a fantastic imaginary world as an ironic hoax, a tradition going back to Poe that characterized the New Romance and its twentieth-century successors.[117]

Like Poe's *The Narrative of Arthur Gordon Pym*,[118] this performance was painstakingly crafted to blur fact and fiction, and it paralleled the newspaper reporter's incredible eye-witness account in many important ways.

The findings of the expedition adhere to Pratt's thesis that the act of discovery is brought "into being through texts."[119] Challenger's claims are verified for a skeptical public by Malone's first-person eyewitness accounts in the *London Gazette*, published by Malone's editor, McArdle, along with the corroborative photographic evidence collected by Malone. In the series of events that repeat mishaps from Challenger's original expedition, however, the bulk of the photographic evidence is lost, damaged, or destroyed. In the course of the expedition to investigate the interior of the lost world, the explorers are attacked by pterodactyls and captured by the tribe of ape-men. After the explorers make a narrow escape, they join a tribe of humans inhabiting the other side of the plateau, and ultimately help them defeat their ape-like nemeses and take control of the entire plateau. The few negatives that survive the series of ordeals are heavily damaged. Their veracity is subsequently questioned, but, when the Committee of Investigation of the Zoological Institute convenes, in London, to test the claims of Professor Challenger's latest expedition, they become an important focus of the proceedings. In one reporter's "fairly accurate, if florid, account

THE STRAND MAGAZINE

Vol. xliii.   APRIL, 1912.   No. 256.

THE LOST WORLD.

Being an account of the recent amazing adventures of Professor George E. Challenger, Lord John Roxton, Professor Summerlee, and Mr. E. D. Malone of the "Daily Gazette."

BY

ARTHUR CONAN DOYLE.

Illustrated by
Harry Rountree and the late Maple White.

" THE LOST WORLD."

The Leader of the Explorers, with some of their Adventures.

Figure 4.6a Harry Rountree, Illustrated Frontispiece, *The Lost World*, "The Leader of the Explorers, with some of their Adventures" (*The Strand Magazine*, April 1912).

of the proceedings," Malone recounts a portion of the speech made by Challenger to the Committee:

> I have safely conducted these three gentlemen to the spot mentioned, and I have, as you have heard, convinced them of the accuracy of my previous account. We had hoped that we should find upon our return that no one was so dense as to dispute our joint conclusion. Warned, however, by my previous experience, I have not come without such proofs as may convince a reasonable man. As explained by Professor Summerlee, our cameras have been tampered with by the ape-men when they ransacked our camp, and most of our negatives ruined. . . . In spite of the destruction of so many invaluable negatives, there still remains in our collection a certain number of corroborative photographs showing the conditions of life on the plateau. Did they accuse them of having forged these photographs? . . . The negatives were open to the inspection of experts.[120]

Although the members of the expedition do mount a strong case based on their evidence—which includes photographs, entomological specimens, and

" THE LOST WORLD."

The Leader of the Explorers, with some of their Adventures.

Figure 4.6b Harry Rountree, Illustrated Frontispiece, *The Lost World*, "The Leader of the Explorers, with some of their Adventures" (*The Strand Magazine*, April 1912).

the eyewitness reports of Malone—many in the crowd of scientists, experts, and journalists dismiss the story as a complete fabrication, along with Challenger's original story. Even with the corroborative materials that many would expect a legitimate expedition to produce—the maps, charts, sketches, and photographs, for example—the story and the expedition are inevitably charged with forgery.

Doyle casts his novel as a supposedly true account that was accurately reported to him by a member of the exploring party. Although he was never asked to submit his negatives to the "inspection of experts,"[121] to the untrained eye, the photographs used for *The Strand* serialization of *The Lost World* do appear thoroughly believable. Not actually expected to believe any of this evidence, the reader is encouraged to play along with the game. For the sake of enjoying a good yarn, an imaginative reader can always believe and still not take it too seriously. In accepting the premise on which the fantastic story is based—what if, somewhere in South America, there was a lost world of dinosaurs—Doyle's readers economize on the suspension of disbelief that is crucial to his narrative technique. Before the expedition sets out on the dangerous journey to the jungle, Lord Roxton comments to Malone:

> "Now, down here in the Matto Grosso"—he swept his cigar over a part of the map—"or up in this corner where three countries meet, nothin' would surprise me ... there are fifty thousand miles of water-way runnin' through a forest that is very near the size of Europe.... Why shouldn't somethin' new and wonderful lie in such a country? And why shouldn't we be the men to find it out?"[122]

The lost world remains a fictional place, but its imaginary discovery is realistically and painstakingly crafted to appear as though this world were brought "into being through texts."[123] Actual, though incredible, contemporary discoveries of the period included the giant Komodo Dragon (referred to by Komodo Islanders in 1912 as the "land crocodile"); the "lost" Inca city of Machu Picchu, discovered by the American explorer Hiram Bigham in 1911; and Doyle's own discovery of several Iguanodon footprints in a quarry close to his Windlesham home in Sussex in 1909. In this context, the actual discovery of a lost world in the South American jungle is not outside the realms of possibility.

In the opening chapters of *The Lost World*, Doyle echoes his own speech to The Royal Society Club in 1910, honoring Admiral Peary as the first explorer to reach the geographical North Pole. When Malone initially approaches McArdle for an assignment "that had adventure and danger in it,"[124] he explains his desire to "break ... away ... from the life he knows, and venture ... forth into the wonderful mystic twilight land where lie the great adventures and the great rewards."[125] The salty old newspaper editor chides the young reporter, "I'm afraid the day for that sort of thing is rather past. . . . The big blank spaces in the map are all being filled in, and there's no room for romance anywhere."[126] Doyle's novel responds to this closing of the final undiscovered global frontiers with its sophisticated gag, one that marshaled all the epistemological weight of visual evidence associated by his readers with the medium of photography. Presenting his newest novel as the factual account of an actual journey, Doyle gathered scientific facts and evidence regarding an imaginary geography, documented its discovery with trick photographs, and capitalized on the popular credibility of this visual proof.

Doyle's expert appropriation of the photograph's status as the mimetic reproduction of a true event and material reality brought into being his discovery of an imaginary frontier deep in the South American jungle. His performance exploited the apparent veracity of the photograph's proof as the "silent witness" of the fact. It opened up a new and powerful imaginary avenue for the extension of geographical adventure into this destabilized, mechanically mediated world. A visual image is a powerful statement of fact, but this medium also challenges the verifiability of what it sees and records. In an 1898 article in *The Harmsworth Magazine*, an anonymous author remarked on the "worthlessness of the camera as a witness," claiming it only produced "lies."[127] Romance writers' claims were predicated on a paucity of evidence to prove the contrary, in fact, and lack of evidence plagued explorers returning from faraway places, as they often brought home tales that few people could believe as well. For Doyle, photography, and its representation in the illustrated magazines, extended the adventure narrative's viability as a twentieth-century literary form by exploiting this problematic relationship of proof and visual verification. In one of the twentieth century's most contested, and innocuous, documentary media, moreover, Doyle had proven the contradictory claim. Presenting proof of having been there, whether "there" was an actual or imaginary place, depended on the glossy, slick-paper pages of an illustrated popular monthly such as *The Strand Magazine*, in order that the photographs could be reproduced in enough fine detail for the performance to be believable. So, contrary to Conrad's trepidations, the "great cloud of fatuous daily photographs . . . under whose shadow no traveler could live"[128] altered the modern adventure narrative's prospects for the good. This "great cloud" became a popular new medium that extended, and expanded, the horizons of possibility for adventure into the new century.

Doyle's early essays for *The British Journal of Photography* show that he was fascinated with photography as a medium, and skill, to be perfected. But, for Doyle, photography was also the impetus for getting out of the city and into the open air. This proved significant for a writer who began writing both adventure and detective stories within the next few years. For *The Strand*'s serialization of *The Lost World* throughout 1912, Doyle again turned his curiosity toward photography, this time as a technology of documentation, while the subject to be documented was an imaginary, undiscovered location beyond the boundaries of the civilized world. His earlier essays already point the way toward that imaginary intersection between photography and adventure.

Leaving the claustrophobic confines of Southsea, to visually document the rural English countryside world around him, is mundane by comparison. But, Doyle's first published essays for *The British Journal of Photography* laid the intellectual groundwork for the author's exploitation of the photograph's ability to postulate the existence of new, parallel worlds by recording their discovery. The first serialization of *The Lost World* in *The Strand Magazine* presented Doyle with the opportunity to extend adventure's domain. His early involvement with amateur photography and developing techniques pitted the photograph's proof and documentary evidence against the romance writers' need to expand avenues for escape and adventure in the modern world. Its performance would not have worked without the serialization and illustrated representation of it in the popular illustrated monthly magazines.

In a period of aggressive commercial expansion for the publishing industries in Britain and the United States, the modern adventure story also developed conflicting and contradictory strains, contemporaneously. Genres of modern adventure proliferated in the pages of magazines, in response to competition in the marketplace. They adapted to meet the needs and expectations of reading audiences, and they responded to the invention of new technologies. Adventure stories have always existed—they were likely the first stories ever told—but the modern adventure story operated in a world that was materially more hostile to the spirit of adventure than ever before.[129] In the fifth and final chapter of this study, I show that modern adventure's dread of an ominous and ubiquitous media threat developed its own powerful aesthetic as well, and in the pages of un-illustrated, all-fiction, American pulp-paper magazines.

Notes

1　"DINOSAURS CAVORT IN FILM FOR DOYLE; Spiritist Mystifies World-Famed Magicians With Pictures of Prehistoric Beasts. KEEPS ORIGIN A SECRET. Monsters of Other Ages Shown, Some Fighting, Some at Play, in Their Native Jungles," *The New York Times* (June 3, 1922), p. 1. See also Russell Miller, *The Adventures of Arthur Conan Doyle: A Biography*, New York: Thomas Dunne Books, 2008, pp. 418–19.

2　Ibid.

3　Miller, pp. 418–19.

4　*The Lost World* was originally serialized across eight installments, from April to November 1912, in *The Strand Magazine*. The chapters appeared as follows: Chaps. I–IV, Vol. 43, No. 256 (April 1912): pp. 363–82; Chaps. V–VII, Vol. 43, No. 257 (May 1912): pp. 483–500; Chaps. VIII–IX, Vol. 43, No. 258 (June 1912): pp. 603–22; Chaps. X–XI, Vol. 44, No. 259 (July 1912): pp. 3–14; Chaps. XI–XII, Vol. 44, No. 260 (August 1912): pp. 123–37; Chaps. XII–XIV, Vol. 44, No. 261 (September 1912): pp. 243–55; Chaps. XIV–XV, Vol. 44,

No. 262 (October 1912): pp. 363–75; and Chaps. XV–XVI, Vol. 44, No. 263 (November 1912): pp. 483–96.

5 *The Lost World*, dir. Harry O. Hoyt, perfs. Bessie Love and Wallace Beery, First National Pictures, 1925.

6 Less than a decade later, Willis O'Brien created the award-winning special effects for the original version of *King Kong* (1933), which starred Fay Wray, Robert Armstrong, and Bruce Cabot, and was directed by Merian C. Cooper and Ernest B. Schoedsack for RKO Radio Pictures.

7 'DINOSAURS CAVORT IN FILM FOR DOYLE,' Ibid.

8 Ibid.

9 By 1922, Doyle was not only a world-famous literary author, but also a celebrated fixture on the American, European, and Australian lecture circuits, delivering speeches and demonstrations on a variety of non-literary subjects, which included spiritualism, Zionism, divorce reform, the occult, international politics, philosophy, and prehistoric man.

10 See Michael Saler, "Delight Without Delusion: The New Romance, Spectacular Texts, and Public Spheres," Ch. 2 from *As If: Modern Enchantment and the Literary Prehistory of Virtual Reality*, Oxford, UK, and New York: Oxford University Press, 2012, pp. 57–104.

11 John M. Lynch, "Introduction," *The Coming of the Fairies* (1921), Arthur Conan Doyle, Lincoln, NE, and London: University of Nebraska Press, 2006, p. xvii.

12 Joseph Conrad, *Lord Jim: A Tale*, Edinburgh and London: William Blackwood & Sons, 1900. "Lord Jim: A Sketch" was originally serialized across 14 installments of *Blackwood's Magazine*, from October 1899 to November 1900.

13 Stephen Donovan, "The Muse of *Blackwood's*: Charles Whibley and Literary Criticism in the World," *Print Culture and the Blackwood Tradition, 1805–1930*, Ed. David Finkelstein, Toronto: University of Toronto Press, 2006, p. 263.

14 H.G. Wells, *Tono-Bungay: A Romance of Commerce*, London: Macmillan, 1909. The novel was first serialized, as a simultaneous transatlantic serialization in both U.S. and UK magazines. They were Street & Smith's *The Popular Magazine* (September 1908–January 1909) and Ford Maddox Hueffer's *The English Review* (December 1908–March 1909).

15 See Bernard Bergonzi, *The Turn of a Century: Essays on Victorian and Modern English Literature*, London: Macmillan, 1973, pp. 95–98.

16 "Chapter IX: How I Stole the Heaps of Quap from Mordet Island," *Tono-Bungay*, Part 3, *The Popular Magazine* Vol. 12, No. 2 (December 1908), pp. 125–39, and "Book the Third, Chapter the Fourth: How I Stole the Heaps of Quap from Mordet Island," *Tono-Bungay*, Part 3, *The English Review* Vol. I, No. 4 (March 1909), pp. 723–49.

17 Mike Ashley, *The Age of the Storytellers: British Popular Fiction Magazines 1880–1950*, London: The British Library, 2006, p. 1.

18 The phrase "Boy's Own Paper stuff," which first gained popularity in the wake of the Second World War, referred to that familiar matrix of ethical codes and cultural archetypes in Victorian and Edwardian literature that regarded manliness as a moral attribute, requiring adherence to a strict concept of masculinity. It is still commonly associated with British boys' fiction, and especially with *BOP* (1879–1967), the British institution that formed a bulwark of early reading matter for generations of British schoolboys, soldiers, sailors, and gentlemen.

19 H.G. Wells, *Tono-Bungay* (1909; Macmillan), New York: Modern Library Classics, 2003, p. 305.

20 Ibid., p. 313.
21 Joseph Conrad, "Travel," *Last Essays*, London and Toronto: J.M. Dent, 1926, p. 129.
22 John Buchan, *The Last Secrets: The Final Mysteries of Exploration*, London, Edinburgh, and New York: Thomas Nelson, 1923, p. 18.
23 By the 1920s, images and advertisements had made places such as Llasa, the Congo, and Timbuktu familiar to the point of saturation, inundation, and consequent innocuousness.
24 H. Greenhough Smith, "Letter to Conan Doyle" (1912), quoted in Saler, *As If*, pp. 78, 81.
25 Nicholas Daly, *Modernism, Romance and the Fin de Siècle: Popular Fiction and British Culture, 1880–1914*, Cambridge, UK: Cambridge University Press, 1999, p. 155.
26 Saler, p. 67.
27 Ibid.
28 *The Graphic* was a British illustrated weekly newspaper that ran between 1869 and 1932. It first serialized Rider Haggard's *She: A History of Adventure* (1886) in 14 installments, from October 2, 1886 to January 1, 1887, at which time, circulation figures could rival even those of the more popularly priced weekly, *The Illustrated London News* (1842–1971).
29 *Le Voyage dans la Lune*, dir. Georges Méliès, perfs. Georges Méliès, Victor André, Bleuette Bernon, Jeanne d'Alcy, and Henri Delannoy, Star Film, 1902. The film is a satire of the conservative French scientific community and was inspired by Jules Verne's *From the Earth to the Moon* (1865) and H.G. Wells's *The First Men in the Moon* (1901).
30 Saler, p. 69.
31 Neil Harris, "Iconography and Intellectual History," in John Higham and Paul Conkin, Eds., *New Directions in American Intellectual History*, Baltimore, MD: Johns Hopkins University Press, 1979, p. 179.
32 Saler, p. 69.
33 J. Habakuk Jephson was the narrator of Doyle's "J. Habakuk Jephson's Statement," first published anonymously in *The Cornhill Magazine* (January 1884), and reprinted by the editors of the *Boston Herald* in 1885. The reportedly "eye-witness" account, which purported to have been written by a passenger aboard the doomed ship *Mary Celeste*, was so convincing that the newspaper's readers accepted it as fact.
34 Conan Doyle, "After Cormorants with a Camera," *The British Journal of Photography* 28 (October 14, 21), 1881, pp. 533–34, 544–46. References made to Doyle, "After Cormorants with a Camera," in John Michael Gibson and Richard Lancelyn Green, Eds., *The Unknown Conan Doyle: Essays on Photography*, London: Secker & Warburg, 1982, pp. 1–12.
35 William Burton was himself an accomplished Victorian photographer.
36 *Anthony's Photographic Bulletin*, Summer 1882.
37 Richard Lancelyn Green and John Michael Gibson, "Introduction," *The Unknown Conan Doyle*, p. xii.
38 Leaving the claustrophobic confines of Southsea, to visually document the rural English countryside world around him, is mundane by comparison. But, Doyle's first published essays for *The British Journal of Photography* laid the intellectual groundwork for the author's later, modern, far more fantastic experiments in adventure writing, which exploited the photograph's ability to postulate the existence of, and record the act of discovering, new, parallel worlds.

39 Journals such as *The American Amateur Photographer* (1889) helped arrange "outings" for their readers, sponsored the formation of amateur camera clubs, and encouraged contests between them "with suitable prizes."

40 Erskine Childers, *The Riddle of the Sands* (1903), Oxford, UK, and New York: Oxford University Press, 1998, pp. 11–16. See also the opening paragraphs of John Buchan, *The Thirty-Nine Steps* (1915), Oxford and New York: Oxford University Press, 1993, pp. 7–8.

41 Doyle, "After Cormorants with a Camera," p. 1.

42 Ibid., pp. 1–2.

43 In the following decade, installments of the series routinely encouraged readers to strike out into the countryside, and out of the city.

44 Doyle, "After Cormorants with a Camera," p. 2.

45 Ibid., pp. 6–7.

46 Ibid., p. 7.

47 Ibid.

48 Ibid., p. 9.

49 Ibid., p. 7.

50 Ibid.

51 Ibid., pp. 7–8.

52 Ibid., p. 8.

53 Ibid.

54 Ibid.

55 Green and Gibson, p. xii.

56 Doyle, "On the Slave Coast with a Camera," *The British Journal of Photography* 29 (March 31, April 7, 1882), pp. 185–87, 202–3. References are to Doyle, "On the Slave Coast with a Camera," *The Unknown Conan Doyle*, pp. 13–22.

57 Doyle, "On the Slave Coast with a Camera," p. 14.

58 Doyle, "With a Camera on an African River," *The British Journal of Photography* 32 (October 30, 1885), p. 697.

59 Ibid.

60 See Jennifer Green Lewis, *Framing the Victorians: Photography and the Culture of Realism*, Ithaca, NY: Cornell University Press, 1996; Jonathan Smith, *Charles Darwin and Victorian Visual Culture*, Cambridge, UK: Cambridge University Press, 2006; and also Elizabeth Heyert, *The Glasshouse Years: Victorian Portrait Photography, 1839–1870*, Montclair, NJ: Allanheld & Schram, 1979.

61 Smith, *Charles Darwin and Victorian Visual Culture*, p. 216.

62 Ibid.

63 Michael T. Saler, "Modernity, Disenchantment, and the Ironic Imagination," *Philosophy & Literature* Vol. 28, No. 1 (April 2004), pp. 137–49.

64 Three of the thirteen articles narrate photographic outings on the west coast of Africa. Two articles are on strictly technical matters. The others describe short photographic jaunts around the English countryside or Scottish coasts.

65 Childers, p. 20.

66 Doyle, "Easter Monday with the Camera," *The British Journal of Photography* 31 (May 23, 1884), pp. 330–32. References are to Doyle, "Easter Monday with the Camera," *Unknown Conan Doyle*, pp. 67–72.

67 Doyle, "Easter Monday with the Camera," p. 69.

68 Ibid., p. 71.

69 The first Kodak "Brownie" was introduced by Eastman-Kodak in February 1900.

70 Thomas Sutton, *The British Journal of Photography* (January 17, 1868), qtd in W. Jerome Harrison, *Chapters in the History of Photography*, "Ch. 8:

Gelatine Emulsion With Bromide Of Silver," *The Photographic Times* Vol. XVII, No. 296 (May 20), 1887, p. 260.

71 "Report on the Inventions Exhibition 1885," *The Times*, London (Tuesday, August 11, 1885), p. 3.

72 The first model of Kodak camera was introduced by the Eastman Dry Plate Co. in 1888. It took round pictures 6.4 cm (2.5 inches) in diameter, and came preloaded with a roll of film enough for 100 exposures.

73 Alexander Black, *Photography Indoors and Out: a Book for Amateurs*, Boston, MA, and New York: Houghton-Mifflin, 1894, p. 58.

74 M. John Stuart, "Address to the Photographic Convention of the United Kingdom," *The Photographic Times: an Illustrated Monthly Magazine* Vol. 30 (1898), p. 468.

75 A. Horsley Hinton, "Notes and Comments," *The Amateur Photographer* Vol. 46, No. 1208 (Tuesday, November 26, 1907), p. 501. Italics are mine.

76 See John Spiller, "Recollections of the First Photographic Exhibition," *Yearbook of Photography* (1882), p. 41; Alan Elliott, *A Century Exposed: One Hundred Years of the Melbourne Camera Club*, Melbourne Camera Club, 1991; "Meetings of Societies," *The British Journal of Photography* Vol. LIV, No. 2439 (Friday, February 1, 1907), pp. 88–89; and Elizabeth Edwards, *The Camera as Historian: Amateur Photographers and Historical Imagination, 1885–1918*, Durham, NC: Duke University Press, 2012, *passim*.

77 Harrison, *A History of Photography*, London: Trubner, 1888, p. 67.

78 Morgan & Kidd ad, "Special Instantaneous" plate, *The Photographer's World* (December 15, 1886), cover.

79 Stereoscopic Company ad, "Free Lessons in Photography," *The Strand Magazine* 2 (1891), p. iii.

80 Kodak camera ad, "You Press the Button. We Do the Rest," *The Strand Magazine* 2 (1891), p. viii.

81 Meagher's "Improved Portable Camera" ad, *The Year-Book of Photography* (1893), p. a.

82 Bausch & Lomb ad, "Perfect Photo Lens," *The Photographic Times-Bulletin* (January 1902), p. ii.

83 *The Photographer's World* (September 15, 1886), p. 15.

84 *The Photographic News for Amateur Photographers* (June 18, 1888), p. 361.

85 See Bernard V. Lightman, *Victorian Science in Context*, Chicago: University of Chicago Press, 1997; and Carla Yanni, *Nature's Museums: Victorian Science and the Architecture of Display*, Princeton, NJ: Princeton Architectural Press, 2005.

86 William G. Fitzgerald, "E.C. Borchgrevink," *The Strand Magazine* Vol. 20, No. 117 (September 1900), p. 257.

87 Paul Martin, *Victorian Snapshots*, New York: Arno Press, 1973, p. vii.

88 See, for example, Walter Benjamin, "A Small History of Photography" (1931), *One Way Street*, Edmund Jephcott and Kingsley Shorter, trans., London: NLB, 1979, pp. 240–57. See also "The Work of Art in the Age of Mechanical Reproduction" (1936), *Illuminations*, London: Fontana, 1968, pp. 214–18; Siegfried Kracauer, "Photography," *The Mass Ornament*, Thomas Y. Levin, trans., Cambridge, MA: Harvard University Press, 1995, pp. 47–63; Theodor W. Adorno, *Aesthetic Theory*, Robert Hullot-Kentor, trans., Minneapolis, MN: University of Minnesota Press, 1997; and Roland Barthes, "The Third Meaning," *The Responsibility of Forms*, Richard Howard, trans., Berkeley, CA: University of California Press, 1991, pp. 41–62.

89 Ibid.

90 The Society's motto—"Organized to 'increase and diffuse geographical know-ledge' "—was an important feature of the magazine's masthead.

91 The accompanying article was titled "Views of *Lhasa*," *National Geographic Magazine* Vol. 16, No. 1 (1905), pp. 27–28.

92 Catherine A. Lutz and Jane L. Collins, *Reading National Geographic*, Chicago and London: University of Chicago Press, 1993, p. 27.

93 John Buchan, *The Last Secrets: The Final Mysteries of Exploration*. Yeovil, UK: Hayne Press, 2007, p. 17.

94 Ibid.

95 "Editorial," *The British Journal of Photography* (December 21, 1880), p. 615.

96 Photographs published in the *National Geographic* in the early decades of the twentieth century, for example, were obtained from scientists, explorers, travelers, or tourists unaffiliated with the magazine in an official capacity. Images of previously undocumented places became the objects of vigorous bidding wars. Competitors vied for first publishing rights, because first publica-tion of the images invariably increased sales and drove up the value of the magazine's advertising space.

97 Buchan, *The Last Secrets*, p. 18.

98 Ibid.

99 Conrad, "Travel," p. 129.

100 The National Geographical Society's motto—"Organized to 'increase and diffuse geographical knowledge' "—is printed on its official letterhead and features on the magazine's masthead.

101 Mary Louis Pratt, *Imperial Eyes: Travel Writing and Transculturation*, London and New York: Routledge, 1992, pp. 203–4.

102 Ibid., p. 204.

103 Ibid., p. 205.

104 Doyle, "Speech to The Royal Society Club," *The London Times* (May 4, 1910).

105 Ibid.

106 Ibid.

107 Doyle, *The Lost World*, Ware, UK: Wordsworth, 1995, p. 39.

108 "Announcement for *The Lost World*," editorial, *The Strand Magazine* (March 1912), p. 360.

109 Rosamund Dalziell, "The Curious Case of Sir Everard im Thurn and Sir Arthur Conan Doyle: Exploration and the Imperial Adventure Novel, *The Lost World*," *English Literature in Transition, 1880–1920* Vol. 45, No. 2 (2002), p. 134.

110 Doyle, *The Lost World*, p. 65.

111 See *King Solomon's Mines* (1885), *Allan Quatermain* (1887), and *She: A History of Adventure* (1887). Other lost world stories include Rudyard Kipling's "The Man Who Would Be King" (1888), Edgar Rice Burroughs's *The Land That Time Forgot* (1918), Abraham Merritt's *The Moon Pool* (1918), H.P. Lovecraft's *At the Mountains of Madness* (1936), and James Hilton's *Lost Horizon* (1933).

112 Even with the advanced printing technologies available to them in 1912, this was an expensive decision for the editor of *The Strand Magazine* to allow. At the insistence of the magazine's most famous literary author, however, he was willing to oblige. H. Greenhough Smith wrote Doyle to say he loved the new serial, "especially when it has the trimmings of faked photos, maps, and plans" (Smith, "Letter to Conan Doyle" (1912), quoted in Saler, *As If*, pp. 78, 81.

113 Doyle, *The Lost World*, pp. 36–37.

114 Ibid.

115 Saler, p. 70.

116   Ibid., p. 78.
117   Ibid.
118   Edgar Allan Poe, *The Narrative of Arthur Gordon Pym of Nantucket*, New York: Harper, 1837. The novel was also partially serialized early in 1837: "[The Narrative of] Arthur Gordon Pym, No. I," *The South Literary Messenger*, Vol. III, No. 1 (January 1837), pp. 13–16; and "[The Narrative of] Arthur Gordon Pym, No. II," *The South Literary Messenger* Vol. III, No. 2 (February 1837), pp. 109–16.
119   Pratt, p. 204.
120   Doyle, *The Lost World*, pp. 175–76.
121   Ibid., p. 176.
122   Ibid., p. 56.
123   Pratt, p. 204.
124   Doyle, *The Lost World*, p. 16.
125   Ibid., p. 15.
126   Ibid., p. 16–17.
127   "Photographic Lies: Proving the Worthlessness of the Camera as Witness," *The Harmsworth Magazine* (1898), p. 259.
128   Conrad, "Travel," p. 129.
129   See Martin Green, *Dreams of Adventure, Deeds of Empire*, London: Kegan Paul, 1979, p. xi; John McClure, *Late Imperial Romance*, London and New York: Verso, 1994, p. 10; Paul Zweig, *The Adventurer*, New York: Basic Books, 1974, pp. 4, 9; Joseph A. Kestner, *Masculinities in British Adventure Fiction 1880–1915*, Farnham, UK: Ashgate, 2010, pp. 2–12; Patrick Brantlinger, *Rule of Darkness: British Literature and Imperialism, 1830–1914*, Ithaca, NY: Cornell University Press, 1988, pp. 227–53; and also Graham Dawson, *Soldier Heroes: British Adventure, Empire and the Imagining of Masculinities*, London and New York: Routledge, 1994, p. 235.

5 Deciphered Codes

John Buchan in *All-Story Weekly*
(1915) and *The Popular*
Magazine (1919)

The broad field of Anglo-American publishing at the turn of the twentieth century was a robust and rapidly expanding juggernaut, but competition within this field remained keen. Desultory sales figures and catastrophic dealings with literary agents were not uncommon in the culture of professional authorship of the period.[1] Faced with the uncertainties of an ever-changing market, authors such as Robert Louis Stevenson, Rider Haggard, Conan Doyle, and John Buchan took surprisingly proactive roles in the direction and management of their own literary careers and in the destinies of their reputations. By contrast, Joseph Conrad was notoriously inept at controlling his finances, as well as at navigating the real-world business of literary marketing and promotion. In October 1897, Conrad reflected on his future prospects as an author: "I have some—literary—reputation but the future is anything but certain, for I am not a popular author and probably I never shall be."[2] When Conrad's first commercial success finally did arrive,[3] it was through the capable efforts of his literary agent, James B. Pinker. In another example, H.G. Wells was too combative to handle his own literary affairs and finances effectively, but he was also notoriously skeptical of agents. Though he employed "as many as five agents ... sometimes several at a time," including both Pinker and Watt, he employed them briefly and only for "specific transactions."[4] Wells insisted that he deal directly with his publishers and editors. As Mary Hammond writes:

> [Wells had an] anxious relationship with the market. For example, he vehemently denied using agents. . . . Wells even took out an advert in the *Author* that ran for a full year, from June 1913 to June 1914 . . .: "Mr. H.G. Wells does not employ an agent for his General Literary Business. Agents to whom he has entrusted specific transactions will be able to produce his authorisation. He will be obliged if Publishers and Editors will communicate directly with him in any doubtful case."[5]

On the other hand, from 1913 to 1930, Sax Rohmer was swindled out of thousands of dollars in royalties by his literary agent, Robert Somerville, and eventually took Somerville to court over it and won, and Arthur Addison Bright cheated J.M. Barrie out of £16,000 before killing himself in 1906.[6] From authorship to agency, promotion, and networking, Stevenson, Haggard, Doyle, and Buchan played a more immediate, pragmatic role in the critical and commercial success of their works. Not only were these writers directly involved on multiple levels in publication and promotion, but they were also quite successful at it. This level of involvement and expertise was particularly useful in navigating the complex field of popular fiction.[7]

Professional authorship at the turn of the twentieth century was defined "in relation to marketplace forces," and it operated within "a modern marketplace culture." This "perpetuated a discourse ... fraught with anxieties."[8] The author of this 1895 editorial in *Chambers's Journal*, for example, states:

> The increase in the demand for fiction has quickened the competition immensely amongst editors and publishers ... and forced up prices in proportion. It is quite possible for a novelist who has a vogue ... to command one thousand pounds, or even fifteen hundred pounds, as the price for serial issue alone.[9]

Noting that the "common method" used by the modern novelist is to "farm out a story through a syndicate or literary agent," the author of the article cautions readers: "But all do not receive the great prizes of literature; the highest work is not the best rewarded. . . . And there are authors who work harder than the average ... business man, who cannot keep their heads above water."[10] And thus the author declares: "In literature, as in other professions, there is always 'plenty of room at the top,' and the best reward there. The struggle is at the foot of the ladder."[11]

Employing terms that evoke Darwinian theories of evolutionary survival, the anonymous author contributes this situation to a "fickleness about the regular novel reader ... ever craving something new; ready to drop a favourite author, when tired of his characters and trick of style, in favour of a fresh hand."[12] The article continues:

> Thus the older writers get elbowed out and forgotten in a surprisingly short space of time ... [S]o many younger men have struggled to the front, that the stage is crowded, and all do not get a proper hearing. Rudyard Kipling, Rider Haggard, Stevenson, Barrie, Crockett, Hall Caine, Dr A. Conan Doyle, Mary E. Wilkins, Stanley Weyman, Gilbert Parker, Anthony Hope, all demand and have received the patronage of the fiction-reading public.[13]

Finally it asks: "So one writer crowds out another, and the question will be, Who is to stay?"[14]

Few authors combined their creative and professional livelihoods as seamlessly and successfully as Buchan. Gary Messinger has remarked on the "pattern of simultaneous interest in both fiction and non-fiction which Buchan was to follow [throughout] his literary career."[15] Robin Winks points out that Buchan's best-selling spy thrillers were just "a small fraction of his total output, his writing as a whole was only one aspect of his total career, and all phases were, generally, going on simultaneously."[16] The author's ability to negotiate several opposing, and even contradictory, literary identities simultaneously was a recurring feature of Buchan's official propaganda work during the First World War. It also informed his arrangements in 1915 for the transatlantic serialization of his 28th book, tenth full-length work of fiction, and first Richard Hannay spy thriller, *The Thirty-Nine Steps*.[17] This chapter not only shows how Buchan's command of literary authorship operated on multiple levels, but also contends that an ability to perform simultaneous roles effectively informs Buchan's development of a new kind of modern adventurer, one whose geography is composed of paper, and whose weapons are printer's ink and the pen. It concludes this study by demonstrating how Buchan, just one of many modern adventure writers of the twentieth century, engaged Conrad's concerns about the threat of new media directly and successfully. Regarding a threat of new media and the end of adventure, I contend that Buchan's spy hero engages with the threat and, by doing so, exerts power and mastery over the new modern forces. In this chapter, I draw connections between the rhetoric and professional discourse of transatlantic periodical publishing on the eve of the First World War and Buchan's development of the modern spy hero as an expert reader of diverse global media and cultural codes. In doing so, I finally suggest that Buchan's own successful career as a publisher, together with his expert navigation of modern media and the competitive transatlantic market for popular fiction, illustrates the sophisticated literary and cultural context from which one of modern spy literature's earliest, and arguably most famous,[18] adventure heroes first emerged.

The Pulp Buchan

Buchan was the prolific author of more than 100 books—26 of them novels, and half of those dealing with themes of modern espionage. He was also a successful publisher, editor, historian, war correspondent for *The Times*, first director of the British Department of Information, and, for nearly 20 years, a regular contributor to the American pulp magazines *Adventure*, *All-Story*, *Argosy*, and S&S's *The Popular Magazine*. The all-fiction, pulp-paper magazines—or the "pulps" as they were later known—were the major source of literary entertainment for most Americans during the first half of the twentieth century. They were printed on low-quality paper, distributed in record numbers, and sold by the millions on newsstands across the US and Canada. Between 1910 and 1928, they were also the medium toward which

Buchan consistently directed most of his new fiction for the North American market. With the extended circulations granted to some of these stories through 1930s and 1940s reprints, Buchan's literary association with pulp magazines would last for nearly half a century.

This two-decade-long bibliographical history of "the pulp Buchan" suggests that a more significant and more symbiotic relationship existed between Buchan and the American pulp magazines than has ever been acknowledged. The periodical contexts that surrounded Buchan's pulp publications, moreover, characterize the author's close association with this medium as one of mutual literary influence. In the transatlantic context of the first North American serializations of his novels in pulp magazines, Buchan—the Scottish poet and historian turned best-selling novelist and celebrity—emerges from the pages of these magazines as an expert navigator of modern media environments and a highly skilled manager of literary returns and reputations.

Buchan was not a "pulp writer" in any conventional sense of the term. His three earliest publications to appear in the pulps were handsomely featured on the covers of *Adventure* and *All-Story Weekly*, an uncommon distinction for any writer's first attempts at breaking into two such competitive markets. Though his earnings would remain consistently middle range by most standards of that period—S&S authors Dane Coolidge and Anna Katherine Green, for example, earned $3,000–$5,000 for long serials—Buchan nonetheless commanded an author's rate in excess of the typical ½ or ⅓ cents per word[19] (see Appendix B). At a time when British popular-fiction writers were in vogue with the editors of American magazines,[20] Buchan occupied a strategic position at the center of the London literary establishment. His professional obligations to Thomas Nelson & Sons, from 1907, and his long-standing ties with the A.P. Watt literary agency[21] afforded him routine access to important contacts within the international export market for British popular fiction. The cultural stereotypes of the pulp "fictioneer" existing at the fringes of literary society and hammering out his daily quota of words for the "fiction factory" certainly did not apply.[22]

Though not a typical pulp writer, Buchan was nonetheless a consistent one. Throughout his career as a best-selling novelist, Buchan maintained literary affiliations with three of the five major pulp publishing houses in New York: the Ridgway Company, Frank A. Munsey Company, and the Street & Smith Corporation. With editors of their magazines, he would arrange, often personally, first North American serializations for no fewer than eight of his novels, including three of the five Hannay novels, and two short stories—a respectable, if not staggering, number of contributions. For a writer of Buchan's caliber, this proportion of first appearances in the pulps occupies a spectrum somewhere between Haggard and H.G. Wells, at the low end, and Edgar Wallace and Talbot Mundy—whose pulp careers were notoriously prolific—at the other.[23]

With only two exceptions, Buchan had published no fiction between January 1901 and February 1909,[24] but, starting in 1910, a pattern of trans-atlantic serialization in popular periodicals, followed by book publication in both hardcover and paperback, would chart the author's steady rise through the ranks of contemporary best-selling British novelists such as H. de Vere Stacpoole and Baroness Orczy. Since 1907, Buchan had been reading copious amounts of periodical fiction as literary advisor for Nelson & Sons. He scrutinized contemporary popular-fiction magazines to see what was selling, to identify trends, and to scout out potential new writers for Nelson's series of cheap reprints he was developing. According to Kate Macdonald, this new and systematic exposure to the popular writing of the day gave Buchan the renewed impetus to write his own fiction again.[25]

Buchan's first American serializations after 1910 demonstrate a marked preference for pulp magazine publication, but, in Britain, those same novels would appear simultaneously across a much wider class of periodical and range of perceived audiences. Between April and September 1910, *Prester John* was first serialized in George Newnes's illustrated boys' magazine, *The Captain*. In December 1913, *The Power-House* was published in *Blackwood's Magazine*, and, from July to September 1915, this same conservative Edinburgh monthly serialized *The Thirty-Nine Steps*. Also in 1915, *Salute to Adventurers* appeared in the *Sunday Chronicle*,[26] a large-circulation provincial newspaper. From July 6 to November 9, 1916, the second Hannay novel, *Greenmantle*, was serialized in Hillaire Belloc's weekly sixpenny military broadsheet, *Land & Water*. And, though *Mr. Standfast* (1919) was never serialized in the UK, the fourth Hannay novel, *The Three Hostages*, would appear in *The Graphic* from April 25 to August 9, 1924. This illus-trated weekly from 1869, a former rival of *The Illustrated London News*, had also first serialized Haggard's *She: A History of Adventure*, from October 2, 1886 to January 1, 1887. From March to August 1922, Alfred Harmsworth's *London Magazine*, a popular all-fiction magazine added to Harmsworth's burgeoning empire in 1900, had serialized *Huntingtower*.[27]

Such diversity was not the case with Buchan's first American serializa-tions. In the US, *Prester John* was serialized in Ridgway Co.'s *Adventure* magazine (March–June 1911), *The Thirty-Nine Steps* and *Salute to Adventurers*[28] in Frank Munsey's *All-Story Weekly* (June 5–12, 1915; and August 14–September 11, 1915), and *Mr. Standfast* in S&S's *The Popular Magazine* (January 7–February 20, 1919), all famous pulps from major pulp publishing houses.

From February 18 to May 18, 1921, *Adventure* then serialized *The Path of the King* and, in April 1928, published Buchan's short story "Skule Skerry."[29] Also in 1921, *The Popular Magazine* serialized *Huntingtower* (August 20–September 7), and, in 1926, *The Goddess of the Shades* (May 7–June 20). After the 1915 serialization of *The Thirty-Nine Steps*, the popularity of the Hannay novels persisted for Munsey's readers across other titles and title changes: in 1924, *Argosy All-Story Weekly* serialized

Figure 5.1 Four Covers: *The Captain* (September 1901); *Blackwood's Magazine* (July 1915); *Land & Water* (July 10, 1919); and *London Magazine* (February 1923).

The Three Hostages (June 14–August 2), and, in December 1938, *Argosy Weekly* reprinted *The Thirty-Nine Steps*—an acknowledgment of the growing international threat of Nazi Germany. This time, however, the first issue in the novel's three-part serialization featured "10,000 Readers Asked for It! The 39 Steps,"[30] stamped in bright red and yellow across the front cover.[31] By then, Buchan had become a "pulp celebrity."[32]

The extant bibliography of Buchan's known pulp publications ends in December 1949, when the Munsey reprint magazine, *Famous Fantastic Mysteries*, published his short story "No-Man's Land." This had been his first accepted publication for *Blackwood's* and had appeared over half a century earlier, in January 1899, when the author was just 23 years old.[33]

Figure 5.2 Six Covers: *Adventure* (March 1911); *All-Story Weekly* (June 5, 1915); *Argosy All-Story Weekly* (June 14, 1924); *The Popular Magazine* (January 7, 1919); *Argosy* (December 10, 1938); and *Famous Fantastic Mysteries* (December 1949).

Buchan was certainly not the only British author to take advantage of the American pulp market through simultaneous transatlantic serializations.[34] In 1905, Haggard's *Ayesha*—a much-anticipated sequel to his best-selling *She* (1886–87)—was published simultaneously by *The Windsor Magazine* in London and, in New York, by *The Popular Magazine*.[35] In 1908, S&S's flagship title also purchased first American serial rights to Wells's sprawling, condition-of-England novel *Tono-Bungay*, whereas, in the UK, this novel first appeared in a very different class of periodical altogether, Ford Maddox Hueffer's *The English Review*, a struggling, no-frills monthly literary magazine featuring art and criticism. Sax Rohmer adopted a different approach during the First World War and simultaneously published his early Fu Manchu stories (1912–16) in both *Collier's Weekly* and Cassell & Co.'s *The Story-Teller*—one of Britain's earliest, non-reprint, "pulp-paper," all-fiction magazines. And, in 1919–20, Joseph Conrad's *The Rescue* would be first serialized in both *Land & Water* and, in the United States, throughout the first seven issues of *Romance* magazine, the Ridgway Co.'s latest addition to a burgeoning post-war pulp market and its companion title to *Adventure*.[36]

Doyle, Kipling, Anthony Hope, and G.K. Chesterton all, at one point or another, had fiction or non-fiction published in pulp magazines, including *People's*, *The Popular*, *Top-Notch*, *Romance*, *10 Story Book*, and *Triple-X Magazine*. Their work was also reprinted—through the 1920s, 1930s, and 1940s—in magazines such as *Amazing Stories*, *Famous Stories*, *Famous Fantastic Mysteries*, *Pioneer Tales*, and *Ghost Stories*. The full list of frequent contributors would read like a "Who's Who" of British popular-fiction writers of the day and include, not only Haggard, Wells, Rohmer, Wallace, Orczy, and Mundy, but also Stacpoole, A.E.W. Mason, Max Pemberton, Ethel M. Dell, E. Phillips Oppenheim, and H.C. "Sapper" McNeile, along with William Le Queux, Rafael Sabatini, and many others.[37]

Authors on both sides of the Atlantic benefitted greatly from the practice. Serialization across multiple markets not only secured international copyright protection for their works, but also increased their readerships abroad, provided valuable marketing for their upcoming publications, and ultimately expanded book sales. In effect, authors were also being paid twice for the same work.[38] Backed by the financial resources of their corporate publishers, pulp-magazine editors such as Trumbull White, Bob Davis, and Charles Agnew Maclean[39] could often offer even better terms than many of the more respectable British illustrated monthlies; their circulations, moreover, numbered in the millions. Readers of pulp magazines represented a modern American equivalent to what Wilkie Collins had termed, half a century earlier, the "Unknown public."[40] And, during the early decades of the twentieth century, pulp magazines became an attractive and increasingly sought-after medium for the serialization of British popular fiction in the North American market.

What is most remarkable in Buchan's case is that he personally fulfilled the roles of author, publisher, and literary agent himself. Unlike Haggard and Doyle, for example, who relied on third-party representation for their American serializations through A.P. Watt, Buchan's pulp publications were a product of the author's own contacts and negotiations. Buchan's knowledge of transatlantic periodical markets and his expert talent for targeting and exploiting those markets had been sharpened and developed through his own experiences working in the publishing business: first, as a publisher's reader for John Lane's The Bodley Head, from 1895 to 1898, and, more importantly, as both a literary advisor, from 1907, and, after 1915, a director for Nelson & Sons. According to Macdonald, it was in late 1906 that Buchan signed a contract to become the London-based literary advisor for the Scottish publishing house. When the First World War began, he used his experience in journalism to establish and nearly single-handedly compose a fortnightly magazine for the firm, *The War*. And, it was Buchan's work on this magazine that earned him a coveted position as correspondent on the Western Front for both *The Times* and the *Daily News* in 1915.[41] Buchan's talent for writing, editing, and publishing fiction and non-fiction operated on multiple levels. This ability to perform simultaneous roles effectively, even to make them complementary, informs his seemingly contradictory career as both Member of Parliament for the Scottish Universities and wildly popular American-pulp-magazine author. It also frames Buchan's development of a new kind of modern adventurer, the South African expatriate turned soldier and secret-service agent, Richard Hannay.

In the transatlantic context of Buchan's first North American serializations of the Hannay novels in pulp magazines, Buchan's protagonist emerges as an expert navigator of modern media environments and manager of texts and information. The rhetoric of transatlantic publishing on the eve of the First World War strongly resonates in Hannay's development over the course of the "war-time trilogy,"[42] charting his progression as an expert reader of new media and textual and cultural codes. This is not surprising, given that pulps and the transatlantic market exerted a powerful gravitational pull on Buchan's sensibilities as a writer of popular fiction. In May 1914, for example, he wrote to his publishing partner, George Brown: "I have picked up two detective stories out of an American magazine, which seem to me rather a new species." The stories were by Clinton H. Stagg and featured the blind detective Thornley Colton, whose modern scientific methods solved otherwise hopelessly elaborate crimes. Stagg's "new species" of detective story had first appeared in S&S's *People's Magazine*, from February to October 1913. In June 1915, the first installment of Buchan's own "new species" of detective story, *The Thirty-Nine Steps*, was published in Frank Munsey's *All-Story Weekly*.

In the following section, I examine more closely the complex commercial context and transatlantic publication history of *The Thirty-Nine Steps*. I focus, not only on the novel's book form, but also, importantly, on the two distinct magazine serializations that preceded publication of the first edition of the book. In subsequent sections of the chapter, I then demonstrate the ways in which Buchan's own expert navigation of the transatlantic market for popular periodical fiction best illustrates the sophisticated literary and cultural context from which his early fictional spy hero first emerged. From Hannay's first appearance as an accidental secret agent in *The Thirty-Nine Steps*, my examination then turns to Buchan's third novel in the Hannay series, *Mr. Standfast* (1919), which, I argue, is the culmination of Hannay's training as a master reader of media and cultural codes. This formula for a twentieth-century hero, the international secret agent, is shown also to be an example of the modern evolution of the nineteenth-century adventurer. The crucial difference here is that, for Buchan, by the start of the First World War, the imaginary geographies required for adventure had all disappeared or else were radically transformed—explored, mapped, connected, and thus replaced by new media landscapes. The nineteenth-century adventurer was a hero in search of a genre, and magazines became this site of adventure for Buchan, because they offered him a place for a character such as Hannay to explore a widely expansive media landscape.

British Institutions, American Pulps

Negotiating contracts, identifying trends, understanding markets, and placing manuscripts accordingly, the professional literary agent served an important mediating role between authors, publishers, and the constantly shifting and mercurial reading public. Agents decoded and helped navigate the mysteries of an increasingly fragmented print culture field. They maximized profits, crafted literary reputations, and targeted constellations of readers through a bewildering variety of new publishing options. And yet, in December 1914, having just finished the manuscript of his 28th book and his tenth full-length work of fiction, *The Thirty-Nine Steps*,[43] Buchan chose to capably forego the services of his own literary agency and personally forward the manuscript to his friend and professional mentor George Blackwood, editor of *Blackwood's* and director of the old, established Edinburgh publishing house, William Blackwood & Sons.

Delighted with the manuscript, Blackwood contracted *The Thirty-Nine Steps* for £100 for first British serial rights and 12.5 percent royalty on all book sales.[44] The novel appeared first serially that summer[45] and then in book form in October. An immediate best-seller, two more editions followed in rapid succession,[46] and, in just 3 months, *The Thirty-Nine Steps* had sold more than 33,000 copies in England alone, an impressive figure at a time when sales of most novels did not reach 1,000 copies.[47]

In the same 3-month period, the combined sales figures for all British pocket reprints of Kipling's works could be estimated at 15,000–20,000 copies, and Conrad would have to wait 2 years (1914–16) before sales of his own first commercial success, *Chance* (1914), finally approached half

Figure 5.3 The Thirty-Nine Steps, 1st UK Edition Dust-Wrapper (Edinburgh: Blackwood & Sons, 1915).

that number.[48] These were solid figures for literary fiction at the time.[49] All combined, they still did not approach the astronomical 500,000 copies of Captain Ian Hay's wartime memoir, *The First Hundred Thousand*, sold that year in book form. Serialized in *Blackwood's* across 12 parts throughout 1915, and then published in book form in November, Hay's memoir topped best-seller lists in both England and the United States within the year. To put these figures in perspective, English major-league football matches during the 1914–15 season could draw from 30,000 to 50,000 spectators per match;[50] the latest single-sided Victor phonograph record of the Italian tenor Enrico Caruso—priced at $3—would sell up to a million copies;[51] and regular daily movie attendance in Britain was estimated at 3–4 million.[52] The wartime market for literary fiction of any kind seems small in comparison.

But, when we consider the first American serialization of *The Thirty-Nine Steps* from that same summer, the numbers dramatically increase. From the Munsey Co., Buchan received $1,000–1,500 for all North American serial rights,[53] or more than two to three times the amount earned by the *Blackwood's* serialization. Within 2 weeks of its appearance in the June 5 and June 12 issues of *All-Story Weekly*, the novel had reached a verified circulation of 400,000—more than three times the circulation of *Blackwood's* for the entire previous 12 months combined.[54] Multiply these figures by between three and five—which was standard industry practice at the time[55]—and we can calculate an estimated audience of nearly 1.5 million readers by the end of June 1915—and all before the novel's first UK appearance in the July issue of *Blackwood's*.

In the summer of 1915, few magazines might have seemed more oddly juxtaposed. Established nearly a century before, *Blackwood's* was a recognizable Victorian institution. The magazine's plain, unembellished cover design was in direct opposition to the momentous visual and technological changes occurring in the market around it. In contrast to the new, brightly covered magazines published each year, *Blackwood's* maintained associations with tradition and stability in an ever-changing market.[56] Annual subscription rates were £3, and the magazine's individual cover price of 2½ shillings—which was just over 50 cents—placed it well out of range of affordable reading matter for the majority of readers[57] and limited the magazine's circulation to just under 6,500 copies per month in 1915.[58]

Having weathered the explosion of new and cheaper periodicals of the 1880s and 1890s, by the First World War, *Blackwood's* had successfully targeted a much narrower, but socially more secure, network of readers, ensuring that the magazine's cultural influence surpassed its circulation. Institutional affiliations with private clubs, libraries, universities, and government organizations sustained a continuing readership for each new issue well out of proportion to its initial sales.[59] Subscribers to *Blackwood's* included members of the government, military, and colonial elite, soldiers and Navy men across Europe and the Empire, the professional and upper middle classes, and the Conservative political and literary establishments. In 1915, a novel serialized in *Blackwood's* would have been read by the publishers, editors, and writers of Britain's most prestigious literary reviews; as far away as Johannesburg, Melbourne, Calcutta, and San Francisco; and by thousands of soldiers serving in Europe and around the world.[60]

By comparison, Munsey's *All-Story Weekly* represented a decidedly lower, more democratic class of periodical altogether. It was populist and pluralistic,[61] priced at just 10 cents per issue.[62] It was printed on rough, untreated paper made directly from pulpwood—softwood trees grown quickly and specifically for this purpose. In 1905, the magazine's inaugural issue had proudly displayed a bright red banner promising readers "Something New."

Only a decade old in 1915, *All-Story* had already gone through several manifestations. It began as a monthly, carried 60 pages of advertisements, and, by its third issue, could claim a circulation of 200,000 copies. By 1912, advertisers had virtually abandoned the title altogether. The October issue from that year, featuring the first of the many *Tarzan* novels by Edgar Rice Burroughs, carried fewer than ten pages of advertisements.[63] In March 1914, the publisher converted the magazine into a weekly, and, 2 months later, with plummeting circulations, *All-Story* was combined with a third, more successful weekly title from 1908, *The Cavalier*. This third manifestation of the magazine's title lasted until May 1915, when *All-Story* again became a separate weekly publication, with a confirmed steady circulation of 200,000

Figure 5.4 First Issue of "Something New," *The All-Story Magazine* (January 1905).

copies.[64] That June, the magazine began its two-part serialization of Buchan's *The Thirty-Nine Steps*; by this time, it had come to epitomize the class of cheap, erratic, and modern market-driven periodicals against which *Blackwood's* identified and perpetuated its own uncompromising brand.[65] In terms of cultural associations, accessibility, political orientations, and constructed readerships, these magazines occupied opposite ends of the cultural spectrum.

If the literary reputations of pulp magazines were suspect, their large circulations more than compensated for that. In 1915, the top five best-selling pulp magazines had a combined circulation of more than 2.26 million copies per month.[66] For an author attempting to reach a wide, popular audience, *Blackwood's* would have seemed a much less appealing prospect for immediate return.[67] Buchan's own experiences in the publishing industry from 1907 involved an aptitude for recognizing and appreciating such differences. The transatlantic serialization of *The Thirty-Nine Steps* allowed him to effectively play both sides. Striking a balance between the symbolic capital of *Blackwood's* and the actual business of marketing and selling literary fiction to a wide, popular audience, Buchan maximized his novel's potential return by exploiting the strengths and weaknesses of each of the novel's distinct periodical contexts.[68]

By 1915, Buchan's multivalent career in publishing had entered its third decade in fact. His first published works had appeared as early as 1893, and his early business relationship with John Lane was established just 2 years later. In addition to his role as literary advisor for Nelson & Sons from 1907, Buchan had also been "a columnist, a book reviewer, and a political pundit (and a failed Parliamentary candidate in the 1910 election)"[69] throughout the period 1904–13. Buchan had been a prolific reviewer for *The Spectator* for the past 14 years, moreover, and, in the meantime, he was "developing a new way of writing fiction that would appeal strongly to the market."[70]

Buchan's letters to Blackwood and the A.P. Watt agency throughout 1915–16 portray the writer, publisher, and literary adviser at work simultaneously, offering advice on what might sell, in what market, how to sell it, and for how much.[71] Letters to Blackwood reference proposed dates for serialization of *The Thirty-Nine Steps*,[72] ongoing arrangements with "the American people,"[73] retail price on the first edition, publication, royalties, and terms.[74] Buchan recommends new writers[75] and even suggests ways that Blackwood might market his novel in book form.[76] In his role as publisher at Nelson & Sons, Buchan negotiates terms with Blackwood for *The Thirty-Nine Steps*[77] and with Watt, his own literary agency, for Hay's *The First Hundred Thousand*.[78] Both titles are requested by Buchan for inclusion in Nelson's Continental Library of Reprints.

We might ask ourselves: at what point does Buchan draw the line between his role as publisher, author, and literary agent, when, as representative of Nelson's, Buchan is negotiating with his own publisher for the rights to his own book? For most authors, such complicated and potentially sensitive negotiations conducted simultaneously across two continents over a period of months would require the services of a professional mediator. That Buchan handled all the arrangements himself offers a familiar template for the author's imagining of the kinds of textual skill necessary for a fictional spy hero's success. The role of the professional literary agent—a complicated synthesis of knowing markets, identifying openings, negotiating terms, mediating interests, and positioning works in an attempt to shape and organize impressions—is paralleled in the novel's growing proliferation of texts and the protagonist's own developing mastery over them. From colonial outsider to intelligence insider, Hannay's dramatic arc of development can be traced through his changing relationship to print media and growing mastery over the instability of texts, and is registered in a series of dramatic breakthroughs that center on the act of reading.

A Master of Pace: *The Thirty-Nine Steps* (1915)

The plot of *The Thirty-Nine Steps* involves the mysterious murder of an American spy that takes place one night in Hannay's flat in London, the discovery of a secret black notebook, and an international plot to steal top-secret Allied documents on the eve of the First World War. Falsely accused of the murder, Hannay must evade capture, decode the notebook, and ultimately help secure the information contained in the top-secret documents. In his desperate flight north to the borderlands of Scotland, Hannay moves quickly from one hiding place to another, only to discover each time that his arrival is preceded by the developing story of his supposed crime in the front-page headlines of the daily newspapers. When Hannay unravels the coded information contained in the secret black notebook, by correctly interpreting the cryptic phrase "Thirty-nine steps . . . 10.17 P.M." (p. 615),[79] he identifies the location of the Black Stone's coastal hideaway and directs the way for British authorities.[80] Only then does Hannay finally evade this ominous threat of ubiquitous media.

Hannay is an example of the persistence of modern adventure, and his successful defiance of both the official authorities and a powerful international network of highly trained German spies certainly defies credulity. His desperate flight north to the Scottish borderlands propels the plot of the novel forward, while opening up new ways of thinking about modernity. Situated almost entirely along railways, highways, and country roads, the fast-paced action of *The Thirty-Nine Steps* celebrates high-speed velocity and modern technologies of speed. In his description of Buchan as "a master of pace," John Keegan contends that:

> Hannay's rush from London to Galloway to the Highlands to the Thames Valley to London again and finally to the Channel coast, by express train, high-powered motor car and on his own fleet feet, leaves the reader breathless, but also panting to know what lies beyond.[81]

The various means of locomotion, the automobile and the express train in particular, are then pitted against the seemingly universal reach of the police, an international organization of German spies, and especially modern mass media. The plot is propelled forward several times by this third situation. Hannay attempts to outrun both the police and the Black Stone and flees almost immediately after the murder of Franklin Scudder at his flat in London, but the knowledge of the event travels even faster.

Even in a remote cottage in rural Scotland, the news of the crime is waiting for him on the front page of the morning's newspaper as he arrives. Several times, at various train stations along the way, it is the developing story of Hannay's suspected crime, which appears in the daily newspapers, that pursues him from one ill-chosen hiding place to another. The author gestures here towards a seemingly universal proliferation and inescapability of the technological changes of modernity. It is an international playing field, constantly shifting, inundated by technologies of high-speed, seemingly ubiquitous information, and there is no place to hide. Invariably, the police arrive at each location soon after Hannay, and he is forced to flee yet again, never actually able to outrun the seemingly universal knowledge of a crime he supposedly committed.[82]

It is significant that Hannay's desperate flight takes him to some of the remotest areas of the UK. Like Conrad's faraway South Seas district of Patusan, the setting for his protagonist's escape in *Lord Jim* (1900), and the remote, unnamed village in the South of France from Wells's *Tono-Bungay* (1909), described by Ponderevo as "that queer corner of refuge out of the world [that] was destined to be my uncle's deathbed,"[83] these harsh landscapes in the north of the island become Buchan's version of a foreign setting, beyond surveillance. A crucial characteristic shared between the texts by both Buchan and Wells, moreover, is that the narrators' descriptions of their inevitable discoveries take place as a result of the mass medium of the daily newspapers. Hannay's attempts to evade pursuit are constantly foiled, once the newspapers "tip" strangers off as to his real identity.

Mark Wollaeger addresses this characteristically modern dilemma, along with the challenges it posed to adventure fiction in the early twentieth century, when he writes:

> To recover traces of what might have existed prior to the global reach of new media and colonialism, late imperial romance had to effect an "imaginary unmapping" of the world in order to escape from the grid of the rational and the known.[84]

For an exemplary register of this "imaginary unmapping" of the modern globally mediated world, Wollaeger offers Doyle's *The Lost World* (1912), in which Professor Challenger and his band of explorers discover an uncharted prehistoric plateau hidden deep in the South American jungles. Literary efforts such as these involve the creation of parallel worlds for imaginary discovery or escape and recuperate a lost sense of faraway fringes beyond the boundaries of civilization. Buchan's own "imaginary unmapping" of modernity relies on Hannay's ability to evade capture, through technological expertise and mastery, rather than escape to geographical pockets of resistance.[85] Encoded messages regarding top-secret plans for world domination signify a radical otherness within this globalized, systematized, mass-mediated modernity, or what Keegan calls "a hint of presences just beyond the boundary of consciousness . . . unseen, undefined powers whose intervention can never be discounted."[86] Hannay evades capture and survives a string of harrowing ordeals by learning to navigate modernity's technologies of high-speed travel and read its ubiquitous flows of information. He escapes technology, in effect, by learning to read, interpret, and manipulate it.

By the end of *The Thirty-Nine Steps*, all three of the narrative's critical texts have been brought safely under control: the notebook is decoded, the headlines of the daily newspapers are no longer a threat, and stolen information contained in the top-secret Allied documents is finally secure.[87] Unravelling the clues, capturing the Black Stone, and securing the top-secret Allied plans represent a significant series of master strokes for Hannay and the British government, but events in *The Thirty-Nine Steps* are only the opening salvo of a much greater clandestine German offensive.

Breaking the Pulp Code: *Mr. Standfast* (1919)

Mr. Standfast (1919) is the third wartime installment of the Hannay spy series, the stakes of which involve a villain's plot to spread anthrax throughout the Allied armies. In Part Two of the novel, Hannay's evolving expert ability to identify and correctly interpret encoded texts is called into service again by the British government and draws critical connections between seemingly unrelated texts across multiple networks of print media. This reading becomes truly compelling, when we consider the initial publication context of *Mr. Standfast* as a four-part serialization in S&S's *The Popular Magazine*.

Mr. Standfast operates as a self-consciously hyper-literary text. The novel is densely packed with direct references and subtle allusions, not only to the author's own works—including *The Thirty-Nine Steps*, Buchan's Wellington House-sponsored *Nelson's History of the War* (1914–18), his war correspondence for *The Times*, and another previous Hannay novel, *Greenmantle* (1916)—but also the *King James Bible*, John Bunyan's *The Pilgrim's Progress* (1678), Romantic German poetry (1815), Izaak Walton's *The Compleat Angler* (1653–76), and the works of Stevenson and Walter Scott. Frequently during the novel, characters read or discuss having read an edition of William Hazlitt's *Essays*, the *Golden Treasury* book series, *A Missionary Child in China*, a *Life of David Livingstone*, and *Ghost Stories of an Antiquary*. An array of magazine and newspaper titles appears, including *Punch, Justice for All, The Critic, Herald, Scotsman, Vossische Zeitung, Weser Zeitung, New York Sentinel*, the *United Free Church Monthly, Frankfurter Zeitung, Der Grosse Krieg, L'illustration*, and the *Temps*.[88] The novel continually draws the reader's attention to both fictional and non-fictional sources outside the text and emphasizes the text's situation within a complex network of other texts.

Even an abbreviated plot summary of *Mr. Standfast* reveals the increasing complexity of the international political situation contextualizing the last part of the wartime trilogy. It also reveals the increasing complexity of Buchan's narrative capabilities. Part One of the novel opens three-and-a-half years into the war. Brigadier-General Richard Hannay is stationed with his men on the Western front. He is summoned by spymaster Sir Walter Bullivant and asked to return to "the great game." Hannay accepts and, posing as a South African named Cornelius Brand, is sent back to England to receive further instructions. From his contact in England, Hannay learns that he must infiltrate a local pacifist community. Here, he meets both Moxon Ivery, described by the narrator as "colourless" and suspiciously "nondescript,"[89] and John Blenkiron, an American spy. Blenkiron hands a message to Hannay, and the two arrange to meet in London. Blenkiron reveals that he has been working undercover around the world. He is hot on the trail of an international network of German spies, whose leader is known to be located in Britain. Blenkiron believes that Ivery, in fact, is the "spider at the center of the web," leaking secrets and vital information to the Germans. Unable to prove it, he suggests using Ivery to feed misinformation to the enemy and then tells Hannay to proceed to Scotland and meet up with an American named Abel Gresson. Blenkiron believes that the stolen information is being sent that way, before being forwarded on to Germany.

In Glasgow, Hannay finds Gresson and learns that Gresson makes frequent boat trips up the Scottish coast. Hannay books passage on the next boat, but then, realizing he needs a passport to travel north, he instead treks inland, only to find he is now wanted by the authorities. Hurrying to Skye and then towards Ranna, Hannay catches up again with the boat, before spotting Gresson on shore. Hannay tracks him to a hidden cave on the coast. The next morning, Hannay searches the area and finds the deep water of the bay ideal for submarines. He also discovers that the cave is actually a secret hiding place used by the German spies to forward messages, via submarine, back to Germany.

The news of this discovery leads Hannay back to England, now disguised as a traveling bookseller. When Hannay is recognized by police in the train station and forced to flee yet again, he stumbles upon Archie Roylance, a British fighter pilot, who flies him south in his aeroplane. The aeroplane breaks down, and Hannay flees once more on foot. He crashes a film set, steals a bicycle, and eventually makes his way to London, now disguised as an Allied soldier. In London, Hannay encounters Ivery in the midst of a

German bombing raid and recognizes him as one of the members of the Black Stone, the international organization of German spies he first tangled with in *The Thirty-Nine Steps*.

When, in the course of the novel, Hannay becomes involved in examining and deciphering several encoded messages ingeniously embedded in the pages of international newspapers, this event assumes a more meaningful and dramatic dimension within the novel's own already dense intertextuality. At the beginning of Part Two, which first appeared as the third installment of the novel's four-part serialization in the February 7, 1919 issue of S&S's *The Popular Magazine*, Hannay returns to the Western Front from counter-espionage activities in England. He remains here for several months, until, stricken by "a bout with malaria" (p. 139),[90] he is placed in a makeshift military hospital to recover. Confined to his bed and growing increasingly restless, he comes across several suspicious-looking advertisements in the English and German newspapers, although Hannay does not immediately suspect they may be some kind of coded communication.

Reading through the "English papers twice and a big stack of German ones," Hannay is first "struck by the tremendous display of one advertisement in the English press" (p. 140),[91] and records:

> It was a thing called "Gussiter's Deep-breathing System," which, according to its promoter, was a cure for every ill, mental, moral, or physical, that man can suffer. Politicians, generals, admirals, and music-hall artists all testified to the new life it had opened up for them. I remember wondering what these sportsmen got for their testimonies, and thinking I would write a spoof letter myself to old Gussiter.
>
> (p. 140)[92]

The ad for patent medicine in the English newspaper assumes further dimensions when Hannay compares it with "an advertisement of the same kind in the *Frankfurter Zeitung*," several more in "one or two rather obscure *Volkstimmes* and *Volkszeitungs*," and "in *Der Grosse Krieg*, the official German propagandist picture paper" (p. 140).[93] Hannay reflects:

> It was not Gussiter this time, but one Weissmann, but his game was identical—"deep breathing." The Hun style was different from the English . . . [b]ut the principal was the same. . . . That made me ponder a little, and I went carefully through the whole batch.
>
> (p. 140)[94]

At this point, Hannay reflects: "[The ads] were all the same but one, and that one had a bold variation, for it contained four of the sentences used in the ordinary English advertisement" (p. 140).[95]

For several paragraphs, the full implications of his discovery remain unclear. Across a two-column page of an installment that runs for only

20 pages, he carefully analyzes, pursues, and discards one hypothesis after another. First, he suspects a possible "case of trading with the enemy," or perhaps that lurking behind "Mr. Gussiter's financial backing" one "might find a Hun syndicate" (p. 140).[96] He then remarks: "And then I had another notion. . . . I went through the papers again" (p. 140),[97] but this time, in order to solve the puzzle, Hannay closely examines and analyzes the context of the ad's several variations and the distinctive features of the newspapers in which those variations appear:

> The English ones which contained the advertisement were all good, solid bellicose organs; the kind of thing no censorship would object to leaving the country. I had before me a small sheaf of pacifist prints, and they had not the advertisement. That might be for reasons of circulation, or it might not.
>   The German papers were either Radical or Socialist publications, just the opposite of the English lot, except the *Grosse Krieg*. Now we have a free press, and Germany has, strictly speaking, none. All her journalistic indiscretions are calculated. Therefore the Bosche has no objections to his rags getting to enemy countries. He wants it.
>
> (p. 140)[98]

This line of reasoning finally leads Hannay to his startling revelation. "Puzzl[ing] over the subject," Hannay records that, "conclusions began to form."[99] The ads are an illicit form of communicating across enemy lines in order to avoid the PO censors who examine the wartime mail. Mr. A places an ad with a "cipher in it," and the paper containing it enters Germany by Holland in 3 days. Mr. B then replies in the *Frankfurter*, and, 3 days later, editors, intelligence officers, and Mr. A are reading it in London, but only Mr. A knows "what it really mean[s]" (p. 140).[100]

Intending to follow what the Germans are saying in several enemy newspapers, Hannay gleans his most useful information, ironically, from the seemingly innocuous ads for patent medicines alongside the articles and editorials.[101] Secret messages hidden in the ads betray the international communications network used by the Wild Birds, a gang of German spies operating between hideouts in England and in several parts of Europe. The Allies exploit this discovery to spread counter-information to the enemy and ultimately capture the novel's central antagonist, the criminal mastermind Moxon Ivery. Such large-scale consequences assert a utopian potential in Hannay's sophisticated form of media mastery. His ability to read correctly across networks of information, connect otherwise disparate forms, and draw meaningful inferences from multiple texts originating from seemingly distant and unrelated sources ultimately helps win the war for the Allies.

Reinserting this pivotal scene into its first publication context in S&S's *The Popular Magazine,* and reading it again alongside the stories, editorials, and adverts that originally appeared alongside it will not reveal anything

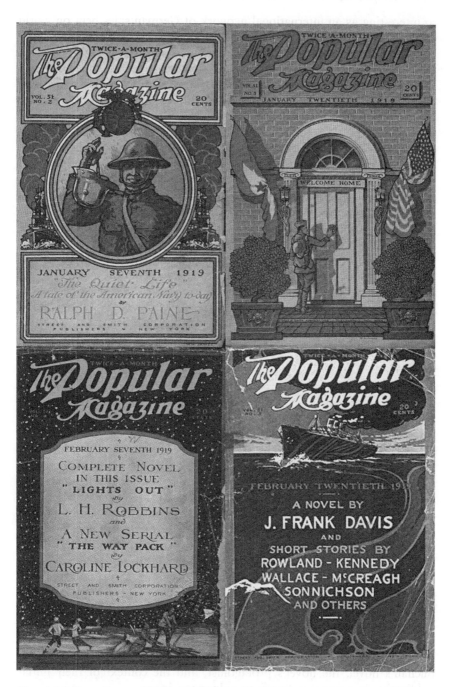

Figure 5.5 Four Covers: *The Popular Magazine* from January 7; January 20; February 7; and February 20, 1919.

so interesting as an international network of German spies bent on world domination.

However, it does suggest a radical reorientation in Buchan's approach to the kinds of adventure still available in the modern world. The new media landscapes of the early twentieth century were defined by what was then the predominant new media form, a burgeoning volume of print in Britain and the United States from 1880 to the First World War. The magazines of that period, and especially American pulp magazines, became a site of creativity and artistic exploration for Buchan, but magazines were not simply a place to explore this widely expansive media landscape. They also had their own kinds of cultural work to perform, and, although Buchan's Hannay certainly influenced some of the writing subsequently done in pulp magazines, especially throughout the 1920s, the pulps had a much more profound influence on Buchan's creation and development of Hannay. Read in the cultural and material context of the pulp magazines, Buchan's development of this hugely popular spy hero, whose talents revolve around fantasies of close reading and mastering media and cultural codes, registers profoundly the anxieties of under-trained and under-skilled members of the modern, evolving, corporate society.

Hannay's cross-examination of English and German newspapers, leading to his discovery and analysis of the varied ads for Gussiter's, first appears on page 140 of the February 7, 1919 issue. Selling for 20 cents a copy, *The Popular Magazine* at this time was a twice-monthly magazine and the flagship publication of the Street & Smith Corporation of New York. The writing was top quality, and *The Popular Magazine* attracted some of the best British popular-fiction writers of its day, including Haggard, Wells, Stacpoole, and Wallace; it also featured covers from artists Charles M. Russell, N.C. Wyeth, Leslie Thrasher, and Norman Rockwell.[102] This issue features 192 pages of fiction[103] and 18 pages of advertisements, and includes a complete novel, six stories, two serial installments, an article on starting a newspaper, and 7 pages of editorial content spread across the issue's middle and back pages. Framing Buchan's contribution, the fiction featured in the magazine is an eclectic mix of modern adventure and intrigue. Editorial subtitles include "an American's adventures in London," "Sherlock Holmes-ing off the Maine coast," "[t]he real West," "behind the scenes in Washington," and "denizens of the underworld are surprised." But, the advertising sections of the magazine best demonstrate the kinds of hypothetical consumer that S&S and their advertising department hoped to locate among *The Popular Magazine*'s 1 million plus readership.[104] And, like Hannay, we can read and examine these ads for clues, while drawing tentative conclusions regarding the level of reciprocal influence at work between Buchan's novel, the novel's protagonist, and the context of their initial publication in a popular American pulp magazine.

Advertisements for patent medicines such as "Gussiter's 'Deep-Breathing' System" were ubiquitous at the turn of the twentieth century, but had largely disappeared from the nationally distributed U.S. magazines by the end of the First World War.[105] In their place, another type of ad had emerged: the mail-order coupon for self-improvement, physical-conditioning, or job-training courses requiring "just 15 minutes a day" and completed entirely by correspondence. Some of the largest and most prominent of them were famous ads for the International Correspondence Schools of Scranton, Pennsylvania. ICS offered more than 400 courses covering some 2,000 subjects, including drawing, languages, salesmanship, engineering, architecture, and engine and radio repair. Conforming to patterns common in American pulp magazines from 1919, the four issues of *The Popular Magazine* that serialized Buchan's novel contain significantly fewer ad pages than more upscale, mass-market magazines of the same period, such as *Scribner's Magazine* or the *Cosmopolitan*, although the products and services advertised also show a familiar pattern: self-improvement, physical conditioning, job training, health supplements, and personal-hygiene products account for just over 51 percent of the entire number, and this includes a prominent half-page ad for ICS (see Appendix G).

Featured in the ICS ad, a frustrated husband proclaims to his wife that a colleague at work was made "manager today, at a fine increase in salary . . . the fourth man in the office to be promoted since January." But, he urges, "I've thought it all out. . . . I'm as good a man as any one of them. All I need is special training—and I'm *going to get it*." The boxed text of the ad reads: "Thousands of men . . . let the [ICS] prepare them. . . . Pick the position you want in the work you like best and the I.C.S. will prepare you."[106] Most ICS ads of the time adopt a similar approach, featuring several different categories of hypothetical client: from manual laborers trying to make ends meet to frustrated office men at the bottom of the corporate ladder. Other ads feature the up-and-coming worker on the brink of a major promotion—or the man just recently promoted: the quintessential ICS success story.

Read in the cultural and material context of these ads, Buchan's fantasy of mastery registers profoundly the anxieties of potentially under-trained and under-skilled members of the modern, evolving, corporate society that, following the First World War, became increasingly integrated in world economies. When Hannay discovers secret communications hidden in the ads for "Gussiter's," this act of sophisticated reading involves the successful navigation of the material artifacts of this complex global media environment—and control over this potentially intimidating textual and technological field. When this pivotal scene from the novel is read alongside prominently placed ads for correspondence schools, job-training courses, 100 ways to improve stamina, memory enhancements, dietary aids, and a variety of guaranteed methods for learning a diverse catalogue of practical skills, the utopian dimensions of this fantasy become much clearer. The spy hero as a super-reader of political, economic, and social codes is an ideal modern subjectivity; Hannay's ability to correctly read and interpret a complex network of mediated signs qualifies him as the exemplary ICS success story.

Organized international networks of spies, and criminal masterminds bent on world domination frame a potentially precarious position for the rest of us, but Hannay's successful discovery satisfies readers' imaginative agency and rewards their participation in the fantasy. This masterful reading of codes, media, and global information flows also operates as an imaginary surrogate for the reader's own desire to successfully navigate complex social and economic environments, the same dynamic at work in job-training ads from ICS on a less abstract, but no less romantic level. ICS ads interpolate the reader—always as a future client—by framing a potentially anxious and precarious social and economic position, then refocusing those insecurities onto more aggressive ways of pursuing financial improvement. In exchange for the clients' time, effort of studying, motivation, self-discipline, and above all direct engagement with their own personal economic destinies—although it required just "15 minutes a day" set aside for reading, exercises, and self-improvement—these ads promise a sense of future mastery, command, and control in the form of personal achievement, the admiration of colleagues, and a rewarding domestic life.[107]

Such fantasies were not exclusive to pulp magazines, American readers, or even under-employed or under-skilled workers, but a popular dimension of a well-subscribed cultural and economic ethos in the early decades of the twentieth century. It was this ethos that Richard Ohmann identifies at work in the modern courtship tale,[108] "valorizing a living modernity" and "expressed in freedom from social conventions, and familiarity with modern technologies ... an indicator of the young, active, aspirational protagonist."[109] Helping also to ease the anxieties and trauma of transitioning between the horizontal industrial economies of the nineteenth century and increasingly bureaucratic, diversified, vertical corporate cultures, such an ethos idealized upward mobility, self-reliance, and personal initiative. The implied audience of readers for a pulp-paper magazine such as S&S's *The Popular Magazine* is interpolated by these ads, not as members of any one class or occupation, but as a significant proportion of a national culture of self-improvement, technical education, and diversified interests leading to greater job prospects. With the magazine's audited circulation in 1919 of more than 370,000 copies every 2 weeks,[110] the estimated readership of a single monthly issue of *The Popular Magazine* was more than 1.5 million. The numbers alone preclude any single class, occupation, gender, or ethnicity being the specific target for these famous ads.

Conclusion

Buchan entered publishing and authorship when transatlantic book and magazine markets were undergoing significant changes.[111] By the start of the First World War, the demise of the three-decker novel and the expansion of new media markets such as cinema, reprints, and pulp magazines had led to organized professional efforts to read, interpret, and control untapped audiences of popular readers as potential consumers. The rising circulation figures and staggering proliferation of new titles demanded increasingly specialized skills for decoding, managing, and navigating this complex commercial environment. Advertising agents analyzed circulations, attempting to anticipate and organize public spending habits; literary agents and newspaper syndicates directed increasingly international flows of fiction, feature essays, fashion advice columns, illustrations, comic strips, political cartoons, photographs, and even crossword puzzles across multiple media and markets, balancing the financial and cultural gains of their clients. Growing numbers of potential buyers of fiction and non-fiction, through books and the magazines, gained more access to greater amounts of disposable income with which to supply new habits of reading for pleasure, for information, for self-improvement, and for relaxation.[112]

Buchan's adventuring secret agent, Richard Hannay, emerges from the rough-paper pages of the iconic American pulp magazines as yet another of these modern mediating subjectivities. As an expert navigator of modern media environments and sophisticated manager of texts and information, Hannay addresses the anxieties of dis-organization and overproduction of print and visual material within a modern culture of specialized marketing and dissemination. In the Paper Age,[113] where simultaneous national access to information and culture was finally made possible through technology, network infrastructure, mass-mediation, and superfluity-by-design, culture's commerce required the increasingly skilled and complex operations of armies of professional mediators, who shaped and organized market responses to an otherwise unmanageable overabundance of print and visual material.

Notes

1 See John T. Soister, *Up from the Vault: Rare Thrillers of the 1920s and 1930s*, Jefferson, NC: McFarland, 2004, pp. 9–10; Cecily Close, "Arthur Greening, Publisher of *The Scarlet Pimpernel*," *The La Trobe Journal* No. 78 (Spring 2006), p. 51; and Cay Van Ash and Elizabeth Rohmer, *Master of Villainy: A Biography of Sax Rohmer*, London: Tom Stacey, 1972, pp. 132, 158, 169, 174, 180, 204.

2 Joseph Conrad, "Letter to Baroness Janina De Brunnow" (2 October 1897), *The Collected Letters of Joseph Conrad, Volume 1*, Eds. Frederick Robert Karl and Laurence Davies, Cambridge, UK: Cambridge University Press, 1983, p. 390.

3 *Chance* (1914) sold 13,000 copies over a period of 2 years, a fourfold increase in Conrad's usual sales figures.

4 Mary Hammond, *Reading, Publishing and the Formation of Literary Taste in England, 1880–1914*, Aldershot, UK: Ashgate, 2006, p. 180.

5 Ibid.

6 Van Ash and Rohmer, pp. 132, 158, 169, 174, 180, 204; and Jonathan Rose, "Modernity and Print I: Britain 1890–1970," *A Companion to the History of the Book*, Eds. Simon Eliot and Jonathan Rose, Chichester, UK: Wiley-Blackwell, 2009, p. 342.

7   At the same time, opportunities offered in the field of popular fiction were far more numerous and diverse. See Introduction.

8   See Christopher Wilson, *The Labor of Words: Literary Professionalism in the Progressive Era*, Athens, GA: University of Georgia Press, 1985; Thomas Strychacz, *Modernism, Mass Culture, and Professionalism*, Cambridge, UK: Cambridge University Press, 1993; and Susanna Ashton, *Collaborators in Literary America, 1870–1920*, New York and Basingstoke, UK: Palgrave Macmillan, 2003.

9   Anonymous, "The Modern Novel," *Chambers's Journal* Vol. 12, No. 591 (April 27, 1895), p. 263; a selection from the article was reprinted as "The Fickleness Of Novel Readers," *Tuapeka Times* Vol. 23, No. 4292 (November 13, 1895), p. 5.

10   Ibid.

11   Ibid.

12   Ibid.

13   Ibid.

14   Ibid.

15   Gary Messinger, *British Propaganda and the State in the First World War*, Manchester, UK: Manchester University Press, 1992, p. 87.

16   Robin W. Winks, "John Buchan: Stalking the Wilder Game," in *The Four Adventures of Richard Hannay*, Ed. Robin W. Winks, Boston, MA: David R. Godine, 1988, p. v.

17   Buchan's "strain of duplicity" would be challenged in the early months of 1915, when competing demands of the First World War involved Buchan as writer of both the official, Wellington House-sponsored *Nelson's History of the War* and a series of unsigned articles for *The War Picture Weekly*, criticizing Britain's official control of war-related information. The author's hectic schedule and colossal work load routinely involved multiple projects. Not only did he write, proofread, and fact-check most of his own material personally, but he also handled the distribution, marketing, sales, and translations of his own work and the work of several others.

18   Examples of "earliest" modern spy hero also include David Carruthers (Erskine Childers, *The Riddle of the Sands*, London: Smith, Elder, 1903); the "most famous" would probably be James Bond (Ian Fleming, *Casino Royale*, London: Cape, 1953).

19   Data regarding authors' rates, derived from a variety of sources, are compiled at The Pulp Magazines Project, "Authors' Rates," at www.pulpmags.org/print-culture (accessed May 5, 2012).

20   This was particularly the case for late-Victorian heavyweights Rider Haggard, Rudyard Kipling, and Conan Doyle.

21   A.P. Watt & Son was the foremost literary agency at that time. Its clients included the most successful British fiction writers of the period: Walter Besant, Marie Corelli, Haggard, Kipling, Doyle, and Winston Churchill.

22   For iconic memoirs of pulp writers, see Frank Gruber's *The Pulp Jungle*, Los Angeles, CA: Sherbourne, 1967; and Paul Powers's *Pulp Writer: Twenty Years in the American Grub Street*, Lincoln, NE: University of Nebraska Press, 2007.

23   For bibliographies of the magazine publications of Haggard, Wells, Wallace, Mundy, and hundreds of other fiction writers, see The FictionMags Index, at www.philsp.com/homeville/fmi/0start.htm (accessed September 5, 2011).

24   Buchan's short story "The Outgoing of the Tide" (January 1902) had been written while Buchan was at Oxford (Andrew Lownie, *John Buchan: The Presbyterian Cavalier*, Boston, MA: Godyne, 1995, p. 83), and his short story "The Kings of Orion" (January 1906) was published in *Blackwood's Magazine*, but under a pseudonym.

25 Kate Macdonald, "John Buchan's Breakthrough: The Conjunction of Experience, Markets and Forms that Made *The Thirty-Nine Steps*," *Publishing History* Vol. 68 (2010), pp. 25–106.

26 The novel was serialized under an alternate title, *New Lands in the Sunset*.

27 Data are derived from several sources, including Lownie, pp. 137–41, 161–82; The FictionMags Index; Kenneth Hillier's "Buchanalia: A Private Collection of John Buchan's Works," unpublished catalogue; the John Buchan Society's "Writings" page, at www.johnbuchansociety.co.uk/thewritingsf.htm (accessed September 5, 2011); and my own collection of 500+ periodicals.

28 The novel was serialized, across five issues, under the alternate title *Andrew Garvald-Tidewater Trader*. On the cover of the August 14, 1915 issue, the novel is mistakenly attributed to "James Buchan."

29 In the UK, this story first appeared in the May 1928 issue of the *Pall Mall Magazine*, which published (from September 1927) six of the stories later included in *The Runagates Club* (Hodder & Stoughton, 1928).

30 The novel was reprinted, across three installments, in the issues for December 10, 17, and 24. The altered title on the magazine's cover was likely a belated tie-in with the 1935 Alfred Hitchcock film of the same name. Inside the magazine, the novel's proper, full-length title, *The Thirty-Nine Steps*, is used instead.

31 A good indication of Buchan's respectable, but decidedly "pulp-ish," literary reputation with readers of American pulp magazines is the company of serials flanking his novel's 1938 reprinting. *The Thirty-Nine Steps* (December 10–24) follows directly on the heels of A. Merritt's *The Ship of Ishtar* (October 29–December 3), runs consecutively alongside Max Brand's *Young Dr. Kildaire* (December 17–31), and precedes Johnston McCulley's *Black Grande* (December 31–January 21) and Edgar Rice Burroughs's *The Synthetic Men of Mars* (January 7–February 11).

32 See also J. Randolph Cox's "Bibliographical Notes: John Buchan in the American Pulp Magazines," *Dime Novel Round-Up* (February/April 2010).

33 John Buchan, "No-Man's Land," *Blackwood's Magazine* Vol. 165, No. 999 (January 1899), pp 1–36.

34 Particularly after *McClure's Magazine* was sold and restyled as a women's periodical in 1911, the pulps became *the* American market for British popular-fiction writers of action, adventure, and romance of every kind.

35 Haggard would soon become a familiar feature in American pulp magazines, with popular serializations of many of his novels appearing in *The Blue Book*, *Cavalier Weekly*, *Gunter's*, and *New Story Magazine*.

36 Data are derived from The FictionMags Index, my own collection of 500+ periodicals, and Mike Ashley's *The Age of the Storytellers: British Popular Fiction Magazines, 1880–1950*, London: The British Library, 2006.

37 Ibid.

38 At least, this was the case in theory. For the American serial rights to *Tono-Bungay*, for example, Wells promptly received a check from S&S for £100, or twice the annual salary of a British laborer employed in the printing trade (*Hazell's Annual for 1910*, Ed. Hammond Hall, London: Hazell, Watson, & Viney, 1910, p. 435.) His contract with *The English Review*, on the other hand, was based on a 20 percent profit share on the magazine's first four issues; when sales of the *Review* failed to live up to Hueffer's expectations, Wells would be left empty-handed. See Chapter 3: The Technological Scene of H.G. Wells's *Tono-Bungay*.

39 White, Davis, and Maclean were the editors of *Adventure*, *All-Story*, and *The Popular Magazine*, published by Ridgway, Munsey, and S&S, respectively.

40 See Wilkie Collins, "The Unknown Public," *Household Words*, No. 439 (Saturday, August 21, 1858), pp. 217–22.
41 Macdonald, pp. 3–4.
42 Joseph A. Kestner, "Masculinities in the Richard Hannay 'War Trilogy' of John Buchan," *John Buchan and the Idea of Modernity*, Eds. Kate Macdonald and Nathan Waddell, London: Pickering & Chatto, 2013; reference is made to the unpublished manuscript of the essay, p. 1.
43 The manuscript was originally titled *The Black Stone*. George Blackwood suggested that a different title be used, and he and Buchan finally settled on *The Thirty-Nine Steps*.
44 Blackwood routinely paid his magazine's contributors according to a "per-page" rate. The payment of £100 was based on the novel's 80-page manuscript. As Blackwood also planned to publish the novel in book form later, his purchase of first UK serial rights and agreement to 12.5 percent on all book sales were included in the same contract.
45 The novel was serialized across three installments in the July, August, and September issues of the magazine.
46 As recorded in the Blackwood ledgers archived in the National Library of Scotland, a first impression of 15,750 copies was ordered in September 1915. A second impression of 10,500 copies was ordered in November, and a third impression of 10,500 copies was ordered in December. Of the 36,750 copies produced, Blackwood recorded 11,620 copies "on hand" at the end of the year (December 31, 1915).
47 Philip Waller, *Writers, Readers, and Reputations: Literary Life in Britain 1870–1918*, Oxford, UK: Oxford University Press, 2006, p. 638.
48 By the end of 1916, *Chance* had gone through seven sold-out editions, totaling 13,000 copies. Stock Ledgers for *Chance*. Methuen MSS. 1892–1944: Methuen Archives; Special Collections, Lilly Library at Indiana University.
49 For contrast, James Joyce's *Dubliners* would sell just 536 copies between 1914 and 1916, and Virginia Woolf's 1915 novel, *The Voyage Out*, would sell fewer than 2,000 in its first 15 years of publication. The novels of Joyce and Woolf were by no means competing with sales of *The Thirty-Nine Steps*, of course, but rather demonstrate the level of disconnect between what people actually did read and what is now deemed worthy of university scholarship.
50 After the 1914–15 season, the FA Cup and virtually all national league play was suspended until the 1919–20 season. Two thousand of Britain's five thousand professional football players enlisted for the war (*Spalding's Official Football Guide*, Ed. Thomas Cahill, New York: American Sports Publishing, 1915, pp. 107–8).
51 John Bolig, *The Victor Red Seal Discography, Vol. I: Single-side Series (1903–1925)*, Denver, CO: Mainspring Press, 2004, p. xvi.
52 Ticket prices averaged 6d (US$.10). See *The Cinema: Its Present Position and Future Possibilities*, The National Council of Public Morals, London: Williams & Norgate, 1917, p. 3.
53 An exact figure for this novel is not yet determined; only a single cancelled check for partial payment of $478.69, endorsed by Buchan, has been located in the personal archives of a pulp collector. Based on Buchan's known record of earnings from pulp publishers, however, payment in the range of $1,000–1,500 seems likely. That same year, for example, Buchan received $1,200 in four increments for *All-Story Weekly*'s serialization of *Andrew Garvald—Tidewater Trader* (August 14–September 11, 1915). In 1919, Buchan was paid $1,500 for the serialization of *Mr. Standfast* in S&S's *The Popular Magazine* (January 7–February 20), and, in 1924, he received $1,500 from *Argosy All-Story Weekly* for the serialization of *The Three Hostages* (June 14–August 2).

54 Circulation figures for *All-Story Weekly* are from *N.W. Ayer & Son's American Newspaper Annual and Directory*, 1915, Vol. 1. Philadelphia: N.W. Ayer, 1915, p. 649. Figures for *Blackwood's* are from David Finkelstein's *The House of Blackwood*, University Park, PA: The Pennsylvania State University, 2002, Appendix 2, p. 166.

55 David M. Earle, *Re-Covering Modernism: Pulps, Paperbacks, and the Prejudice of Form*. Farnham, UK: Ashgate, 2009, p. 63.

56 See Laurel Brake's "Maga, the Shilling Monthlies, and the New Journalism," *Print Culture and the Blackwood Tradition, 1805–1930*, Ed. David Finkelstein, Toronto: University of Toronto Press, 2006, pp. 184–211.

57 From 1859 to 1860, *Macmillan's* and *The Cornhill Magazine* would set a standard cover price for monthlies at 1 shilling, hence the term "shilling monthlies." By the 1890s, single issues of *The Strand, Windsor, Pearson's*, and *Cassell's Magazine* were priced at just 6d; the *Pall Mall Magazine* retained a cover price of 1 shilling until January 1905, then it too dropped to 6d; by 1910, there were several popular magazines on the British market priced even lower, from 4 to 4½d, including *The Novel, Story-Teller, Grand, Royal*, and *Red Magazine*. See Ashley.

58 This number would double by the end of the war, but still represent a fraction of the readers of an average popular illustrated monthly at the time. It was a magazine intended for subscriptions and bookshops, rather than the stalls of W.H. Smith & Son.

59 Many private clubs in London and Edinburgh, for example The Garrick and Savage Clubs, maintained perpetual subscriptions.

60 For a discussion of *Blackwood's* upper-middle-class audience and global distribution, see David Finkelstein's *The House of Blackwood*, pp. 101–12.

61 For a discussion of Munsey's populist politics, see Nathan Madison's "Munsey: The Man Who Made the *Argosy*," in *Blood 'n' Thunder*, Ed. Ed. Hulse, No. 30 (Summer 2011), pp. 62–86.

62 At $.10 per issue in 1915, the cover price of a Munsey pulp was one-fifth that of *Blackwood's* and comparable to the price of *Munsey's, Cosmopolitan*, and UK magazines such as *The Strand, Windsor, Pearson's*, and *Pall Mall Magazine*.

63 Some titles of the period, such as *Harper's* or *McClure's*, could carry as many as 80–140 pages of advertisements per issue, or 50–60 percent of the magazine's entire page count.

64 Munsey was notorious for "fidgeting" with his magazines' formats. See Madison, pp. 69–70. For circulation figures of the *All-Story Weekly* in 1915, see *N.W. Ayer & Son*, p. 649.

65 See Brake, pp. 193–98.

66 Circulation figures for the top five best-selling pulp titles from 1915 are based on *N.W. Ayer & Son*, which records *The Popular Magazine*: 380,000, bi-weekly; *Argosy*: 275,000, monthly; *Red Book*: 250,000, monthly; *All-Story*: 200,000, weekly; and *Blue Book*: 175,000, monthly. Combined monthly circulation for all five titles is thus 2,260,000 copies. Circulation × 3–5 (which was the industry standard) = 6,780,000–11,300,000 (projected readership).

67 For a writer such as Buchan—who was Scottish, Conservative, and brought up on *Maga*—publishing in the pages of this prestigious Edinburgh magazine entailed significant benefits other than a mass readership. Besides considerable sentimental value, it would have offered a sense of having arrived, an ambition realized.

68 This strategy worked and delivered the author his first real commercial success. According to Janet Adam Smith, "Up to 1915 Buchan had not sold more than

2000 copies of any of his novels or books of short stories" (Janet Adam Smith, *John Buchan: A Biography*, Oxford, UK, and New York: Oxford University Press, 1965, p. 293).

69 Macdonald, p. 5.
70 Ibid., p. 8.
71 Copies of letters from Buchan to Blackwood are held in special collections at the University of Stirling Library, in Stirling, UK. All references to correspondence with Blackwood are made to The John Buchan Papers, 1910–1972. Presented by J. MacGlone, Esq., 1983. Special Manuscripts, Classmark MS 44. Reference to Buchan's correspondence with Watt is made to the University of North Carolina's Louis Round Wilson Library, A.P. Watt Records, 1888–1982 (Collection # *11036)*, Series 1, Folders 171–12 & 172–12, in Chapel Hill, NC.
72 Letter from Buchan to Blackwood, March 18, 1915.
73 Ibid., April 9, 1915.
74 Ibid., June 16, 1915.
75 Ibid., March 20, 1915.
76 Ibid., undated.
77 Ibid., November 25, 1915.
78 Letters from Buchan to Watt, December 20, 1915; February 2, 5, & 8, 1916.
79 In-text citation refers to the novel's serialization in *The All-Story Weekly* (Part One, June 5, 1915). The phrase "Thirty-nine steps ... 10.17 P.M." occurs initially in the Penguin paperback edition on page 39. John Buchan, *The Thirty-Nine Steps*, London and New York: Penguin, 2004.
80 All three events occur, in quick succession, in the final two chapters of the novel: Chapters IX, "The Thirty-Nine Steps," and X, "Various Parties Converging on the Sea."
81 John Keegan, Introduction, *The Thirty-Nine Steps* (1915), New York: Penguin, 2004, p. xvii.
82 In 1935, Alfred Hitchcock put this frenetic pace and pervasive sense of paranoia to good use in his cinematic adaptation of Buchan's novel.
83 H.G. Wells, *Tono-Bungay* (1909), New York: Penguin, 2005, p. 358.
84 Mark A. Wollaeger, *Modernism, Media, and Propaganda: British Narrative from 1900 to 1945*, Princeton, NJ: Princeton University Press, 2006, p. 34.
85 I also contend that dilemmas such as Hannay's (attempted and often failed escapes) are more common instances of twentieth-century responses (in both film and literature) to modernity's "grid of the rational and the known." The innocent protagonist charged with a crime he did not commit, who attempts to escape the authorities, or a criminal organization, only to be hunted down relentlessly through the global reach of new media and telecommunications technologies, has by now become a well-worn cliché.
86 Keegan, p. xvii.
87 In the novel, a member of the Black Stone poses as the First Sea Lord Alloa, head of the British Navy, infiltrates a top-secret meeting of high-ranking government officials, and commits the naval plans to photographic memory.
88 These are all titles of actual contemporary periodicals published in the First World War (1914–18).
89 John Buchan, *Mr. Standfast* (1919), London and New York: Oxford University Press, 1993, p. 33.
90 In-text citations refer to the novel's serialization in *The Popular Magazine* (Part 3, February 7, 1919). For page numbers from the book, refer to the endnotes below. John Buchan, *Mr. Standfast* (1919), London and New York: Oxford University Press, 1993, p. 173.
91 Ibid., p. 174.

92 Ibid.
93 Ibid.
94 Ibid.
95 Ibid.
96 Ibid.
97 Ibid.
98 Ibid., pp. 174–75.
99 Ibid., p. 175.
100 Ibid.
101 This scene has a real-life equivalent in Buchan's journalistic writing. See "The Spy Peril," *The War: Nelson's Picture Weekly*, No. 4 (September 19, 1914), p. 16.
102 For a listing of magazine cover paintings by these artists, see The FictionMags Index.
103 For a discussion of the competition between early pulp magazines for the title "The Largest Magazine in the World," see R.D. Mullen's "From Standard Magazines to Pulps and Big Slicks: A Note on the History of US General and Fiction Magazines," *Science Fiction Studies* #65, Appendix, Vol. 22, Pt. 1 (March 1995).
104 During this time, issues of *The Popular Magazine* sometimes featured the phrase "Over a Million Readers Every Issue" across the top of the magazine's masthead.
105 "Muck-raking" reports in the national magazines such as *Collier's Weekly*, *Munsey's*, and *McClure's Magazine* had revealed the fraudulent claims of patent medicine advertising and helped bring about the establishment of the U.S. Pure Food and Drug Act in 1906. This brand of popular, and *populist*, investigative journalism, which had emerged in the magazines of the United States after 1900, would continue to be influential long after the First World War.
106 Ad for International Correspondence Schools, *The Popular Magazine* Vol. 51, No. 4 (February 7, 1919), unnumbered ad pages.
107 In a sense, all Buchan's novels convey this message of worldly success as the prize for hard work and dedication.
108 Richard Ohmann, *Selling Culture: Magazines, Markets and Class at the Turn of the Century*, London: Verso, 1996, 1998, p. 313, *passim*.
109 Macdonald, p. 6.
110 Circulation for *The Popular Magazine* in 1919 is taken from N.W. Ayer & Son's American Newspaper Annual and Directory, Vol. 2, Philadelphia, PA: N.W. Ayer, 1919, p. 675.
111 Macdonald, p. 4.
112 Ibid.
113 Earle, p. 6.

Conclusion

Lost in Transit: Sax Rohmer, Conan Doyle, and Baroness Orczy's *Eldorado* (1913) in Africa

In the May 15, 1913 issue of *The Kenya Gazette*, the POs of Mombasa and Nairobi took out the following notice (for full-text page images, see also Appendix H), which they designated "General Notice No. 307":

> POST OFFICE NOTICE. List of Magazines, Newspapers, etc, found loose at the Mombasa and Nairobi Post Offices during the month of April 1913.[1]

What follows this headline is a three-page listing of more than 200 periodical issues in a dozen languages from around the world. Most are wrapped subscriptions made undeliverable for any number of reasons—for example, the address label has been lost or rubbed away in transit. Alerting readers to the status of these hundreds of periodical issues currently lost in postal transit, this general notice asks readers to come in person to claim their magazines and newspapers:

> Owners of the above should make early application to this Office, together with proof of ownership.[2]

Among the 182 titles listed[3] in the PO announcement are eight mail-order catalogues, including the April 1913 issue of *W.H. Smith & Son's Library Catalogue*. There are also several dozen British, French, and Canadian magazines; three American daily newspapers (from New York, Houston, TX, and Des Moines, IA); Irish, German, Italian, and Jamaican newspapers; and newspapers and magazines published as far away as India, Australia, and New Zealand. The list seems a striking reminder of the sheer travelling power of early twentieth-century periodicals, and, for scholars in the fields of periodical studies and print culture history, it offers insights, clues, and information that might not be otherwise available. Alexis Weedon makes an important case for the scholarly value of such "historical records" and "lists of quantities," when she writes:

Because text production—in the past and now—frequently aimed at multiplying and spreading its product as much as possible, and because those texts commonly became subject to markets and market forces, historical records of books and the book trade sometimes take the form of lists of quantities. Particularly since the invention of printing, we sometimes have information about the fee paid to an author, the cost of paper, the cost of composition, print runs, the cost and rate of binding, the costs of advertising and distribution, and sales figures. [. . .] This historical information is usually patchy, the way it was recorded varied a great deal, and much more has been lost than survives, but, even so, the data available are rich enough and important enough to be treated seriously. This is where the quantitative history of the book, or *bibliometrics*, comes in. It does not answer all the questions, and often its answers need careful interpretation, but it does give us access to parts of book history that would otherwise be wholly inaccessible.[4]

As archival evidence of the reading habits of one globally connected (albeit imperial) reading community in Kenya from May 1913, this list also suggests a number of connections that might be made between the expansion of the British Empire and the periodical publishing industries that expanded alongside it. Sources such as these can tell us a lot about book and periodical readers, allow us to compare trends between domestic and foreign production, and show colonial market perspectives that challenge conventional notions of the print culture field's cosmopolitan focus.[5] The variety of subscriptions listed, moreover, is surprisingly broad. If representative of colonial readers' preferences in other parts of the world, this snapshot of a single node in that much larger network of subscribers reveals that audiences for British middlebrow periodicals such as *The Strand*, *Punch*, and *The Illustrated London News* were considerably large and variegated outside of England. Over the remaining months of 1913 (June–December), *The Kenya Gazette* ran no fewer than six additional notices taken out monthly by the POs of Mombasa and Nairobi. Combined, they alert readers to a revolving confluence of more than 900 periodicals from around the world, "found loose" in the PO sorting rooms.

There are 272 titles listed for the month of August alone.[6] These include two issues of *The Windsor Magazine* (June and July 1913), featuring the first half of Gertrude Page's latest "novel of Rhodesian life," *The Pathway*; Chapters 7–8 of Halliwell Sutcliff's *The Open Road: A Romance of High Adventure*; Albert Kinros's *The Fortunes of Virginia Bright*—about the young American girl's experiences living on a farm in Kent—and John Barnett's "Black Ivory," set in the Sudan.[7] There is one issue of *Pearson's Magazine* (July 1913), which includes May Edgington's short story "The Piracy: An Adventure Story" and Donald Francis McGrew's "Bunga Doo: A Soldier Story," set deep in the Philippines jungles. Margaret Strickland's horror story about a werewolf, "The Case of Sir Alister Moeran," appears in the previous month's issue of *The Novel Magazine* (July 1913), and celebrity authors G.K. Chesterton, Elinor Glyn, E. Phillips Oppenheim, Bruno Lessing, and Hall Caine all had items published in a 3-month-old copy of *Nash's Magazine* (May 1913). *The Story-Teller* (July 1913) features the long-awaited tenth and final installment of Sax Rohmer's popular detective novel *The Mystery of Dr. Fu Manchu*, and consecutive issues of *The Grand Magazine* (July and August 1913) feature installments 5 and 6 from H.G. Wells's *The Passionate Friends*. In *The Wide World Magazine* (June 1913), articles of famous explorer-naturalists such as Roy Sharpe, Douglas Carruthers, and Captain W. Brooke describe shipwrecks off the coast of Australia, nomadic tribes in Mongolia, and shark hunting through the South Pacific. There are multiple copies listed of *The Strand Magazine* issue of July 1913,[8] which features the final installment of Conan Doyle's second novel in the Professor Challenger series, *The Poison Belt*; additional titles include *Punch*, *Tit-Bits*, and *John Bull*, for example—all are recognizably British institutions. All are established, metropolitan, and middlebrow. They are the same sorts of magazine we could expect to find just about anywhere that English people gathered socially and domestically in the first decades of the twentieth century. It is just the sort of popular best-selling fiction we would associate with Edwardian England, and this would seem unremarkable on the racks of a W.H. Smith & Son at the Manchester train station. Last month's issue of *The Strand Magazine* "found loose" in the POs of Mombasa and Nairobi is seemingly out of place, however, in the sense that the material artifact is so far from the original site of printing or manufacture. Yet, given how little we actually know of the systems of distribution that delivered monthly parcels of subscriptions more than 7,000 miles away in just a matter of weeks, the moment of archival discovery quickly gives way to reflection—and disappointment. The finding only whets the appetite for more complete and exhaustive records. For scholars to ever truly understand the full extent and global dynamics of the print and periodical cultures of the period, the full records of agents, editors, publishers, advertisers, and news-dealers are needed. These should be located, archived, and digitized in order that the complex print cultures and relations they record might be at least partially reconstructed. In many cases, however, it is unlikely that complete records have survived, for, as Simon Eliot observes: "the sources of information [on periodical publication] are neither consistent nor continuous[; and] the sources are very few."[9]

  This is one of the main challenges to book history approaches to studying the production and distribution of popular periodicals from the late nineteenth and early twentieth centuries—the absence of "historical records" in the form of "lists of quantities."[10] In the meantime, a "working [set of] hypotheses" can be made.[11] Examining the notices posted for consecutive months, during the periods when issues are available, it is possible to discern patterns based on such information given.[12] The July increase (to 272) is 55 percent over the June number (120) of listings, for example; this would reflect the general pattern in the annual sales and circulation of British magazines in the domestic market. The long-standing tradition of special summer and holiday fiction numbers accounted for a similar spike in sales each summer and in late November–early December. More than half of the periodical issues "found loose" in the POs of Mombasa and Nairobi also have covers dated from within 4–6 weeks of the current issue of *The Kenya Gazette* (a weekly paper) in which they were listed. And, as noted, these represent only a fraction of the total traffic passing regularly through the Colonial PO, that is, they are the 900 *undeliverable* periodical issues that arrived during the course of the previous 6 months at just two PO locations.[13] To put these figures in perspective, there were a total of 118 PO locations operating in the East Africa and Uganda Protectorates in 1913.[14]

Based just on the available data, I want to end my study of the globalization of magazines in the early twentieth century with the following final conclusions. By the start of the First World War, periodical print cultures, whether at home or abroad, had been organized around roughly the same annual patterns of production and distribution. When sales and subscription circulations of British periodicals increased during the year—an event that typically coincided with the spring (April), summer (July), and Christmas (November) book sales seasons—these monthly notices in the *Kenya Gazette* listing periodicals "found loose" at the Mombasa and Nairobi POs reflected a similar increased volume of print subscription traffic (see Appendix I). Subscribers to *Cassell's Magazine of Fiction* living in Nairobi in 1913 received their copies of February's issue, featuring Sax Rohmer's *The Sins of Séverac Bablon,* Ep. 10,[15] within weeks of their cosmopolitan London contemporaries who purchased copies from their local bookstalls at Victoria Station.[16] Following the exciting 11-part serialization of Baroness Orczy's latest historical romance, *Eldorado* (June 1912–April 1913), colonial subscribers to *The Grand Magazine* living in Mombasa participated directly in linked global reading communities from a considerable geographical distance, and yet they participated in close approximation to "real time". Through the Colonial POs of the East Africa and Uganda Protectorates,[17] readers subscribed to the same magazines, read the same new fiction, and basically read it around the same time. This series of PO notices from a single colonial gazette in 1913—and the more than 900 lost periodicals recorded—serves as a sitemap for further studies of the networked relationships in early twentieth-century popular print culture in a global context. Such ephemera are certainly very valuable sources of data to be "mined," but data's own ability to reveal convergences and underlying structures is far more important still.

POs brought books, magazines, and newspapers to readers around the world with astonishing rapidity, and the postal service became a critical factor in the phenomenal expansion of published titles, volumes, and issues of British and American magazines produced at the turn of the twentieth century. A central conceit of this study has been that "communities in Australia, India, England, and South Africa developed common literary vernaculars with their counterparts living many thousands of miles away in New Zealand, Barbados, Hong Kong, and across the American Midwest."[18] This moment in the convergence of newspapers, magazines, the PO, and the colonial gazette in 1913 Kenya shows complex systems of modern trade, transportation, and communications at work. These systems made linked, global reading communities possible, and yet the PO notices in the *Kenya Gazette* show only a snippet of the moment that those systems broke down, and their usefulness to scholars is further limited to a specific time and place. The networks that made these global reading communities possible have been notoriously difficult to map, because the archived records of colonial administrations, POs, distributors, shipping agents, and subscription managers either no longer exist, or they are inaccessibly packed away in physical archives. With the expansion of digital projects amid the growth of the field of digital humanities, however, we can expect this current state of things to change, dramatically, and for the better. Major indexing projects such as the *Waterloo Directory of English Newspapers and Periodicals, 1800–1900*[19] and the FictionMags Index—the largest, most comprehensive index of twentieth-century magazines available[20]—oblige scholars to set studies of individual titles and publishers in a broad context of the hundreds of periodicals available. Archival recovery projects, including the Modernist Journals Project, Pulp Magazines Project, and Blue Mountain Project,[21] are bringing a fuller range of twentieth-century periodicals to the attention of literary scholars, and projects such as the Reading Experience Database (RED), 1450–1949—which, as of October 2016, "has amassed over 30,000 records of reading experiences of British subjects, both at home and abroad"[22]—provide additional, much-needed perspectives into what readers of these periods were actually buying and reading. Together, such initiatives are changing the way scholars access, manage, and communicate their own research. With the next generation of digital humanities projects built on RDF (Resource Description Framework), while embracing the principles of linked and open data, we will eventually be able to link hundreds of individual projects together through combined user interfaces, in order to share and compare data across and between them.[23]

Seemingly ephemeral materials such as these Colonial PO notices, crudely digitized for online viewing via Google Books (see Appendix H), not only enrich our understanding and research into early twentieth-century periodicals, but also demonstrate the value of open-access digital archives. Providing access to otherwise unknown or inaccessible materials, they can help expand existing research into new areas of inquiry, offer new, more efficient ways of asking the traditional questions of humanities researchers, while creating new opportunities for other kinds of questions to one day be asked.

Notes

1   "Gen. Notice No. 307, POST OFFICE NOTICE. List of Magazines, Newspapers, etc, found loose at the Mombasa and Nairobi Post Offices during the month of April 1913," *The Kenya Gazette* (May 15, 1913), pp. 455–57.

2   Ibid., p. 457.

3   There are 200+ individual items listed in the announcement, but many of these are multiple copies of the same title and issue.

4   Alexis Weedon, "The Uses of Quantification," in *A Companion to the History of the Book*, Eds. Simon Eliot and Jonathan Rose, Malden, MA, and Oxford, UK: Wiley-Blackwell, 2009, p. 33.

5   For a similar perspective, see also Patrick Collier's "Imperial/Modernist Forms in the *Illustrated London News*," *Modernism/Modernity* Vol. 19, No. 3 (September 2012), pp. 487–514; Collier suggests further that: "establishing a causal link between imperial expansion, newspaper aesthetics, and modernist form in various media would suggest deep and substantive connections between two currently separate and non-communicative—not to say hostile—enterprises in contemporary modernist criticism: on one hand work that focuses on global modernisms, transnational exchange, and modernism's imbrication with empire, on the other work that focuses on modernism's complex relations with [mass media]" (487).

6   The announcements are dated June 15, 1913: 104; July 15, 1913: 40 bundles (each bundle contains on average 4–5 periodicals); August 15, 1913: 272; September 15, 1913: 96; October 15, 1913: [No Notice]; November 15, 1913: 108; and December 15, 1913: 200 (including the November 1913 issue of *The All-Story Magazine*).

7   The July issue of *The Windsor Magazine* also includes an abundance of advertising, glossy full-color illustrations, a comic short story by Dornford Yates, titled "Private View," and essays by Charles G.D. Roberts and A.E. Fletcher. Detailed black-and-white reproductions of photographs taken by telescope at the Lick Observatory accompany H.C. O'Neill's "The Problem of Mars."

8   In fact, notices posted each month for 1913 list multiple "lost" copies of the previous month's issue of *The Strand*, an unscientific, but most likely accurate, measure of the total number of copies passing through the mail each month.

9   Simon Eliot, "Section E: Periodical Publication," *Some Patterns and Trends in British Publishing 1800–1919*, Occasional Papers of the Bibliographical Society, Number 8 (1994), p. 78.

10 Weedon, p. 33.

11 Eliot, p. 5.

12 The itemized lists are organized in columns. Each row includes a full title, number of copies, and the date of issue.

13 Although *The Kenya Gazette* was published once a week, PO notices alerting readers to periodicals "found loose" in the sorting rooms appeared on a monthly basis and refer to periodicals found "during the month of [. . .]."

14 *COLONIAL REPORTS*—Annual. No. 840. East Africa Protectorate. Report for 1913–14. London: HMSO, 1915.

15 Sax Rohmer, *The Sins of Séverac Bablon*, London: Cassell, 1914 (first appeared in *Cassell's Magazine of Fiction* [June 1912–August 1913]).

16 For a study of the connection between periodical expansion and train-station bookstalls, see Charles Wilson, *First with the News: The History of W.H. Smith 1792–1972*, Garden City, NY: Doubleday, 1986.

17 East Africa and Uganda Protectorates was the name used by the combined postal services of the protectorates of East Africa and Uganda between April 1, 1903 and July 22, 1920.

18   See Introduction: Print in Transition.
19   See the Waterloo Directory of English Newspapers and Periodicals 1800–1900 (Series Three), online, at www.victorianperiodicals.com/series3/index.asp (accessed October 22, 2016).
20   See the FictionMags Index, at www.philsp.com/homeville/fmi/0start.htm (accessed October 22, 2016).
21   See the Modernist Journals Project (at http://modjourn.org/), Pulp Magazines Project (at www.pulpmags.org/), and Blue Mountain Project (at http://blue mountain.princeton.edu/index.html; all accessed October 22, 2016 at their respective URLs, listed above).
22   See Shafquat Towheed, Edmund King, Francesca Benatti, Jonathan Gibson, Carl Cottingham, Helen Chambers, and Rachel Garnham, the Reading Experience Database (RED), 1450–1949, at www.open.ac.uk/Arts/RED/ (accessed October 18, 2016).
23   See the following projects in twentieth-century literary studies: Linked Modernisms (at http://linkedmods.uvic.ca/), Modernist Networks (at www.modnets. org/), and the ModNets's umbrella organization, the Advanced Research Consortium (at http://idhmcmain.tamu.edu/arcgrant/; all accessed on October 18, 2016 at their respective URLs, listed above).

Appendix A

British and American Books, Magazines, and Newspapers: Titles by Year (1860–1922)

Table A.1 British and American Books, Magazines, and Newspapers: Titles by Year (1860–1922)

Year	United Kingdom					United States		Magazines (UK & US; Total)
	Magazines	Newspapers	Books	Books + Editions	Periodicals (Total)	Magazines	Periodicals (Total)	
1860	500	1,000	1,132	4,564	1,500	650	5,000	1,150
1861	500	1,000	1,263	4,303	1,500	650	5,253	1,150
1862	500	1,000	1,399	3,938	1,500	700	5,500	1,200
1863	500	1,000	1,539	3,943	1,500	700	5,500	1,200
1864	537	1,250	1,615	4,136	1,787	750	5,500	1,287
1865	554	1,271	1,720	4,426	1,825	750	5,500	1,304
1866	557	1,257	1,963	4,388	1,814	750	5,500	1,307
1867	588	1,294	2,273	4,371	1,882	750	5,500	1,338
1868	621	1,324	2,729	4,536	1,945	800	5,500	1,421
1869	655	1,372	3,602	4,372	2,027	800	5,500	1,455
1870	626	1,390	3,617	4,656	2,016	800	5,500	1,426
1871	638	1,450	3,254	4,830	2,088	850	6,000	1,488
1872	639	1,456	3,258	4,568	2,095	884	6,992	1,523
1873	630	1,536	2,230	4,749	2,166	875	7,291	1,505

continued . . . .

Table A.1 Continued

| Year | United Kingdom | | | | | United States | | Magazines (UK & US; Total) |
	Magazines	Newspapers	Books	Books + Editions	Periodicals (Total)	Magazines	Periodicals (Total)	
1874	639	1,585	2,392	4,312	2,224	890	7,500	1,529
1875	643	1,609	2,731	4,903	2,252	910	7,500	1,553
1876	720	1,645	2,036	4,888	2,365	1,682	8,129	2,402
1877	808	1,692	2,340	5,095	2,500	1,613	8,427	2,421
1878	839	1,744	2,360	5,305	2,583	1,661	8,832	2,500
1879	953	1,763	2,458	5,834	2,716	1,700	9,225	2,653
1880	1,033	1,835	2,695	5,718	2,868	2,148	10,674	3,181
1881	1,097	1,886	2,645	5,406	2,983	2,246	11,232	3,343
1882	1,180	1,817	2,845	5,124	2,997	2,358	11,805	3,538
1883	1,311	1,962	3,369	6,145	3,273	2,494	12,605	3,805
1884	1,260	2,015	3,773	6,375	3,275	2,555	13,343	3,815
1885	1,298	2,052	3,836	5,640	3,350	2,633	13,958	3,931
1886	1,368	2,093	4,054	5,210	3,461	2,752	14,908	4,120
1887	1,462	2,135	4,202	5,686	3,597	2,811	15,600	4,273
1888	1,508	2,177	4,536	6,591	3,685	2,905	16,604	4,413
1889	1,593	2,186	4,376	6,067	3,779	3,068	17,265	4,661
1890	1,752	2,234	4,300	5,735	3,986	3,304	18,531	5,056
1891	1,778	2,234	4,557	5,706	4,012	3,600	19,323	5,378
1892	1,901	2,255	4,849	6,254	4,156	3,843	20,115	5,744
1893	1,961	2,268	4,827	6,382	4,229	3,852	20,774	5,813
1894	2,061	2,291	5,249	6,485	4,352	3,852	20,774	5,913
1895	2,081	2,304	5,126	6,516	4,385	3,721	21,142	5,802

Year								
1896	2,097	2,355	4,922	6,573	4,452	3,578	21,325	5,675
1897	2,186	2,396	5,033	7,926	4,582	3,671	21,955	5,857
1898	2,225	2,396	4,677	7,516	4,621	3,981	22,092	6,206
1899	2,290	2,364	4,782	7,567	4,654	3,985	22,308	6,275
1900	2,328	2,471	4,872	7,239	4,799	4,026	22,436	6,354
1901	2,446	2,468	5,513	6,044	4,914	4,128	22,687	6,574
1902	2,486	2,437	5,762	6,941	4,923	4,230	22,839	6,716
1903	2,531	2,412	6,122	8,381	4,943	4,336	23,221	6,867
1904	2,597	2,936	5,937	8,334	5,533	4,786	23,385	7,383
1905	2,597	3,461	5,982	8,252	6,058	4,628	23,480	7,225
1906	2,663	3,716	5,959	8,603	6,379	4,660	23,595	7,323
1907	2,663	2,777	5,825	9,914	5,440	4,645	23,819	7,308
1908	2,729	3,039	5,724	9,821	5,768	4,633	23,726	7,362
1909	2,762	2,322	6,196	10,725	5,084	4,686	23,894	7,448
1910	2,795	2,353	6,167	10,804	5,148	4,867	24,089	7,662
1911	3,216	2,395	5,968	10,914	5,611	4,902	24,235	8,118
1912	3,915	3,333	3,195	12,067	7,248	5,065	24,315	8,980
1913	4,815	2,546	2,500	12,379	7,361	5,083	24,381	9,898
1914	4,870	2,504	2,000	11,537	7,374	5,191	24,527	10,061
1915	4,756	2,398	2,000	10,665	7,154	5,261	24,724	10,017
1916	4,791	2,421	2,000	9,149	7,212	5,336	24,589	10,127
1917	4,867	2,366	2,500	8,131	7,233	5,558	24,868	10,425
1918	4,790	2,319	3,000	7,716	7,109	5,600	24,252	10,390
1919	5,000	2,342	4,000	8,622	7,342	5,368	23,074	10,368
1920	5,000	2,293	4,000	11,004	7,293	5,379	22,428	10,379
1921	5,500	2,319	4,000	8,622	7,819	5,327	22,373	10,827
1922	5,500	2,225	4,000	8,988	7,725	5,486	22,353	10,986

Note: Figures in italics are estimated, based on the author's research

Appendix B

Representative Authors' Payments for First UK & U.S. Serial Rights (1884–1938)

Table B.1 Representative Authors' Payments for First UK & U.S. Serial Rights (1884–1938)

Year	Publisher (Magazine)	Title of Work	Author	Payment Received
1880s				
1884	*The Cornhill Magazine*	"J. Habakuk Jephson's Statement"	Arthur Conan Doyle	£30
1887	*Beeton's Christmas Annual*	A Study in Scarlet	Arthur Conan Doyle	£25
1890s				
1890	*Lippincott's Magazine*	*The Sign of Four*	Arthur Conan Doyle	£100
1890	*Lippincott's Magazine*	*The Light That Failed*	Rudyard Kipling	$800
1891	*The Strand Magazine*	"A Scandal in Bohemia"	Arthur Conan Doyle	£36
1891	*The Strand Magazine*	"The Red-Headed League"	Arthur Conan Doyle	£36
1894	*McClure's Magazine*	*The Ebb-Tide*	R.L. Stevenson	£400
1894	*The Pall Mall Magazine*	*Joan Haste*	Rider Haggard	£1,500
1895	*The New Review*	*The Time Machine*	H.G. Wells	£100
1896	*McClure's Magazine*	*Captains Courageous*	Rudyard Kipling	£3,000
1896	*Pearson's Magazine*	*Captains Courageous*	Rudyard Kipling	£2,500
1896	*The Strand Magazine*	*Rodney Stone*	Arthur Conan Doyle	$7,300
1896	*The Savoy*	"The Idiots"	Joseph Conrad	£38

Year	Magazine	Title	Author	Price
1897	McClure's Magazine	St. Ives	R.L. Stevenson	$8,000
1897	Pearson's Magazine	The War of the Worlds	H.G. Wells	£200
1897	The Cornhill Magazine	"The Lagoon"	Joseph Conrad	£10
1897	Cosmopolis	"An Outpost of Progress"	Joseph Conrad	£40
1897	Blackwood's Magazine	"Karain"	Joseph Conrad	£40
1898	Blackwood's Magazine	"Youth"	Joseph Conrad	£35
1899	Blackwood's Magazine	(The) Heart of Darkness	Joseph Conrad	£100
1899	Blackwood's Magazine	Lord Jim	Joseph Conrad	£300
1899	McClure's Magazine	The Life of the Master	Ian Maclaren	$10,000

1900s

Year	Magazine	Title	Author	Price
1900	McClure's Magazine	Kim	Rudyard Kipling	$25,000
1901	The Illus. London News	"Amy Foster"	Joseph Conrad	$195
1901	The Strand Magazine	The Hound of the Baskervilles	Arthur Conan Doyle	£6,000
1902	The Pall Mall Magazine	Typhoon	Joseph Conrad	£75
1903	The Sat. Evening Post	The Call of the Wild	Jack London	$750
1903	Collier's Weekly	The Return of Sherlock Holmes	Arthur Conan Doyle	$45,000
1905	Blackwood's Magazine	"In Captivity"	Joseph Conrad	$64
1905	The Popular Magazine	Ayesha	Rider Haggard	£200
1906	The All-Story Magazine	The Man in Lower Ten	Mary Roberts Rinehart	£400
1906	Blackwood's Magazine	"Initiation"	Joseph Conrad	$105
1906	The Popular Magazine	"In Sheep's Clothing"	A.M. Chisolm	$25
1907	The Popular Magazine	"A Forlorn Hope"	A.M. Chisolm	$25
1908	The English Review	Tono-Bungay	H.G. Wells	***
1908	The Popular Magazine	Tono-Bungay	H.G. Wells	£100
1908	The English Review	Some Reminiscences	Joseph Conrad	£780
1909	The Popular Magazine	The House of the Whispering Pines	Anna Katherine Green	$5,000
1909	The Cavalier	Morning Star	Rider Haggard	$800

continued . . .

Table B.1 Continued

Year	Publisher (Magazine)	Title of Work	Author	Payment Received
1910s				
1910	*The Cavalier*	*The Wizard of the Peak*	Thomas E. Grant	$175
1910	*The Popular Magazine*	"The Winning Ball"	Zane Grey	$125
1910	*The Popular Magazine*	*The Heritage of the Desert*	Zane Grey	$1,800
1910	*The Popular Magazine*	"The Rubber Hunter"	Zane Grey	$360
1911	*The Scrap-Book*	"A Transaction in Diamonds"	Talbot Mundy	$60
1911	*The Cavalier*	*The Second Deluge*	Garrett P. Serviss	$750
1911	*The Popular Magazine*	*Initials Only*	Anna Katherine Green	$5,000
1912	*The All-Story Magazine*	*Under the Moons of Mars*	Edgar Rice Burroughs	$400
1912	*The All-Story Magazine*	*Tarzan of the Apes*	Edgar Rice Burroughs	$700
1913	*The Strand Magazine*	*Captain Scott's Journals*	Robert Falcon Scott	£2,000
1913	*New Story Magazine*	*The Return of Tarzan*	Edgar Rice Burroughs	$1,000
1914	*The All-Story Weekly*	"The Rose Orchid"	Rex Stout	$200
1915	*The All-Story Weekly*	*Andrew Garvald—Tidewater Trader*	John Buchan	$1,200
1915	*Blackwood's Magazine*	*The Thirty-Nine Steps*	John Buchan	£100
1915	*The All-Story Weekly*	*The Thirty-Nine Steps*	John Buchan	+/-£200
1915	*The Popular Magazine*	"Mounty Price's Nightingale"	Zane Grey	$125
1915	*The Sat. Evening Post*	*Uneasy Money*	P.G. Wodehouse	$5,000
1917	*The All-Story Weekly*	"An Officer and a Lady"	Rex Stout	$45
1917	*The All-Story Weekly*	*When Bearcat Went Dry*	Charles Neville Buck	$1,400
1918	*The Popular Magazine*	"Fusileer Ballads"	H. de Vere Stacpoole	$60
1918	*The Sat. Evening Post*	*Picadilly Jim*	P.G. Wodehouse	$7,500

Year	Title	Magazine	Author	Price
1918	*The Land That Time Forgot*	*The Blue Book*	Edgar Rice Burroughs	$3,000
1918	*The Country of Strong Men*	*The Popular Magazine*	A.M. Chisolm	$1,600
1919	*Mr. Standfast*	*The Popular Magazine*	John Buchan	$1,500
1919	*The Secret City*	*The Popular Magazine*	Roy Norton	$2,000
1920s				
1920	*Picaroons*	*The Popular Magazine*	H. de Vere Stacpoole	$2,500
1921	*The Voice of La Paloma*	*Western Story Magazine*	Max Brand	$660
1921	*Tarzan the Terrible*	*Argosy All-Story Weekly*	Edgar Rice Burroughs	$3,000
1922	"Blessed Are the Meek"	*People's Magazine*	Thomas Curry	$25
1922	*Smiling Charlie*	*Western Story Magazine*	Max Brand	$4,000
1924	*The Three Hostages*	*Argosy All-Story Weekly*	John Buchan	$1,500
1924	"Spear and Fang"	*Weird Tales*	Robert E. Howard	$18
1927	*Thunder Moon*	*Western Story Magazine*	Max Brand	$4,000
1928	*The Skylark of Space*	*Amazing Stories*	Clark Ashton Smith	$125
1928	"The Metal Man"	*Amazing Stories*	Jack Williamson	$25
1930s				
1931	"Washington and Lee University"	*College Stories*	Richard Sale	$100
1932	*Man of Bronze*	*Doc Savage Magazine*	Lester Dent	$500
1933	The G-8 Novels	*G-8 and His Battle Aces*	Robert J. Hogan	$700
1934	"At the Bottom of Every Mess"	*Black Mask*	Dwight Babcock	$100
1936	"The Cat Woman"	*Dime Mystery*	Bruno Fischer	$60
1937	"Eagles Over Crooked Creek"	*Western Story Magazine*	Max Brand	$112
1938	*Trigger Law*	*Western Story Magazine*	Ney Geer	$325

Appendix C

Average Delivery Time of Mail Packet Steamers by Decade (1840–1920)

Table C.1 Average Delivery Time of Mail Packet Steamers by Decade (1840–1920)

		1840s	1850s	1860s	1870s	1880s	1890s	1900s	1910s	1920s	Change, %
N. America	New York	14		8			5	5		5	−280
	Kingston				19		16				−119
	St. Thomas	18			14	14					−129
S. America	Panama		32	20							−160
	Rio de Janeiro		45	25				17	16		−281
	Buenos Aires		36					20			−180
Africa	Alexandria	30	13					5			−600
	Port Said				13	10	9	5			−260
	Cape Town		38	36	34	20	18	17	16		−238
British India	Aden		17								NA
	Calcutta	45	45	45	38				14		−321
	Madras				34						NA
	Ceylon				23						NA
E. Asia	Bombay	60	42	42	28	22	18	15	14		−429
	Hong Kong	100	80	68	54	42	38	34			−294
	Shanghai				60	29					−207
	Yokohama				54						NA
S.E. Asia	Singapore	102	44	42	38						−268
	Java		110	42				30		21	−524
	Penang				36						NA
Australasia	Sydney	125	65	65	56	42	35	34			−368
	Melbourne	134	64		53	42		32			−419
	Wellington	158	55	55	42						−376

Note: Figures in italics are estimated, based on the author's research

Appendix D
Major International Copyright Legislation Affecting Authors (1880–1920)

Table D.1 Major International Copyright Legislation Affecting Authors (1880–1920)

Year	Full Title of Act
1886	Berne Convention for the Protection of Literary and Artistic Works
1891	U.S. International Copyright Treaty (Chace Act)
1896	Berne Convention revised in Paris
1897	U.S. Copyright Office established, separate from Library of Congress
1903	U.S. Copyright extended to posters and advertisements
1908	Berne Convention revised in Berlin
1908	U.S. signs Mexico City Convention (1902)
1909	U.S. Copyright terms are extended to 56 years
1911	Imperial Copyright Act extended U.K. copyright to the Empire, abolished the requirement for registration at Stationers' Hall, and implemented 1908 Berlin revisions to the Berne Convention
1912	U.S. Copyright (Townsend Amendment) extended to motion pictures
1913	U.S. Copyright (Housekeeping Amendment) required additional information for foreign copyright applications, principally with respect to the place and date of first publication and the country of origin
1914	Berne Convention completed in Berne
1914	U.S. signs Buenos Aires Convention (1910)
1919	U.S. Retroactive Protection and Ad Interim Amendment

Appendix E

Commercial Statistics of the Principal Countries of the World (1904–06)

Table E.1 Commercial Statistics of the Principal Countries of the World (1904–06)

Country	Railways		Telegraphs			# of Post Offices	Sent	
	Date	Miles	Date	Miles			Printed Matter	Letters
				Line	Wire			
Argentina	1906	12,230	1905	32,387	75,204	2,282	218,522,784	206,981,296
Commonwealth of Australia	1906	14,988	1906	45,220		6,654	159,775,452	281,160,737
New Zealand	1906	2,520	1906	8,355	25,116	1,898	30,293,672	66,292,441
Austria, including Bosnia-Herzegovina	1905	24,338	1904	25,714	116,915	9,007	255,121,690	1,067,413,613
Hungary	1905		1904	14,572	77,133	5,209	52,754,428	318,815,338
Belgium	1905	4,375	1905	4,117	23,079	1,330	363,419,138	237,205,863
Bolivia	1905	701	1904	2,778	481		374,547	1,018,028
Brazil	1905	600	1904	15,502	30,686	2,871	28,638,000	36,782,000
Bulgaria	1905	972	1904	3,272	6,918	2,035	11,977,534	20,040,388
Canada	1905	21,280	1905	37,804	103,165	10,879	50,820,000	331,792,500

Country								
Costa Rica	294	1906	1905	946				
Guatemala	400	1905	1905	3,230		281		
Honduras	57	1905		3,811		256	57,116	451,824
Nicaragua	171	1904		3,152		133		
Salvador	104	1905		1,872		82		
Chile	2,939	1906		9,312		1,010	2,835,705	59,128,481
China	3,435	1905		22,183	33,989	1,626	5,620,556	24,693,010
Columbia	411	1904		6,475			1,233,313	2,794,069
Cuba	1,583	1905				479	2,472,780	23,671,684
Denmark	2,043	1905		2,353	8,823	1,332	107,867,789	101,863,682
Ecuador	186	1905		2,566				
Egypt	3,233	1905		2,752	11,400	1,137	13,324,150	22,450,000
France	29,018	1906		97,941	369,851	11,920	1,463,024,819	1,119,488,834
Algeria		1905		7,416	21,638	594	17,039,328	18,017,184
Tunis		1904		2,143	6,385	349	5,317,992	12,757,176
French East Indies	1,549	1905		7,798	13,005	264	2,359,106	6,743,516
French Colonies	998	1905		9,370		464	805,383	4,358,092
German Empire	34,526	1905		89,348	331,547	47,525	2,730,625,402	3,263,325,080
German Colonies		1901		2,077	2,210	108		
Greece	695	1905			5,899	597	10,347,037	14,261,206
Haiti	140	1905		3,916		31		

continued . . .

Table E.1 Continued

Country	Railways		Telegraphs			# of Post Offices	Sent	
	Date	Miles	Date	Miles			Printed Matter	Letters
				Line	Wire			
India, British	1905	28,221	1904	61,684	227,749	16,033	69,141,957	553,887,150
Italy, including Eritrea	1905	10,120	1905	30,094	117,216	8,917	583,367,500	359,587,384
Japan	1905	4,693	1905	19,015	88,811	4,650	200,534,624	871,077,817
Formosa	1905	231	1905	942	3,321	121		397,322
Congo Free State	1905	297				49	60,852	
Korea	1905	536	1905	2,170		100	7,131,794	8,802,582
Luxemburg			1905	683	1,414			
Mexico	1905	12,227	1906	34,996		2,466	77,807,143	64,752,789
Netherlands	1905	2,133	1905	4,346	19,868	1,388	206,782,075	181,420,390
Dutch East Indies	1905	1,430	1904	8,420	11,321	1,517	10,510,948	15,190,398
Dutch Possessions in America	1905	37	1904			18	272,192	989,890
Norway	1905	1,515	1905	6,104	12,073	2,836	67,529,664	51,504,494
Paraguay	1905	157	1905	1,136		157		
Persia	1905	34	1905	6,459	10,393	106		
Peru	1905	1,299	1906	374	1	369		

Country	Year			Year				
Portugal	1905	1,550	5,369	1904	12,123	3,081	34,411,136	47,585,189
Portuguese Colonies	1905	667	2,336	1904	2,546	189	507,467	2,837,922
Romania	1905	1,975	4,358	1905	11,502	3,278	36,849,216	49,833,680
Russia	1906	39,591	112,244	1904	380,196	13,094	486,042,945	716,124,511
Finland	1906	2,069				1,441	23,142,552	21,242,712
Santo Domingo	1905	117	429	1897		69		
Serbia	1905	439	2,039	1905	4,799	1,241	7,861,374	10,509,993
Siam	1905	446	3,287	1904		111		
Spain	1905	8,782	20,053	1904	47,424	4,734	182,442,940	194,414,149
Sweden	1905	7,815	10,770	1904	32,071	3620	179,682,732	144,923,270
Switzerland	1905	2,640	3,892	1905	14,012	3,942	194,452,977	214,402,137
Turkey	1905	3,110	26,488	1904	42,358	1,407	4,620,400	22,656,260
UK	1906	22,907	52,115	1905	588,164	23,073	1,023,100,000	3,359,100,000
British Colonies	1906	11,121	33,144			3,711		
US	1905	218,291	202,959	1906	1,256,147	65,600	4,774,700,000	6,465,850,000
Philippine Islands	1903	200	6,966	1906		476		
Puerto Rico	1906	200	517	1905		79		
Uruguay	1905	1,210	4,919	1905		762	14,894,658	
Venezuela	1905	634	4,033	1903		214		5,227,538
Total		564,073	1,144,090			279,683	13,720,454,867	20,603,823,919

Appendix F
American Pulp Magazine Circulations (1900–22)

Table F.1 American Pulp Magazine Circulations (1900–22)

Title	1900	1901	1902	1903	1904	1905	1906	1907	1908	1909	1910
10 Story Book					52,869	52,121	52,516	64,700	75,700	75,700	70,000
Adventure											
All-Story										250,000	250,000
Argosy	90,000	81,000	111,777	300,000	335,000	400,000	413,667	413,667	413,667	425,000	500,000
Black Mask											
Blue Book										200,000	200,000
Breezy Stories											
The Cavalier											
Detective Story											
Green Book											
Live Stories											
Love Story											
New Story											
Parisienne											
People's											80,000
The Popular							265,000	265,000	300,000	300,000	330,000
Red Book										300,000	350,000
Romance											
Saucy Stories											
Snappy Stories											
Short Stories	26,000	14,700	14,700	14,700	14,700	14,700	14,700	14,700	75,000	75,000	75,000
Thrill Book											
Top-Notch											
Western Story											
Totals	116,000	95,700	126,477	314,700	402,569	466,821	745,883	758,067	864,367	1,625,700	1,855,000

1911	1912	1913	1914	1915	1916	1917	1918	1919	1920	1922
89,714	88,913	88,913	88,000	85,000	85,000					58,586
100,000	100,000	125,000	128,000	139,044	200,000	150,000	146,083	194,868		
250,000	251,370	180,000	170,000	200,000	200,000	175,000	330,000	331,669		
450,000	500,000	300,000	240,000	275,000	275,000	221,000			448,810	470,280
										50,000
200,000	200,000	175,000	175,000	175,000	175,000	175,000	175,000	175,000	175,000	200,000
							128,000	110,000	113,000	
	125,966	125,000	120,000							
						131,436	100,000			
		95,000	95,000	95,000		60,000	60,000	60,000	70,000	
						100,000				130,000
		150,000	140,000	140,000						
						180,000	162,678	150,000	140,000	
175,000	180,000	180,000	190,000	175,482	172,191	169,989	169,989			
400,000	400,000	369,801	375,000	380,000	393,744	387,079	372,884	372,884		
300,000	300,000	300,000	250,000	250,000	320,000	350,000	369,896	405,132	604,534	733,576
						35,000				
							125,000	125,000	120,000	
			60,000	175,000	200,000	200,000	200,000		175,000	175,000
	120,000			95,000	95,000	85,000	85,000		75,890	174,899
				220,000	195,957	196,694	197,938	200,000		
									850,000	779,718
1,689,714	2,161,249	1,968,714	1,993,000	2,405,000	2,338,183	2,476,008	2,707,821	2,349,674	2,918,317	2,966,927

Appendix G
Advertising Ratios in Representative British and American Magazines (1919)

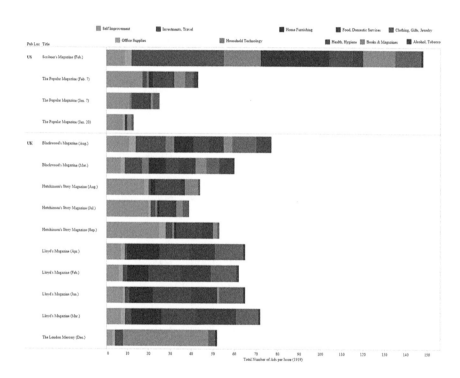

Figure AG.1 Advertising Ratios, Representative Issues of British and American Magazines (1919).

Appendix H

List of Magazines, Newspapers, etc., Found Loose (*Kenya Gazette*, May 1913)

Figure AH.1 "List of Magazines, Newspapers, etc., found loose at the Mombasa and Nairobi Post Offices," *Kenya Gazette*, May 15, 1913, pp. 455–57.

Appendix I

Combined Monthly Totals from "List of Magazines, Newspapers, etc.," *Kenya Gazette*, 1900–22

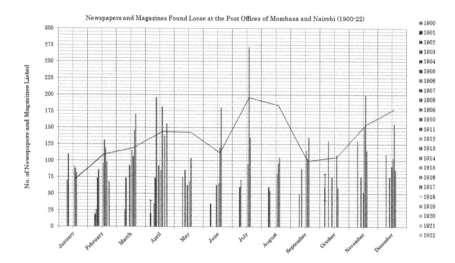

Figure AI.1 Combined Monthly Totals from "List of Magazines, Newspapers, etc.," *Kenya Gazette*, 1900–22 (with 2 Period Moving Avg. Trendline).

Bibliography

Adorno, Theodor W. *Aesthetic Theory*. Trans. Robert Hullot-Kentor. Minneapolis, MN: University of Minnesota Press, 1997.

Allingham, Phillip V. "The Initial Publication Context of Joseph Conrad's *Heart of Darkness* in *Blackwood's Edinburgh Magazine*," The Victorian Web. Site last accessed on February 3, 2012: www.victorianweb.org/authors/conrad/pva46.html

" 'Almayer's Folly': To the Editor of the 'Straits Times,' " *The Straits Times* (January 17, 1896).

Altick, Richard D. *The English Common Reader*. Chicago, IL: University of Chicago Press, 1957.

The American and European Railway and Steamship Guide. New York: J. Disturnell, 1853.

Andree, Richard, Ed. "British Empire, Showing the Commercial Routes of the World and Ocean Currents," map. *The Times Atlas of the World*. London: The Office of *The Times*, 1900.

"Announcement for *The Lost World*," editorial, *The Strand Magazine* (March 1912), p. 360.

Anonymous. "Almayer's Folly. A Romance of the Indian Archipelago," *The Straits Times* (January 16, 1896).

——. "Review of *An Outcast of the Islands*," *The Straits Budget* (May 19, 1896).

A.P. Watt Records, 1888–1982 (Collection # 11036), Series 1, Folders 171–12 & 172–12. Louis Round Wilson Library, University of North Carolina, Chapel Hill, NC.

Arewa, Olufunmilayo B. "Culture as Property: Intellectual Property, Local Norms, and Global Rights," *Northwestern Public Law Research Paper*, Nos. 07–13 (April 2007).

"Around the World," advertisement, *Time Magazine* Vol. 7, No. 26 (June 28, 1926), p. 3.

Ashcroft, Bill, Gareth Griffiths, and Helen Tiffin, Eds. *The Post-Colonial Studies Reader*. New York: Routledge, 1995.

Ashley, Mike. *The Age of the Storytellers: British Popular Fiction Magazines 1880–1950*. London: The British Library, 2006.

——. "Blue Book—The Slick in Pulp Clothing," *Pulp Vault* No. 14. Barrington Hills, IL: Tattered Pages Press, 2011, pp. 210–53.

——. *The Time Machines: The Story of the Science-Fiction Pulp Magazines from the Beginning to 1950*. Liverpool, UK: Liverpool University Press, 2000.

Ashton, Susanna. *Collaborators in Literary America, 1870–1920*. New York and Basingstoke, UK: Palgrave Macmillan, 2003.

Australia To-day. Sydney: United Commercial Travellers' Association of Australia, 1917.

Bainbridge, William Sims. *Dimensions of Science Fiction*. Cambridge, MA: Harvard University Press, 1986.

Bancroft, Hubert. *The New Pacific*. New York: Bancroft, 1914.

Banham, Christopher. " 'England and America Against the World': Empire and the USE in Edwin J. Brett's *Boys of England*, 1866–99," *Victorian Periodicals Review* Vol. 40, No. 2 (2007), pp. 151–71.

Barnes, Alan. *Sherlock Holmes on Screen: The Complete Film and TV History*. Chicago, IL: Reynolds & Hearn, 2009.

Barnicoat, Constance. "What Did the 'Colonial Girl' Read?," *The Nineteenth Century* (1906), qtd. in *A History of the Book in Australia, 1891–1945*. Marton Lyons and John Arnold, Eds. Brisbane: QLD: University of Queensland Press, 2001.

Barrett, Gerard. "The Ghost of Doubt: Writing, Speech, and Language in *Lord Jim*," *Master Narratives: Tellers and Telling in the English Novel*. Richard Gravil, Ed. Aldershot and Burlington, VT: Ashgate, 2001.

Barthes, Roland. "The Third Meaning," *The Responsibility of Forms*. Trans. Richard Howard. Berkeley, CA: University of California Press, 1991, pp. 41–62.

Batchelor, John. *The Edwardian Novelists*. London: Duckworth, 1982.

Beasley, Edward. *Empire as the Triumph of Theory: Imperialism, Information and the Colonial Society of 1868*. London: Routledge, 2005.

Beck, Ulrich. *Cosmopolitan Vision*. Trans. Ciaran Cronin. Cambridge, UK: Polity Press, 2006.

Belk, Patrick Scott. "John Buchan and the American Pulp Magazines," *John Buchan and the Idea of Modernity*. Kate Macdonald and Nathan Waddell, Eds. London: Pickering & Chatto, 2013, pp. 155–68.

——, contributor. "Research Society for Victorian Periodicals Bibliography 2009–2011," *Victorian Periodicals Review* 45.3 (2012): 320–57.

——, The Pulp Magazines Project. Site last accessed on December 22, 2016, www.pulpmags.org/.

Bell, David, and Gill Valentine, Eds. *Mapping Desire: Geographies of Sexualities*. London: Routledge, 1995.

Benjamin, Walter. "A Small History of Photography" (1931), *One Way Street*. Trans. Edmund Jephcott and Kingsley Shorter. London: NLB, 1979, pp. 240–57.

——. "The Work of Art in the Age of Mechanical Reproduction" (1936), *Illuminations*. London: Fontana, 1968, pp. 214–18.

Bergonzi, Bernard. *The Turn of a Century: Essays on Victorian and Modern English Literature*. London: The Macmillan Press, 1973.

Bishop, W.H. "Story-Paper Literature," *The Atlantic Monthly* 44: 263 (September 1879), p. 383.

Black, Alexander. *Photography Indoors and Out: A Book for Amateurs*. Boston, MA, and New York: Houghton-Mifflin, 1894.

Blackburn, William, Ed. *Joseph Conrad: Letters to William Blackwood and David S. Meldrum*. Durham, NC: Duke University Press, 1958.

Blackwood Papers, MSS30001-30976: "1804–1986: Correspondence, Book Files, Agreements and Legal Papers, Financial Records, Misc. Family Papers" (NRA 10824 Blackwood). National Library of Scotland, Manuscript Collections.

The Blue Mountain Project. Site last accessed on December 22, 2016, www.bluemountain.princeton.edu/.

Bloom, Clive, Ed. *Spy Thrillers From Buchan to Le Carré*. London: Macmillan, 1990.

Bode, Katherine. *Reading by Numbers: Recalibrating the Literary Field*. London and New York: Anthem Press, 2014.

Boehmer, Ellenke. *Empire Writing: An Anthology of Colonial Literature, 1870–1918*. Oxford, UK: Oxford University Press, 1998.

Bolig, John. *The Victor Red Seal Discography, Vol. I: Single-side Series (1903–1925)*. Denver, CO: Mainspring Press, 2004.

Booker, M. Keith. *The African Novel in English: An Introduction*. London: Heinemann, 1998.

——. *Colonial Power, Colonial Texts: India in the Modern British Novel*. Westport, CT: Praeger Publishers, 2002.

——. *The Dystopian Impulse in Modern Literature*. Westport, CT: Greenwood Press, 1994.

——. *Dystopian Literature: A Theory and Research Guide*. Westport, CT: Greenwood Press, 1994.

Boyd, Kelly. *Manliness and the Boys' Story Paper in Britain: A Cultural History, 1855–1940*. London: Palgrave Macmillan, 2003.

Bradshaw's Through Routes to the Capitals of the World and Overland Guide to India, Persia, and the Far East. London: Henry Blacklock, 1903.

Brake, Laurel. "Maga, the Shilling Monthlies, and the New Journalism," *Print Culture and the Blackwood Tradition 1805–1930*. David Finkelstein, Ed. Toronto: University of Toronto Press, 2006, pp. 184–211.

——. *Print in Transition 1850–1910*. Basingstoke, UK, and New York: Palgrave, 2001.

Brake, Laurel, and Demoor, Marysa, Eds. *Dictionary of Nineteenth-Century Journalism in Great Britain and Ireland*. Ghent, Belgium, and London: Academia Press, 2009.

Brantlinger, Patrick. *The Reading Lesson: The Threat of Mass Literacy in Nineteenth-Century British Fiction*. Bloomington and Indianapolis, IN: Indiana University Press, 1998.

——. *Rule of Darkness: British Literature and Imperialism, 1830–1914*. Ithaca, NY: Cornell University Press, 1988.

Brett, George. *Forty Years—Forty Millions: The Career of Frank A. Munsey*. New York: Farrar & Rinehart, 1935.

Bristow, Joseph. *Empire Boys: Adventures in a Man's World*. Derek Longhurst, Ed. London: Harper Collins Academic, 1991.

Buchan, John. *The Last Secrets: The Final Mysteries of Exploration*. London, Edinburgh, and New York: Thomas Nelson, 1923.

——. *The Last Secrets: The Final Mysteries of Exploration*. Yeovil, UK: Hayne Press, 2007.

——. *Mr. Standfast* (1919). London and New York: Oxford University Press, 1993.

——. "Mr. Standfast," *The Popular Magazine* Vol. 51, Nos. 2–4, and Vol. 52, No. 1 (January 7–February 20, 1919).

——. "No-Man's Land," *Blackwood's Magazine* Vol. 165, No. 999 (January 1899), pp. 1–36.

——. "The Spy Peril," *The War: Nelson's Picture Weekly*, No. 4 (September 19, 1914), p. 16.

——. *The Thirty-Nine Steps* (1915). London and New York: Penguin, 2004.

——. *The Thirty-Nine Steps* (1915). Oxford, UK, and New York: Oxford University Press, 1993.

——. "The Thirty Nine Steps: A Two-Part Story," *The All-Story Weekly* Vol. 45, No. 4, and Vol. 46, No. 1 (June 5 and 12, 1915).

Buckley, Jerome Hamilton. *William Ernest Henley: A Study in the "Counter-Decadence" of the 'Nineties*. Princeton, NJ: Princeton University Press, 1945.

Bunn, David. "Embodying Africa: Woman and Romance in Colonial Fiction," *English in Africa* Vol. 15, No. 1 (1988), pp. 1–28.

Burroughs, Edgar Rice. *The Land That Time Forgot* (Chicago, IL: A.C. McClurg, 1924), *The Blue Book Magazine* Vol. 27, No. 4–Vol. 28, No. 2 (August, October, and December 1918). Chicago, IL: The Story-Press Corporation.

Butts, Dennis. "Introduction," *King Solomon's Mines* (1885), Rider Haggard. Oxford, UK, and New York: Oxford University Press, 1989.

Calder, Jenni, Ed. *Stevenson and Victorian Scotland*. Edinburgh: Edinburgh University Press, 1981.

Cannadine, David. *Orientalism: How the British Saw Their Empire*. Oxford, UK: Oxford University Press, 2000.

Cantor, Paul, and Peter Hufnagel. "The Empire of the Future: Imperialism and Modernism in H.G. Wells," *Studies in the Novel* Vol. 38, No. 1 (Spring 2006), pp. 36–37.

"Captain Scott's Expedition," *The London Times*, Issue 39747 (November 20, 1911), p. 9, col. C.

Cawleti, John G. *Adventure, Mystery, and Romance*. Chicago, IL: University of Chicago Press, 1976.

Cawleti, John G., and Bruce A. Rosenberg. *The Spy Story*. Chicago, IL: University of Chicago Press, 1987.

Charles Agnew Maclean: Editor of the Popular Magazine, 1904–1928. New York: Bartlett Orr Press, 1928.

"Cheap Editions for the Colonies," *The Colonial Book Circular and Bibliographical Record* Vol. 1, No. 1 (September 1887).

Cheng, John. *Astounding Wonder: Imagining Science and Science Fiction in Interwar America*. Philadelphia, PA: University of Pennsylvania Press, 2012.

Chesterton, G.K. "A Defense of Penny Dreadfuls," *The Speaker*, New Series, Vol. III, No. 76 (March 16, 1901), pp. 648–49.

Childers, Erskine. *The Riddle of the Sands* (1903). Oxford, UK, and New York: Oxford University Press, 1998.

Clegg, James, Ed. *Clegg's International Directory of the World's Book Trade*, Vols. 6 and 7. London: Elliot Stock, 1903, 1906.

Close, Cecily. "Arthur Greening, Publisher of *The Scarlet Pimpernel*," *The La Trobe Journal*, No. 78 (Spring 2006).

Cohen, Scott A. " 'Get out!': Empire Migration and Human Traffic in 'Lord Jim,' " *NOVEL: A Forum on Fiction* Vol. 36, No. 3, Modernisms (Summer 2003), pp. 374–97.

Colley, Ann C. *Victorians in the Mountains: Sinking the Sublime*. Farnham, UK: Ashgate, 2010.

Collier, Patrick. *Modernism on Fleet Street*. Farnham, UK: Ashgate, 2006.

——. "Imperial/Modernist Forms in the *Illustrated London News*," *Modernism/Modernity* Vol. 19, No. 3 (September 2012), pp. 487–514.

Collins, Wilkie. "The Unknown Public," *Household Words*, No. 439 (Saturday, August 21, 1858), pp. 217–22.

"The Colonial Library," *The Bookseller*, No. CCCCLVI (November 6, 1895), p. 1073.

COLONIAL REPORTS—Annual. No. 840. East Africa Protectorate. Report for 1913–14. London: HMSO, 1915.

Conrad, Joseph. "An Outpost of Progress," *Tales of Unrest*. New York: Doubleday, Page, 1920.

———. *Heart of Darkness* (1899). Paul B. Armstrong, Ed. Norton Critical Ed. New York: W.W. Norton, 2006.

———. *Lord Jim* (1900). New York: Bantam Books, 1981.

———. *Lord Jim* (1900). Thomas C. Moser, Ed. Second Norton Critical Ed. New York and London: W.W. Norton, 2006.

———. "Lord Jim: A Sketch," *Blackwood's Edinburgh Magazine* Vols. 166–68 (October 1899–November 1900).

———. *Lord Jim: A Tale*. Edinburgh and London: William Blackwood, 1900.

———. "Preface," *Last Essays*. Richard Curle, Ed. London: J.M. Dent, 1926.

———. "Travel," *Last Essays*. Richard Curle, Ed. London and Toronto: J.M. Dent, 1926.

Cook's Australasian Travellers' Gazette and Tourist Advertiser. London: Thomas Cook, 1892.

"Cook's, Clark's, etc. Travel Adverts, *Harper's Magazine Advertiser*," Back Matter. *Harper's Magazine* Vol. 121 (August 1910), New York and London: Harper, p. 15.

Cooper, John. "A Heavy Handicap. A Canadian Outlook. Imperial Rates on Newspapers and Magazines," *The Author* Vol. XII, No. 10 (May 1, 1902), p. 190.

Cox, J. Randolph. "Bibliographical Notes: John Buchan in the American Pulp Magazines," *Dime Novel Round-Up* (February/April 2010).

Cox, Tom. *Damned Englishman: A Study of Erskine Childers (1870–1922)*. New York: Exposition Press, 1975.

Crone, Rosalind. "Attempts to (Re)shape Common Reading Habits: Bible Reading on the Nineteenth-century Convict Ship," *A Return to the Common Reader: Print Culture and the Novel, 1850–1900*. Beth Palmer and Adelene Buckland, Eds. Farnham, UK: Ashgate, 2011, pp. 103–20.

———. "The Dimensions of Literacy in Victorian England: A Reappraisal," *Journal of Victorian Culture* (forthcoming)

———, Katie Halsey, and Shafquat Towheed. "Examining the Evidence of Reading: Three Examples from the Reading Experience Database, 1450–1945," *Reading in History: New Methodologies from the Anglo-American Tradition*. Bonnie Ciunzenhauser, Ed. London: Pickering & Chatto, 2010, pp. 29–45.

Cryle, Denis. "A British Legacy? The Empire Press Union and Freedom of the Press, 1940–1950," *History of Intellectual Culture* Vol. 4, No. 1 (2004), p. 1.

———. "The Ebb and Flow of the Tasman Mediasphere: A Century of Australian and New Zealand Print Media Development, 1840–1940," paper presented at the Australian Media Traditions Conference: Politics Media History, and the University of Canberra, November 24–25, 2005.

Daly, Nicholas. *Modernism, Romance and the Fin de Siècle: Popular Fiction and British Culture, 1880–1914*. Cambridge, UK: Cambridge University Press, 1999.

Dalziell, Rosamund. "The Curious Case of Sir Everard im Thurn and Sir Arthur Conan Doyle: Exploration and the Imperial Adventure Novel, *The Lost World*," *English Literature in Transition, 1880–1920* Vol. 45, No. 2 (2002), pp. 131–57.

Daniell, David. *The Interpreter's House: A Critical Assessment of John Buchan.* London: Nelson, 1985.

Dawson, Graham. *Soldier Heroes: British Adventure, Empire and the Imagining of Masculinities.* London and New York: Routledge, 1994.

DeForest, Tim. *Storytelling in the Pulps, Comics, and Radio: How Technology Changed Popular Fiction in America.* Jefferson, NC: McFarland, 2004.

Delany, Samuel R. "Critical Methods: Speculative Fiction," *Quark 1.* Samuel R. Delany and Marilyn Hacker, Eds. New York: Paperback Library, 1970.

"DINOSAURS CAVORT IN FILM FOR DOYLE; Spiritist Mystifies World-Famed Magicians With Pictures of Prehistoric Beasts. KEEPS ORIGIN A SECRET. Monsters of Other Ages Shown, Some Fighting, Some at Play, in Their Native Jungles," *The New York Times* (June 3, 1922), p. 1.

Donovan, Stephen. Conrad First: The Joseph Conrad Periodical Archive. Site last accessed on February 3, 2012: www.conradfirst.net/view/serialisation?id=93

——. *Joseph Conrad and Popular Culture.* Basingstoke, UK, and New York: Palgrave Macmillan, 2005.

——. "The Muse of *Blackwood's*: Charles Whibley and Literary Criticism in the World," *Print Culture and the Blackwood Tradition, 1805–1930.* David Finkelstein, Ed. Toronto: University of Toronto Press, 2006, pp. 259–86.

Doyle, Conan. "After Cormorants with a Camera," *The British Journal of Photography* 28 (October 14 and 21, 1881), pp. 533–34, 544–46.

——. "Easter Monday with the Camera," *The British Journal of Photography* 31 (May 23, 1884), pp. 330–32.

——. "J. Habakuk Jephson's Statement," *The Cornhill Magazine* (January 1884).

——. "Mr Stevenson's Methods in Fiction," *The National Review* 14 (1890), pp. 646–57.

——. "On the Slave Coast with a Camera," *The British Journal of Photography* 29 (March 31, April 7, 1882), pp. 185–87, 202–3.

——. "Speech to The Royal Society Club," *The London Times* (May 4, 1910).

——. "The Lost World," *The Strand Magazine* Vol. 43, No. 256–44, No. 263 (April–November 1912).

——. *The Lost World* (1912). Ware, UK: Wordsworth, 1995.

——. "With a Camera on an African River," *The British Journal of Photography* 32 (October 30, 1885), p. 697.

Dryden, Linda. "At the Court of *Blackwood's*," *Print Culture and the Blackwood Tradition, 1805–1930.* David Finkelstein, Ed. Toronto: University of Toronto Press, 2006.

——. " 'The Difference Between Us': Conrad, Wells, and the English Novel," *Studies in the Novel* Vol. 45, No. 2 (Summer 2013), pp. 214–33.

——. *Joseph Conrad and the Imperial Romance.* Basingstoke, UK, and New York: Palgrave Macmillan, 2000.

Duffy, Enda. *The Speed Handbook: Velocity, Pleasure, Modernism.* Durham, NC: Duke University Press, 2009.

Dugan, Sally. *Baroness Orczy's The Scarlet Pimpernel: A Publishing History.* Farnham, UK: Ashgate, 2014.

Earle, David M. *Re-Covering Modernism: Pulps, Paperbacks, and the Prejudice of Form.* Farnham, UK: Ashgate, 2009.

Early, Julie English. "Technology, Modernity, and 'The Little Man': Crippen's Capture by Wireless," *Victorian Studies* Vol. 39, No. 3 (Spring 1996), pp. 309–37.

"Earth's Unknown Lands Beckon Explorers," *Popular Science Monthly* (December 1925), p. 24.

"Editorial," *The British Journal of Photography* (December 21, 1880), p. 615.

Edwards, Elizabeth. *The Camera as Historian: Amateur Photographers and Historical Imagination, 1885–1918.* Durham, NC: Duke University Press, 2012.

Eggert, Paul. "Robbery Under Arms: The Colonial Market, Imperial Publishers, and the Demise of the Three-Decker Novel," *Book History* Vol. 6. Ezra Greenspan and Jonathan Rose, Eds. University Park, PA: Pennsylvania State University Press, 2003.

"Egypt and How To See It," advertisement, *The English Review* Vol. I, No. 4 (March 1909), p. iii.

Eldridge, C.G. *Victorian Imperialism*, Atlantic Highlands, NJ: Humanities Press, 1978.

Eliot, Simon. "Reading Experience Database: Or, What are we to do about the history of reading?" Site last accessed on May 1, 2012: www.open.ac.uk/Arts/RED/redback.htm

——. *Some Patterns and Trends in British Publishing 1800–1919*, Occasional Papers of the Bibliographical Society, No. 8 (1994).

——. "Some Trends in British Book Production, 1800–1919", *Literature in the Marketplace: Nineteenth-Century British Publishing and Reading Practices.* John O. Jordan and Robert L. Patten, Eds. Cambridge, UK: Cambridge University Press, 2003, pp. 19–43.

—— and Jonathan Rose, Eds. *A Companion to the History of the Book.* Oxford, UK: Wiley-Blackwell, 2009.

Elliott, Alan. *A Century Exposed: One Hundred Years of the Melbourne Camera Club.* Melbourne: Melbourne Camera Club, 1991.

Encyclopedia of Exploration, 1800–1850: A Comprehensive Reference Guide to the History and Literature of Exploration, Travel, and Colonization between the years 1800 and 1850. Raymond John Howgego, Ed. Potts Point, NSW: Horden House, 2004.

Erdinast-Vulcan, Daphna. "The Failure of Myth: *Lord Jim*," *Lord Jim* (1900), Joseph Conrad. Thomas Moser, Ed. Second Norton Critical Ed. New York and London: W.W. Norton, 1996.

——. *The Strange Short Fiction of Joseph Conrad: Writing, Culture, and Subjectivity.* Oxford, UK: Oxford University Press, 1999.

——, Allan H. Simmons, and J.H Stape, Eds. *Joseph Conrad: The Short Fiction.* Amsterdam: Editions Rodopi, 2004.

Evans, A.B. *Jules Verne Rediscovered: Didacticism and the Scientific Novel.* Westport, CT: Greenwood Press, 1988.

Feather, John. *A History of British Publishing*, 2nd Ed. Oxford, UK, and New York: Routledge, 2006.

Ferguson, DeLancey, and Marshall Waingrow, Eds. *RLS: Stevenson's Letters to Charles Baxter.* New Haven, CT: Yale University Press, 1956.

"The Fickleness Of Novel Readers," *Tuapeka Times* Vol. 23, Issue 4292 (November 13, 1895), p. 5.

The FictionMags Index. Site last accessed on May 9, 2011: www.philsp.com/.

Finkelstein, David. "Appendix 2: Blackwood's Magazine Sales, 1856–1915," *The House of Blackwood: Author–Publisher Relations in the Victorian Era.* University Park, PA: Pennsylvania State University Press, 2002, pp. 165–66.

——. "The Globalization of the Book 1880–1970," *A Companion to the History of the Book*. Simon Eliot and Jonathan Rose, Eds. London: John Wiley, 2011.

——. *The House of Blackwood: Author–Publisher Relations in the Victorian Era*. University Park, PA: Pennsylvania State University Press, 2002.

——. "Imperial Self-Representation: Constructions of Empire in *Blackwood's Magazine*, 1880–1900," *Imperial Co-Histories: National Identities and the British and Colonial Press*. Julie F. Codell, Ed. London: Associated University Presses, 2003, pp. 95–108.

——. "Introduction," *Print Culture and the Blackwood Tradition 1805–1930*. Toronto: University of Toronto Press, 2006.

Finkelstein, David, and Alistair McCleery, Eds. *An Introduction to Book History*. New York and London: Routledge, 2005.

Fisher, Margery. *The Bright Face of Danger: An Exploration of the Adventure Story*. Boston, MA: The Horn Book, 1986.

——, and James Fisher. *Shackleton and the Antarctic*. Boston, MA: Houghton Mifflin, 1958.

Fitzgerald, William G. "E.C. Borchgrevink," *The Strand Magazine* Vol. 20, No. 117 (September 1900), p. 257.

Fleming, Ian. *Casino Royale*. London: Cape, 1953.

Fleming, Sir Sandford. "Our Empire Cables," *The Empire Club of Canada Speeches 1903-1904*. Toronto: The Empire Club of Canada, 1904, pp. 84–94.

"Frank Presbrey's Address, Transportation and Advertising." Delivered at the annual dinner of the Atlas Club, Chicago (November 1902). *Printers' Ink: A Journal for Advertisers* Vol. XLII, No. 2. (January 14, 1903). New York: Geo. P. Rowell, 1903.

Fraser, Robert. *Victorian Quest Romance: Stevenson, Haggard, Kipling and Conan Doyle*. Plymouth, UK: Northcote House, 1998.

"Free Lessons in Photography," Stereoscopic Company ad, *The Strand Magazine* Vol. 2 (1891), p. iii.

Friedman, Susan Stanford. "Periodizing Modernism: Postcolonial Modernities and the Space/Time Borders of Modernist Studies," *Modernism/Modernity* Vol. 13, No. 3 (September 2006), pp. 425–44.

"From Darkest Africa, *The Railroad Man's Magazine—Advertising Section*," Back Matter. *The Railroad Man's Magazine* Vol. XIV, No. 4 (May 1911), p. 18.

Fulton, Richard. "Boys' Adventure Magazines and the Discourse of Adventure, 1860–1885," *Australasian Journal of Victorian Studies* Vol. 15, No. 1 (2010).

Fyfe, Aileen. *Steam-Powered Knowledge: William Chambers and the Business of Publishing, 1820–1860*. Chicago, IL: University of Chicago Press, 2012.

Geppert, Alexander. *Fleeting Cities: Imperial Expositions in Fin-de-Siècle Europe*. Basingstoke, UK: Palgrave Macmillan, 2010.

Gernsback, Hugo. "A New Kind of Fiction," *Amazing Stories* (April 1926), p. 1.

Gervais, Daniel J. "The 1909 Copyright Act in International Context," Vanderbilt Public Law Research Paper No. 10-23: 2010.

Gettman, Royal. *A Victorian Publisher: A Study of the Bentley Papers*. Cambridge, UK: Cambridge University Press, 1960.

Gibson, John Michael, and Richard Lancelyn Green, Eds. *The Unknown Conan Doyle: Essays on Photography*. London: Secker & Warburg, 1982.

Giddings, Robert, Ed. *Literature and Imperialism*. New York: St. Martin's Press, 1991.

Gillies, Mary Ann. *The Professional Literary Agent in Britain, 1880–1920.* Toronto: University of Toronto Press, 2007.

Glissant, Edouard. *Poetics of Relation.* Trans. Betsy King. Ann Arbor, MI: University of Michigan Press, 1997.

Gorra, Michael. "Joseph Conrad," *The Hudson Review* Vol. LIX, No. 4 (Winter 2007), pp. 1–31.

Graham, Gerald S. *A Concise History of the British Empire.* London: Thames & Hudson, 1978.

Graver, Lawrence. *Conrad's Short Fiction.* Berkeley and Los Angeles, CA: University of California Press, 1969.

Gray, Stephen. *Southern African Literature: An Introduction.* New York: Harper & Row, Barnes & Noble Import Division, 1979.

Green, Martin. *The Adventurous Male: Chapters in the History of the White Male Mind.* University Park, PA: Pennsylvania State University Press, 1993.

——. *Dreams of Adventure, Deeds of Empire.* New York: Basic Books, 1979.

——. *The Robinson Crusoe Story.* University Park, PA: Pennsylvania State University Press, 1990.

——. *Seven Types of Adventure Tale.* University Park, PA: Pennsylvania State University Press, 1991.

Green, Richard Lancelyn and John Michael Gibson. "Introduction," *The Unknown Conan Doyle: Essays on Photography.* London: Secker & Warburg, 1982.

Green, Roger Lancelyn. "Introduction," *The Prisoner of Zenda* (1894), Anthony Hope. London: J.M. Dent, 1966.

——. *Tellers of Tales.* London: Edmund Ward, 1946.

Greenspan, Ezra. *George Palmer Putnam.* University Park, PA: Pennsylvania State University Press, 2000.

Griffith, Penny, Keith Maslen, and Ross Harvey, Eds. *Book & Print in New Zealand: A Guide to Print Culture in New Zealand.* Wellington, NZ: Victoria University Press, 1997.

Gruber, Frank. *The Pulp Jungle.* Los Angeles, CA: Sherbourne, 1967.

Gurr, Andrew. *Writers in Exile: The Identity of Home in Modern Literature.* Brighton, UK: Harvester Press, 1981.

Haggard, H. Rider. "About Fiction," *Contemporary Review* Vol. 51, No. 302 (February 1887), pp. 172–80.

——. *Diary of an African Journey: The Return of H. Rider Haggard.* Stephen Coan, Ed. New York: New York University Press, 2000.

——. "'Elephant Smashing' and 'Lion Shooting'," *The African Review* (June 9, 1894), pp. 762–63.

——. *King Solomon's Mines.* London: Cassell, 1885.

——. *She: A History of Adventure.* London: Longmans, Green, 1887.

Hall, Donald, Ed. *Muscular Christianity: Embodying the Victorian Age*, Cambridge Studies in Nineteenth-Century Literature and Culture. Cambridge, UK: Cambridge University Press, 1994.

"Hamburg-American Line," advertisement, *Scribner's Magazine* Vol. 47, No. 2 (February 1910), p. 58.

Hammond, Mary. *Reading, Publishing and the Formation of Literary Taste in England, 1880–1914.* Aldershot, UK: Ashgate, 2006.

Hampson, Robert. *Cross-Cultural Encounters in Joseph Conrad's Malay Fiction.* New York and Basingstoke, UK: Palgrave Macmillan, 2001.

——. "The Physical Presence of Conrad in Certain Works by H.G. Wells," *The Conradian* Vol. 6, No. 2 (June 1981), pp. 16–19.

Hardman, Thomas. *A Parliament of the Press: The First Imperial Press Conference.* With preface by the Rt. Hon. the Earl of Rosebery. London: Constable, 1909.

Harlow, Alvin F. *Old Wires and New Waves: The History of the Telegraph, Telephone, and Wireless.* London: D. Appleton-Century, 1936.

Harlow, Barbara, and Mia Carter. *Imperialism and Orientalism: A Documentary Sourcebook.* Oxford, UK: Blackwell, 1999.

Harman, Claire. *Myself and the Other Fellow: A Life of Robert Louis Stevenson.* New York: Harper Perennial, 2005.

Harris, Neil. "Iconography and Intellectual History," *New Directions in American Intellectual History.* John Higham and Paul Conkin, Eds. Baltimore, MD: Johns Hopkins University Press, 1979.

Harrison, W. Jerome. *A History of Photography.* London: Trubner, 1888.

——. "Gelatine Emulsion with Bromide Of Silver," *The Photographic Times* Vol. XVII, No. 296 (May 20, 1887).

Hartley, J. *Popular Reality: Journalism, Modernity and Popular Culture.* London: Arnold, 1996.

Haynes, Christine. *Lost Illusions: The Politics of Publishing in Nineteenth-Century France.* Cambridge, MA: Harvard University Press, 2010.

Hazell's Annual for 1910. Hammond Hall, Ed. London: Hazell, Watson, & Viney, 1910.

Headrick, Daniel R. *The Tentacles of Progress: Technology Transfer in the Age of Imperialism, 1850–1940.* Oxford, UK: Oxford University Press, 1988.

——. *The Tools of Empire: Technology and European Imperialism in the Nineteenth Century.* Oxford, UK: Oxford University Press, 1981.

——. *When Information Came of Age: Technologies of Knowledge in the Age of Reason and Revolution, 1700–1850.* Oxford, UK: Oxford University Press, 2000.

Henderson, Louise. " 'Everyone will die laughing': John Murray and the Publication of David Livingstone's Missionary Travels," Livingstone Online. Site last accessed on December 27, 2011: www.livingstoneonline.ucl.ac.uk/companion.php?id=HIST2 (no longer available).

Hepburn, James G. *The Author's Empty Purse and the Rise of the Literary Agent.* London and New York: Oxford University Press, 1968.

Hersey, Harold. *Pulpwood Editor.* Westport, CT: Greenwood Press, 1974.

Heyert, Elizabeth. *The Glasshouse Years: Victorian Portrait Photography, 1839–1870.* Montclair, NJ: Allanheld & Schram, 1979.

Heyns, Michiel. "Like People in a Book: Imaginative Appropriation in *Lord Jim*," *Under Postcolonial Eyes: Joseph Conrad after Empire.* Gail Fincham and Myrtle Hooper, Eds. Capetown, SA: Juta, 1996.

Hilton, James. *Lost Horizon.* London: Macmillan, 1933.

Hinton, A. Horsley. "Notes and Comments," *The Amateur Photographer* Vol. 46, No. 1208 (Tuesday, November 26, 1907), p. 501.

Ho, Janice. "The Spatial Imagination and Literary form of Conrad's Colonial Fictions," *Journal of Modern Literature* Vol. 30, No. 4, Reading from the Margins of Modernism (Summer 2007), pp. 1–19.

Hoberman, Ruth. *Museum Trouble: Edwardian Fiction and the Emergence of Modernism.* Charlottesville, VA: University of Virginia Press, 2011.

Hobsbawm, Eric. *The Age of Empire*. New York: Pantheon, 1987.

Hopkins, J.C. *The Canadian Annual Review of Public Affairs*, 9. Toronto: Annual Review Publishing Company, 1910, pp. 61–76.

Horsley, Lee. *Fictions of Power in English Literature: 1900–1950*. New York: Longman, 1995.

"How Best to Promote the Sale of Pure Literature in Our Schools," *The Sunday School Chronicle: A Weekly Journal of Help and Intelligence for Sunday School Workers* (January 19, 1877), p. 36.

Howarth, Patrick. *Play Up and Play the Game: The Heroes of Popular Fiction*. London: Methuen, 1973.

Howe, Susanne. *Novels of Empire*. New York: Columbia University Press, 1949.

Hugon, Anne. *The Exploration of Africa: From Cairo to the Cape*. New York: Harry Abrams, 1993.

Hulme, Peter, and Tim Youngs, Eds. *The Cambridge Companion to Travel Writing*. Cambridge, UK: Cambridge University Press, 2002.

Hunter, Jefferson. *Edwardian Fiction*. Cambridge, MA: Harvard University Press, 1982.

Hyam, Ronald. *Empire and Sexuality: The British Experience*. Manchester, UK: Manchester University Press, 1990.

"Improved Portable Camera," Meagher's ad, *The Year-Book of Photography* (1893), p. a.

"International Correspondence Schools," ad, *The Popular Magazine* Vol. 51, No. 4 (February 7, 1919), unnumbered ad pages.

"International Statistics of Book and Periodical Production, UK, Book Production," *The American Library Annual 1914–1915*. New York: R.R. Bowker, 1915.

Jameson, Fredric. "Romance and Reification," *The Political Unconscious: Narrative as a Socially Symbolic Act*. Ithaca, NY: Cornell University Press, 1981, pp. 194–270.

Jeal, Tim. *Stanley: The Impossible Life of Africa's Greatest Explorer*. New Haven, CT: Yale University Press, 2007.

Johanningsmeier, Charles A. *Fiction and the American Literary Marketplace: The Role of Newspaper Syndicates in America, 1860–1900*. Cambridge, UK: Cambridge University Press, 1997.

The John Buchan Papers [1910–1972]. Presented by J. MacGlone, Esq., 1983. Special Manuscripts, Classmark MS 44. University of Stirling Library, Stirling, UK.

Jones, Susan. "Into the Twentieth Century: Imperial Romance from Haggard to Buchan," *A Companion to Romance From Classical to Contemporary*. Corinne Saunders, Ed. Malden, MA: Blackwell Publishing, 2004.

Joshi, Priya. *In Another Country: Colonialism, Culture, and the English Novel in India*. New York: Columbia University Press, 2002.

——. "Trading Places: The Novel, the Colonial Library, and India," *Print Areas: Book History in India*. Abhijit Gupta and Swapan Chakravorty, Eds. Delhi: Permanent Black, 2004, pp. 17–64.

Karl, Alissa. *Modernism and the Marketplace*. London: Routledge, 2013.

Karl, Frederick R. "Conrad, Wells, and the Two Voices," *PMLA* Vol. 88, No. 5 (October, 1973), pp. 1049–65.

——, and Laurence Davies, Eds. *The Collected Letters of Joseph Conrad, Volume 1: 1861–97*. Cambridge, UK: Cambridge University Press, 1983.

——. *The Collected Letters of Joseph Conrad, Volume 2: 1898–1902*. Cambridge, UK: Cambridge University Press, 1986.

——. *The Collected Letters of Joseph Conrad, Volume 3 1903–1907*. Cambridge, UK: Cambridge University Press, 1988.

——. *The Collected Letters of Joseph Conrad, Volume 4: 1908–1911*. Cambridge, UK: Cambridge University Press, 1990.

——, and Owen Knowles, Eds. *The Collected Letters of Joseph Conrad, Volume 6: 1917–1919*. Cambridge, UK: Cambridge University Press, 2003.

Katz, Wendy R. *Rider Haggard and the Fiction of Empire: A Critical Study of British Imperial Fiction*. Cambridge, UK: Cambridge University Press, 1987.

Kaul, Chandrika. *Reporting the Raj: The British Press and India, c. 1880–1922*. Manchester, UK: Manchester University Press, 2003.

Keegan, John. "Introduction," *The Thirty-Nine Steps* (1915), John Buchan. New York: Penguin, 2004.

Kestner, Joseph A. *The Edwardian Detective, 1901–1915*. Farnham, UK: Ashgate Publishing, 1999.

——. *Masculinities in British Adventure Fiction, 1880–1915*. Farnham, UK: Ashgate, 2010.

——. "Masculinities in the Richard Hannay 'War Trilogy' of John Buchan," *John Buchan and the Idea of Modernity*. Kate Macdonald and Nathan Waddell, Eds. London: Pickering & Chatto, 2013.

Kiberd, Declan. *Inventing Ireland: The Literature of the Modern Nation*. Cambridge, MA: Harvard University Press, 1996.

Kiely, Robert. *Robert Louis Stevenson and the Fiction of Adventure*. Cambridge, MA: Harvard University Press, 1964.

Killam, G.D. *Africa in English Fiction, 1874–1939*. Ibadan, Nigeria: Ibadan University Press, 1968.

Kimmel, Michael S. *Changing Men: New Directions in Research on Men and Masculinity*. Newbury Park, CA: Sage, 1987.

Kimmel, Michael S., and Michael A. Mesner. *Men's Lives*. New York: Macmillan, 1992.

King, Lynda J. *Best-Sellers by Design*. Detroit, MI: Wayne State University Press, 1988.

Kipling, Rudyard. "The Man Who Would Be King," *The Phantom Rickshaw and other Eerie Tales*. Vol. 5 of the Indian Railway Library. Allahabad, India: A.H. Wheeler, 1888.

Klein, Bernhard, Ed. *Fictions of the Sea: Critical Perspectives on the Ocean in British Literature and Culture*. Aldershot, UK, and Brookfield, VT: Ashgate, 2002.

Knight, Ian. *Rorke's Drift, 1879*. Westport, CT: Praeger, 2005.

Knox-Shaw, Peter. *The Explorer in English Fiction*. New York: St. Martin's Press, 1986.

Kracauer, Siegfried. "Photography," *The Mass Ornament*. Trans. Thomas Y. Levin. Cambridge, MA: Harvard University Press, 1995, pp. 47–63.

Kupinse, William. "Wasted Value: The Serial Logic of H.G. Wells's *Tono-Bungay*," *NOVEL: A Forum on Fiction* Vol. 33, No. 1 (Autumn 1999), pp. 51–72.

Lane, Christopher. *The Burdens of Intimacy: Psychoanalysis and Victorian Masculinity*. Chicago, IL: Chicago University Press, 1999.

Latham, Sean, and Mark Morrison. "Introduction," *Journal of Modern Periodical Studies* Vol. 1, No. 1 (2010). University Park, PA: Penn State University Press.

Lazarsfeld, P., and Wyant, R. "Magazines in 90 Cities: Who Reads What?" *Public Opinion Quarterly* (October 1837), pp. 29–41.

Le Voyage dans la Lune, dir. Georges Méliès, perfs. Georges Méliès, Victor André, Bleuette Bernon, Jeanne d'Alcy, and Henri Delannoy, Star Film, 1902.

Ledger, Sally, and Roger Lockhurst, Eds. "Anthropology and Racial Science," *The Fin de Siècle: A Reader in Cultural History c. 1880–1900*. Oxford, UK: Oxford University Press, 2000.

Lee, Robert. "Potential Railway World Heritage Sites in Asia and the Pacific." York, UK: Institute of Railways Studies, University of York, 2003.

Lewis, Jennifer Green. *Framing the Victorians: Photography and the Culture of Realism*. Ithaca, NY: Cornell University Press, 1996.

Lightman, Bernard V. *Victorian Science in Context*. Chicago, IL: University of Chicago Press, 1997.

"Literary Affairs in London," *The Dial* Vol. 61, No. 726 (October 5, 1915), p. 251.

Lomazow, S. *American Periodicals: A Collector's Manual and Reference Guide*. West Orange, NJ: Horowitz Books, 1996.

The Lost World, dir. Harry O. Hoyt, perfs. Bessie Love and Wallace Beery, First National Pictures, 1925.

Lothe, Jakob. *Conrad's Narrative Method*. Oxford, UK: Clarendon Press, 1989.

Lovecraft, H.P. *At the Mountains of Madness* (Sauk City, WI: Arkham House, 1939). *Astounding Stories* Vol. 16, No. 6–Vol. 17, No. 2 (February, March, and April 1936). New York: Street and Smith.

Lownie, Andrew. *John Buchan: The Presbyterian Cavalier*. Boston, MA: Godyne, 1995.

Lutz, Catherine A., and Jane L. Collins. *Reading National Geographic*. Chicago, IL, and London: University of Chicago Press, 1993.

Lynch, John M. "Introduction," *The Coming of the Fairies* (1921), Arthur Conan Doyle. Lincoln, NE, and London: University of Nebraska Press, 2006.

Lyons, Martyn. "Britain's Largest Export Market," *A History of the Book in Australia, 1891-1945*. Marton Lyons and John Arnold, Eds. Brisbane: QLD: University of Queensland Press, 2001.

———. "Reading Practices in Australia," *A History of the Book in Australia, 1891–1945*. Marton Lyons and John Arnold, Eds. Brisbane: QLD: University of Queensland Press, 2001.

Macdonald, Kate, "John Buchan's Breakthrough: The Conjunction of Experience, Markets and Forms that Made *The Thirty-Nine Steps*," *Publishing History* Vol. 68 (2010), pp. 25–106.

———. "Thomas Nelson & Sons and John Buchan: Mutual Marketing in the Publisher's Series," *The Culture of the Publisher's Series*, Vol. 1, *Authors, Publishers, and the Shaping of Taste*. John Spiers, Ed. London: Palgrave Macmillan, 2011, pp. 156–70.

Macdonald, Kate, and Nathan Waddell, "Introduction," *John Buchan and the Idea of Modernity*. London: Pickering & Chatto, 2013, pp. 1–16.

Mack, E.C. *Public Schools and British Opinion Since 1860: The Relationship Between Contemporary Ideas and the Evolution of an English Institution*. Westport, CT: Greenwood Press, 1971.

Mackenzie, John M. *Propaganda and Empire: The Manipulation of British Public Opinion, 1880–1960*. Manchester, UK: Manchester University Press, 1986.

Mackenzie, John M., Ed. *Imperialism and Popular Culture*. Manchester, UK: Manchester University Press, 1986.

MacLaren, Eli. " 'Against All Invasion': The Archival Story of Kipling, Copyright, and the Macmillan Expansion into Canada, 1900–1920," *Journal of Canadian Studies* Vol. 40, No. 2 (2006), pp. 139–62.

Macmillan, Frederick. *The Net Book Agreement 1899 and the Book War 1906–1908*. Glasgow, UK: Robert MacLehose, 1924

Madison, Nathan. "Munsey: The Man Who Made the *Argosy*," *Blood 'n' Thunder*, No. 30 (Summer 2011), pp. 62–86.

Mangan, J.A. *The Games Ethic and Imperialism: Aspects of the Diffusion of an Ideal*. London: Frank Cass, 1998.

Mangan, J.A., and James Walvin, Eds. *Manliness and Morality: Middle-Class Masculinity in Britain and America, 1800–1940*. New York: St. Martin's Press, 1987.

Mark, Thomas. "Unpublished notes," Morgan Source Files, Macmillan Archives, British Library, box M75d.

Martin, Paul. *Victorian Snapshots*. New York: Arno Press, 1973.

Mayer, Ruth. *Serial Fu Manchu: The Chinese Supervillain and the Spread of Yellow Peril Ideology*. Philadelphia, PA: Temple University Press, 2014.

May's British and Irish Press Guide. London: F.L. May, 1880–1915.

McClure, John. *Late Imperial Romance*. London and New York: Verso, 1994.

McClure, S.S. *My Autobiography*. New York: Frederick A. Stokes, 1913.

McKitterick, David. *A History of Cambridge University Press: New Worlds for Learning, 1873–1972*. Cambridge, UK, and London: Cambridge University Press, 2004.

"Meetings of Societies," *The British Journal of Photography* Vol. LIV, No. 2439 (Friday, February 1, 1907), pp. 88–89.

Merritt, Abraham. *The Moon Pool* (New York: G.P. Putnam, 1919) [First published in two parts as "The Moon Pool" in *All-Story Weekly* Vol. 85, No. 3 (June 22, 1918), and "The Conquest of the Moon Pool," *All-Story Weekly* Vol. 94, No. 1 (February 15, 1919) to Vol. 95, No. 2 (March 22, 1919). New York: Frank A. Munsey].

Messinger, Gary. *British Propaganda and the State in the First World War*. Manchester, UK: Manchester University Press, 1992.

Meyers, Jeffrey. *Fiction and the Colonial Experience*. Ipswich, UK: Boydell Press, 1972.

Mickalites, Carey. *Modernism and Market Fantasy*. London: Palgrave Macmillan, 2012.

Middleton, Peter. *The Inward Gaze: Masculinity and Subjectivity in Modern Culture*. London: Routledge, 1992.

Miers, H.A. *Geological Magazine*, New Series Vol. II, No. X (October 1905), pp. 473–78.

Miller, David. *W.H. Hudson and the Elusive Paradise*. New York: St. Martin's Press, 1990.

Miller, Russell. *The Adventures of Arthur Conan Doyle: A Biography*. New York: Thomas Dunne Books, 2008.

Mitchell, W.J.T. "Postcolonial Culture, Postimperial Criticism," *The Post-Colonial Studies Reader*. Bill Ashcroft, Ed. New York: Routledge, 1995, pp. 475–79.

Mitchell's Newspaper Press Directory. London: Mitchell, 1880–1915.

"The Modern Novel," *Chambers's Journal* Vol. 12, No. 591 (April 27, 1895), p. 263.

The Modernist Journals Project. Site last accessed on December 22, 2016, www.modjourn.org/.

The Modernist Versions Project. Site last accessed on December 22, 2016, http://web.uvic.ca/~mvp1922/.

Mongia, Padmini. " 'Ghosts of the Gothic': Spectral Women and Colonized Spaces in *Lord Jim," Conrad and Gender.* Andrew Michael Roberts, Ed. Amsterdam and Atlanta, GA: Rodopi, 1993, pp. 1–16.

Monsman, Gerald. *H. Rider Haggard on the Imperial Frontier: The Political and Literary Contexts of his African Romances.* Greensboro, NC: ELT Press, 2006.

Moore-Gilbert, B.J. *Kipling and "Orientalism."* New York: St. Martin's Press, 1986.

Moretti, Franco. *Distant Reading.* London and New York: Verso Books, 2013.

Morris, James. *Pax Britannica.* New York: Harcourt, 1980.

Morrison, Mark. *The Public Face of Modernism.* Madison, WI: University of Wisconsin Press, 2001.

Moser, Thomas C., Ed. "The Division, by Chapters, of the Monthly Installments of *Lord Jim: A Sketch* in *Blackwood's Edinburgh Magazine," Lord Jim* (1900), Second Norton Critical Ed. New York and London: W.W. Norton, 2006, p. 308.

Moskowitz, Sam. *Under the Moons of Mars: A History and Anthology of "The Scientific Romance" in the Munsey Magazines, 1912–1920.* New York: Holt, Rinehart, 1970.

Moss, Robert F. *Rudyard Kipling and the Fiction of Adolescence.* London: Macmillan, 1982.

Mott, Frank Luther. *A History of American Magazines, 1885–1905.* Boston, MA: Harvard University Press, 1957.

Mullen, R.D. "From Standard Magazines to Pulps and Big Slicks: A Note on the History of US General and Fiction Magazines," *Science Fiction Studies* #65, Appendix, Vol. 22, No. 1 (March 1995).

Munsey, Frank A. *The Story of the Founding and Development of the Munsey Publishing-House.* New York: Frank A. Munsey, 1907.

Murdock, Graham, and Peter Golding. "The Structure, Ownership and Control of the Press," *Newspaper History: From the 17th Century to the Present Day.* G. Boyce, J. Curran and P. Wingate, Eds. London: Constable, 1978, p. 130.

Murphy, Sharon. " 'Quite Incapable of Appreciating Books Written for Educated Readers': the Mid-nineteenth-century British Soldier," *A Return to the Common Reader: Print Culture and the Novel, 1850–1900.* Beth Palmer and Adelene Buckland, Eds. Farnham,UK: Ashgate, 2011, pp. 121–32.

Myers, Janet C. *Antipodal England: Emigration and Portable Domesticity in the Victorian Imagination.* Albany, NY: The State University of New York Press, 2009.

Najder, Zdzisław. *Joseph Conrad: a Life.* Rochester, NY: Camden House, 2007.

Nansen, Fridtjof. *In Northern Mists: Arctic Exploration in Early Times,* Vol. 1–2. Trans. Arthur G. Chater. New York: Frederick A. Stokes, 1911.

National Council of Public Morals. *The Cinema: Its Present Position and Future Possibilities.* London: Williams & Norgate, 1917.

Neuberg, Victor E. *Popular Literature: A History and Guide.* London: The Woburn Press, 1977.

The New Zealand Official Year-Book, Vols. 2, 22. Wellington, NZ: John Mackay Government Printer, 1893, 1913.

Noakes, Richard. "The *Boy's Own Paper* and late-Victorian juvenile magazines," *Science in the Nineteenth-Century Periodical*. Cambridge, UK: Cambridge University Press, 2007, pp. 151–283.

North, Michael. *Camera Works: Photography and the Twentieth-Century Word*. Oxford, UK: Oxford University Press, 2005.

N.W. Ayer & Son's American Newspaper Annual and Directory. Philadelphia, PA: N.W. Ayer, 1880–1915.

"Oceanic Steamship Co.," ad, *Scribner's Magazine* Vol. 47, No. 2 (February 1910), p. 58.

The Official Year Book of the Commonwealth of Australia (1901–1907, –1912). No. 1, 6. Melbourne, VIC: McCarron, Bird, 1908, 1913.

O'Hara, Glen. "New Histories of British Imperial Communication and the 'Networked World' of the 19th and Early 20th Centuries," *History Compass* Vol. 8, No. 7 (2010), pp. 609–25.

Ohmann, Richard. *Selling Culture: Magazines, Markets and Class at the Turn of the Century*. London and New York: Verso, 1996.

Oliphant, Margaret. *Annals of a Publishing House: William Blackwood and His Sons, Their Magazine and Friends*, 2 vols. London and Edinburgh: Blackwood, 1897; 3 vols. New York: Scribner's Sons, 1897–98.

Orel, Harold. *Critical Essays on Rudyard Kipling*. Boston, MA: G.K. Hall, 1989.

Osborne, G., and G. Lewis. *Communication Traditions in Twentieth-Century Australia*. Melbourne, VIC, and Oxford, UK: Oxford University Press, 2001.

Osborne, Roger. "A National Interest in an International Market: The Circulation of Magazines in Australia during the 1920s," *History Australia* Vol. 5, No. 3 (2008), pp. 75.1–75.16.

———. "Joseph Conrad's *Under Western Eyes:* The Serials and First Editions," *Studies in Bibliography: Papers of the Bibliographical Society of the University of Virginia* Vol. 54 (2001), pp. 301–16.

Palmer, Beth, and Adelene Buckland, Eds. *A Return to the Common Reader: Print Culture and the Novel, 1850–1900*. Farnham, UK: Ashgate, 2011.

Parker, George. "Distributors, Agents, and Publishers: Creating a Separate Market for Books in Canada 1900–1920: Part I," *Papers of the Bibliographical Society of Canada* Vol. 43, No. 2 (2005), pp. 7–65.

Parry, Benita. *Delusions and Discoveries: India in the British Imagination, 1880–1939*. New York: Verso Press, 1998.

Peck, John. *Maritime Fiction: Sailors and the Sea in British and American Novels, 1719–1917*. Basingstoke, UK, and New York: Palgrave, 2001.

"Perfect Photo Lens," Bausch & Lomb ad, *The Photographic Times-Bulletin* (January 1902), p. ii.

Peterson, Theodore. *Magazines in the Twentieth Century*. Urbana, IL: University of Illinois Press, 1956.

Phillips, Richard. *Mapping Men and Empire: A Geography of Adventure*. New York: Routledge, 1996.

"Photographic Lies: Proving the Worthlessness of the Camera as Witness," editorial, *The Harmsworth Magazine* (1898), p. 259.

Pilot, Roy, and Alvin E. Rodin. "Introduction," *The Annotated Lost World*. Indianapolis, IN: Wessex Press, 1996.

Piper, Leonard. *Dangerous Waters: The Life and Death of Erskine Childers*. London: Hambledon and London, 2003.

"Pleasure Pirate Pilgrimages," ad, *Time* Vol. 7, No. 26 (June 28, 1926), p. 22.

Plotz, John. *Portable Property: Victorian Culture on the Move*. Princeton, NJ: Princeton University Press, 2008.

Pocock, Tom. *Rider Haggard and the Lost Empire: A Biography*. London: Weidenfield & Nicolson, 1993.

Poe, Edgar Allan. *The Narrative of Arthur Gordon Pym of Nantucket*. New York: Harper, 1837.

——. "[The Narrative of] Arthur Gordon Pym, No. I," *The South Literary Messenger* Vol. III, No. 1 (January 1837), pp. 13–16.

——. "[The Narrative of] Arthur Gordon Pym, No. II," *The South Literary Messenger* Vol. III, No. 2 (February 1837), pp. 109–16.

Porch, Douglas. *Wars of Empire*. London: Cassell, 2000.

"Postal Statistics of Papua, 1905–06 and 1909–10," *The Official Year Book of the Commonwealth of Australia*. No. 4. Melbourne, VIC: McCarron, Bird, 1911, p. 1110.

Pound, Reginald, and Geoffrey Harmsworth. *Northcliffe*. London: Cassell, 1959.

Powers, Paul. *Pulp Writer: Twenty Years in the American Grub Street*. Lincoln, NE: University of Nebraska Press, 2007.

Pratt, Mary Louis. *Imperial Eyes: Travel Writing and Transculturation*. London and New York: Routledge, 1992.

Preston, Thomas. *The Elementary Education Act, 1870: Being the Act to Provide Public Elementary Education in England and Wales*. London: William Amer, 1870.

Purdy, Dwight H. "The Chronology of *Lord Jim*," *Lord Jim* (1900), Joseph Conrad. Thomas Moser, Ed. Second Norton Critical Ed. New York and London: W.W. Norton, 1996, p. 385.

Quayle, Eric, Ed. *The Collector's Book of Boys' Stories*. London: Studio Vista, 1973.

Raiskin, Judith L. "Preface," *Wide Sargasso Sea* (1966), Jean Rhys. Norton Critical Ed. New York: W.W. Norton, 1999.

Raven, James. *The Business of Books: Booksellers and the English Book Trade, 1450–1850*. New Haven, CT, and London: Yale University Press, 2007.

Rawson, Rawson W. "An Inquiry into the Condition of Criminal Offenders in England and Wales with Respect to Education," *Journal of the Statistical Society of London* Vol. 3 (January 1841).

Ray, Martin. "Conrad, Wells, and 'The Secret Agent': Paying Old Debts and Settling Old Scores," *The Modern Language Review* Vol. 81, No. 3 (July 1986), pp. 560–73.

Reed, David. *The Popular Magazine in Britain and the United States 1880–1960*. Toronto and Buffalo, NY: University of Toronto Press, 1997.

"Report on the Inventions Exhibition 1885," *The Times*, London (Tuesday, August 11, 1885), p. 3.

Richards, Jeffrey, Ed. *Imperialism and Juvenile Literature*. Manchester, UK: Manchester University Press, 1989.

Richards, Thomas. *The Imperial Archive: Knowledge and the Fantasy of Empire*. New York: Verso Books, 1993.

Ridley, Hugh. *Images of Imperial Rule*. New York: St. Martin's Press, 1983.

Rieder, John. *Colonialism and the Emergence of Science Fiction*. Middleton, CT: Wesleyan University Press, 2008.

Riviere, Jacques. *The Ideal Reader*. Blanche A Price, Ed. and trans. New York: Meridian Books, 1960.

Roberts, Adam. "Late Twentieth-Century Science Fiction: Multimedia, Visual Science Fiction and Others," *The History of Science Fiction*. Basingstoke, UK: Palgrave Macmillan, 2005, pp. 326–40.

Roberts, Andrew Michael. *Conrad and Masculinity*. Basingstoke, UK, and New York: Palgrave Macmillan, 2000.

Roberts, Andrew Michael, Ed. *The Conradian: Conrad and Gender*. Amsterdam: Editions Rodopi, 1993.

Rohmer, Sax. *The Sins of Séverac Bablon* (London: Cassell, 1914) [First appeared in *Cassell's Magazine of Fiction* (June 1912–August 1913)].

Roper, Michael, and John Tosh, Eds. *Manful Assertions: Masculinities in Britain since 1800*. London: Routledge, 1991.

Rose, Jonathan. *The Intellectual Life of the British Working Classes*, 2nd Ed. New Haven, CT, and New York: Yale University Press, 2010.

——. "Modernity and Print I: Britain 1890–1970," *A Companion to the History of the Book*. Simon Eliot and Jonathan Rose, Eds. Chichester, UK: Wiley-Blackwell, 2009, pp. 341–53.

Ross, P.D. "Some Deductions from the Imperial Press Conference: An Address by Mr. P.D. Ross, Chief Editor of the *Ottawa Journal*, before the Empire Club of Canada," *The Empire Club of Canada Addresses* (Toronto, Canada), February 17, 1910, p. 149–60.

Ross, Stephen. *Conrad and Empire*. Columbia, MO: University of Missouri Press, 2004.

Ruppert, Peter. *Reader in a Strange Land: The Activity of Reading Literary Utopias*. Athens, GA: University of Georgia Press, 1986.

Said, Edward W. *Culture and Imperialism*. New York: Alfred A. Knopf, 1993.

——. *Joseph Conrad and the Fiction of Autobiography* (1966). New York: Columbia University Press, 2008.

——. *Orientalism*. New York: Vintage Books, 1979.

Saler, Michael. *As If: Modern Enchantment and the Literary Prehistory of Virtual Reality*. Oxford, UK, and New York: Oxford University Press, 2012.

——. "Modernity, Disenchantment, and the Ironic Imagination," *Philosophy & Literature* Vol. 28, No. 1 (April 2004), pp. 137–49.

"Sales," Stock Ledgers for *Chance*. Methuen MSS. 1892–1944: Methuen Archives; Special Collections, Lilly Library at Indiana University.

Salmonson, Jessica Amanda. "An Annotated Bibliography of H. Rider Haggard's Fantasies in 1st Editions, Alphabetically Arranged." Site last accessed on December 27, 2011: www.violetbooks.com/haggard-bib.html (no longer available).

Sandison, Alan. *The Wheel of Empire: A Study of the Imperial Idea in Some Late Nineteenth and Early Twentieth-Century Fiction*. New York: St. Martin's Press, 1967.

Schmidt, Barbara Quinn. "Novelists, Publishers, and Fiction in Middle-Class Magazines: 1860–1880," *Victorian Periodicals Review* Vol. 17, No. 4 (Winter 1984), pp. 142–53.

Scholes, Robert and Cliff Wulfman. *Modernism in the Magazines: An Introduction*. New Haven, CT: Yale University Press, 2011.

Schwarz, Daniel R. *Conrad: The Later Fiction*. London: Macmillan Press, 1982.

Sconce, Jeffrey. *Haunted Media: Electronic Presence from Telegraphy to Television*. Durham, NC, and London: Duke University Press, 2000.

Scott, William R. *Scientific Circulation Management for Newspapers*. New York: Ronald Press, 1915.

"Section D—No. 7, Correspondence Relative to the Establishment of a Mail Service Between England and the Australian Colonies," *Appendix to the Journals of the House of Representatives of New Zealand*. Auckland, NZ: Robert J. Creighton, 1863.

Seymour-Smith, Martin. *Rudyard Kipling*. London: Macdonald-Queen Anne Press, 1989.

Sherry, Norman, Ed. *Conrad: The Critical Heritage*. London: Routledge & Kegan Paul, 1973.

Showalter, Elaine. *Sexual Anarchy: Gender and Culture at the Fin de Siècle*. New York: Penguin, 1990.

Silverman, Kaja. *Male Subjectivity at the Margins*. London: Routledge, 1992.

Simmel, Georg. *On Individuality and Social Forms*. Donald N. Levine, Ed. Chicago, IL: University of Chicago Press, 1971.

Simmons, Alan H. *Joseph Conrad*, Critical Issues Series. Basingstoke, UK, and New York: Palgrave Macmillan, 2006.

Smith, Janet Adam. *John Buchan: A Biography*. Oxford, UK, and New York: Oxford University Press, 1965.

Smith, Jonathan. *Charles Darwin and Victorian Visual Culture*. Cambridge, UK: Cambridge University Press, 2006.

Snyder, Katherine W. *Bachelors, Manhood, and the Novel, 1850–1925*. Cambridge, UK: Cambridge University Press, 1999.

Soister, John T. *Up from the Vault: Rare Thrillers of the 1920s and 1930s*. Jefferson, NC: McFarland, 2004.

Spalding's Official Football Guide. Thomas Cahill, Ed. New York: American Sports Publishing, 1915.

"Special Instantaneous" plate, Morgan & Kidd ad, *The Photographer's World* (December 15, 1886), cover.

Spiers, John. "'Must Not Be Sold or Imported . . .': British Colonial Editions, 1843–1972," *The Colonial and Postcolonial History of the Book, 1765–2005: Reaching the Margins*, exhibition pamphlet. London: Open University, 2005.

Spiller, John. "Recollections of the First Photographic Exhibition," *Yearbook of Photography* (1882), p. 41.

Spurr, David. *The Rhetoric of Empire: Colonial Discourse in Journalism, Travel Writing, and Imperial Administration*. Durham, NC: Duke University Press, 1993.

Stape, J.H. *The Cambridge Companion to Joseph Conrad*. Cambridge, UK: Cambridge University Press, 1996.

——. *The Several Lives of Joseph Conrad*. New York: Pantheon Books, 2007.

Stead, W.T. "The Editors of the Empire at Home," *The Contemporary Review* (July 1909), p. 48.

——. "The Wasted Wealth of *King Demos*," *Review of Reviews* (July 15, 1893), pp. 83–87.

Stephen, Daniel. *The Empire of Progress: West Africans, Indians, and Britons at the British Empire Exhibition, 1924–25*. Basingstoke, UK: Palgrave Macmillan, 2013.

Stetz, Margaret Diane. "Sex, Lies, and Printed Cloth: Bookselling at the Bodley Head in the Eighteen-Nineties," *Victorian Studies* 35 (Autumn 1991), pp. 80–81.

Stevenson, Robert Louis. "A Gossip on Romance," *Longman's Magazine* Vol. 1 (February 1882), pp. 69–79.

Stiebel, Lindy. *Imagining Africa: Landscape in H. Rider Haggard's African Romances.* Westport, CT: Greenwood Press, 2001.

Stocking, George W., Jr. *Victorian Anthropology.* New York: Simon & Schuster, 1991.

Stockwell, Anthony J. "The White Man's Burden and Brown Humanity: Colonialism and Ethnicity in British Malaya," *Journal of the Malaysian Branch of the Royal Asiatic Society* Vol. 10, No. 1 (1982).

Street, Brian V. *The Savage in Literature: Representations of "Primitive" Society in English Fiction, 1858–1920.* London: Routledge & Kegan Paul, 1975.

Strychacz, Thomas. *Modernism, Mass Culture, and Professionalism.* Cambridge, UK: Cambridge University Press, 1993.

Stuart, M. John. "Address to the Photographic Convention of the United Kingdom," *The Photographic Times: an Illustrated Monthly Magazine* Vol. 30 (1898), p. 468.

Sullivan, Zohreh T. *Narratives of Empire: The Fictions of Rudyard Kipling.* Cambridge, UK: Cambridge University Press, 1993.

Sussman, Herbert. *Victorian Masculinities: Manhood and Masculine Poetics in Early Victorian Literature and Art.* Cambridge, UK: Cambridge University Press, 1995.

Terry, T. Philip. *Terry's Mexico: Handbook for Travellers.* Sonora, CA: Sonora News, 1909.

"Terry's Mexico," ad, *Scribner's Magazine* Vol. 47, No. 2 (February 1910), p. 59.

Thompson, Andrew S. *Imperial Britain: The Empire in British Politics, c. 1880-1932.* London: Routledge, 2014.

Thompson, J. Lee. "Selling the Mother Country to the Empire: The Imperial Press Conference of June 1909," *Imperial Co-Histories: National Identities and the British and Colonial Press.* Julie F. Codell, Ed. Cranbury, NJ, and London: Associated University Presses, 2003, pp. 109–24.

Thompson, Robert L. *Wiring a Continent: The History of the Telegraph Industry in the United States, 1832–1866.* Princeton, NJ: Princeton University Press, 1947.

Thurston, Herbert. "An Old-Established Periodical," *The Month* Vol. XXV, No. 212 (February 1882), p. 153.

Towheed, Shafquat. "Geneva v. Saint Petersburg: Two Concepts of Literary Property and the Material Lives of Books in *Under Western Eyes*", *Book History* 10, (2007), pp. 169–91.

Trainor, Luke. "Colonial Editions," New Zealand Electronic Text Centre. Site last accessed on January 20, 2011: www.nzetc.org/tm/scholarly/tei-GriBook-_div3-N11A1D.html

"Travelling Companion," ad, *Scribner's Magazine* Vol. 47, No. 2 (February 1910), p. 58.

Trevelyan, G.M. "The White Peril," *Nineteenth Century* Vol. 50 (December 1901), pp. 1049–50.

Trollope, Anthony. *Australia and New Zealand,* 2 vols. London: Chapman & Hall, 1873–74.

Turner, E.S. *The Shocking History of Advertising.* New York: Penguin, 1953.

Turner, Frederick Jackson. "The Significance of the Frontier in American History," *A Report of the American Historical Association* (1893), pp. 199–227.

Usborne, Richard. *Clubland Heroes: A Nostalgic Study of Some Recurrent Characters in the Romantic Fiction of Dornford Yates, John Buchan, and Sapper.* London: Barrie & Jenkins, 1953.

"Vacation Thoughts on Heating, *The Railroad Man's Magazine—Advertising Section*," Back Matter. *The Railroad Man's Magazine* Vol. XIV, No. 4 (May 1911), p. 1.

Van Ash, Cay, and Elizabeth Rohmer. *Master of Villainy: A Biography of Sax Rohmer*. London: Tom Stacey, 1972.

"Views of *Lhasa*," *National Geographic* Magazine Vol. 16, No. 1 (1905), pp. 27–28.

Waller, Philip J. *Writers, Readers, and Reputations: Literary Life in Britain, 1870–1918*. New York and Oxford, UK: Oxford University Press, 2006.

Wark, Wesley K., Ed. *Spy Fiction, Spy Films, and Real Intelligence*. London: Frank Cass, 1991.

Watt, Ian. *Conrad in the Nineteenth Century*. Berkeley, CA: University of California Press, 1979.

——. *Essays on Conrad*. Cambridge, UK: Cambridge University Press, 2000.

Watts, Cedric. "Introduction," *Lord Jim* (1900), Joseph Conrad. New York: Penguin, 1986, p. 15.

Weedon, Alexis. *Victorian Publishing: The Economics of Book Publishing for a Mass Market 1836–1916*, Farnham, UK: Ashgate, 2003.

Wells, H.G. "Book the Third, Chapter the Fourth: How I Stole the Heaps of Quap from Mordet Island," *Tono-Bungay*, Part 3, *The English Review* Vol. I, No. 4 (March 1909), pp. 723–49.

——. "Chapter IX: How I Stole the Heaps of Quap from Mordet Island," *Tono-Bungay*, Part 3, *The Popular Magazine* Vol. 12, No. 2 (December 1908), pp. 125–39.

——. *Tono-Bungay: A Romance of Commerce*. London: Macmillan, 1909.

——. *Tono-Bungay* (1909). New York: Modern Library Classics, 2003.

——. *Tono-Bungay* (1909). New York: Penguin, 2005.

West, James. "The Chace Act and Anglo-American Literary Relations," *Studies in Bibliography* Vol. 45 (1992), pp. 303–11.

"What Influenced the N.K. Fairbank Company," Street & Smith advert. *Life* Vol. 51 (March 19, 1908), front pp.

"What Makes an Edition?" *The Publisher's Weekly* Vol. 84, No. 9 (August 30, 1913), pp. 575–76.

"Where Are You Going This Summer?" ad for *Munsey's* "Special Summer Resort Number," *All-Story Weekly* Vol. XLV, No. 4 (June 5, 1915), p. iii.

Whibley, Charles. "Musings Without Method," *Blackwood's Magazine* (February 1900–December 1929).

White, Andrea. *Joseph Conrad and the Adventure Tradition*. Cambridge, UK: Cambridge University Press, 1993.

Wilson, Charles. *First with the News: The History of W.H. Smith 1792–1972*. Garden City, NY: Doubleday, 1986.

Wilson, Christopher. *The Labor of Words: Literary Professionalism in the Progressive Era*. Athens, GA: University of Georgia Press, 1985.

Winks, Robin W. "John Buchan: Stalking the Wilder Game," *The Four Adventures of Richard Hannay*. Robin W. Winks, Ed. Boston, MA: David R. Godine, 1988.

Winks, Robin W., and James Rush, Eds. *Asia in Western Fiction*. Honolulu, HI: University of Hawaii Press, 1990.

Winseck, Dwayne A., and Robert M. Pike. *Communication and Empire: Media, Markets, and Globalization, 1860–1930*. Durham, NC: Duke University Press, 2007.

Wollaeger, Mark A. *Joseph Conrad and the Fictions of Skepticism*. Stanford, CA: Stanford University Press, 1990.

——. *Modernism, Media, and Propaganda: British Narrative from 1900 to 1945*. Princeton, NJ: Princeton University Press, 2006.

Worth, Aaron. *Imperial Media: Colonial Networks and Information Technologies in the British Literary Imagination, 1857–1918*. Columbus, OH: Ohio State University Press, 2014.

Wright, Alex. *Cataloging the World: Paul Otlet and the Birth of the Information Age*. Oxford, UK: Oxford University Press, 2014.

Wynne, Catherine. *The Colonial Conan Doyle: British Imperialism, Irish Nationalism, and the Gothic*. Westport, CT: Greenwood Press, 2002.

Yanni, Carla. *Nature's Museums: Victorian Science and the Architecture of Display*. Princeton, NJ: Princeton Architectural Press, 2005.

"You Press the Button. We Do the Rest," Kodak camera ad, *The Strand Magazine* Vol. 2 (1891), p. viii.

Zweig, Paul. *The Adventurer: The Fate of Adventure in the Western World*. New York: Basic Books, 1974.

Index

Taylor & Francis eBooks

Helping you to choose the right eBooks for your Library

Add Routledge titles to your library's digital collection today. Taylor and Francis ebooks contains over 50,000 titles in the Humanities, Social Sciences, Behavioural Sciences, Built Environment and Law.

Choose from a range of subject packages or create your own!

Benefits for you

» Free MARC records
» COUNTER-compliant usage statistics
» Flexible purchase and pricing options
» All titles DRM-free.

REQUEST YOUR FREE INSTITUTIONAL TRIAL TODAY

Free Trials Available
We offer free trials to qualifying academic, corporate and government customers.

Benefits for your user

» Off-site, anytime access via Athens or referring URL
» Print or copy pages or chapters
» Full content search
» Bookmark, highlight and annotate text
» Access to thousands of pages of quality research at the click of a button.

eCollections – Choose from over 30 subject eCollections, including:

Archaeology	Language Learning
Architecture	Law
Asian Studies	Literature
Business & Management	Media & Communication
Classical Studies	Middle East Studies
Construction	Music
Creative & Media Arts	Philosophy
Criminology & Criminal Justice	Planning
Economics	Politics
Education	Psychology & Mental Health
Energy	Religion
Engineering	Security
English Language & Linguistics	Social Work
Environment & Sustainability	Sociology
Geography	Sport
Health Studies	Theatre & Performance
History	Tourism, Hospitality & Events

For more information, pricing enquiries or to order a free trial, please contact your local sales team: www.tandfebooks.com/page/sales

 Routledge
Taylor & Francis Group

The home of
Routledge books

www.tandfebooks.com

For Product Safety Concerns and Information please contact our EU representative GPSR@taylorandfrancis.com Taylor & Francis Verlag GmbH, Kaufingerstraße 24, 80331 München, Germany

Printed and bound by CPI Group (UK) Ltd, Croydon, CR0 4YY
01/05/2025
01858422-0008